Global Trade Policy

Global Trade Policy

Questions and Answers

Pamela J. Smith

WILEY Blackwell

This edition first published 2014
© 2014 John Wiley & Sons, Inc

Wiley-Blackwell is an imprint of John Wiley & Sons, formed by the merger of Wiley's global
Scientific, Technical and Medical business with Blackwell Publishing.

Registered Office
John Wiley & Sons Ltd, The Atrium, Southern Gate, Chichester, West Sussex, PO19 8SQ, UK

Editorial Offices
350 Main Street, Malden, MA 02148-5020, USA
9600 Garsington Road, Oxford, OX4 2DQ, UK
The Atrium, Southern Gate, Chichester, West Sussex, PO19 8SQ, UK

For details of our global editorial offices, for customer services, and for information about how to
apply for permission to reuse the copyright material in this book please see our website at www.
wiley.com/wiley-blackwell.

The right of Pamela J. Smith to be identified as the author of this work has been asserted in
accordance with the UK Copyright, Designs and Patents Act 1988.

Library of Congress Cataloging-in-Publication Data
Smith, Pamela J.
Global trade policy: questions and answers/Pamela J. Smith.
pages cm
Includes bibliographical references and index.
ISBN 978-0-470-67128-3 (hardback: alk. paper) – ISBN 978-1-118-35765-1 (pbk.: alk. paper) – ISBN
1. Commercial policy. 2. International trade. I. Title.
HF1411.S4965 2013
382'.3–dc23
2013006411

A catalogue record for this book is available from the British Library.

Cover image: Earth at night China / Japan, detailed view of the earth from space with night lights.
© Matthias Kulka/Corbis.
Cover design by Design Deluxe

Set in 10.5/13 pt Minion by Toppan Best-set Premedia Limited
Printed in Singapore by Ho Printing Singapore Pte Ltd

1   2014

Contents

Acknowledgments

This book in many ways is not a sole authored text, but rather the cumulative product of the research and teaching of economists who have shaped the field of international trade. I have been blessed to have some of the leaders in the field as my mentors and colleagues. What these individuals have in common is their generosity with their time, their infectious enthusiasm for the topic of international trade, and their human kindness to me as their student (in earlier years) and colleague (in later years). While the content of this book has been shaped by these leaders, the format is my response to the learning styles and feedback of students in my courses over the past 20 years.

The seeds of my interest in international economics were first planted by *Shirley Gedeon* and *Douglas Kinnard*, professors at the University of Vermont. I began my path at Vermont in 1978 as a political science major, and gravitated naturally toward political economy courses with significant international content. While at Vermont, *Shirley Gedeon* provided extensive feedback on my written work on comparative economics and was the first to propose that I should consider a PhD in economics. *Douglas Kinnard* selected me to participate in a special course in International Relations requiring competitive admission and a non-traditional teaching format. Although three decades have passed, I credit these two mentors for planting the seeds of my interest in international economics.

In 1985, I began my graduate work in economics in the Master's program at Tufts University in Boston. At Tufts, I learned the fundamentals of microeconomic and macroeconomic theory, as well as econometrics, from a number of gifted teachers. This was an important time in my professional development as I had come to economics from political science and did not have the mathematics background that graduate economics programs require. While at Tufts, I took a course on Math for Economists from *Drusilla Brown*. She recognized my non-traditional background and aggressively called on me in her class and offered extra office hours to help me close the gap. I am grateful to her for her advising in mathematics. Also while at Tufts, I elected to take my field courses at the Fletcher School of Law and Diplomacy. This is where I took my first graduate courses in international economics.

After completing my Master's degree, I decided to explore the policy world before moving on to a doctoral program. During this intermission in my schooling, I worked as a research assistant with *Lester Gordon* at the Harvard Institute for Economics Development. Together we generated curriculum materials for a program on public budgeting and financial management for government officials in sub-Saharan African countries. This experience was my first exposure to the applied aspects of economic research and deepened my interests in international and development aspects of economic policy. After completing this project, I was offered a position as the Deputy Director of the Office of Science and Technology of the Executive Office of Economic Affairs for the State of Massachusetts. In this position, I worked closely with the Executive Director and wonderful mentor *Greg Watson*, on science and technology initiatives to promote the economic development of the state, including trade competitiveness. I also had the opportunity to translate our work into speech writing for Governor Michael Dukakis who was then pursuing the Democratic presidential nomination. These practical policy experiences were fundamental in shaping my later research work in international trade, economic growth and development, and intellectual property rights.

In 1989, I began my doctoral work in economics at the University of Wisconsin. During the next four years, I took multiple courses in international trade with *Bob Baldwin* and *Dave Richardson*, both leaders in the field and extraordinary mentors. These courses significantly expanded the breadth and depth of my knowledge of international trade and inspired me to become an international trade economist. I was also blessed with the opportunity to work as a research assistant with both *Bob Baldwin* and *Dave Richardson* for a substantial portion of my time at Wisconsin. Under their guidance, I learned a great deal about the political economy of trade (from Baldwin) and innovative empirical applications of trade theory (from Richardson). My work with Dave Richardson contributed substantially to my thesis research on the effects of knowledge capital and spillovers on international trade. This guidance was augmented by the strong econometric teaching and advising I received from *Arthur Goldberger*. These three outstanding role models left a legacy that I am grateful to carry forward.

After completing the doctoral program, I joined the economics faculty at Concordia University in Montreal, Quebec, Canada (1992–93), and then the University of Delaware (1993–98). During this time, I was invited by Dave Richardson to participate in a conference of the National Bureau of Economic Research (NBER) on international trade and growth. This initial experience lead to numerous subsequent research opportunities through the NBER, invited lectures at universities and the Federal Reserve Banks, and presentations at national and international conferences on economics including the American Economics Association meetings, among others. These conferences during the 1990s were enormously influential in shaping the character of my research and teaching.

During the 1990s, the international trade literature was evolving in significant ways to explain new patterns of trade including intra-industry trade and intra-firm trade. I was inspired by numerous leaders in the emerging areas of New trade theory, the economic geography of trade, growth and trade, and trade and multinationals, including *Robert Feenstra, Gene Grossman, Elhanan Helpman, Paul Krugman*, and *James Markusen*. I was also inspired by the work of *Paul Romer* on endogenous growth and *Zvi Griliches* on the economics of technical change, and *Jeffrey Bergstrand* on the Gravity model. In Part One of this book, I cover the traditional theme of inter-industry trade as well as the research on intra-industry and intra-firm trade inspired by these economists.

The 1990s was also an important decade in terms of the rapidly changing character of trade policy. The policy focus on tariffs had shifted to non-tariff measures including export subsidies and "trade-related" policies such as intellectual property rights, environmental policies, labor policies, and growth and development policies, among others. Applied research in these areas took a new prominence in the field of international trade. I have been particularly influenced by the research of *Keith Maskus* and database development of *Walter Park* on intellectual property rights, *Scott Taylor* on the environment, and *Robert Feenstra* on labor. These trade and trade-related policies are the focus of Parts Two and Three of this book, respectively.

Finally, the 1990s was a pivotal decade in terms of the character of arrangements for managing trade policy. A voluminous number of regional trade arrangements emerged as well as the establishment of the World Trade Organization (WTO) in 1995 as the successor of the Generalized Agreement on Tariffs and Trade (GATT). These arrangements focused more extensively on trade-related policies than did previous arrangements. The rapid economic integration via international trade also focused new attention on the forms and effects of alternative institutional arrangements (e.g., free trade areas, customs unions, multilateral arrangements) and political economy aspects of these arrangements. The evolution of this literature was advanced by foundational research by *Bob Baldwin, Anne Krueger*, and *Robert Stern*, among others. These institutional arrangements are the focus of Part Four of this book.

In 1998, I joined the faculty at the University of Minnesota in the Department of Applied Economics. Building on the foundations provided by many of the leaders, I have pursued research in the areas of international trade and policy, intellectual property rights, and trade and multinationals. My most recent research extends these themes to policy aspects of international trade in crops that are intensive in genetically modified organisms. My interests in applied research on agricultural trade and policy has been influenced by *Vernon Ruttan*, my colleague and role model for over a decade. I was blessed with the opportunity to work alongside *Vernon Ruttan*, who was a leader in research on agricultural development and science and technology policy. I will long remember his kindness, and curious and engaged mind.

I have also benefited at the University of Minnesota from the opportunity to concentrate my teaching almost exclusively in the area of international trade and policy, with periodic deviations into the fields of macroeconomics, and science and technology policy. For this teaching, I have benefited from several outstanding textbooks including Robert C. Feenstra, *Advanced International Trade: Theory and Evidence* (Princeton University Press, 2004); Robert C. Feenstra and Alan M. Taylor, *International Trade* (Worth, 2011); Paul R. Krugman, Maurice Obstfeld, and Marc J. Melitz, *International Economics: Theory and Policy* (Pearson-Addison Wesley, 2010); James R. Markusen, James R. Melvin, William H. Kaempfer, and Keith E. Maskus, *International Trade: Theory and Evidence* (McGraw-Hill, 1995), Dominick Salatore, *International Economics* (Wiley, 2007), among others. My own book does not seek to be a substitute for these texts, but rather a complement. The emphasis on "applied economics" in my teaching has shaped the format of this book, which emphasizes the prominent questions that trade theory seeks to answer and the guidance that trade theory can provide in assessing alternative policy choices. My hope is that this format will be accessible for students of economics, business, public policy, and fields of applied economics.

I have worked with some outstanding students over the past 20 years. These students have challenged me to dig deeper into my understanding of international trade and policy. I believe that we teach what we need to learn. I have learned a tremendous amount from teaching undergraduate, masters, and doctoral students from various disciplines and from around the world. These students remind me of two fundamental questions: *So what, and who cares?* or *What's at stake, and for whom?* With these questions in mind, I have written this book with explicit attention to the multiple perspectives both within countries and across countries, as well as the perspectives of countries influenced by the policies of their trading partners.

Finally, I am grateful to the reviewers whose input has improved this book, to the editors at John Wiley and Sons, and to Augustine Mok for creating the electronic versions of the tables and figures in this book. I take credit for all remaining errors.

Last but not least, I am thankful for the support of my dear friends Mindy Goldman, Margot Giblin, Kristen Harrington, and Darcie McCann, and my family Teagan Burch, Kurt Burch, Henry Smith, Mary Jane Smith, Kathy Shelley, Chuck Smith, and Betsy Campeau, who have witnessed and blessed my path for decades.

List of Tables

List of Figures

Preface

This book is intended for Master's level (or advanced undergraduate) courses in business, public policy, economics, and applied economics. I assume that readers have completed undergraduate courses in microeconomics and/or macroeconomics. My goal is to bring the reader from that common point up to the recent research on international trade policy. The material covered will give the reader the foundation needed to understand the current debates in international trade policy as well as current research in the field. This book is particularly suitable for courses covering topics in international trade, international economics, economic policy, global economy, theory of international trade, globalization, managing international trade and investment, and other international policy concerns. The website http://www.wiley.com/go/globaltradepolicy provides materials to support instructors in using this book in a variety of environments at the graduate and advanced undergraduate levels.

The book is designed to reflect the evolution of international trade policy in terms of real-world practice and the academic literature. During the past two decades, the character of international trade and policy has changed in unprecedented ways. Trade in different goods across countries (i.e., inter-industry trade) has been augmented by trade in similar goods (i.e., intra-industry trade) and trade between foreign affiliates of multinational firms (i.e, intra-firm trade). At the same time, the instruments of trade policy have evolved. Attention has turned from traditional trade policies (such as tariffs, quantitative restrictions, and export subsidies) to "trade-related policies" (such as intellectual property rights, labor policies, environmental policies, and growth and development policies). The institutional arrangements for these policies continue to evolve with substantial international debate. This book offers an accessible coverage of these topics and an economic framework for thinking.

The book is organized into four parts. The *first* part covers topics that are typically found in theory books on international economics. The intent of this part is to provide the background in trade theory that is useful to guide discussions of trade policy. The material includes traditional theories of inter-industry trade as well as newer theories of intra-industry and intra-firm trade. The *second* part of the book covers trade policies and their effects. This part focuses on widely used policies that are designed to affect international trade flows directly. These policies include tariffs, export subsidies, and quantitative restrictions. The intent of this part is to explore the effects (at the national, subnational, and global levels) of both imposing and liberalizing these policies. The *third* part of the book covers trade-related policies. This part focuses on policies that are designed for a purpose other than targeting trade. However, these policies still have a significant effect on international trade flows. These trade-related policies include intellectual property rights, environmental policies, labor policies, and growth and development policies. The *fourth* part of the book explores the arrangements within which trade policies are designed, adopted and managed. This part covers multilateral and regional arrangements including customs unions and free trade areas.

The book also provides supplemental materials to deepen the reader's understanding of trade policy. *Applied problems* provide the reader with the opportunity to explore the overarching themes of each part and to apply these themes to issues of current policy debate. These problems do not have definitive answers. Rather, they are designed to allow the reader to apply the theories/models to explore open-ended questions of policy debate. These applied problems are a particularly important component of the book. They allow to the reader apply the frameworks developed to country and industry scenarios that match with their interests. They also help the reader to identify the perspective of alternative arguments in policy debates and to articulate explicitly the underlying assumptions of these perspectives. Because the applied problems do not have right or wrong answers, they require a level of critical thinking particularly valuable in graduate environments.

The book also provides rich listings of *further reading* associated with the topics of each chapter. These provide the reader with the classic and recent literature on topics of trade policy and include journal articles, books, reports and working papers that may prompt further graduate research in topics of trade policy. They emphasize the literature that is on the frontier of the field of trade policy. These readings can be used as the core content of PhD courses in international trade policy. In such advanced graduate settings, this book can be used as the foundation or springboard for the advanced research found in the journal articles.

The book is unique in several ways. First, to my knowledge, there are no other books on international trade policy that target a Master's level audience in business, public policy, economics, and applied economics. Because the book targets a multidisciplinary audience, it is written using accessible language, realistic applications, and applied problems. It is designed particularly for readers who are learning to integrate concepts and apply their knowledge/thinking to open-ended questions of policy debate.

Second, the book focuses on international trade policy (a subfield of international economics) and broadens the definition of policy to include trade-related policies, which are the subject of much current debate. This book gives substantial attention to these trade-related policies, including intellectual property rights, environmental policies, labor policies, and growth and development policies. It also gives considerable attention to multilateral and regional trade policy arrangements.

Third, the format of the book is designed around questions, rather than on the traditional model-based format. That is, the models are covered in the book for the purpose of providing the tools and skills to answer the questions. However, these models are presented in the context of the questions to which they apply. This is important because readers can learn the models (using traditional book formats) without much understanding of how to apply the models to real-world questions. They are then unable to take the next step, which is to select the appropriate modeling frameworks to analyze real-world policy questions. This book provides an alternative, in that its organization around questions is designed to support this leap in learning to apply knowledge.

Fourth, the book is designed to explicitly identify perspectives, including the aggregate national, subnational, and global perspectives, as well as the perspectives of consumers, producers, governments, and others who comprise the aggregates. These perspectives are often implicit in discussions of international trade policy and thus can lead to confusion. By making the perspective explicit, this book seeks to help the reader place alternative viewpoints within the larger overarching framework for thinking about trade policy. The book considers the effects of national policies on countries that impose the policies, as well as the effects on trading partners and globally. For example, discussions of international trade policy typically focus on national-level effects, such as the effects of a tariff on the country that imposes the tariff. In contrast, this book covers these national effects as well as the international effects, such as the effects of a tariff on the trading partners of the country that imposes the policy. These perspectives are useful as they help explain opposing views on trade policy and liberalization.

Finally, the applied problems are a particularly distinctive component of the book. These applied problems allow the reader to apply the models and concepts in the book to answer a broad range of contemporary policy issues. These problems require that readers identify the underlying assumptions, choose between alternative frameworks for thinking, and apply the frameworks to open-ended questions that do not have right or wrong answers. The applied problems cover a broad range of issues of interest to a multidisciplinary audience. Examples include: the effects of export subsidies in Europe and North America on farmers in the developing world; the national and international implications of intellectual property rights for genetically modified crops; the use of trade policy to address domestic and global externalities such as water pollution and global warming; the effects of trade policy on income inequality between skilled and unskilled labor in developed and developing countries; and the role of trade in promoting growth and development that is welfare improving.

The ultimate goal of this book is to provide readers with the ability to identify the divergent perspectives around current trade policy debates, clarify what is at stake and for whom, and develop creative policy solutions.

Part One

Trade Theory as Guidance to Trade Policy

1

Preliminaries
Trade Theory

1.1   What Are the Core Questions Asked by International Trade Economists?

The field of *international economics* within the economics discipline explores transactions that occur across national borders. Flows across national borders include movements of goods, services, factors of production, and financial assets. Flows of goods, services, and factors of production are considered to be "real" movements and fall under the subfield of *international trade*. Flows of financial assets are considered to be "nominal" movements and fall under the subfield of *international finance*. These two subfields are the primary branches of the field of international economics. This book focuses on international trade – real flows of goods, services and factors of production across national borders. Furthermore, it focuses specifically on the policy dimensions of international trade, that is, policies that alter international trade in some way.

We begin our study of *international trade policy* with the basics of trade theory in Part One. The topics of trade theory address three primary dimensions of trade. The first dimension is the *patterns of trade*. That is, why do countries export and import what they do? The second dimension is *gains from trade*. That is, who wins and who loses from trade? The third dimension is *protectionism*. That is, what are the effects of adding or removing policies that distort trade? Our goal in exploring these questions is to show how trade theory can provide guidance to trade policy.

Global Trade Policy: Questions and Answers, First Edition. Pamela J. Smith.
© 2014 John Wiley & Sons, Inc. Published 2014 by John Wiley & Sons, Inc.

1.2   How Can Trade Theory Provide Guidance to Trade Policy?

Trade theory provides guidance to trade policy in a direct way. Trade theories that explain the patterns of trade and gains from trade typically compare two hypothetical states – autarky and free trade. *Autarky* is a state of no trade, which cannot be observed in our current reality. *Free trade* is a state of trade that is undistorted by policies, which also cannot be observed in our current reality. Trade theories typically predict the patterns and gains from trade when we move from the hypothetical state of autarky to free trade or, conversely, when we move from the hypothetical state of free trade to autarky.

In reality, the state of trade lies somewhere in between these two hypothetical extremes. However, understanding the effects of moving between the two extremes in theory provides guidance for understanding trade policy in practice. That is, when barriers to trade are added, we take one step closer to autarky; and when barriers to trade are removed, we take one step closer to free trade. In other words, the direction of the effects of moving from autarky to free trade corresponds with the effects of liberalizing policy barriers to trade. Similarly, the direction of the effects of moving from free trade to autarky corresponds with the effects of adding protectionist policies.

Trade theory also provides guidance to trade policy in several indirect ways. For example, analysis of the patterns of trade involves exploring the sources of comparative advantage. Understanding the sources of comparative advantage is a prerequisite to designing policies that seek to alter the patterns of trade. For example, if we know that an abundance of skilled labor provides a comparative advantage in services, then we can predict that countries abundant in skilled labor will export services. National policies that promote this comparative advantage would be those that seek to increase a country's abundance of skilled labor. Similarly, if we know that an abundance of forests provides a comparative advantage in paper products, then we can predict that countries abundant in forests will export paper products. National policies that promote this comparative advantage would be those that seek to increase a country's abundance of forests for use in manufacturing paper.

Second, analysis of the distribution of gains and losses from trade helps us to understand the economic incentives behind the sometimes contentious viewpoints on trade policy. This understanding is prerequisite to efforts to reach a consensus across divergent groups, and for designing redistribution policies. For example, if we know that trade liberalization will result in an uneven distribution of gains and losses across countries, and within countries, then policies can be adopted for redistribution purposes, or for assistance during the transition periods following liberalization. Furthermore, if we understand the distributional effects of trade, then this understanding can provide guidance as countries negotiate individual policy changes or changes in portfolios of policies. That is, this understanding is prerequisite to designing policies and policy portfolios where gains and losses are counterbalanced in some equitable manner.

Finally, analysis of the effects of alternative trade policy instruments and alternative policy arrangements is prerequisite for making optimal choices between these instruments and arrangements. For example, two policy instruments, (such as tariffs and quotas) may both be effective in achieving a goal (such as protection of a domestic industry). However, one of the two instruments may have fewer side effects in the form of new distortions or welfare losses. Similarly, two policy arrangements (such as customs unions and free trade areas) may both be effective in achieving a goal (such as trade liberalization). However, one of the two arrangements may be relatively more trade-creating while the other may be trade-diverting. Understanding such effects of policies and policy arrangements is a prerequisite to making optimal policy choices in a coordinated manner.

1.3 How Has International Trade Evolved over Time in Practice?

Before turning to our discussion of trade theory, it is important to note that the character of international trade in *practice* has evolved over time. The character of international trade *theory* has also evolved in response to the real-world changes in trade. In the remainder of this preliminary chapter, we describe these changes. First, we describe how trade has changed in practice. Then we described how the trade theory literature has evolved to address these changes. Finally, we describe how this book is organized in relation to this evolution.

So, how has international trade evolved over time? First, the volume and value of international trade have *grown* dramatically. From a global perspective, growth in international trade corresponds with an increase in the interconnectedness of national economies. However, from a national perspective the importance of international trade varies considerably. One way to assess the importance of trade to a particular country is to consider whether the country is open or closed in an economic sense. In a political sense, whether a country is open or closed refers to the degree to which the country institutes policy barriers to trade. The economic interpretation of openness is somewhat different. Countries that are *open* in an economic sense are those for which trade is a relatively large share of their overall economic activity. Countries that are *closed* to trade are those for which trade is a relatively small share of their overall economic activity. Countries that are relatively open to trade are more economically sensitive to changes in international markets, including policy changes.

Second, the *composition* of international trade has evolved over time. There is a long history of trade in agricultural and manufactured goods. However, in the last two decades, trade in services has grown dramatically, particularly since the 1980s. Trade in services is defined broadly to include all modes of conducting international transactions. For example, trade in services includes financial services, accounting services, insurance services, and technical assistance services. It also includes foreign investments in telecommunications and transportation. And it includes movements of people across borders for the purpose of education, medical, and educational services. The expansion of trade in services is due in large part to advances in information technologies and telecommunications.

Third, the character of the *firm* has changed. In the past, firms were characterized as national firms that were associated with the geographic location of production. However, with the emergence of *foreign direct investment*, the location of the production of subsidiaries no longer corresponds with the location of ownership of the firm. Further, with the emergence of *multinational firms*, both the location and ownership of firms can span multiple countries throughout the world. This new character of firms is also associated with movements across countries of factors of production. For example, a parent firm may transfer factor inputs such as knowledge capital or labor to subsidiaries located in other countries.

Fourth, along with the changes in the character of firms, the *type* of international trade has evolved over time. Types of trade include inter-industry trade, intra-industry trade, inter-firm trade, and intra-firm trade. *Inter-industry trade* occurs when countries trade dissimilar goods with one another. *Intra-industry trade* occurs when countries trade different varieties of similar goods with one another. *Inter-firm trade* occurs between different national firms. *Intra-firm trade* occurs when the trade across countries occurs within the same multinational firm. For example, if a country exports manufactured goods to another country in exchange for agricultural goods, this is inter-industry trade because the goods are distinct. However, if a country exports one variety of electronics to another country in exchange for a different variety of electronics, this is intra-industry trade. If this trade occurs between different national firms with ownership in the different countries, then this is inter-firm trade. However, if the trade occurs between a parent firm and a subsidiary, or two firms under the same multinational umbrella, then this is intra-firm trade.

Early patterns of trade were predominantly inter-industry and inter-firm. However, the predominance of intra-industry trade has increased, particularly since the 1970s and 1980s. And intra-firm trade has increased with the rise of foreign direct investment and multinational firm activities, particularly since the late 1980s.

1.4   How Has Trade Theory Evolved over Time?

Trade theory has evolved in response to these real-world changes. The international trade literature includes distinct bodies of research that reflect this evolution. These include traditional trade theory, New trade theory, and Trade and Multinationals theory. The literature also includes applications of trade theory that account for the effects of policy instruments and policy arrangements.

Traditional trade theory is grounded on the core concept known as the *law of comparative advantage*. This states that countries tend to export those goods that have a lower relative cost, and therefore price, in autarky (i.e., the state of no trade). Conversely, countries tend to import those goods that have a higher relative cost, and therefore price, in autarky. So what does this mean? If we could observe the costs – and thus prices – of producing all goods in all countries in a state of autarky, then we could predict which goods each country would import and export when we allow for trade.

For example, suppose that the cost of producing good x is low relative to the cost of producing good y in country A; and the cost of producing good y is low relative to the cost of producing good x in country B. Then, the law of comparative advantage would predict that country A will specialize in producing good x, and will export x and import y. Similarly, country B will specialize in producing good y, and will export y and import x. Furthermore, when each country specializes in this manner in their sector of comparative advantage, their joint output is higher. Consequently, with trade, their joint consumption is higher. In this sense, the well-being of the two countries increases as a consequence of their trade based on comparative advantage.

This concept of comparative advantage is often confused with the concept of *absolute advantage*. This describes the case where a country can produce a good or many goods at lower costs than another country or countries. In contrast, the concept of comparative advantage compares the *relative costs* of producing goods within a given country. If a country has an absolute advantage in many goods, one might argue that this country should produce all of these lower cost goods. However, the weakness of this argument is that countries face resource constraints. That is, factor inputs are not available in infinite supply, thus trade offs in production must be made. That is, a country with an absolute advantage can still specialize based on comparative advantage and gain from trade.

Extending our prior example, suppose that country A has an absolute advantage in producing both good x and good y. In other words, country A can produce goods x and y at a lower absolute cost than country B. However, in relative terms, suppose that country A can produce good x at a lower cost relative to good y; and country B can produce good y at a lower cost relative to good x. The presence of an absolute advantage does not conflict with the presence of a comparative advantage. That is, a country (such as A) can have an absolute advantage in goods x and y and a comparative advantage in good x. Similarly, a country (such as B) can have an absolute disadvantage in goods x and y and a comparative advantage in good y.

Gains from specialization and trade result when countries specialize based on comparative advantage. The intuition is that countries specialize in the goods that they can produce at a lower relative cost and export these goods. Similarly, countries import goods that they would otherwise produce themselves at a higher relative cost. When multiple countries specialize and trade, there are gains from trade. These gains are reflected in the lower costs and prices, and the higher overall output and consumption of the trading countries in aggregate. The gains in consumption correspond with improvements in economic well-being (or welfare).

Traditional trade theory is based on this core concept of comparative advantage as an explanation for inter-industry trade. The various models found in the traditional trade literature differ primarily in the source of the comparative advantage. That is, the theories differ in their explanations of what causes the relative cost and price differences across countries. For example, in the Ricardian model, relative differences in technologies across countries are the source of comparative advantage. In the Heckscher-Ohlin model, relative differences in endowments across countries are the source of comparative advantage. In the specific factors model, relative differences in immobile factors of production are the source of comparative advantage. Each of these traditional models explains the patterns of inter-industry trade based on comparative advantage arising from these various sources.

These traditional trade models share several underlying assumptions. For example, they assume a market structure of perfect competition. They assume constant returns to scale technologies. They assume a world in which trade occurs between the national firms of different countries. And, they typically assume that factors of production are immobile across countries. Furthermore, the traditional trade models have in common the type of trade that they predict, which is *inter-industry* and *inter-firm* trade. As we depart from traditional trade theory, we relax these core underlying assumptions to reflect changes in trade in practice.

New trade theory emerged as an extension of traditional trade theory in the late 1970s and early 1980s. It was originally associated with work by Paul Krugman, who along with other international trade economists observed that countries with similar technologies and similar endowments were trading with each other. Furthermore, they observed that similar countries were trading different varieties of similar goods. This new form of trade was *intra-industry* rather than inter-industry. But, traditional trade theory could not explain this real-world behavior. For example, countries that are similar in technologies or endowments would not trade different varieties of similar goods according to traditional explanations of comparative advantage. This observation prompted the emergence of research studies on economies of scale and product differentiation in imperfectly competitive markets, as an explanation for intra-industry trade. In this New trade theory literature, intra-industry trade could occur independently of the patterns of comparative advantage explained by traditional trade theory.

Trade and Multinationals theory also emerged in the 1980s as an extension of earlier trade theories. This new theory has its foundations in research on the multinational firm by John Dunning. This research was later linked to international trade by James Markusen and Elhanan Helpman, among others. International trade economists observed that firms could no longer be characterized as national firms. With the emergence of *foreign direct investment,* the location of the production of subsidiaries no longer corresponded with the location of ownership of the firm. Further, with the emergence of *multinational firms,* both the location and ownership of firms could span multiple countries throughout the world. Large volumes of trade now occured between parent firms and their subsidiaries, or between firms under the same multinational umbrella. These changes required a re-conception of the unit of analysis in international trade away from the country-based firm to the firm that spans multiple countries. Economists also observed intra-firm flows of factors of production, particularly mobile factors such as knowledge assets. These real-world changes gave rise to studies of new forms of *intra-firm trade*, including trade between parent firms and their subsidiaries, trade within multinational firms, and outsourcing and offshoring.

Each of these three theory literatures (traditional trade theory, New trade theory, and Trade and Multinationals theory) has been applied to examine the effects of policy instruments and policy arrangements. These applications of trade theory have evolved to reflect the evolution of policy instruments and arrangements in practice. By policy instruments, we mean measures that can be manipulated by governments to achieve social or economic outcomes. By policy arrangements we mean the methods by which different national governments coordinate the use of policy instruments.

Early research on policy instruments focused on tariffs as the primary policy tool. All other policy instruments were categorized under the broad heading of non-tariff measures (NTMs) or non-tariff barriers (NTBs). *Non-tariff measures* are defined as policies, rules, regulations, and practices – other than tariffs – that distort international trade. *Non-tariff barriers* comprise a subset of NTMs that reduce rather than augment trade. Non-tariff measures include policies that are designed specifically to affect trade. These include export subsidies that artificially increase trade and quantitative restrictions such as quotas that artificially decrease trade. Non-tariff measures also include trade-related policies. *Trade-related policies* are instruments that are designed for non-trade purposes, but affect trade as a side effect. These include policies related to intellectual property rights, the environment, labor, and growth and development, among many others. The application of trade theory to examine a broad range of non-tariff measures has grown along with the use of these instruments, particularly since the 1980s, and is an ongoing area of research for international trade economists.

Finally, research has evolved with the changing nature of policy arrangements. Such arrangements include bilateral treaties, regional trade arrangements such as customs unions and free trade areas, and multilateral agreements, among others. Prominent examples of customs unions include the European Union (EU) and the Central American Common Market (CACM). Prominent examples of free trade areas include the North American Free Trade Area (NAFTA) and the Free Trade Area of the Americas (FTAA). Prominent examples of multilateral arrangements include the General Agreement on Tariffs and Trade (GATT) and its successor, the World Trade Organization (WTO). These arrangements govern trade between their member countries. The prominence and membership of such arrangements have grown dramatically, particularly since the 1990s. The research literature has evolved to reflect these changes in trade arrangements.

1.5 How Is the Book Organized?

The overarching organization of this book is based on this evolution of international trade and policy, in terms of real-world practice and in terms of academic research.

Part One of the book focuses on trade theory as guidance to trade policy. This part is divided into two core chapters. Chapter 2 covers three prominent models from traditional trade theory that explain *inter-industry trade*. These include the Ricardian model, the Heckscher-Ohlin model, and the Specific Factors model. We use the Ricardian model to assess the question: What are the effects of trade in the long run, when countries differ in technologies? We use the Heckscher-Ohlin model to assess the question: What are the effects of trade in the long run, when countries differ in endowments? We use the Specific Factors model to examine the question: What are the effects of trade in the short run, when countries differ in immobile endowments? Further, we use the Heckscher-Ohlin and Specific Factors models to assess the distributional effects of trade within and across countries in the long and short run, respectively.

Chapter 3 then covers explanations of *intra-industry trade* and *intra-firm trade*. We use frameworks from the New trade theory literature to examine the questions: What is intra-industry trade and its effects? Specifically, what are the patterns and gains from intra-industry trade? We use frameworks from the Trade and Multinationals literature to examine the questions: What is intra-firm trade and its effects? Specifically, what are the patterns and motives for foreign direct investment? How is trade related to foreign direct investment? What are the patterns and motives for outsourcing and offshoring?

We then turn to specific trade policies. Part Two covers *traditional trade policies* and their effects. Traditional trade policies are policies that are specifically targeted to affect trade. Chapter 4 provides preliminary background on traditional trade policies. This chapter includes a discussion of approaches used to examine trade policy. It also includes an overarching discussion of the concept of welfare (or well-being), and the welfare effects of liberalizing trade policy. The remaining chapters in Part 2 focus on prominent traditional trade policies. In each chapter we examine the questions: What are the effects of the policy? What are the effects of liberalizing the policy? Chapter 5 considers these questions for tariffs, Chapter 6 covers export subsidies, and Chapter 7 covers quantitative restrictions, including import quotas, voluntary export restraints, and bans. Chapter 8 then provides policy comparisons of these traditional trade measures. The comparisons are used to assess the relative effects of liberalizing policies, as well as the effects of substituting one policy (such as a quantitative restriction) for another policy (such as a tariff). These comparisons provide a foundation for understanding modern hybrid policies such as tariff rate quotas.

Part Three then covers *trade-related policies* and their effects. Trade-related policies are policies designed for non-trade purposes that also affect trade as a side effect. Chapter 9 provides preliminary background on trade-related policies. This chapter considers how trade-related policies toward goods have evolved over time in practice. It also considers how policies toward services trade have evolved over time in practice, given the rapid growth of this sector. The remaining chapters in Part Three focus on prominent trade-related policies. In each chapter we ask the two-way questions: What are the effects of the trade-related policies on trade?

What are the effects of trade policies on the conditions that are the targets of the trade-related policies? Chapter 10 considers these questions for intellectual property rights policies, Chapter 11 covers environmental policies, Chapter 12 covers labor policies, and Chapter 13 covers growth and development policies. Each of these policies are intimately connected to trade. These policies have been the source of heated debates between developed and developing countries in recent trade negotiations.

Part Four covers the *institutional arrangements* for trade policy. Chapter 14 begins by considering alternative forms of arrangement for trade policy, including bilateral and multilateral arrangements, as well as regional arrangements such as free trade areas and customs unions. This chapter also covers the prominent multilateral arrangements in practice, including the evolution of policies negotiated under the GATT and its successor the WTO. The chapter then considers the effects of alternative arrangements for trade policy. Questions considered include: What are the effects of regional liberalization? What are the effects of multilateral liberalization? What are the effects of country exclusion from multilateral arrangements? Finally, this chapter considers whether or not regional arrangements facilitate the movement toward broader multilateral liberalization; that is: Are regional arrangements stepping stones or stumbling blocks to multilateral liberalization?

This book is titled *Global Trade Policy* rather than the more traditional *International Trade Policy*. There are two reasons for this choice. First, the words "global trade" better reflect the contemporary version of trade that we observe in the real world. "International trade" refers to trade that is common to or affecting two or more countries. "Global trade" is more comprehensive and general, and places weaker boundaries on what is conceived of as trade (such as intra-firm flows, or regional versus multilateral flows). Second, this book seeks to encourage a shift in thinking away from the national perspective toward a more purely global perspective. The national perspective tends to have an "us versus them" flavor that is often implicit rather than explicit in discussions of trade policy. In contrast, this book takes great care to make the perspective explicit and to generalize to the global perspective whenever feasible.

Throughout the book, the ultimate goal is to illustrate the implications of trade and policy for the economic well-being of people at the subnational, national, and global levels. Thus, the book gives explicit attention to these multiple perspectives, which include the perspectives of consumers, producers, and governments associated with a trading country, countries in relation to one another, and the global economy. The overarching questions of the book are: *What is at stake, and for whom?* The answers are: *economic well-being, and it depends*.

Further Reading

Feenstra, Robert C. 2004. *Advanced International Trade: Theory and Evidence*. Princeton, NJ: Princeton University Press.

Feenstra, Robert C., and Alan M. Taylor. 2011. *International Trade*, 2nd edn. New York: Worth Publishing.

Feenstra, Robert C., and Alan M. Taylor. 2012. *International Economics*, 2nd edn. New York: Worth Publishing.

Helpman, Elhanan. 2011. *Understanding Global Trade*. Cambridge: Harvard University Press.

Krugman, Paul R., Maurice Olstfeld, and Marc J. Melitz. 2010. *International Economics:Theory and Policy*, 9th edition. New York: Pearson-Addison Wesley.

Markusen, James R., J. R. Melvin, K. E. Maskus, and W. Kempfer. 1995.*International Trade: Theory and Application*. New York: McGraw Hill.

Salvatore, Dominick. 2007. *International Economics*, 9th edn. New York: John Wiley and Sons, Inc.

2
Inter-Industry Trade

This chapter presents three traditional models of inter-industry and inter-firm trade. *Inter-industry trade* is two-way trade between countries in dissimilar goods. *Inter-firm trade* is trade between national firms of different countries. For example, inter-industry trade occurs when country A exports good x to country B and imports good y from country B, where x and y are dissimilar goods. When this trade is between national firms of countries A and B, then it is inter-firm trade. Traditional models of inter-industry, inter-firm trade include the Ricardian model, the Heckscher-Ohlin model, and the Specific Factors model.

All three of these traditional models are grounded on the concept of comparative advantage. However, the models differ in their source of comparative advantage. The source of comparative advantage in the Ricardian model is country differences in technologies; in the Heckscher-Ohlin model, it is country differences in endowments; and in the Specific Factors model it is country differences in endowments that are immobile across industries (i.e., "specific factors"). Furthermore, the Ricardian and Heckscher-Ohlin models are both long-run models because they assume that factors of production are mobile across industries. In contrast, the specific factors model is a short-run variation of the Heckscher-Ohlin model, where the Specific Factors are endowments that are immobile across industries. All three models focus on the supply side and leave demand-side considerations to extensions.

In this chapter, we use these three models to evaluate three core questions: (1) What are the effects of trade in the long run, when countries differ in technologies? (2) What are the effects of trade in the long run, when countries differ in endowments? (3) What are the effects of trade in the short run, when countries differ in immobile endowments?

Global Trade Policy: Questions and Answers, First Edition. Pamela J. Smith.
© 2014 John Wiley & Sons, Inc. Published 2014 by John Wiley & Sons, Inc.

2.1   What Are the Effects of Trade in the Long Run, When Countries Differ in Technologies?

We begin our analysis of the long-run effects of trade by presenting the Ricardian model. This model is the most basic general equilibrium model of international trade. The source of comparative advantage in the Ricardian model is technology differences across countries. These technology differences determine the production possibilities, and relative costs and prices of the goods that countries produce in autarky. As a consequence, these technology differences determine the patterns of trade across countries. These are the patterns of trade that occur in the long run after resources (i.e., factors of production) have been reallocated across the various industries in the countries.

As we work through this model, we consider five component questions for a representative home and foreign country: (1) What are the production possibilities? (2) What are the relative costs and prices in autarky? (3) What are the world prices with trade and patterns of trade? (4) What are the gains from trade? (5) What are the effects of liberalizing trade policy? We introduce the model here by laying out the core underlying assumptions. We then consider the questions above by evaluating and comparing the hypothetical state of autarky (no trade) with the hypothetical state of free trade (no barriers).

To begin, the Ricardian model differs from other traditional models in that it relaxes the assumption that *technologies* are similar across countries. In the Ricardian model, technologies are reflected in the factor productivities or the amount of an input required to produce a given amount of output. Typically and historically, the Ricardian model is articulated in terms of labor productivity as an expression of these technology differences. However, this is illustrative only. Indeed, the technology differences can be expressed in terms of any factor input. Thus, in the following example, we refer to a generic factor of production (f).

For illustrative purposes, we present a simple expression of the Ricardian model. But keep in mind, this expression can be extended to more complicated scenarios and produce similar results. The basic expression presented here assumes the following: There are two countries – home and foreign. (Throughout this book we will denote the foreign country with an asterisk.) There are two goods – x and y. There is one homogeneous factor of production – f. The market structure is perfect competition, such that goods are priced at the cost of production. The mobility of the factor of production is such that it is immobile across countries, but is mobile across industries within a country. The productivity of the factor differs across countries. This last assumption reflects technology differences across countries.

Further, the technologies are constant returns to scale. This means that a fixed amount of the factor is required to produce a unit of output. The productivities (or technologies) are reflected in *unit input requirements*. These express the amount of the factor required to produce a unit of the output. For example, a_x is the amount of the generic factor f required to produce one unit of good x; and a_y is the amount of the generic factor f required to produce one unit of good y. These tech-nologies can be expressed in relative terms as a_y/a_x or a_x/a_y. And these relative technologies can differ across countries. For example, we may observe that $a_y/a_x < a_y^*/a_x^*$, where the term on the left-hand side reflects relative productivities in the home country and the term on the right reflects relative productivities in the foreign country. In this case, the amount of factor f required to produce good y is relatively low in the home country and relatively high in the foreign country. Similarly, the amount of factor f required to produce good x is relatively high in the home country and relatively low in the foreign country.

2.1.1   What are the production possibilities?

We can determine the production possibilities of countries using our knowledge of their technology differences and their factor supplies. The *production possibilities frontier* (PPF) shows the trade off between production of good x (Q_x) and good y (Q_y) given the technologies and factor supplies of each country. Equations (2.1) and (2.2) show the production possibilities for the home and foreign countries:

$$a_x Q_x + a_y Q_y \leq F \tag{2.1}$$

$$a_x^* Q_x^* + a_y^* Q_y^* \leq F^* \tag{2.2}$$

where F and F* are the total supply of the generic factor in the home and foreign countries respectively; and the other variables are defined as above. Equation (2.1) shows that the amount of the generic factor used to produce outputs of good x plus good y must be less than or equal to the amount of the factor supply within the country. Equation (2.2) shows the same relationship for the foreign country. Assum-ing that the generic factor is fully employed within each country (e.g., there is no unemployment of the factor), then equations (2.1) and (2.2) hold with equality.

Figure 2.1 shows these production possibilities of the home (a) and foreign (b) countries, respectively. This illustration is a plotting of equations (2.1) and (2.2) derived by rearranging the equations as follows:

$$Q_x = F/a_x - (a_y/a_x)Q_y \tag{2.3}$$

$$Q_x^* = F^*/a_x^* - (a_y^*/a_x^*)Q_y^* \tag{2.4}$$

The figures and equations show the trade off between producing goods x and y, given the relative technologies reflected in the slopes of the frontiers (a_y/a_x) and (a_y^*/a_x^*). Intuitively, the slopes reflect the opportunity cost of producing good x in terms of the amount of good y foregone, and vice versa. In this illustration, the home country's technology favors production of good y and the foreign country's technology favors production of good x, since $a_y/a_x < a_y^*/a_x^*$.

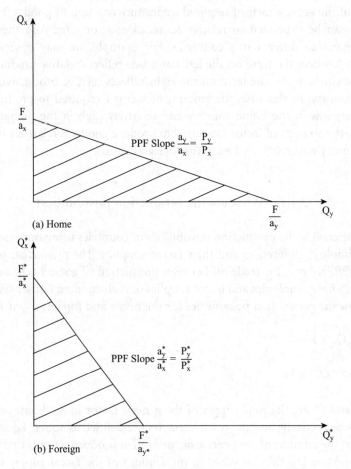

Figure 2.1 Ricardian model – production possibilities of home and foreign.

2.1.2 What are the relative costs and prices in autarky?

We can now use the production possibilities frontiers to answer questions about the hypothetical state of autarky. Specifically, what are the relative costs and prices in autarky for each country? Recall that these relative costs and prices tell us about the comparative advantage of each country (as discussed in Chapter 1).

In our example, we have one factor (f) and two goods (x and y). When we refer to relative costs, we mean the relative price of factor f in the two industries. We refer to the price of this generic factor as the rental rate (r). Further, P_x is the price of good x and P_y is the price of good y. These goods prices and factor prices are related to each other. Specifically, given the assumption of perfect competition, profits are zero and the price of the factor equals the value of the factor's marginal product. This gives the following relationships:

$$r_x = P_x / a_x \tag{2.5}$$

$$r_y = P_y / a_y \tag{2.6}$$

where r_x and r_y are the price of the generic factor used to produce goods x and y, respectively.

Further, given the assumption that the generic factor is mobile across industries, we know that $r_x = r_y$. This is because mobile factors of production move freely to the industry with the highest rental rate. For example, if $r_x \geq r_y$, then the generic factor will move from industry y to industry x. This movement puts downward pressure on the rental rate in industry x and upward pressure on the rental rate in industry y. This movement continues until the factor prices (rental rates) equalize across the industries. Similarly, if $r_x \leq r_y$ then the factor will move from industry x to industry y until the factor prices (rental rates) equalize across the two industries. When we equate the factor prices shown in equations (2.5) and (2.6), we get

$$r_x = r_y = P_x / a_x = P_y / a_y \tag{2.7}$$

When factor prices equate in this manner, then countries are indifferent between producing goods x and y. Intuitively this means that the home and foreign countries may choose to produce anywhere along their production possibilities curves, shown in Figure 2.1 (a) and (b).

We can now determine the relative prices of goods in autarky by rearranging equation (2.7) as

$$P_y / P_x = a_y / a_x \tag{2.8}$$

where the left-hand term is the relative price of good y to x and the right-hand term is the relative factor input requirement. This equation shows that in autarky, the relative prices of goods equals the relative technologies of a country. This relationship also appears in Figures 2.1 (a) and (b), where the slope of the production possibilities curves equates with both the relative technologies and the relative autarky prices of the goods in the home and foreign countries. In this illustration, the home country has a lower relative price of good y to x; and the foreign country has a lower relative price of good x to y. These are the relative goods prices in autarky that arise from the country differences in technologies.

2.1.3   What are the world prices with trade and patterns of trade?

We can now extend our analysis to the hypothetical state of free trade. This is the counter extreme to the state of autarky. In this state of free trade, what are the relative prices of goods x and y? How do these relative prices compare with the autarky prices? What are the patterns of trade at the world prices?

Continuing our prior example, we assume that there are technology differences across the home and foreign countries such that

$$a_y/a_x < a_y^*/a_x^* \qquad\qquad\qquad (2.9)$$

That is, the amount of factor f required to produce good y is relatively low in the home country and relatively high in the foreign country. And, the amount of factor f required to produce good x is relatively low in the foreign country and relatively high in the home country. Combining equations (2.8) and (2.9), we also know that

$$P_y/P_x < P_y^*/P_x^* \qquad\qquad\qquad (2.10)$$

where the price of good y is relatively low in the home country and high in the foreign country. Alternatively stated, the price of good x is relatively high in the home country and low in the foreign country. These are the relative autarky prices.

What then is the relative price of goods at which trade will occur in the world market? The intuitive answer is that countries will only trade at prices that are more favorable then their internal prices in the state of autarky. That is, countries will export goods at higher prices and import goods at lower prices relative to autarky. To illustrate this intuition, we must look at the world market for goods x and y.

The world market comprises the combined supply and demand of the countries of the "world". Given our model of two countries, the world quantities supplied of goods x and y are the sums of the quantities of the two countries. Thus

$$Q_x^w = Q_x + Q_x^* \qquad\qquad\qquad (2.11)$$

$$Q_y^w = Q_y + Q_y^*$$

where Q_x^w is the world output of good x and Q_y^w is the world output of good y.

Figure 2.2 illustrates the determination of world prices. This figure presents the familiar supply and demand curves expressed alternatively in relative terms. That is, this figure plots the world relative supply S^w and demand D^w curves for goods x and y. The relative demand curve shows that the relative world demand for good y increases as the relative price of good y falls. The relative supply curve is discontinuous. When the relative world price (P_y^w/P_x^w) equals the home country's relative autarky price (P_y/P_x), then the home country is indifferent between supplying good x and y. Similarly, when the relative world price (P_y^w/P_x^w) equals the foreign country's relative autarky price (P_y^*/P_x^*), then the foreign country is indifferent between supplying good x and y. These flat segments along the relative supply curve in Figure 2.2 correspond with the positions along the production possibilities curves in Figure 2.1 (a) and (b).

The set of possible equilibrium world relative prices falls within the range between the two countries' autarky prices $(P_y/P_x$ and $P_y^*/P_x^*)$. In this range, the home country will specialize in good y because the world relative price of good y is higher

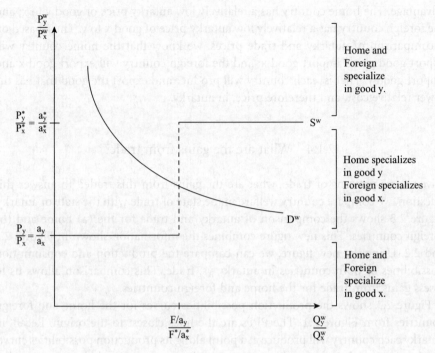

Figure 2.2 Ricardian model – world relative supply and demand.

than the home country's autarky relative price. Similarly, the foreign country will specialize in good x because the world relative price of good x is higher than the foreign country's relative autarky price. Thus, the two countries will specialize and trade for all prices such that

$$P_y^*/P_x^* > P_y^w/P_x^w > P_y/P_x \qquad (2.12)$$

$$a_y^*/a_x^* > P_y^w/P_x^w > a_y/a_x$$

Within this price range, trade is advantageous over autarky for both countries.

For all other world relative prices, there is disequilibrium. That is, for world prices greater than P_y^*/P_x^*, both countries will specialize in good y. Similarly, for world prices less than P_y/P_x, both countries will specialize in good x. In these cases, there is no trade. That is, trade is not favorable to both countries simultaneously.

Intuitively, Figure 2.2 illustrates that world relative price (P_y^w/P_x^w) must fall between the home and foreign country's relative autarky prices $(P_y^*/P_x^*$ and $P_y/P_x)$ in order for trade to occur. Since the relative autarky prices reflect the underlying technologies, these technologies create a lower and upper bound for the equilibrium relative world price. At these world prices, trade will occur based on comparative advantage. The home country has a relatively low autarky price of good y to x; and the foreign country has a relatively low autarky price of good x to y. Thus, based on a comparison of autarky and trade prices, we know that the home country will export good y and import good x; and the foreign country will export good x and import good y. That is, each country will produce and export the good that has the lower relative cost, and therefore price, in autarky.

2.1.4   What are the gains from trade?

Given these patterns of trade, what are the gains from this trade? To answer this question, we compare country welfare in the state of trade with the state of autarky. Figure 2.3 shows the comparison of autarky and trade for the (a) home and (b) foreign countries. This new figure combines the information shown in Figures 2.1 and 2.2. Using the new figure, we can compare the production and consumption possibilities of both countries in autarky vs. trade. This comparison allows us to assess gains from trade for the home and foreign countries.

Figure 2.3 shows the production possibilities curves for the home and foreign countries from Figure 2.1. The PPFs are the lines closest to the origin. Recall, in autarky each country will produce at a point along its production possibilities curve. Furthermore, each country will consume at this same point, such that consumption equals production. That is, in the absence of trade, a country can only consume as much as it produces. The relative price of the goods equals the ratios of factor input requirements in each country. This is the slope of the production possibilities curves (e.g., $P_y/P_x = a_y/a_x$ and $P_y^*/P_x^* = a_y^*/a_x^*$). Thus, in autarky the consumption opportunities of a country equate with the production possibilities of that country.

If we have knowledge about the preferences of the countries, then we can determine the exact production and consumption of each country at the autarky prices. For example, if we assume similar preferences across countries as represented by the indifference curves i and i*, then consumption equals production in autarky at the point $c_a = p_a$ for the home country and $c_a^* = p_a^*$ for the foreign country. This represents the points where consumption is maximized subject to the constraint that consumption cannot exceed production in autarky.

In contrast, with trade a country's consumption possibilities are no longer limited by its production possibilities. With trade, both countries will produce on their production possibilities frontier. However, they will consume outside their frontier at the new world relative price. This world relative price is represented by the trade lines in Figure 2.3 (a) and (b). The trade line is further from the origin and has a slope that corresponds with the world relative price (P_y^w/P_x^w). This world price is the same for the home and foreign countries.

So how do production and consumption change when we allow for trade? With trade, countries will specialize based on their comparative advantage. Recall that this pattern reflects the relative costs and prices that arise from the differences in technologies that is the source of comparative advantage in the Ricardian model.

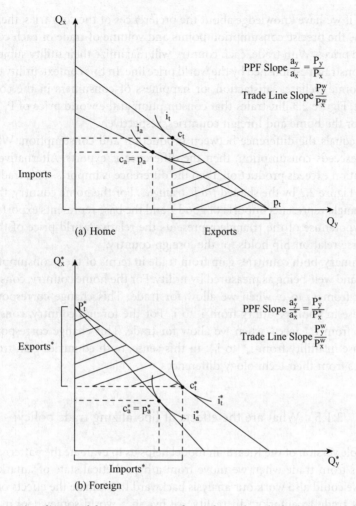

Figure 2.3 Ricardian model – comparison of autarky and trade for home and foreign.

Specifically, the home country will specialize in good y and produce at point p_t. In contrast, the foreign country will specialize in good x and produce at point p_t^*. Each country will specialize completely in their sector of comparative advantage and produce none of the other good. Specialization is complete because the autarky prices are constant at all points along the production possibilities frontiers.

The countries will then trade at the relative world price $(P_y/P_x)^w$ established in Figure 2.2. Recall that the equilibrium relative world price must fall between the autarky prices of the two countries. In Figure 2.3, this relative world price is illustrated by the slope of the trade line, which is the same for both countries. With trade, both countries can consume at points along the trade line, while they produce at points along their production possibilities curves. That is, consumption need not equal production. Thus, with trade the consumption possibilities increase for each country.

Again, if we have knowledge about the preferences of the countries, then we can determine the precise consumption points and volume of trade of each country at the world prices. With trade, each country will maximize their utility subject to the budget constraint established by the world price line. In this context, utility describes the economic welfare, satisfaction, or happiness of consumers in the country in aggregate. Figure 2.3 illustrates that consumption at the world price of P_y^w/P_x^w is c_t and c_t^* for the home and foreign countries, respectively.

Trade equals the difference between production and consumption. When production exceeds consumption, then the difference is exports. Alternatively, when consumption exceeds production, then the difference is imports. This trade is illustrated in Figure 2.3 by the shaded *trade triangles*. For the home country, the height of the triangle represents imports of good x and the base represents exports of good y. The hypotenuse of the triangle represents the relative world price of this trade. The reverse relationship holds for the foreign country.

In summary, both countries gain from trade in terms of their consumption possibilities and well-being as measured by utility. For the home country, consumption increases from c_a to c_t when we allow for trade. This change corresponds with an increase in country utility from i_a to i_t. For the foreign country, consumption increases from c_a^* to c_t^* when we allow for trade. This change corresponds with an increase in utility from i_a^* to i_t^*. In this sense, both countries gain from trade that arises from their technology differences.

2.1.5   What are the effects of liberalizing trade policy?

This simple version of the Ricardian model helps us to evaluate the patterns of trade and gains from trade when we move from a hypothetical state of autarky to free trade. (We could also work our analysis backward to evaluate the effects of moving from free trade to autarky.) In reality, we live in a world somewhere in between these two extremes. However, the model provides guidance for understanding what happens if we move closer to free trade (or closer to autarky). Moving toward autarky represents cases of protectionism where policy barriers reduce trade. Moving toward free trade represents cases of liberalization where trade increases as policy barriers are eliminated.

So, what are the effects of liberalizing trade policy in the long run when countries differ in technologies?

First, the *patterns* of production and trade are unambiguous. Countries will produce and export goods that have a lower relative opportunity cost (and therefore price) in autarky. These goods are the sectors of comparative advantage. The factor of production will move into the sectors of comparative advantage in each country and out of the sectors of comparative disadvantage. Concomitantly, production will increase in each country in the sectors of comparative advantage and decrease in the sectors of comparative disadvantage. Countries will then export goods in the sectors of comparative advantage and import the goods in their sectors of comparative disadvantage.

Second, the *gains* from trade are also unambiguous. Table 2.1(a) summarizes these gains. Countries gain from trade as long as the relative world price with trade falls in between the countries' autarky prices. In this case, countries have an incentive to trade. As a consequence of specialization and trade, world output and thus world consumption increases. These gains are accrued to each country in aggregate. That is, the consumption possibilities and aggregate utility of each

Table 2.1 Comparative welfare effects of trade.

(a) Ricardian

Home/Foreign	Welfare effects
Aggregate gains	Increase consumption possibilities and utility in Home and Foreign.
Distribution within countries	Increase price (wage or rent) of mobile factors used in sector of comparative advantage. Decrease price of these same factors used in sector of comparative disadvantage. Factor prices change until they equalize across sectors.

(b) Heckscher-Ohlin

Home/Foreign	Welfare effects
Aggregate gains	Increase consumption possibilities and utility in Home and Foreign.
Distribution within countries	Increase nominal and real price (rent or wage) to the country's abundant factor endowments. Decrease in the nominal and real price to the country's scarce endowments (Stolper-Samuelson theory). Factor prices change until they equalize across countries (Factor-Price Equalization theory).

(c) Specific factors

Home/Foreign	Welfare Effects
Aggregate gains	Increase consumption possibilities and utility in Home and Foreign.
Distribution within countries (mobile factors)	Increase nominal price (rent or wage) to the country's mobile factors. Increase real price to mobile factor in terms of purchasing power of imported good. Decrease real price to mobile factor in terms of purchasing power of exported good.
Distribution within countries (immobile factors)	Increase real price to the country's abundant immobile factors. Decrease in the real price to the country's scarce immobile factors.

Note: Factor prices include wages to labor, rents to capital and land owners, etc.

country increase. The aggregate utility captures the well-being of consumers in the country.

The model provides only modest insight into the *distribution* of gains from trade within countries. This is because the model assumes that the generic factor is mobile across industries within each country. This generic factor is often assumed to be labor. Prior to trade, the rental rate (or price) paid to the generic factor is low in the sector of comparative advantage and high in the sector of comparative disadvantage. As countries liberalize trade, the rental rate rises in the sector of comparative advantage and falls in the sector of comparative disadvantage. These movements in the rental rates (or prices) paid to the factors continue until the rates equate across the sectors; that is, the rental rate paid to the factor is the same in all industries when we allow for trade. If we assume that this generic factor is labor, then trade results in an increase in the relatively low wage paid to labor in the sector of comparative advantage and a decrease in the relatively high wage paid to labor in the sector of comparative disadvantage.

These results taken together show that trade produces gains for countries in aggregate. However, the distribution of these gains can vary across economic agents (such as labor) within a country. This later finding prompted trade economists to ask the question: can gains be *redistributed* within a country such that the well-being of all agents within the country increases as a consequence of trade? Samuelson (1939) first addressed this question. He showed that all consumers within a trading country are potentially better off under free trade since those who gain can compensate those who lose while remaining better off than in autarky. That is, he showed that with redistribution, trade can increase the consumption possibilities of all agents within an economy. This theoretical result applies in the context of the Ricardian model as well as the subsequent models considered in this book. The issue of gains from trade and redistribution of gains are also addressed at greater length in Chapters 4 and 12.

Finally, it should be noted that the results of the Ricardian model are *long-run* results. The long run corresponds with the time that it takes for the factor of production to move out of sectors of comparative disadvantage and into sectors of comparative advantage as countries specialize their production for trade.

2.2   What Are the Effects of Trade in the Long Run, When Countries Differ in Endowments?

We continue our analysis of the long-run effects of trade by presenting the Heckscher-Ohlin (HO) model. Like the Ricardian model, the HO model is a general equilibrium model that explains inter-industry trade. Furthermore, the HO model explains trade in the long run.

The HO model differs from the Ricardian model in several prominent ways. First, the source of comparative advantage in the HO model is differences across countries in *endowments*. Endowments are the aggregate of factors of production available to an economy. These endowments are often referred to as *factor endowments*. They differ from factor inputs in that they are not specific to a given industry. The relative abundance (or scarcity) of these endowments is the source of comparative advantage. Second, the HO model assumes that there are multiple endowments that are used to produce outputs whereas the Ricardian model assumes one factor input. The consequence of this difference is that the HO model tells us more about the effects of trade on income distribution within countries. Third, whereas the Ricardian model assumes technology differences across countries, the HO model assumes that technologies are the same across countries. In the HO model, it is endowment differences across countries – rather than technology differences – that drive comparative advantage.

As we work through the HO model, we consider several component questions for a representative home and foreign country: (1) How are endowments and outputs related? (2) How are goods prices and factor prices related? (3) What are the production possibilities? (4) What are the relative costs and prices in autarky? (5) What are the world prices with trade and the patterns of trade? (6) What are the gains from trade? (7) What are the effects of liberalizing trade policy? (8) How does factor mobility change the trade patterns? We introduce the model by summarizing four theories that emerge from the model, and by laying out the core underlying assumptions. We then consider the questions above by evaluating and comparing the state of autarky (no trade) with the state of free trade (no barriers).

Four theorems emerge from the HO model. Two of these explain the patterns of production and trade; the other two explain gains from trade within a country and across trading countries.

First, the *Heckscher-Ohlin theory* says that countries will produce and export goods that are intensive in the country's abundant factor endowments, and will import goods that are intensive in the country's scarce factor endowments. Thus, this theory links endowments to the patterns of trade.

Second, the *Rybczynski theory* says that an increase in an endowment leads to an increase in the output of the good that is intensive in the use of that endowment, and leads to a decrease in the output of the good that is not intensive in the use of that endowment. Thus, this theory links endowments to production. This relationship between endowments and outputs (articulated in the Rybczynski theory) underlies the relationship between endowments and trade (articulated in the HO theory).

Third, the *Stolper-Samuelson theory* says that trade (and the associated price changes) leads to an increased factor price (or rental rate) paid to a country's abundant endowments and a decreased factor price paid to a country's scarce endowments. Thus, this theory links trade with gains from trade within countries.

Fourth, the *Factor-Price equalization theory* says that factor prices (or rental rates) are equalized across countries as a result of trade. Thus, this theory links trade with gains from trade across trading partners.

In the discussion that follows, we illustrate these theorems of the HO model.

The key assumption of the HO model is that endowments differ across countries. These endowments are typically defined to include capital and labor. However, broader definitions of endowments may include natural and other resources. Broader definitions also may detail endowments by type, such as physical and knowledge capital, or high-skilled and low-skilled labor, or forest and range land.

In this section, we present a simple expression of the HO model. The assumptions of this expression are as follows. There are two countries – home and foreign. There are two goods – x and y. There are two endowments – capital and labor. The market structure is perfect competition. There are constant returns to scale. The mobility of factors is such that they are immobile across countries, but are mobile across industries within a country. The technology is such that both endowments are used in the production of both goods. Furthermore, there is only one combination of the endowments used to produce each good. The combination is referred to as a fixed coefficients technology.

The *fixed coefficients technologies* appear in unit input requirements. *Unit input requirements* express the amount of a factor endowment required to produce a unit of the output. For example, k_x is the amount of capital required to produce one unit of good x; l_x is the amount of labor required to produce one unit of good x; k_y is the amount of capital required to produce one unit of good y; and l_y is the amount of labor required to produce one unit of good y. These technologies differ across industries; however, they are the same across countries. This is a key assumption. For example, we may observe that good x is capital intensive and good y is labor intensive. This means that good x requires a relatively higher ratio of capital to labor; and good y requires a relatively higher ratio of labor to capital. These assumptions about factor intensities can be written as

$$k_x/l_x > k_y/l_y, \text{ or} \tag{2.13}$$

$$k_x/k_y > l_x/l_y$$

We can determine the production possibilities of a country using our knowledge of relative abundance of endowments and factor intensities. In our example, the PPF shows the trade off between the outputs of good x (Q_x) and good y (Q_y) given the factor intensities of each good and the factor endowments of the country. The production possibilities are constrained by the factor endowments available in the country as follows:

$$k_x Q_x + k_y Q_y \leq K \tag{2.14}$$

$$l_x Q_x + l_y Q_y \leq L \tag{2.15}$$

Equation (2.14) shows that the amount of capital used to produce output of good x plus good y must be less than or equal to the supply of capital (K) within the country. Similarly, equation (2.15) shows that the amount of labor used to produce

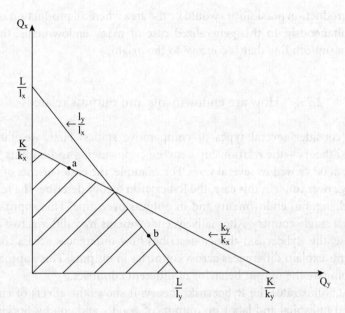

Figure 2.4 Heckscher Ohlin model – production possibilities.

output of good x plus good y must be less than or equal to the supply of labor (L) within the country. Assuming that capital and labor are fully employed within the country (i.e., no unemployment), then equations (2.14) and (2.15) hold with equality.

Figure 2.4 shows these production possibilities for good x and good y for the country. This is a simple diagrammatic plotting of equations (2.14) and (2.15) that we derive by rearranging the equations as follows:

$$Q_x = K/k_x - (k_y/k_x)Q_y \tag{2.16}$$

$$Q_x = L/l_x - (l_y/l_x)Q_y$$

The diagram shows the trade off between producing good x and good y, given the relative factor intensities of the two goods reflected in the slopes (k_y/k_x and l_y/l_x) of the production constraints. Given that both resource constraints must hold simultaneously, the production possibilities set is the shaded area where both equations (2.16) hold.

Intuitively, the slope of each constraint reflects the opportunity cost of producing good x in terms of good y foregone, and vice versa. Because there are multiple factors of production (two in this simple version), the opportunity cost differs at various points along the frontier in the HO model (such as points a and b in the figure). In this simple version, the frontier is kinked and has two slopes. If we were to generalize our simple two-factor model to one with many factors of production, then our production possibilities would be the area where all production constraints hold simultaneously. In this generalized case of many endowments, the frontier would be a smooth line that is concave to the origin.

2.2.1   How are endowments and outputs related?

Next, we consider several types of comparative statics. First, we illustrate the Rybczynski theory – the relationship between endowments and outputs. This relationship can be viewed in several ways. For example, the endowments of a country may change over time. In this case, the Rybczynski theory describes the relationship between changes in endowments and in outputs over time. This approach can be applied to a single country. Alternatively, endowments may differ across countries. In this case, the Rybczynski theory describes how differences across countries in endowments explain differences across countries in outputs. This approach can be used to compare the output behavior of different countries.

Figure 2.5 illustrates the Rybczynski theory. It shows the effects of changes (or differences) in capital and labor on outputs of good x and good y. Specifically, the figure shows the effect of an increase in the supply of capital on production possibilities. We can see that an increase in capital from K_0 to K_1 results in an increase in production possibilities for good x, which uses capital intensively in production.

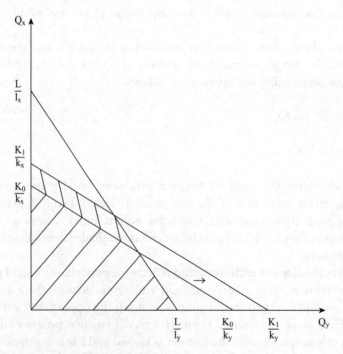

Figure 2.5   Heckscher Ohlin model – Rybczynski effect.

Alternatively, if we had relaxed the labor constraint, then we would have seen an increase in the output of the labor intensive good y.

We can draw two general conclusions here. First, an increase in an endowment over time leads to an increase in the output of goods that are produced using the endowment intensively. This is a cross-time effect. In this case, the changes shown in Figure 2.5 represent two points in time. Second, countries that differ in endowments will produce goods that use their abundant endowments intensively in production. This is the cross-country effect. In this case, the differences shown in the figure represent two countries.

2.2.2 How are goods prices and factor prices related?

Next, we illustrate the Stolper-Samuelson theory – the relationship between goods prices and factor prices. As above, this relationship can be viewed in several ways. For example, goods prices may change over time. In this case, the Stolper-Samuelson theory would describe the relationship between changes in goods prices and changes in factor prices over time. This approach can be applied to a single country. Alternatively, goods prices may differ across countries. In this case, the Stolper-Samuelson theory describes how differences across countries in goods prices explain differences across countries in factor prices. These differences can be the result of trade. This approach can be used to compare the price behavior of countries.

To illustrate the Stolper-Samuelson theory, we must examine equilibrium in the factor market. Given the HO model assumption of perfect competition, we know that goods prices equal the sum of factor prices in each sector in equilibrium. In our example, this equilibrium condition is

$$P_x = k_x r + l_x w \tag{2.17}$$

$$P_y = k_y r + l_y w$$

where r is the rental rate paid to capital, w is the wage rate paid to labor (i.e., wage), and P_x and P_y are the prices of goods x and y, respectively.

To plot these equations, we simply rearrange to get

$$r = P_x / k_x - (l_x / k_x) w \tag{2.18}$$

$$r = P_y / k_y - (l_y / k_y) w$$

Furthermore, we need to apply our knowledge about factor intensities. For example, we may observe that good x is capital intensive and good y is labor intensive. In this case, the relationship shown in equation (2.13) holds. Figure 2.6 shows the labor market equilibrium under these conditions; that is, it shows equations (2.18) with the factor intensity assumption in equation (2.13). The equilibrium factor prices are r_0 and w_0.

Here we know if we had reduced the labor constraint, then we would have a similar increase in the scaling of the other but have good Y ...

We can draw two lines also discussed here, that an increase in the return to one factor type leads to a decrease in the output per unit of that type represented with the end of each ... above. Table 2.6 confirms ... with the axes through origin. Shown in Figure 2.6 represent both points ... if ... economy ... the other in either ...

... firm will ... more goods that ... the ... at ... the ... respectively, in ... would. This is ... the cross ... only value. In this case, the r_0 will ... be ... is ... the reason ... equilibrium ...

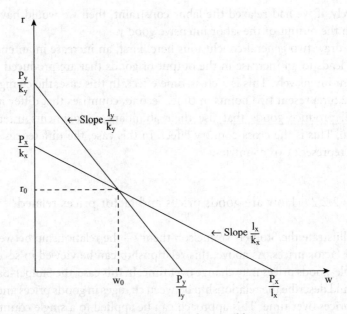

Figure 2.6 Heckscher Ohlin model – factor market equilibrium.

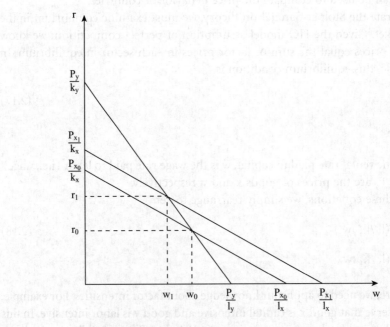

Figure 2.7 Heckscher Ohlin model – Stolper-Samuelson effect.

We can now illustrate the Stolper-Samuelson theory. Figure 2.7 shows the effects of changes (or differences) in goods prices on factor prices. Specifically, the figure shows the effect of an increase in the price of good x (from P_{x0} to P_{x1}) on the rental rate paid to capital and labor. We can see that this change leads to an increase in the rental rate paid to capital owners (r_0 to r_1) and a decrease in the wage paid to labor (w_0 to w_1). Alternatively, we could have shown that an increase in the price of good y leads to an increase in the wage rate paid to labor and a decrease in the rental rate paid to capital owners. These are changes in *nominal* returns to capital and labor.

We can also examine the effect of changes in goods prices on *real rates* paid to capital and labor. To do this, we need to look at factor prices relative to goods prices. For example, the real rental rates paid to capital owners in terms of goods x and y are r/P_x and r/P_y, respectively. Similarly, the real wage rates paid to labor in terms of good x and y are w/P_x and w/P_y, respectively. Thus, to determine real wages and rental rates, we need to consider changes in factor rates relative to changes in goods prices. In Figure 2.7, we see that the changes in the rent and wage are larger than the change in the price of good x. That is

$$|(r_1 - r_0)| > |(P_{x1} - P_{x0})| \tag{2.19}$$

$$|(w_1 - w_0)| > |(P_{x1} - P_{x0})|$$

Thus, the real rental rate paid to capital owners increases in terms of good x and the real wage rate paid to labor decreases in terms of good x. Also, since the price of good y does not change in our example, the real and the nominal changes in rental and wage rates paid to capital and labor are the same in terms of good y.

We can draw two general conclusions. First, an increase in the price of a good over time leads to an increase in the nominal and real rates paid to the factor endowment that is used intensively in the production of that good. This is a cross-time effect. In this case, the changes shown in Figure 2.7 represent two points in time. Second, when goods prices differ (or change) across countries, the nominal and real rental rates paid to factors will also differ (or change) across countries. This is the cross-country effect. In this case, the differences shown in the figure represent two countries.

Furthermore, there is a *magnification effect*. That is, the magnitude of the changes in nominal factor prices (rental and wage rates) exceeds the magnitude of changes in goods prices. Consequently, both real and nominal factor prices move in the same direction as a result of changes in goods prices.

We can now examine the effects of moving from autarky to trade in the HO model. To illustrate, assume there are two countries – home and foreign. These two countries have identical technologies such that

$$(k_x/l_x) = (k_x^*/l_x^*) \tag{2.20}$$

$$(k_y/l_y) = (k_y^*/l_y^*)$$

However, the technologies differ across industries as shown in equation (2.13) such that

$$(k_x/l_x) > (k_y/l_y) \qquad\qquad (2.21)$$

$$(k_x*/l_x*) > (k_y*/l_y*)$$

where good x is capital intensive and good y is labor intensive. Further, the countries differ in their relative abundance of endowments. Specifically, the home country is abundant in capital and the foreign country is abundant in labor. Thus, the production constraints shown in equations (2.14) and (2.15) differ across the two countries such that

$$K/L > K*/L* \qquad\qquad (2.22)$$

where K/L is the capital/labor ratio of the home country and K*/L* is the capital/labor ratio of the foreign country.

2.2.3   What are the production possibilities?

We can illustrate these differences by plotting PPFs for the two countries. Figure 2.8 shows the PPF for the home and foreign countries under these conditions. As shown, the capital constraint for the home country is further from the origin, reflecting the home country's abundance in capital. Similarly, the labor constraint for the foreign country is further from the origin, reflecting the foreign country's abundance of labor. However, the slopes of the constraints are identical across the two countries, reflecting their identical technologies. The shaded areas show the production possibilities. We can see that the outputs of the two countries are biased toward the sectors that use the abundant endowment intensively in production.

2.2.4   What are the relative costs and prices in autarky?

The production and consumption of the two countries in autarky may be any point along the PPFs. The specific point depends on preferences. We can envision an indifference curve tangent to each country's PPF such as i and i*. This is the indifference curve that would maximize country utility, given the constraint that each country can only consume what it produces in a state of autarky. In this case, the home country will produce and consume along the portion of the frontier with slope l_y/l_x; and the foreign country will produce and consume along the portion of the frontier with slope k_y/k_x.

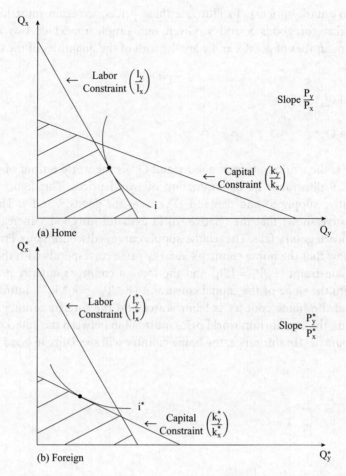

Figure 2.8 Heckscher Ohlin model – production possibilities of home and foreign.

We can then see that goods prices differ across the countries in autarky. As in the Ricardian model, goods prices are determined by the technologies and are reflected in the slopes of the PPFs. As shown, in autarky the price of good x is relatively low in the home country and the price of good y is relatively low in the foreign country.

2.2.5 What are the world prices with trade and the patterns of trade?

What then is the (relative) price of goods at which trade will occur in the world market? As in the Ricardian model, the intuitive answer is that countries will only trade at prices that are more favorable then the prices in autarky. That is, countries are willing to export goods at higher prices and import goods at lower prices (relative to autarky prices). To illustrate these prices, we again must look at the world market for goods x and y. Given our simple model of two countries, the world quantities of good x and y are the sum of the quantities of the two countries. Thus

$$Q_x^w = Q_x + Q_x^*$$ (2.23)

$$Q_y^w = Q_y + Q_y^*$$

where Q_x^w is the world output of good x and Q_y^w is the world output of good y.

Figure 2.9 illustrates the determination of world prices. This figure plots the world relative supply S^w and demand D^w curves for goods x and y. The relative demand curve shows that the relative world demand for good y increases as the relative price of good y falls. The relative supply curve is discontinuous. From Figure 2.8, we know that the home country's autarky price corresponds with the slope of the labor constraint ($P_y/P_x = l_y/l_x$) and the foreign country's autarky price corresponds with the slope of the capital constraint ($P_y^*/P_x^* = k_y^*/k_x^*$). Intuitively, this reflects that the home country is labor scarce and the foreign country is capital scarce. Thus, the equilibrium world price must fall in between the autarky prices of the two countries. In this range, the home country will specialize in good x because

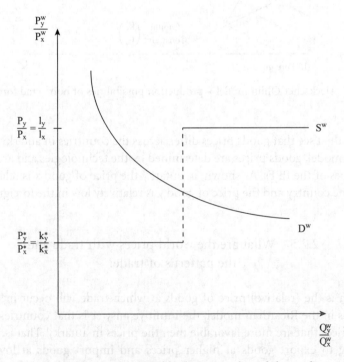

Figure 2.9 Heckscher Ohlin model – world relative supply and demand.

the world relative price of good x is higher than the home country's autarky relative price. Similarly, the foreign country will specialize in good y because the world relative price of good y is higher than the foreign country's relative autarky price. Thus, the two countries will specialize and trade for all prices such that

$$P_y{}^*/P_x{}^* < P_y{}^w/P_x{}^w < P_y/P_x \text{ or} \qquad (2.24)$$

$$k_y{}^*/k_x{}^* < P_y{}^w/P_x{}^w < l_y/l_x$$

For all other world relative prices, there is a disequilibrium. That is, for world prices greater than P_y/P_x, both countries will specialize in good y. Similarly, for world prices less than $P_y{}^*/P_x{}^*$, both countries will specialize in good x. In these cases, there is no trade. That is, trade is not favorable to both countries simultaneously.

We can see the HO patterns of production and trade by looking back at our production possibilities and considering the equilibrium world prices. That is, with trade, the home country will move along its frontier to increase production of good x and decrease production of good y. Similarly, the foreign country will move along its frontier to increase production of good y and decrease production of good x. The home country will export good x and the foreign country will export good y at a world price as described in equation (2.24). This trade will allow both countries to consume at a point somewhere outside their respective PPFs.

Stated more generally, countries will produce and export goods that are intensive in the country's abundant factor endowments, and will import goods that are intensive in the country's scarce factor endowments.

2.2.6 What are the gains from trade?

So, what are the gains from this trade? At the aggregate country level, we know that both countries gain from trade because their consumption possibilities increase as a result of specialization and trade. Specifically, at equilibrium world prices, both countries can consume on indifference curves that are outside of their respective PPFs (shown in Figure 2.8).

We can also observe the distribution of these gains within countries. To this end, we revisit our labor market constraints. We consider the effects of changes in goods prices resulting from trade on changes in factor prices. Figure 2.9 and equation (2.24) describe the changes in prices that result when each country moves from autarky to trade. Specifically, we know that the home country will experience an increase in the relative price of good x and the foreign country will experience an increase in the relative price of good y, as a result of trade.

What are the effects of these goods price changes on the rental and wage rates paid to capital and labor in each country? Figure 2.10 illustrates the effects of trade for the (a) home and (b) foreign countries. For the home country, the price of good x rises relative to good y. We show this relative change by increasing the price of

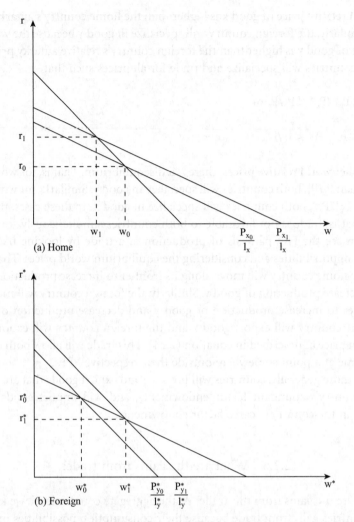

Figure 2.10   Heckscher Ohlin model – comparison of autarky and trade for home and foreign.

good x and leaving the price of good y unchanged. The results include an increase in the nominal rental rate paid to capital owners (r) as well as an increase in the real rental rate paid to capital owners (r/P_x and r/P_y). The results also include a decrease in the nominal wage rate paid to labor (w) and real wage rate paid to labor (w/P_x and w/P_y). That is, capital owners gain in terms of their purchasing power of both goods and wage earners lose in terms of their purchasing power of both goods.

In contrast, for the foreign country, the price of good y rises relative to good x. We show this relative change by increasing the price of good y and leaving the price of good x unchanged. The results include a decrease in the nominal rental rate paid to capital owners (r) as well as a decrease in the real rental rate paid to capital owners (r/P_x and r/P_y). The results also include an increase in the nominal wage rate paid to labor (w) and real wage rate paid to labor (w/P_x and w/P_y). That is, capital owners lose in terms of their purchasing power of both goods and wage earners gain in terms of their purchasing power of both goods.

Finally, we can describe gains from trade in terms of the differences in factor prices across countries. Specifically, the *Factor-Price Equalization theory* says that factor prices (or wage and rental rates) are equalized across countries as a result of trade. This is the consequence of the changes in goods prices that result from trade (as shown in Figure 2.9). These changes in goods prices lead to changes in factor prices (as shown in Figure 2.10). In our example, the capital abundant home country has a relatively low rental rate and high wage in autarky. As the home country opens to trade and specializes in the capital intensive good x, the rent rises and the wage falls (in real and nominal terms). Similarly, the labor abundant foreign country has a relatively low wage and high rental rate in autarky. As the foreign country opens to trade and specializes in the labor intensive good y, the wage rises and the rental rate falls (in real and nominal terms). Through this process, the rental rates and wages of the two countries continue to change (in theory) until they are equalized across the two countries. With trade, the world equilibrium prices are

$$P_x^w = w^w l_x + r^w k_x \qquad\qquad (2.25)$$

$$P_y^w = w^w l_y + r^w k_y$$

where world wages and rental rates equal the wages and rental rates in the home and foreign countries ($w^w = w = w^*$ and $r^w = r = r^*$).

2.2.7 What are the effects of liberalizing trade policy?

The simple version of the HO model presented here helps us to evaluate the patterns of trade and gains from trade when we move from a hypothetical state of autarky to free trade (or visa versa). As noted earlier, we live in a world somewhere in between these two extremes. Thus, the model provides guidance for understanding what happens if we move closer to autarky or closer to free trade by changing policies.

So, what are the effects of liberalizing trade policy in the long run when countries differ in endowments?

First, the patterns of production and trade are unambiguous. Countries will produce and export goods that have a lower relative opportunity cost (and therefore price) in autarky. These are the goods that are intensive in the country's relatively abundant endowments.

Second, the gains from trade are also unambiguous. Table 2.1(b) summarizes these gains. Countries gain from trade as long as the relative world price with trade falls in between the countries' autarky prices. In this case, countries have an incentive to trade. As a consequence of specialization and trade, world output and thus world consumption increases. These gains are accrued to each country in aggregate. That is, the aggregate utility (or well-being) of each country increases.

The model also tells us about the distribution of gains from trade within countries. Specifically, those who gain from trade are the owners of the countries' abundant factor endowments. Those who lose from trade are the owners of the countries' scarce factor endowments. In theory, the changes in factor prices continue to change as a result of trade until factor prices equalize across countries.

These results of the HO model are *long-run* results. The long run corresponds with the time that it takes for the factor of production to move out of sectors of comparative disadvantage and into sectors of comparative advantage as countries specialize their production for trade.

2.2.8   How does factor mobility change the trade patterns?

The *Factor-Content* expression of the HO model extends the above results in one important way, by relaxing the assumption that factor endowments are immobile across countries. Given this alternative assumption, a country may either export the good in which it has a comparative advantage or it may export the factor endowment that is used intensively to produce that good. Similarly, a country may either import the good in which it has a comparative disadvantage or it may import the factor endowment that is used intensively to produce that good. This trade is referred to as "trade in factor services". The primary implication of the factor-content expression is that factor endowments can flow across countries instead of, or in addition to, goods.

To illustrate, consider an extension of our prior example. We assumed that the home country is abundant in capital and the foreign country is abundant in labor. We assumed that good x is produced using capital intensively and good y is produced using labor intensively. We assumed that capital and labor are immobile across countries. Now, let's relax this assumption and allow capital and labor to be mobile across countries. Accordingly, the factor-content expression of the HO theory says the following. The home country will export either good x or capital and import either good y or labor. Similarly, the foreign country will export either good y or labor and import either good x or capital. The factor endowments are "embodied" in trade.

The general result of the Factor-Content expression is that a country will export the services of its abundant factor endowments and import the services of its scarce factor endowments. Thus, this interpretation gives us a more generalized prediction of the patterns of trade. The implications of the factor-content interpretation for gains from trade are the same as the traditional HO theory.

2.3   What Are the Effects of Trade in the Short Run, When Countries Differ in Immobile Endowments?

In this section, we continue our analysis of trade by presenting the Specific Factors (SF) model. Like the previous models, the SF model is a general equilibrium model that explains inter-industry, inter-firm trade.

The SF model extends the previous models in several ways. The source of comparative advantage in the SF model is country differences in endowments of specific factors. *Specific factors* are factors of production that are immobile across industries. These factors of production cannot easily be moved from one industry to another in the short run. Thus, the SF model is a short-run model. We can think of this model as a short-run extension of the previously discussed long-run models.

The SF model is similar to the previous models in several key ways. Each is a general equilibrium model of trade. Each shares several underlying assumptions, such as a market structure of perfect competition, and a production process characterized by constant returns to scale. Each focuses on the supply side and leaves the demand side to extensions. Each describes the patterns of inter-industry trade.

However, the SF model differs from the Ricardian and HO models in one significant way. It relaxes the assumption that factors of production are mobile across industries. Instead, the SF model assumes that some factors of production are mobile across industries while others are immobile across industries. The *immobile* factors are referred to as "specific factors" since they are specific to a particular industry. This differs from the previous models, which assume that factors are instantaneously mobile across industries.

The consequence of the factor mobility assumption is that the SF model tells us about the effects of trade on income distribution within countries in the *short run*. Specifically, the model tells us about the effects of trade on the prices of both mobile and immobile factors in the short run. The short run is the period of time when some factors of production cannot easily be moved into the sector of comparative advantage. It is the time required for a factor to be adapted for use in a different industry. Depending on the factor, this adaptation may occur by retooling, retraining, redesigning, or reconfiguring.

As we work through the SF model, we consider several component questions for a representative home and foreign country. These questions are: (1) What are the production possibilities? (2) What are the relative costs and prices in autarky? (3) What are the world prices with trade? (4) What are the patterns of trade? (5) What are the gains and income distribution effects of trade? (6) What are the effects of liberalizing trade policy? We introduce the model by laying out the core underlying assumptions and framework. We then consider the questions above by evaluating and comparing the state of autarky (no trade) with the state of free trade (no barriers).

The key assumption of the SF model is that some factors of production are immobile across industries, while others are mobile. The mobile factors are often defined to include labor while the immobile factors are often defined to include capital and land. However, these definitions are illustrative only. Alternative definitions of mobile and immobile factors are simply variations on applications of the model. For example, one could alternatively define high-skilled labor and low-skilled labor as the immobile specific factors. Such factors may be immobile in the short run but can be interchanged over time.

The second key assumption of the SF model is that industries differ in their use of factors of production. For example, capital may be "specific" to manufacturing, while land may be "specific" to agriculture. The third key assumption is that the mobile factor of production exhibits diminishing marginal returns. That is, as more of the mobile factor is combined with a given specific factor, the marginal output of the mobile factor decreases. For example, the marginal product of labor may decrease as additional units of labor are combined with land to produce agricultural output.

In this section, we present a simple expression of the SF model. The assumptions of this expression are as follows. There are two countries – home and foreign. There are two goods – good x and good y. There are three factor endowments – labor, capital, and land. These factors differ in their mobility across industries. Specifically, we assume that labor is mobile across industries; and capital and land are immobile across industries. Furthermore, we assume that the immobile factors are specific to different industries; that is, capital is specific to good x, and land is specific to good y.

2.3.1   What are the production possibilities?

Now, we can determine the production possibilities for a country in the SF model. We determine the production possibilities using our knowledge of the country's mobile and immobile factor endowments. To begin, we need to determine the constraint on the use of the mobile factor in each industry. In our example, this is the amount of labor supply that can be divided between the production of goods x and y. We also need to determine the production functions of the two industries, given their mobile and immobile factor endowments. In our example, this is the amount of output of goods x and y that can be produced, given the country's resources of both mobile and immobile factor endowments.

Figure 2.11 shows the derivation of the production possibilities for goods x and y for a given country.

The labor constraint for the country is

$$L_x + L_y \leq L \tag{2.26}$$

where L_x is labor used in good x, L_y is labor used in good y, and L is the total labor supply of the country. Assuming no unemployment of labor, this constraint holds

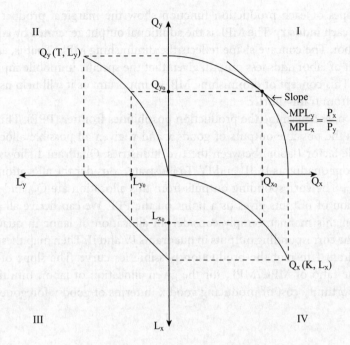

Figure 2.11 Specific factors model – production possibilities.

with equality. Quadrant III in Figure 2.11 shows a plotting of this labor constraint. Intuitively, this constraint shows that the labor used in goods x and y must be less than or equal to the total labor supply. This total labor supply can be allocated in various ways across the two industries. An increase in the use of labor in good x corresponds with a decrease in the use of labor in good y, and visa versa.

Figure 2.11 also shows the production functions. Quadrants II and IV show the production functions for goods y and x, respectively. The production functions show how much output of goods x and y a country can produce, given the country's factors. These factors include capital that is specific to good x, land that is specific to good y, and labor that can be moved between the industries. The production function in quadrant II plots the relationship between the mobile labor input (L_y) and output of good y (Q_y), given fixed amounts of immobile land (T). Similarly, the production function in quadrant IV plots the relationship between the mobile labor input (L_x) and output of good x (Q_x), given a fixed amount of immobile capital (K). These production function are

$$Q_y = f(T, L_y) \tag{2.27}$$

$$Q_x = f(K, L_x)$$

where all terms are defined as above.

The slopes of each production function show the marginal product of labor (MPL) in each industry. The MPL is the additional output generated by adding one unit of labor. The concave shape reflects the diminishing MPL. That is, each additional unit of labor adds less output, given that the specific immobile input is held constant. This concept of diminishing MPL is important as it will help us to assess the gains from trade shortly.

We can now determine the production possibilities frontier (PPF). This frontier represents the possible outputs of goods x and y, given all possible allocations of the mobile factor (labor) between the two industries. Quadrant I shows the PPF derived from quadrants II, III and IV. To illustrate, consider the allocation of labor L_{x0} and L_{y0}. The corresponding outputs from this allocation are Q_{x0} and Q_{y0}. This combination of outputs gives us a point on the PPF. We can derive all points of the PPF in this manner. Simply consider an allocation of labor in quadrant III. Observe the corresponding outputs in quadrants IV and II. Then map these outputs into quadrant I to plot the production possibilities curve. The slope of the PPF reflects the ratio of MPL_y/MPL_x for the given allocation of labor. Intuitively, this is the opportunity cost of producing good x in terms of good y foregone and visa versa.

2.3.2   What are the relative costs and prices in autarky?

We can use the PPF to answer several questions about the state of autarky. Specifically, what are the relative costs and prices in autarky for each country? In other words, what are the patterns of comparative advantage? To answer this question, we first need to look at the prices of factors and goods in autarky.

To this end, we must examine equilibrium in the market for the mobile factor of production. In our example, the mobile factor is labor and the rental rate paid to labor is the wage. The supply of labor for a given country is fixed, as shown in the labor constraint in equation (2.26). The demand for labor is such that the wage paid to labor equals the value of the MPL. Intuitively, labor is demanded at the point where the value of the additional unit of labor equals the cost of the additional unit of labor. This relationship can be written as

$$w_x = P_x MPL_x \tag{2.28}$$

$$w_y = P_y MPL_y$$

where w_x and w_y are the wages paid to labor in industries x and y; and P_x and P_y are the autarky prices of good x and y.

Further, we know that labor is mobile across industries in our example. Thus, the wage paid to labor in the two industries must be equal in equilibrium. For example, if the wage were higher in industry x, then labor would have an incentive to move out of industry y and into industry x. This movement of labor would put downward pressure on the wage in industry x and upward pressure on the wage in industry y, until the two wages equate. Thus, in equilibrium the wage rate paid to labor employed in sectors x and y equate as

$$w = w_x = w_y \qquad\qquad\qquad (2.29)$$

Figure 2.12 illustrates this equilibrium in the market for the mobile factor. The horizontal width of the figure represents the fixed supply of labor (L) that can be allocated between the two industries, as shown in equation (2.26). The amount of labor employed in good x is measured from left to right, and the amount of labor employed in good y is measured from right to left. The vertical axis of the figure represents the wage, which equals the value of the MPL, as shown in equation (2.28). The two curves represent wages in industries x and y, given alternative allocations of labor between the two industries. (The two curves are plotted together in a side-by-side fashion with the wage curve for good y flipped horizontally.) Both curves are convex to their respective origins. The convex shape of the curves reflects the diminishing MPL. That is, as more labor is employed in an industry, the value of the MPL decreases, but at a decreasing rate.

The equilibrium price of the mobile factor (labor) in Figure 2.12 is where the wages paid to labor in the two industries equate at $w_{x0} = w_{y0}$, as shown in equation (2.29). This intersection determines the equilibrium wages paid to labor in both

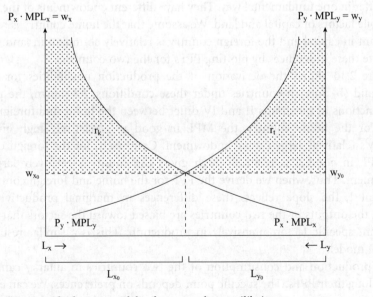

Figure 2.12 Specific factors model – factor market equilibrium.

sectors. The corresponding allocation of labor is such that L_{x0} is the amount of labor employed to produce good x and L_{y0} is amount of labor employed to produce good y.

Figure 2.12 also provides information about the real rental rates to the immobile factors of production that are specific to each industry. These rates include the rental rate paid to capital owners (r_k) and the rental rate paid to land owners (r_t). Recall that capital is specific to good x. Thus, the real rental rate paid to capital owners is the shaded area below the wage curve for good x and above the equilibrium wage. Also recall that land is specific to good y. Thus, the real rental rate paid to land owners is the shaded area below the wage curve for good y and above the equilibrium wage. Intuitively, these rental rates represent the surplus of the value of the MPL above the equilibrium wage for each unit of labor employed in that industry.

Finally, we can now return to Figure 2.11 to observe the equilibrium outputs in the goods market in autarky. To this end, we combine the equilibrium conditions in equations (2.28) and (2.29) to show that

$$P_x / P_y = MPL_y / MPL_x \qquad\qquad (2.30)$$

The right-hand side of this expression is the slope of the PPF shown in Figure 2.11. The left-hand side is a given set of autarky prices in the goods market. For this set of autarky prices, the equilibrium outputs of good x and good y are Q_{x0} and Q_{y0}.

We can now examine the effects of moving from autarky to trade in the SF model. To illustrate, assume there are two countries – home and foreign. These two countries differ in one fundamental way. They have different endowments of the specific immobile factors of capital and land. We assume that the home country is relatively abundant in capital and the foreign country is relatively abundant in land. We can illustrate these differences by plotting PPFs for the two countries.

Figure 2.13 shows the derivation of the production possibilities for the (a) home and (b) foreign countries under these conditions. As shown, the production functions in quadrants II and IV differ between the home and foreign countries. For the home country, the MPL in good x is relatively high given the country's relatively large capital endowment. Conversely, for the foreign country, the MPL in good y is relatively high given the country's relatively large land endowment. Thus, when we derive the PPF for the home and foreign countries in quadrant I, the slope reflects these differences in marginal productivities. As shown, the outputs of the two countries are biased toward the sectors that use the abundant specific factor intensively in production. This is a similar result as in the HO model.

The production and consumption of the two countries in autarky can be any point along their PPFs. The specific point depends on preferences. We can envision an indifference curve tangent to each country's PPF such as i and i*. This is the indifference curve that would maximize country utility, given the constraint that

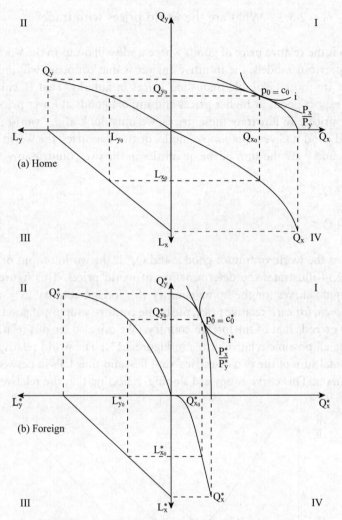

Figure 2.13 Specific factors model – autarky for home and foreign.

each country can only consume what it produces in autarky. In this case, the home country will produce and consume the combination of goods x and y where $p_0 = c_0$. Similarly, the foreign country will produce and consume the combination of goods x and y where $p_0^* = c_0^*$.

We can then see that goods prices differ across the countries in autarky. The goods prices are determined by the MPL in each industry and country and are reflected in the slopes of the PPFs. As shown, in autarky the relative price of good x is low in the home country and the relative price of good y is low in the foreign country. That is, in autarky $P_x/P_y < P_x^*/P_y^*$.

2.3.3   What are the world prices with trade?

What then is the relative price of goods where trade will occur in the world market?
As in the previous models, the intuitive answer is that countries will only trade at
prices that are more favorable than their prices in autarky. That is, countries are
willing to export goods at higher prices and import goods at lower prices, relative
to autarky prices. To illustrate these prices, we must look at the world market for
good x and good y. Given our simple model of two countries, the world quantities
of goods x and y are the sum of the quantities in the two countries or

$$Q_x^w = Q_x + Q_x^* \qquad\qquad\qquad (2.31)$$

$$Q_y^w = Q_y + Q_y^*$$

where Q_x^w is the world output of good x and Q_y^w is the world output of good y.

Figure 2.14 illustrates the determination of world prices. This figure plots the
relative supply curves for the home country (S), foreign country (S*), and world
(S^w). As shown, for each relative price, the home country's supply of good x (relative
to good y) exceeds that of the foreign country. (We can also see this relationship by
considering all possible relative prices in Figure 2.13.) The world relative supply is
the horizontal sum of the two countries' supplies, and thus falls in between the two
country curves. This curve is upward sloping, reflecting that the relative supply of

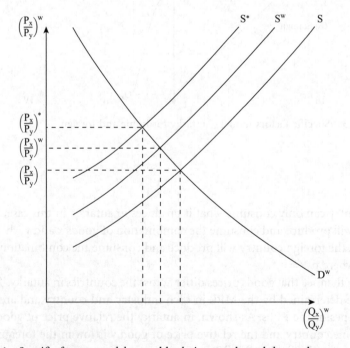

Figure 2.14   Specific factors model – world relative supply and demand.

good x increases as the relative price of good x increases. Alternatively, the world demand for good x (relative to good y) decreases as the price of good x increases (relative to good y). Given similar preferences across countries, the demand curves of the foreign and home countries are the same as the world demand curve.

Figure 2.14 shows that the equilibrium world price falls in between the equilibrium autarky prices in the two countries. For such world prices, the home country will specialize in good x because the world relative price of good x is higher than the home country's autarky relative price. Similarly, the foreign country will specialize in good y because the world relative price of good y is higher than the foreign country's relative autarky price. Thus, the two countries both have an incentive to specialize and trade for all world prices such that

$$P_x/P_y < P_x^w/P_y^w < P_x^*/P_y^* \qquad (2.32)$$

For all other world relative prices, there is a disequilibrium. That is, for world prices greater than P_x^*/P_y^*, both countries will specialize in good x. Similarly, for world prices less than P_x/P_y, both countries will specialize in good y. In these cases, there is no trade, because trade is not favorable to both countries simultaneously.

2.3.4   What are the patterns of trade?

We can now see the patterns of production and trade by revisiting the production possibilities and considering production at the equilibrium world price. Figure 2.15 shows the frontiers in quadrant I of Figure 2.13. In Figure 2.15, we compare the state of autarky to the state of trade for both countries. As shown, with trade the home country (a) moves along its frontier to increase production of good x and decrease production of good y (from p_0 to p_1). Similarly, the foreign country (b) moves along its frontier to increase production of good y and decrease production of good x (from p_0^* to p_1^*). At the new world equilibrium price, the home country exports good x and the foreign country exports good y. This trade allows both countries to consume at a point somewhere outside their PPFs. This is the point where the new world price line is tangent to the country indifference curves (i_1 and i_1^*). The consumption points with trade are c_1 and c_1^* for the home and foreign countries, respectively.

What are the patterns of trade? Each country produces and exports goods that use the country's abundant specific (immobile) factor. And, each country imports goods that use the country's scarce specific (immobile) factor.

2.3.5   What are the gains and income distribution effects of trade?

What are the gains from this trade? At the aggregate country level, we know that both countries gain from trade because their consumption possibilities increase as

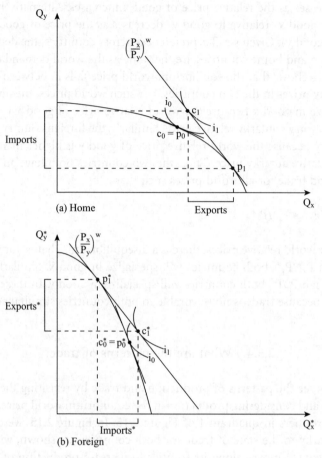

(a) Home

(b) Foreign

Figure 2.15 Specific factors model – gains from trade for home and foreign, in aggregate.

a result of specialization and trade. Specifically, at equilibrium world prices, both countries can consume on indifference curves that are outside of their respective PPFs, as shown in Figure 2.15.

We can also observe the distribution of these gains within countries. To this end, we revisit our labor market figures, and consider the effects of changes in goods prices resulting from trade, on changes in factor prices. Figure 2.14 and equation (2.32) describe the changes in goods prices that result when each country moves from autarky to trade. Specifically, we know that the home country will experience an increase in the relative price of good x and the foreign country will experience an increase in the relative price of good y, as a result of trade. What then are the effects of these goods price changes on the wage paid to labor, and rental rates paid to capital and landowners in each country?

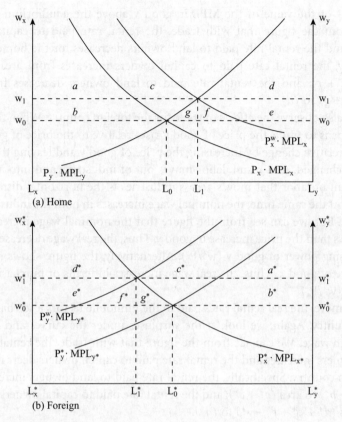

Figure 2.16 Specific factors model – gains from trade for home and foreign, within countries.

Figure 2.16 illustrates the effects of trade for the (a) home and (b) foreign countries. For the home country, the price of good x rises relative to good y. We show this relative change by increasing the price of good x and leaving the price of good y unchanged. As a result of this change, labor moves out of the industry y and into industry x. The amount of labor that moves across industries is the horizontal distance from L_0 to L_1. At the same time, the nominal wage received by labor increases in both industry x and industry y. The amount of the nominal wage increase is w_0 to w_1. But, we can see from Figure 2.16 that the nominal wage increases by an amount less than the price increase in good x. Thus, the real wage decreases in terms of purchasing power of good x (w/P_x). Alternatively, since there is no change in the price of good y, the real wage increases in terms of the purchasing power of good y (w/P_y).

Furthermore, the rental rates of the immobile factors also change. Recall that the rental rate paid to capital owners is the surplus of the value of the MPL in good x above the equilibrium wage. And, the rental rate paid to land owners is the surplus of the value of the MPL in good y above the equilibrium wage. We can see from the figure that with trade, the rental rate paid to capital owners increases and the rental rate paid to land owners decreases for the home country. Specifically, the rental rate paid to capital owners increases from areas $(a + b)$ to area $(a + c)$; and the rental rate paid to land owners decreases from areas $(d + e + f + g)$ to (d).

We can also observe the effects of trade for the foreign country. When the foreign country opens to trade, the price of good y rises relative to the price of good x. We show this relative change by increasing the price of good y and leaving the price of good x unchanged. As a result, labor moves out of industry x and into industry y. The amount of labor that moves across industries is the horizontal distance from L_0^* to L_1^*. At the same time, the nominal wage increases in both the industries from w_0^* to w_1^*. But, we can see from the figure that the nominal wage increases by an amount less than the price increase in good y. Thus, the real wage decreases in terms of purchasing power of good y (w^*/P_y). Alternatively, the figure shows no change in the price of good x. Thus, the real wage increases in terms of purchasing power of good x (w^*/P_x).

Furthermore, the real rental rates paid to the immobile factors also change in the foreign country. Again, we look at the surpluses under the curves and above the equilibrium wage. We can see from the figure that with trade, the rental rate paid to land owners increases and the rental rate paid to capital owners decreases within the foreign country. Specifically, the rental rate paid to land owners increases from areas $(a^* + b^*)$ to area $(a^* + c^*)$; and the rental rate paid to capital owners decreases from areas $(d^* + e^* + f^* + g^*)$ to (d^*).

2.3.6   What are the effects of liberalizing trade policy?

The simple version of the SF model presented here helps us to evaluate the patterns of trade and gains from trade when we move from a hypothetical state of autarky to free trade (or visa versa). As noted earlier, we live in a world somewhere in between these two extremes. Thus, the model provides guidance for understanding what happens if we move closer to autarky or closer to free trade by changing policies.

So, what are the effects of liberalizing trade policy in the short run when countries differ in specific factors?

First, the patterns of production and trade are unambiguous. Countries will produce and export goods that have a lower relative opportunity cost (and therefore price) in autarky. These are the goods that are produced using the country's relative abundant immobile endowments (or specific factors).

Second, the gains from trade are also unambiguous. Table 2.1(c) summarizes these gains. Countries gain from trade as long as the relative world price with trade falls in between the countries' autarky prices. In this case, countries have an incentive to trade. As a consequence of specialization and trade, world output and thus world consumption increases. These gains are accrued to each country in aggregate. That is, the aggregate utility (or well-being) of each country increases.

The model also tells us about the distribution of gains from trade within countries. Specifically, the mobile factor (such as labor) gains in terms of its nominal wage rate. However, in real terms, the mobile factor loses in terms of its purchasing power of the good that the country exports, and gains in terms of its purchasing power of the good that the country imports. The model also shows gains and losses in the rental rates paid to the specific immobile factors (such as capital and land). That is, those that gain from trade are the owners of a country's abundant immobile factors. Those that lose from trade are the owners of a country's scarce immobile factors.

These results of the SF model are *short-run* results. The short run corresponds with the time period when some factors of production cannot be easily moved into use in other industries.

2.4   Summary Remarks

This chapter explored inter-industry, inter-firm trade. This trade is two-way trade in dissimilar goods between the national firms of countries. We examined this trade using three traditional trade models: the Ricardian model, the Heckscher-Ohlin model, and the Specific Factors model. These three models are grounded on the concept of comparative advantage. The law of comparative advantage says that countries will produce and export goods that have a lower relative cost, and therefore price, in autarky. In the Ricardian model, this comparative advantage arises from differences in technologies across countries. In the Heckscher-Ohlin model, comparative advantage arises from differences in endowments across countries. And, in the Specific Factors model, comparative advantage arises from differences in immobile endowments across countries. The Ricardian and Heckscher-Ohlin models are long-term models because they allow factors of production to move freely across industries. The Specific Factors model is a short-term model because it accounts for the immobility of factors of production across industries. Below, we summarize the key findings from each of these models.

What are the effects of trade in the long run, when countries differ in technologies? We used the Ricardian model to examine the effects of trade in the long run, when countries differ in technologies. When countries differ in technologies, the production possibilities of countries are biased toward the industries with relatively high productivities. These industries have relatively low costs and prices in autarky. When we allow for trade, countries export the goods that have relatively low autarky costs/prices and import the goods that have relatively high autarky costs/prices. That is, countries export goods with relatively high productivities and import goods with relatively low productivities. This trade occurs at world prices that are advantageous relative to domestic autarky prices. That is, trade occurs at world prices where the price of exports relative to imports is high in comparison to autarky. As countries specialize in their sectors of comparative advantage and trade, their joint output increases. This pattern of production and trade results in gains. These gains appear as an increase in countries' consumption possibilities and utility (or well-being).

What are the effects of trade in the long run, when countries differ in endowments? We used the Heckscher-Ohlin model to examine the effects of trade in the long run, when countries differ in endowments. When countries differ in endowments, the production possibilities are biased toward the industries that are intensive in the countries' relatively abundant endowments (i.e., Rybczynski theory). These industries have relatively low costs and prices in autarky. When we allow for trade, countries exports the goods that have relatively low autarky costs/prices and import the goods that have relatively high autarky costs/prices. That is, countries export goods that are intensive in their relatively abundant endowments and import goods that are intensive in their relatively scarce endowments (i.e., Heckscher-Ohlin theory). This trade occurs at world prices that are advantageous relative to domestic autarky prices. That is, trade occurs at world prices where the price of exports relative to imports is high in comparison to autarky prices. As countries specialize in their sectors of comparative advantage and trade, their joint output increases. This pattern of production and trade results in gains. These gains appear as an increase in countries' consumption possibilities and utility (or well-being).

Specialization and trade also result in income distribution effects in the long run. That is, trade results in an increase in the factor prices (wages or rental rate) paid to a country's abundant endowments, and a decrease in the factor prices paid to a country' scarce endowments (i.e., Stolper-Samuelson). The magnitude of these factor prices changes exceeds the magnitude of the goods price changes (i.e., the Magnification effect). Consequently, both real and nominal factor prices increase to a country's abundant endowments, and decrease to a country's scarce endowments. Furthermore, factor prices are equalized across countries as a result of trade (i.e., Factor-Price Equalization Theory). This is because the factor prices of abundant endowments are relatively low and the factor prices of scarce endowments are relatively high in autarky. As countries open up to trade, the low factor prices of abundant endowments increase and the high factor prices of scarce endowments decrease until these prices equate across countries.

Finally, if we allow for factor endowments to be mobile across countries in the long run, then the results above can be extended in one additional way. That is, a country can either export the goods in which it has a comparative advantage or export the factor endowments that are used intensively to produce the goods (i.e., Factor Content theory). Thus, with factor mobility, countries can export their abundant endowments and import their scarce endowments in lieu of goods trade or embodied as factor inputs in traded goods.

What are the effects of trade in the short run, when countries differ in immobile endowments? We used the Specific Factors model to examine the effects of trade in the short run, when countries differ in immobile specific factors. In the short run, countries possess endowments that are mobile across industries (such as labor) and immobile across industries (such as capital and land). The immobile endowments are specific factors since they are stuck in a given industry. When countries differ in specific factors, the production possibilities are biased toward the industries that are intensive in the countries' relatively abundant specific factors. These industries have relatively low costs and prices in autarky. When we allow for trade, countries export the goods that have relatively low autarky costs/prices and import the goods that have relatively high autarky costs/prices. That is, countries export goods that are intensive in their relatively abundant specific factors and import goods that are intensive in their relatively scarce specific factors. This trade occurs at world prices that are advantageous relative to domestic autarky prices. That is, trade occurs at world prices where the price of exports relative to imports is high in comparison to autarky prices. As countries specialize in their sectors of comparative advantage and trade, the mobile factor endowment moves to the export sector. Furthermore, the joint output of countries increases. This pattern of production and trade results in gains. These gains appear as an increase in countries' consumption possibilities and utility (or well-being).

Specialization and trade also results in income distribution effects in the short run. That is, trade results in an increase in the factor price (wage or rental rate) of a country's mobile endowments. However, the magnitude of these factor price changes is less than the magnitude of the goods price changes. Consequently, while the nominal factor price increases to a country's mobile endowments, the real factor price decreases in terms of the price of the exported good and increases in terms of the price of the imported good. Thus, whether or not the mobile factor endowment is better or worse off as a result of trade depends on the consumption bias. If consumption is biased toward the exported (imported) good then the mobile factor is worse (better) off in real terms. In contrast, trade results in an increase in the rental rate paid to a country's immobile abundant endowments and a decrease in the rental rate to a country's immobile scarce endowments. It should be noted that these short-run income distribution effects (associated with the Specific Factors model) are somewhat different than the long-run income distribution effects (associated with the Heckscher-Ohlin model).

What are the effects of liberalizing trade policy? The effects of trade liberalization are illustrated in the models by comparing autarky (i.e., no trade) with free trade. How then do these models provide guidance to trade policy?

The Ricardian model is suited to the long-run analysis of trade liberalization between countries that differ in relative technologies. This model can also be used to analyze the effects of changes in technologies over time that alter the relative industry productivities across countries. In contrast, the Heckscher-Ohlin model is suited to the long-run analysis of trade liberalization between countries that differ in endowments, but are similar in technologies. This model can also be used to analyze the effects of changes over time in relative endowments across countries. Finally, the Specific Factors model is suited to short-run analysis of countries that differ in immobile endowments that are specific to an industry. This model can also be used to analyze the effects of changes over time in relative abundance of mobile and immobile factors.

The Heckscher-Ohlin and Specific Factors models are suited to the analysis of the income distribution effects of trade liberalization within countries. These effects include changes in the wages and rental rates paid to the mobile and immobile endowments. Together, these models help us to understand who gains and who loses from trade liberalization (or protectionism) in the short and long run. These results help explain why abundant factor endowments in a country support trade liberalization while scarce factor endowments do not support trade liberalization. They also help explain why mobile factor endowments in the short run may or may not support trade liberalization, depending on their consumption patterns.

Finally, it should be noted that this chapter summarized the effects of trade (or trade liberalization) from the perspective of *countries* in aggregate and from the perspective of *factors* (capital, labor, land owners) within countries. From a *global* perspective, we can add an additional conclusion. With trade liberalization, global output increases. Given the assumptions laid out in this chapter, this results in an increase in global consumption possibilities and utility. In other words, this results in an increase in global well-being.

Applied Problems

2.1   Consider two countries, two industries, and one factor of interest to you. Illustrate the long-run effects of trade liberalization across countries that differ in technologies. Specifically, consider: (a) the patterns of trade; and (b) the gains from trade. Then, consider the alternative effects of protectionist policies.

2.2   Consider two countries, two industries, and two endowments of interest to you. Illustrate the long-run effects of trade liberalization across countries that differ in endowments. Specifically, consider: (a) the patterns of trade; and (b) the gains from trade. Then, consider the alternative effects of protectionist policies.

2.3   Consider two countries, two industries, and three specific factors of interest to you. Illustrate the short-run effects of trade across countries that differ in immobile specific factors. Specifically, consider the income distribution effects of: (a) liberalization policies; and (b) protectionist policies.

2.4   The General Agreement on Tariffs and Trade (GATT) and the World Trade Organization (WTO) have led to substantial liberalization of world trade through multilateral agreement. Use your knowledge of traditional trade theory to evaluate the *long-run* effects of going from a world with restricted trade to a world with free trade on: (a) welfare across countries; and (b) income distribution with countries.

2.5   Consider two groups of countries (industrialized and developing) and two industries (manufactures and agriculture). Use these country groups and industries to answer the following question: what are the effects of liberalizing trade on income distribution: (a) in the short run; and (b) in the long run.

2.6 Politicians sometimes argue in favor of restricting trade. Use your knowledge of traditional trade theory to evaluate the effects of imposing protectionists policies on: (a) income distribution within countries in the short run; (b) income distribution within countries in the long run; and (c) aggregate country welfare in the long run.

2.7 Use your knowledge of traditional trade theory to explain why low skilled labor in the US resisted the NAFTA agreement, while high skilled labor in the US did not resist the agreement.

2.8 Read the journal articles listed under "further reading" at the end of this chapter, then answer the following questions. (a) What real-world economic behaviors do the journal articles attempt to explain? (b) In what ways do the journal articles extend the traditional trade theories presented in this chapter? For example, what assumptions are relaxed? What features are added? (c) What are the implications of these extensions? For example, what are the predictions for the patterns of inter-industry trade, gains from trade, and effects of trade policy?

Further Reading

Bhagwati, Jagdish. 1964. The pure theory of international trade: a survey. *Economic Journal* 74 (293): 1–84.

Collins, Susan M. 1985. Technical progress in a three-country Ricardian model with a continuum of goods. *Journal of International Economics* 19 (1–2): 171–179.

Deardorff, Alan V. 2001. Fragmentation in simple trade models. *North American Journal of Economics and Finance* 12 (2): 121–137.

Dornbusch, Rudiger, Stanley Fischer, and Paul A. Samuelson. 1977. Comparative advantage, trade, and payments in a Ricardian model with a continuum of goods. *American Economic Review* 67 (5): 823–839.

Eaton, Jonathan, and Samuel Kortum. 2002. Technology, geography, and trade. *Econometrica* 70 (5): 1741–1779.

Heckscher, Eli. 1919. The effect of foreign trade on the distribution of income. *Ekonomisk Tidskrift* 21: 497–512.

Hicks, John R. 1953. An inaugural lecture. *Oxford Economic Papers* 5 (2): 117–135.

Jones, Ronald W. 1961. Comparative advantage and the theory of tariffs: a multi-country, multi-commodity model. *Review of Economic Studies* 28 (3): 161–175.

Jones, Ronald W. 1971. A three-factor model in theory, trade, and history. In *Trade, Balance of Payments, and Growth* (eds Jagdish Bhagwati, Ronald Jones, Robert Mundell, and Jaroslav Vanek), Amsterdam: North-Holland.

Jones, Ronald W. 2007. Specific Factors and Heckscher-Ohlin: an intertemporal blend. *Singapore Economic Review* 52: 1–6.

Jones, Ronald W., and Sugata Marjit. 1991. The Stolper-Samuelson Theorem, the Leamer Triangle, and the Produced Mobile Factor Structure. In *Trade, Policy, and International*

Adjustments (eds A. Takayama, M. Ohyama, and H. Ohta), San Diego, CA: Academic Press.

Jones, Ronald W., and Sugata Marjit. 2003. Economic development, trade, and wages. *German Economic Review* 4:1–17.

Kemp, Murray, and Leon Wegge. 1969. On the relation between commodity prices and factor rewards. *International Economic Review* 9: 497–513.

Krugman, Paul R. 1995. Growing world trade: causes and consequences. *Brookings Papers on Economic Activity* 1: 327–362.

Lawrence, Robert Z., and Mathew J. Slaughter. 1993. International trade and American wages in the 1980s: giant sucking sound or a small hiccup? *Brookings Papers on Economic Activity* 2: 161–226.

Magee, Stephen. 1980. Three simple tests of the Stolper-Samuelson Theorem. In *Issues in International Economics* (ed. P. Oppenheimer), London: Oriel Press, pp. 138–153.

Melitz, Marc J. 2003. The impact of trade on intra-industry reallocations and aggregate industry productivity. *Econometrica* 71 (6): 1695–1725.

Neary, J. Peter. 1978. Short-run capital specificity and the pure theory of international trade. *Economic Journal* 88: 488–510.

Ohlin, Bertil. 1933. *Interregional and International Trade.* Cambridge, MA: Harvard University Press.

Panagariya, Arvind. 2000. Evaluating the factor-content approach to measuring the effect of trade on wage inequality. *Journal of International Economics* 50 (1): 91–116.

Ricardo, David. 1817. *The Principles of Political Economy and Taxation,* reprint, 1981. Cambridge: Cambridge University Press.

Ruffin, Roy, and Ronald W. Jones. 1977. Protection and real wages: the neo-classical ambiguity. *Journal of Economic Theory* 14: 337–348.

Rybczynski, T.M. 1955. Factor endowments and relative commodity prices. *Economica* 22 (87): 336–341.

Samuelson, Paul A. 1948. International trade and the equalization of factor prices. *Economic Journal* 58 (230): 163–184.

Samuelson, Paul A. 1971. Ohlin was right. *Swedish Journal of Economics* 73: 365–384.

Sanyal, Kalyan, and Ronald W. Jones. 1982. The theory of trade in middle products. *American Economic Review* 72: 16–31.

Stern, Robert M. 1962. British and American productivity and comparative costs in international trade. *Oxford Economic Papers* 14 (3): 275–296.

Stolper, Wolfgang, and Paul A. Samuelson. 1941. Protection and real wages. *Review of Economic Studies* 9 (3): 58–73.

Wilson, Charles A. 1980. On the general structure of Ricardian models with a continuum of goods. *Econometrica* 48 (7): 1675–1702.

3

Intra-Industry and Intra-Firm Trade

The previous chapter focused on traditional theories of inter-industry and inter-firm trade. In contrast, the current chapter focuses on newer theories of intra-industry and intra-firm trade. *Intra-industry* trade occurs when countries trade different varieties of similar goods with one another. *Intra-firm* trade occurs when the trade across countries occurs within the same firm – such as between a parent firm and affiliates or between different firms under a multinational umbrella. Intra-industry trade need not be intra-firm; and intra-firm trade need not be intra-industry. That is, intra-industry trade can occur between different national firms or between affiliated firms. And intra-firm trade can include trade in different goods or trade in different varieties of the same good. Both intra-industry and intra-firm trade have emerged as prominent and growing new forms of trade in the global economy.

The *New trade theory* literature in economics explores the determinants of intra-industry trade. This literature is distinct from the previous traditional literature in that it relaxes the assumptions of perfect competition market structure and constant returns to scale technologies. Instead, New trade theory assumes imperfect competition market structure and economies of scale. These assumptions help explain the intra-industry trade that could not be explained by traditional trade theories based on comparative advantage.

The *Multinationals theory* literature in economics explores intra-firm trade. This literature is distinct from the traditional trade literature in that it relaxes the assumption that trade occurs between national firms. Instead, Multinationals theory accounts for trade that occurs across countries, but within the same multinational firm or between a parent firm and affiliates. This new assumption alters the conception of the unit of analysis in international trade away from the country-based firm

Global Trade Policy: Questions and Answers, First Edition. Pamela J. Smith.

to a firm that spans multiple countries. Furthermore, Multinationals theory accounts more extensively for the movement of factors of production, such as knowledge assets, across countries within the multinational firm.

The New trade theory and Multinationals theory literatures overlap extensively. These literatures emerged as a result of observed behavior in international trade that could not be explained by the traditional theories. This observed behavior is summarized in the following stylized facts: first, a high and increasing percentage of trade takes place between similar industrialized countries; second, a high percentage of the trade between similar industrialized countries is intra-industry; and third, an increasing percentage of trade is intra-firm trade by multinationals. These stylized facts were articulated by Helpman and Krugman (1985) and others in the early literature on intra-industry and intra-firm trade. Each of these stylized facts is inconsistent with the traditional theories of inter-industry and inter-firm trade that were covered in Chapter 2.

In this chapter, we explore intra-industry trade and intra-firm trade sequentially. We begin by examining intra-industry trade and its effects. Specifically, we consider the question: (1) What are the patterns and gains from intra-industry trade? We then turn to examining intra-firm trade and its effects. We consider the questions: (2) What are the patterns and motives for foreign direct investment? (3) How is trade related to foreign direct investment? (4) What are the patterns and motives for outsourcing and offshoring?

3.1   What Is Intra-Industry Trade and Its Effects?

Intra-industry trade occurs when countries trade different varieties of similar goods with one another. Similarity is typically defined as goods that are included in the same sector. For example, the United States simultaneously exports and imports different varieties of automobiles. However, the varieties of exported and imported autos are different.

This pattern of intra-industry trade is not consistent with the traditional trade theories based on comparative advantage. For example, if the United States had a comparative advantage in producing autos, then it would be an exporter but not an importer of autos. Traditional theory would suggest that the United States would export autos in exchange for dissimilar goods from another country. This traditional form of trade is inter-industry.

Defining the degree of similarity or dissimilarity of goods is challenging as a practical matter. For example, it is possible that a country could have a comparative advantage in one variety of auto but have a comparative disadvantage in another. In this case, two-way trade in autos would be considered inter-industry as the varieties are sufficiently different to give rise to comparative advantage and disadvantage. However, economists also observe two-way trade in goods that are not sufficiently different as to give rise to comparative advantage or disadvantage. This trade is what we mean by intra-industry trade. That is, intra-industry trade cannot be explained by traditional theories based on comparative advantage.

Intra-industry trade includes two types: horizontal and vertical. *Horizontal intra-industry trade* occurs when countries trade similar goods that are at the same stage in processing. For example, these goods may both be final goods (such as autos); but they may differ in minor ways to appeal to consumer demand for product variety (such as safety or design features). In contrast, *vertical intra-industry trade* occurs when countries trade similar goods that are at different stages in processing. For example, a country may import the intermediate inputs that comprise the final goods (such as auto components or materials), and may export the final goods (such as autos).

Empirical evidence of intra-industry trade was first observed in the 1960s and 1970s. Intra-industry trade is typically measured using an index constructed by Gruebel and Lloyd (1975). A common expression of this index is:

$$IIT_i = 1 - (|X_i - M_i|)/(|X_i + M_i|) \tag{3.1}$$

where IIT_i is the index measure for sector i, X_i is exports in sector i, and M_i is imports in sector i. This index takes a value of zero when there is no intra-industry trade within sector i; and it takes a value of one when all trade within sector i is intra-industry. Values greater than 0.50 suggest a predominance of intra-industry trade within sector i.

When applying this index, one needs to make a somewhat arbitrary decision about what constitutes industry i. For example, when industry i is defined as a broad aggregate (such as manufacturing), then more intra-industry trade is observed. Conversely, when industry i is defined as a more detailed subaggregate (such as electronics), then less intra-industry trade is observed.

Despite this measurement difficulty, measures of intra-industry trade do reveal several stylized facts.[1] First, intra-industry trade has increased significantly since the 1980s. Second, intra-industry trade is high for complex manufacturing products. Third, intra-industry trade is high for open economies where trade is a large share of GDP. Fourth, intra-industry trade is positively related to foreign direct investment inflows. Fifth, intra-industry trade is positively related to preferential trade arrangements. Sixth, a large proportion of intra-industry trade is intra-firm trade – trade across countries within the same multinational enterprise.

The theory foundation for this new pattern of trade was developed in the 1980s and 1990s in the New trade theory literature. Models of intra-industry trade in this literature tend to take one of two approaches. The first is to assume a monopolistic competition market structure with differentiated goods.[2] The second approach is to assume oligopoly market structure.[3] Here, we present a simple expression of the monopolistic competition model developed by Paul Krugman. We use the model to examine the question: what are the patterns and gains from intra-industry trade?

3.1.1   What are the patterns and gains from intra-industry trade?

To begin, consider the following *thought experiment* that illustrates the intuition behind models of intra-industry trade. Consider two countries that are identical. Specifically, assume that the two countries have identical technologies, identical endowments, identical immobile specific factors, and identical preferences. Further, assume the technologies are constant returns to scale and the market structure is perfect competition. In other words, none of the traditional sources of comparative advantage are present. Will these countries trade? The answer is no. According to traditional trade theory, the relative costs and prices in autarky are identical across the two countries. There is no source of comparative advantage and there are no gains to be made from trade.

Alternatively, will these identical countries trade if we relax the technology assumption to allow for economies of scale? The answer is yes. With trade, each country can specialize in a different variety of the same good and increase their scale of production in that specific variety. This leads to cost efficiencies due to the economies of scale. The increased scale of production is supported through trade because the national firm now supplies the global market (i.e., both countries) rather than just the domestic market (i.e., the home country). Each country produces a given variety and trades their variety with the other country. This form of trade is intra-industry. However, we cannot predict the direction of this intra-industry trade. That is, we do not know which country will specialize in which variety of the good since the two countries are identical.

In this illustration, the gains from intra-industry trade take two forms. With specialization and trade, the combined outputs of the two countries are higher due to the production efficiencies. Thus, the combined consumption possibilities and utility are higher. Further, if we assume that consumers have preferences for product variety, then consumer utility is also higher with intra-industry trade because consumers have access to an increased variety of products.

Here, we present a simple expression of the monopolistic competition model to illustrate the above intuition for intra-industry trade. This model differs from traditional models in that it relaxes the assumption of constant returns to scale technologies. Instead, this model assumes economies of scale. These economies of scale are *internal economies* that are experienced at the level of the firm. That is, the firm's costs per unit of output depend on the firm's size. As the firm increases its scale of production, it experiences increased efficiency. A common source of such efficiencies is the specialization of factor inputs within the larger firm. Because the efficiencies of scale are internalized by the firm, the firm takes these efficiencies into account in its profit maximization decisions.

Economies of scale at the firm level give rise to imperfect competition market structures. Such market structures include monopoly, oligopoly, and monopolistic competition. The model presented here assumes the monopolistic competition market structure. In this case, there are multiple firms and the behavior of firms affects price. Each firm exercises monopoly power over its specific variety of the good. However, the firm competes with the other firms in the market for close substitutes – other varieties of the same good. Thus, monopolistic competition is a hybrid of monopoly and perfect competition.

We begin by examining the monopoly behavior of firms over their product variety. The traditional monopoly is a single firm that determines the price in the market. We then extend the discussion to a monopolistic competition framework.

The demand that the monopoly faces is

$$x = A - Bp \tag{3.2}$$

where x is the unit of output, p is the price per unit of output, A is a constant intercept term, and B is a constant slope term. The corresponding marginal revenue (MR) is

$$MR = p - (x / B) \tag{3.3}$$

where the terms are as defined above. Conceptually, the marginal revenue is the additional revenue generated from producing one additional unit of the good.

The total costs are the sum of fixed costs plus variable costs defined as

$$C = F + cx \tag{3.4}$$

where C is total costs, F is fixed costs, and cx is variable costs. Dividing total costs by output gives average costs as

$$AC = (C/x) = (F/x) + c \tag{3.5}$$

As shown, these average costs decrease as output increases. This is because the fixed costs are spread across a larger output. This relationship captures the *internal econo-mies of scale*: as the firm increases its scale of production, its average costs fall. Figure 3.1 illustrates this relationship. It shows that as the quantity (Q) of output x increases, average costs (AC) decrease.

Taking the derivative of total costs with respect to output gives the marginal cost as

$$MC = c \tag{3.6}$$

where c is marginal cost. Conceptually, the marginal cost is the additional cost of producing one additional unit of output. Comparing equations (3.5) and (3.6), we see that average costs are greater than marginal costs (AC > MC). We can also see that average costs are negatively related output. That is, as output increases, average costs decrease. This decrease reflects the efficiencies that come from the larger scale of firm production.

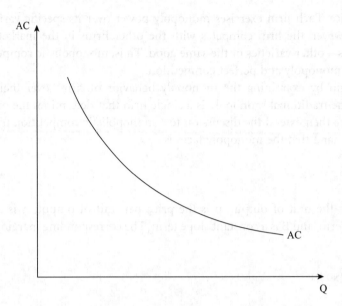

Figure 3.1   Average costs with economies of scale.

The monopolist maximizes profits by setting marginal revenue (3.3) equal to marginal costs (3.6). This gives the equilibrium price and quantity in the monopoly case.

Monopolistic competition is a variation on the above. In this case, the demand curve can be rewritten as

$$x = S[(1/n) - b(p - p')] \qquad (3.7)$$

where S is industry output, n is the number of firms in the industry, p is firm price, p' is the average price of competitors, and b is the slope of the demand curve. Marginal revenue in this case is

$$MR = p - (x/Sb) \qquad (3.8)$$

where $Sb = B$ from the monopoly case in equation (3.3).

Assuming that symmetric firms compete in the market for close substitutes, then firms' prices will equate with the average price of competitors such that $p = p'$. Combining this assumption with the demand relationship in equation (3.7) gives

$$x = S/n \qquad (3.9)$$

which is the output in the symmetric firm case. In this case, each firm has an equal output share in industry output. The more firms in the market, the smaller the output share of each firm.

We can now determine the equilibrium number of firms and equilibrium price in the monopolistic competition case.

First, we substitute firm output in equation (3.9) into the average cost equation (3.5). This gives

$$AC = n(F/S) + c \qquad (3.10)$$

Equation (3.10) shows a positive relationship between the number of firms and the average cost in the monopolistic competition case. That is, as the number of firms decreases, the average cost decreases.

Second, we impose the equilibrium condition that marginal revenue (3.8) equals marginal cost (3.6). This gives

$$c = p - (x/Sb) \text{ or} \qquad (3.11)$$

$$p = c + (x/Sb)$$

Then substituting equations (3.9) into equation (3.11) gives

$$p = c + 1/nb \qquad (3.12)$$

Equation (3.12) shows a negative relationship between the number of firms and price; that is, as the number of firms decreases, the price increases.

Third, we impose the equilibrium condition that p = AC. That is, we equate equilibrium equations (3.12) and (3.10) to determine the equilibrium number of firms and price. This equilibrium condition arises due to free entry and exit of firms into the market.

Figure 3.2 illustrates this equilibrium in the monopolistic competition case. This figure plots the number of firms horizontally and the price and average costs vertically. Equation (3.10) is plotted as the upward sloping CC curve. This curve shows the positive relationship between the number of firms and the average costs. Equation (3.12) is plotted as the downward sloping PP curve. This curve shows the negative relationship between the number of firms and the price. The intersection of the two curves gives the equilibrium number of firms and equilibrium price. To the right of the equilibrium, average costs exceed price and firms exit the market – that is, the number of firms decreases. To the left of the equilibrium, the price exceeds average costs and firms enter the market – that is, the number of firms increases.

What happens in this framework when we allow for trade? Or, what happens when we liberalize trade policies to reduce barriers to trade? The effect of allowing for trade is an increase in the market size. That is, as countries open to trade, the market that firms face is no longer limited to the domestic market, but rather includes the larger global market. Access to a larger market results in a decrease in average costs due to the efficiencies that arise from economies of scale. Equation (3.10) shows this effect. As industry size (S) increases, average costs (AC) decrease.

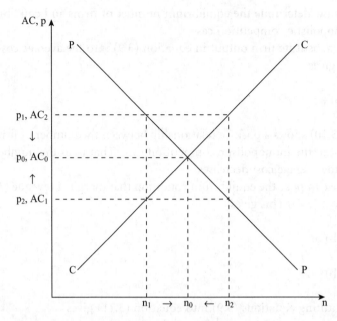

Figure 3.2   Monopolistic competition model – equilibrium number of firms and prices.

Figure 3.3 illustrates the effects of trade on the equilibrium in the monopolistic competition case. An increase in the market output (S) corresponds with an increase in the output of each firm (x) and a decrease in their average costs (AC). As a consequence, the CC curve in Figure 3.3 shifts from $C_0 C_0$ to $C_1 C_1$. This change results in a decrease in the equilibrium price (p_0 to p_1) and an increase in the equilibrium number of firms (n_0 to n_1).

So what are the effects of trade or trade liberalization when technologies exhibit economies of scale? In other words, what are the patterns and gains from intra-industry trade? The patterns of intra-industry trade are ambiguous; that is, intra-industry trade can occur between similar countries that specialize in different varieties of the same good. Because the countries are similar, there is no way to determine which country will specialize in which variety of the good. However, the gains from intra-industry trade are not ambiguous. Intra-industry trade (or trade liberalization) results in an increase in the market size as firms trade their varieties in the larger world market rather than supplying only their smaller domestic market. Firms increase the scale of their production in a given product variety in order to take advantage of economies of scale. As a result of these economies, the price and average costs decrease. Thus, as a result of intra-industry trade, consumers have access to increased product variety and lower prices of these varieties. Consumer utility increases in the trading countries; that is, consumers gain from trade.

Finally, it is important to note that models of intra-industry trade are not incompatible with models of inter-industry trade. Rather, models of intra-industry trade in the New trade theory literature extend the models of inter-industry trade in the

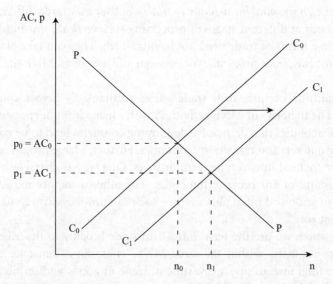

Figure 3.3 Monopolistic competition model – effect of trade on equilibrium.

traditional trade theory literature. Inter-industry trade arises because of sources of comparative advantage – country differences in technologies, endowments, or specific factors. Intra-industry trade arises because of economies of scale – efficiencies associated with the scale of production. These modeling approaches can be combined in more complex frameworks where some industries are subject to economies of scale and others are subject to constant returns. In this way, we can simultaneously observe patterns of inter-industry and intra-industry trade.

3.2   What Is Intra-Firm Trade and Its Effects?

Intra-firm trade is when the trade across countries occurs within the same firm – such as between different affiliates of the same multinational enterprise (MNE). The MNE is a firm that has affiliates in more than one country, and whose operations and activities in different countries are coordinated by one or more headquarters. Most MNEs are organized such that there is one headquarters located in a *home* country and affiliates located in *host* countries. However, alternative organization structures are becoming increasing prominent. The establishment in the home country is often referred to as the *parent firm*. Intra-firm trade includes both trade between the parent firm and affiliates, and trade from affiliate to affiliate.

Intra-firm trade can be either inter-industry or intra-industry, and can also be either horizontal or vertical. In other words, different affiliates of the same MNE may trade different goods (i.e., *inter-industry trade*) or different varieties of similar goods (i.e., *intra-industry trade*). Furthermore, different affiliates of the same multinational firm may trade different varieties of the similar good at similar stages in processing (i.e., *horizontal intra-industry trade*); or they may trade different varieties of similar goods at different stages of processing (i.e., *vertical intra-industry trade*). However, these forms of trade need not be intra-firm. They can take place between national firms (i.e., *inter-firm trade*) or between affiliates of an MNE (i.e., *intra-firm trade*).

The magnitude of intra-firm trade varies substantially across countries and industries. The majority of MNE activities involve firms from developed countries. Those MNE activities that do involve developing countries tend to be concentrated in emerging markets and transition economies. Further, a large proportion of MNE activities are focused in two types of industries. One type is characterized by high growth rates and/or emerging technologies. The other is mature industries where economies of scale and intangible assets – such as knowledge or reputation – play an important role.[4]

In this chapter, we use the term intra-firm trade broadly to describe *flows* that occur across countries within the same MNE. These flows can take a variety of forms, including: foreign direct investment; trade in goods and services; and outsourcing and offshoring. The MNE is the organizational unit that facilitates these flows between affiliates. However, it should be noted that the MNE does not always operate like a queen bee who issues top-down decisions worldwide. Rather, the degree of centralized versus decentralized decision-making varies, with some affiliates having more autonomy than others. The following sections consider the prominent forms of intra-firm flows across countries.

3.2.1   What are the patterns and motives for foreign direct investment?

Foreign direct investment (FDI) is defined as investments in which a firm acquires a majority (or controlling interest) in a foreign firm. As noted earlier, the firm making the foreign direct investments is referred to as an MNE. The terms FDI and MNE are often used synonymously. However, it is more accurate to view FDI as one of the modes by which an MNE can engage in international activities. Other modes include cooperative agreements and offshoring.

Several stylized facts prompted research into FDI in the context of the international trade literature.[5] First, high-income developed countries are the major source *and* recipient of FDI. This pattern contradicts traditional trade theory, which predicts that capital should flow from capital-abundant to capital-scarce countries embodied in goods or as factor inputs. Second, the host country recipients of FDI tend to be large markets. Third, the outputs of FDI tend to be consumed in either in the host country or in a third country within the region of the host country. These three stylized facts suggest that there are demand-side motives for FDI in addition to supply-side motives.

There are two prominent methods of FDI – greenfield and brownfield/acquisition. *Greenfield investments* occur when a firm creates a new foreign enterprise from scratch. *Brownfield or acquisition investments* occur when a firm acquires an existing foreign firm.[6] Furthermore, there are two prominent types of FDI – horizontal and vertical.[7] *Horizontal FDI* occurs when a foreign affiliate replicates the parent firm's activities or goods and services.[8] For example, the foreign firm may modify or adapt products for sale in the foreign market, that were originally developed by the parent firm. Further, the foreign affiliates and headquarters may share assets – such as knowledge capital – that have a public goods quality. Such assets can be used simultaneously in multiple locations without diminishing their value or supply. Horizontal FDI typically occurs between relatively similar countries. The incentives for horizontal FDI mirror the incentives for intra-industry trade, such as the ability to take advantage of economies of scale at the corporate/enterprise level. With horizontal FDI, the firm produces *and* sells the good or service in the foreign market. Thus, horizontal FDI is often referred to as *market-seeking* since this is a prominent underlying motivation.

Alternatively, *vertical FDI* occurs when the foreign affiliates engage in a production activity that is distinct from the home firm's activities.[9] For example, the domestic firm may serve as the headquarters whereas the foreign firm(s) may undertake distinct production activities. The activities in the different locations often have different factor intensities. In this case, the MNE fragments its production process into different parts and locates these parts in different countries. Vertical FDI typically occurs between relatively dissimilar countries. The incentives for vertical FDI mirror the incentives for inter-industry trade, such as the ability to take advantage of factor-price differences across countries. Thus, vertical FDI is often referred to as *resource-seeking* since this is the underlying motivation.

Research on the motives for FDI has benefited significantly from early work in the international business literature by Dunning (1973). The Ownership-Location-Internalization (OLI) framework developed by Dunning describes conditions that give rise to FDI. According to this framework, there are three conditions required for a firm to create or acquire a foreign firm: (1) ownership advantage; (2) location advantage; and (3) internalization advantage. The intuition is as follows.

First, the *ownership advantage* needs to be present in order for a firm to engage in trade or FDI. According to the ownership advantage, the firm must own a firm-specific asset that gives the firm an advantage over other local firms in the host market. This advantage is required since competing local firms have a natural advantage in their local market. Examples of firm-specific assets include proprietary intangible assets, such as knowledge that can be protected via intellectual property rights. Such knowledge assets can be used at multiple production locations simultaneously.[10] This ownership advantage is required for both FDI and trade into a foreign market.

Second, a *location advantage* needs to be present in order for a firm to choose FDI instead of trade as the means for serving the foreign market. According to the location advantage, firms engage in FDI rather than trade into the foreign market when there is a cost advantage to establishing a foreign affiliate rather than exporting into the market. In the case of horizontal FDI, the motive for the FDI is to serve the local market. In this case, the cost advantage of FDI can arise from direct access to the large market and plant-level scale economies. The cost advantage of FDI can also arise from high trade costs associate with policy barriers (such as tariffs) or transportation costs. Alternatively, in the case of vertical FDI, the motive for the FDI is to export the goods and services produced by the foreign affiliate back to the home country or to a third market. In this case, the cost advantage of FDI includes low input costs and trade costs associated with importing intermediate goods and exporting final goods from the location. In other words, firms choose horizontal FDI rather than trade, when the foreign market is large and trade costs are high; and firms choose vertical FDI rather than trade, when trade costs and factor prices are low in the foreign location.

Finally, the *internalization advantage* needs to be present in order for a firm to choose FDI instead of licensing an asset or activity to a non-affiliated firm. Internalization has to do with holding assets or activities within the firm (MNE) rather than transferring the asset or activity to an outside firm. Internalization motivations include: efforts to control product quality and firm reputation, which can be difficult in contracts between national firms; efforts to control proprietary firm-specific knowledge, which can be difficult in licensing contracts between national firms; and efforts to avoid taxes by shifting income to affiliates located in low tax countries. Each of these motivations is influenced by a variety of policies in the host countries. For example, the effort to control proprietary knowledge is particularly important when the intellectual property rights in the host countries are weak.

3.2.2   How is trade related to foreign direct investment?

How is trade in goods and services related to foreign direct investment? As discussed in the previous section, an ownership advantage is required for a firm to decide to engage in either trade or FDI. A location advantage is required for a firm to decide to engage in FDI rather than trade. An internalization advantage is required for a firm to decide to engage in either trade or FDI rather than transferring activities to an unaffiliated firm, such as through a licensing agreement or outsourcing. This section considers the conditions that influence these decisions about the means of servicing the foreign market. Specifically, we consider the conditions under which FDI is a substitute for trade and the conditions under which FDI is a complement to trade. That is, we consider both the negative and positive relationship between FDI and trade. As will be discussed, the conditions for these relationships depend in part on the form of FDI.

When is FDI a substitute for trade? According to Dunning's (1973) OLI framework, FDI is a substitute for trade when there is a location advantage. In this case, there is a cost advantage to locating the production activity in the foreign market where the good or service will be sold. As noted earlier, prominent cost advantages include the ability to avoid trade costs, particularly those associated with policy barriers and transportation. The *proximity-concentration trade-off* refers to this case.[11] This framework suggests that a firm will choose FDI rather than trade when trade costs are high relative to the cost efficiencies associated with plant-level economies of scale from concentrating production in the home country. *Tariff-jumping* is an example of this case. In this case, firms will engage in FDI in order to avoid (e.g., jump) high tariff barriers to trade.

When is trade a complement to FDI? Trade is a complement to FDI in the case where FDI serves to create an export platform. *Export platforms* arise when a free trade agreement results in the liberalization of trade policies within a block of countries, while each country maintains its higher barriers with countries outside the agreement. In such a case, countries outside the block may set up one production facility in a country inside the block. This facility then exports to the other countries within the block. The outside firm engages in FDI to access the block, and then trades to move the goods and services to consumers within the various countries in the block. The FDI is attracted into the lowest cost country within the block. In this case, regional trade liberalization attracts FDI into the block for the purpose of setting up an export platform to trade into the other countries within the block.[12]

Trade and FDI can also be complements in the case of vertical FDI. As discussed previously, vertical FDI occurs when a firm fragments its production activities to take advantage of cost differences across countries. The firm locates each production stage in the lowest cost country. The goods are then exported back to the parent country or to a third country. For this behavior to occur, the cost advantage of fragmenting production must exceed the trade costs associated with the export of the goods to the parent or third country. If this is the case, then lower policy barriers and transportation costs increase both FDI and trade, although it is important to note that the FDI and trade are moving in different directions.

To summarize, FDI and trade are closely related. FDI can be a substitute to trade when there is a location advantage. An example would be when affiliates are located in the country where the good is destined for consumption and the market is large. For example, with horizontal FDI, the varieties of the goods produced by affiliates may be destined for consumers in the host country. However, FDI can also be a complement to trade. This positive relationship occurs when FDI results in new forms of trade. For example, FDI that creates an export platform results in new trade from the platform to countries within a trading block. Furthermore, with vertical FDI, distinct intermediate inputs that comprise a final good are produced in multiple locations. These intermediate inputs then move, in the form of trade, to locations of assembly. Thus, the production and assembly locations may serve as an export platform for trade into third country markets.

3.2.3   What are the patterns and motives for outsourcing and offshoring?

Outsourcing describes the activity where components of a good or service are produced in several countries. Outsourcing need not be international. For example, a firm may move activities to another firm within the same country (i.e., domestic outsourcing) or another firm in a foreign country (i.e., international outsourcing). In contrast, *offshoring* is when a firm moves some of its operations to other countries, but retains ownership of those operations. In this case, operations are moved to affiliates of the same firm. Thus, the difference between outsourcing and offshoring is the ownership of the foreign activities. In practice, the degree of ownership can vary considerably, with some subsidiaries wholly owned and others partially owned. Despite this ownership distinction, the terms outsourcing and offshoring are often used synonymously in the popular literature.

Outsourcing and offshoring have different implications for trade. Trade can be either inter-firm or intra-firm. When the fragmented activities occur within different affiliates of the same MNE, then the corresponding flows can be viewed as "intra-firm". This is the case of offshoring. When the fragmented activities occur across different national firms, then the corresponding flows can be viewed as "inter-firm." This is the case of outsourcing. These fragmented activities can include either production activities or service activities.

A firm's decision to engage in outsourcing versus its decision to engage in offshoring hinges largely on the internalization advantage described earlier. That is, the firm must choose between internalizing its assets and activities or contracting with an external firm. This contracting may involve the licensing of knowledge assets to the unaffiliated foreign firm. Or, it may involve contracting for select production activities to be undertaken by the unaffiliated foreign firm. In the case of offshoring, ownership of the foreign activities is maintained and transferred assets remain internalized. In the case of outsourcing, ownership of the foreign activities is not maintained and transferred assets move outside the boundaries of the firm.

The decisions to outsource and license are similar decisions. Both involve a decision about whether to internalize assets and production activities within the firm or to engage in contractual relationships with an unaffiliated firm in a foreign country. Licensing tends to be related to horizontal FDI. That is, a firm is deciding between setting up a replica of the parent firm in a foreign location or licensing the activities to an unaffiliated foreign firm. Alternatively, outsourcing tends to be related to vertical FDI. That is, a firm is deciding between fragmenting production across locations within the same MNE or outsourcing the fragmented production stages across unaffiliated foreign firms. Both outsourcing and licensing decisions are affected by costs associated with contractual arrangements and information asymmetries with unaffiliated firms. Alternatively, offshoring would serve as a way to fragment production activities across locations while still internalizing the activities within the MNE. Offshoring can be related to vertical FDI.

Empirical evidence of outsourcing and offshoring shows that there was an increase in such activities during the 1980s and 1990s.[13] This evidence is seen in two types of measures: processing trade and intermediate input trade. Measures of *processing trade* show an increase in imports of intermediate inputs for processing and subsequent re-export of a final product. For example, Feenstra and Hanson (2004) show that China's processing exports increased from one-third to over one-half of China's total exports in the decade between 1988 and 1998. Similarly, measures of *intermediate input trade* show an increase in the use of imported inputs as a share of total intermediate input purchases for a country. For example, Campa and Goldberg (1997) show that this share increased for Canada and the United Kingdom by approximately 27% and 61%, respectively, between 1974 and 1993. For these countries, the shares of imported intermediate inputs exceeded 20% of total input purchases by the end of this period.

Much of the recent discussion around this outsourcing/offshoring focuses on the effects on factor prices, particularly wages to skilled and unskilled labor. This research was originally motivated by the observation that wages and employment of skilled labor increased during the 1980s while the wages and employment of unskilled labor fell during the same period. These *relative* wage changes were observed in both developed and developing countries, and corresponded with increasing income inequality globally. Feenstra (2010) provides a synthesis of research on the role of outsourcing as an explanation for these wage changes. This research takes a nuanced approach to examining the skill content of labor used in the range of activities that involve outsourcing. In this approach, the labor that is "relatively unskilled" in developed countries is "relatively skilled" in developing countries. The core findings show that with outsourcing, developed countries shift their relatively less-skilled activities to developing countries, resulting in a decrease in the wage of low-skilled labor (relative to high-skilled labor) in the developed source countries. In the developing countries, the outsourced activities are relatively more skill-intensive compared to their existing activities. Thus, the outsourced activities result in an increase in the domestic wage of the higher skilled labor (relative to low-skilled labor) in the developing host countries. These findings are consistent with the observed evidence of increasing income inequality in both sources and hosts.

3.3 Summary Remarks

This chapter explored intra-industry trade and its effects. This trade occurs when countries trade different varieties of similar goods with one another. Intra-industry trade includes two types. Horizontal intra-industry trade occurs when countries trade similar goods that are at the same stage in processing. Vertical intra-industry trade occurs when countries trade similar goods that are at different stages of processing. These patterns of trade are not consistent with traditional trade theories based on comparative advantage because they can arise between countries that are identical in endowments, technologies and specific factors. The New trade theory literature in economics explores the determinants of this intra-industry trade. This literature extends the traditional trade theories by relaxing the assumption of perfect competition and constant returns to scale technologies. In contrast, models of intra-industry trade allow for imperfect competition market structures and economies of scale. The importance of such intra-industry trade has been demonstrated in empirical studies that use the Grubel and Lloyd index to measure the predominance of intra-industry trade within a given industry. Such studies suggest that intra-industry trade is a significant component of international trade in our contemporary global economy.

What are the patterns and gains from intra-industry trade? To answer this question, we summarized the key findings from the monopolistic competition model of intra-industry trade associated with the work of Paul Krugman. This model illustrates the determination of the equilibrium number of firms and price/average costs. Using this framework, we examined the effects of trade (or trade liberalization) on this equilibrium. The effect of allowing for trade (or trade liberalization) is an increase in market size. Access to a larger market results in a decrease in the average costs, due to the efficiencies that arise from economies of scale. These efficiencies create an incentive for countries to specialize in a given product variety, and to trade this variety in exchange for another variety exported from a trading partner.

The direction of this intra-industry trade is ambiguous. That is, the model does not predict which country will export which variety. However, the gains from intra-industry trade are not ambiguous. With trade (or trade liberalization), firms increase the scale of their production in a given product variety in order to take advantage of the economies of scale. As a result, the price and average cost of these varieties decrease. Consumers have access to increased product variety and lower prices of these varieties. That is, consumer utility increases as a consequence of intra-industry trade.

What is intra-firm trade and its effects? Intra-firm trade occurs when the trade across countries is within the same firm, such as between different affiliates of the same multinational enterprise. This intra-firm trade can take a variety of forms. For example, it can be inter-industry or intra-industry. And, it can be horizontal intra-industry or vertical intra-industry. Furthermore, these forms of intra-firm trade can occur via a variety of methods. These methods include foreign direct investment, trade in goods and services associated with foreign direct investment, and outsourcing and offshoring. Below, we summarize the key findings from our discussion of these various forms and methods of intra-firm trade.

What are the patterns and motives for foreign direct investment? We discussed the types, methods, and motives for foreign direct investment. Foreign direct investment (FDI) is investments in which a firm acquires a majority or controlling interest in a foreign firm. The prominent methods of FDI include greenfield and brownfield/acquisition investments. Greenfield investments occur when a firm creates a new foreign enterprise from scratch. In contrast, brownfield or acquisition investment occur when a firm acquires an exiting foreign firm. Further, the predominant types of FDI include horizontal and vertical FDI. Horizontal FDI occurs when a foreign affiliate replicates the parent firm's activities or goods and services. The prominent underlying motive for horizontal FDI is market-seeking. Vertical FDI occurs when the foreign affiliates engage in a production activity that is distinct from the home firm's activities. The prominent underlying motive for vertical FDI is resource-seeking.

We considered the Ownership-Location-Internalization (OLI) framework for examining the patterns and motivation for these forms of FDI. According to this framework, an ownership advantage must be present in order for FDI and/or trade to take place. That is, an investing firm must own a firm-specific asset (such as knowledge) that gives the firm an advantage over local firms in the host market. A location advantage must be present in order for a firm to choose FDI instead of trade. That is, firms choose FDI rather than trade when there is a cost advantage to establishing a foreign affiliate rather than exporting into the foreign market. For example, firms choose horizontal FDI rather than trade when the foreign market is large and trade costs are high. Alternatively, firms choose vertical FDI rather than trade when trade costs and factor prices are low in the foreign location. Finally, an internalization advantage must be present in order for a firm to choose FDI instead of licensing as a means of servicing the foreign market. That is, firms will choose to hold their assets/activities within the enterprise rather than licensing. For example, this internationalization can allow the firm to control product quality, control proprietary knowledge, and avoid taxes.

How is trade related to foreign direct investment? We discussed the relationship between trade and foreign direct investment. Specifically, we considered the conditions under which trade is a substitute for FDI, and the conditions under which trade is a complement to FDI. Again, we used intuition from the OLI framework to inform our discussion. FDI is a substitute for trade when there is a location advantage. In this case, there is a cost advantage to locating the production activity in the foreign market where the good will be sold. Firms will choose FDI rather than trade for a variety of cost reasons such as the ability to avoid trade barriers (e.g., tariff jumping) or high transportation costs. Alternatively, FDI is a complement to trade when FDI serves to create an export platform. In this case, a firm engages in FDI in order to access a trading block. The firm sets up a production facility in the lowest cost country within the block and then exports the produced goods to consumers in the other countries within the block. FDI is also a complement to trade in the case of vertical FDI. In this case, a firm fragments its production process in order to take advantage of cost differences across countries and then exports the good to the parent or third country. In this case, FDI and trade both respond positively to lower policy barriers and lower transportation costs.

What are the patterns and motives for outsourcing and offshoring? Outsourcing is when a firm moves some of it activities to an unaffiliated firm in another domestic location or country. *Offshoring* is when a firm moves some of its activities to other countries, but retains ownership of those operations. The main difference between outsourcing and offshoring is the ownership of the foreign activities. Outsourcing and offshoring have different implications for trade. With offshoring, the corresponding trade flows are intra-firm; with outsourcing, the corresponding trade flows are inter-firm. The decision of a firm to engage in outsourcing versus offshoring depends on the internalization advantage. With offshoring, any transferred assets remain internalized; with outsourcing, transferred assets move outside the boundaries of the firm. Further, the decisions to outsource and license are closely related. Both involve a decision about whether to internalize assets and production activities within the firm or to engage in contractual relationships with an unaffiliated firm. Both outsourcing and licensing are affected by costs associated with contractual arrangements and information asymmetries with unaffiliated firms. Empirical evidence on outsourcing and offshoring shows that there has been an increase, as evidenced by processing trade and intermediate input trade. There continues to be much debate about the implications of these activities for wages to low- and high-skilled labor in both the source and host countries.

Applied Problems

3.1   Consider theories of intra-industry trade and intra-firm trade to answer the following questions. (a) What is inter-industry trade? (b) What are the patterns and gains from inter-industry trade? (c) What is inter-firm trade? (d) What are the patterns and motives for foreign direct investment? (e) How is trade related to foreign direct investment? (f) What are the patterns and motives for outsourcing and offshoring?

3.2   Consider the monopolistic competition model of trade to answer the following questions. (a) What is the relationship between the number of firms and average costs? (b) What is the relationship between the number of firms and price? (c) What is the equilibrium number of firms, price, and average costs? (d) What are the effects of trade on this equilibrium?

3.3   Consider the monopolistic competition model of trade to answer the following questions. (a) Consider two countries participating in a trade war that decreases the effective market size faced by each country. What are the effects of the trade war on firm output, average costs, price, and number of firms? (b) If the trade war is prolonged, what is the effect on the ability of the countries to benefit from external economies of scale?

3.4   Consider a world where industrialized countries are identical to each other in every way except that they vary in absolute size; and where developing countries are identical to each other in size, but vary in their relative endowments. Further, assume that industrialized countries specialize in high-technology industries that experience economies of scale, whereas developing countries specialize in low-technology industries with no economies of scale. Based on these assumptions, predict the patterns of inter-industry and intra-industry trade within and across industrialized and developing countries.

3.5   John Dunning introduced the concepts of ownership, location, and internalization to explain the motivations behind the activities of multinational enterprises. These concepts have been integrated into the trade and multinationals literature. How do these concepts explain the motivation for trade, foreign direct investment, and licensing?

3.6   The trade theory literature has evolved to include traditional trade theory, Factor Content theory, New trade theory, and Trade and Multinationals theory. Use your knowledge of these literatures to answer the following questions. (a) What are the key assumptions of each of the literatures? In other words, what assumptions are relaxed relative to previous literatures? (b) How do the predictions of the models change as the assumptions are relaxed?

3.7 Consider the evolution of the trade theory literature to answer the following questions. (a) What are the implications for trade of relaxing the assumption of perfect competition to allow for economies of scale? (b) What are the implications for trade of relaxing the assumption of the national firm to allow for multinational firms?

3.8 Over time, four distinctive bodies of trade theory literature have emerged, including traditional trade theory, Factor Content theory, New trade theory, and Trade and Multinationals theory. Consider this evolution of the literature to answer the following questions. (a) What real-world observations prompted the initiation of each of the four bodies of literature? (b) What are the implications of each body of literature for theory predictions in terms of gains from trade, patterns of trade, and protectionist or liberalization policies?

3.9 The Ricardian and Heckscher-Ohlin models are early formal models of international trade. Both of these models rest on assumptions that seem unbelievable in light of contemporary international conditions. Many recent models can be viewed as extensions that relax the assumptions of the earlier models. Briefly describe the contemporary trade behavior that can be examined by relaxing the following assumptions: (a) countries are the appropriate unit of analysis; (b) factors of production are immobile across countries; (c) technologies exhibit constant returns to scale.

3.10 Use your knowledge of Trade and Multinational theory to explain the following stylized facts. (a) A large proportion of trade and foreign direct investment occurs between relatively similar economies – similar in size and relative endowments; that is, flows tend to be north-north or south-south rather than north-south or south-north. (b) A large proportion of trade and foreign direct investment is two-way in similar products – intra-industry trade. (c) Foreign direct investment has grown faster than trade in recent years. (d) A large proportion of foreign direct investment is concentrated among industrialized countries; that is, foreign direct investment tends to flow north-to-north rather than north-to-south or south-to-south. This foreign direct investment tends to be horizontal in character.

3.11 Read the journal articles listed under "further reading" at the end of this chapter, then answer the following questions. (a) What real-world economic behaviors do the journal articles attempt to explain? (b) In what ways do the journal articles extend the trade and multinationals theories presented in this chapter? For example, what assumptions are relaxed? What features are added? (c) What are the implications of these extensions? For example, what are the predictions for the patterns of intra-industry and intra-firm trade, gains from trade, and effects of trade policy?

Further Reading

Amiti, Mary, and Shang-Jin Wei. 2006. *Service Off-shoring and Productivity: Evidence from the United States.* NBER Working Paper No. 11926. Cambridge: MA: National Bureau of Economic Research.

Antras, Pol. 2003. Firms, contracts, and trade structure. *Quarterly Journal of Economics* 118 (4): 1375–1418.

Bergstrand, Jeffrey H., and Peter Egger. 2007. A knowledge-and-physical-capital model of international trade, foreign direct investment, and multinational enterprises. *Journal of International Economics* 73 (2): 278–308.

Borga, Maria, and William J. Zeile. 2004. *International Fragmentation of Production and International Trade of US Multinational Companies.* Bureau of Economic Analysis Working Paper No. 2004-02. Washington, D.C.: BEA.

Braconier, Henrik, Pehr-Johan Norback, and Dieter Urban. 2005. Reconciling the evidence on the knowledge-capital model. *Review of International Economics* 13 (4): 770–786.

Brainard, S. Lael. 1997. An empirical assessment of the proximity-concentration trade-off between multinational sales and trade. *American Economic Review* 87 (4): 520–544.

Brander, James A. 1981. Intraindustry trade in identical commodities. *Journal of International Economics* 11 (1): 1–14.

Campa, Jose, and Linda Goldberg. 1997. *The Evolving External Orientation of Manufacturing Industries: Evidence for Four Countries.* NBER Working Paper No. 5919. Cambridge, MA: National Bureau of Economic Research.

Carr, David L., James R. Markusen, and Keith E. Maskus. 2001. Estimating the knowledge-capital model of the multinational enterprise. *American Economic Review* 91 (3): 693–708.

Caves, Richard E. 2007. *Multinational Enterprises and Economic Analysis.* Cambridge: Cambridge University Press.

Clausing, Kimberly A. 2003. Tax-motivated transfer pricing and US intrafirm trade prices. *Journal of Public Economics* 87 (9/10): 2207–2223.

Clausing, Kimberly A. 2006. International tax avoidance and US international trade. *National Tax Journal* 59 (2): 269–287.

Dixit, Avinash K., and Joseph E. Stiglitz. 1977. Monopolistic competition and optimum product diversity. *American Economic Review* 67 (3): 297–308.

Dunning, John H. 1973. The determinants of international production. *Oxford Economic Papers* 25 (3): 289–336.

Dunning, John H. 1988. *Explaining International Production.* London: Unwin Hyman.

Dunning, John H. 1993. *Multinational Enterprises and the Global Economy.* Wokingham, UK: Addison Wesley.

Dunning, John H., and Rajneesh Narula. 2004. *Multinationals and Industrial Competitiveness: A New Agenda.* Cheltenham, UK: Edward Elgar.

Eaton, Jonathan, and Gene M. Grossman. 1986. Optimal trade and industrial policy under oligopoly. *Quarterly Journal of Economics* 101 (May): 383–406.

Feenstra, Robert C., and Gordon H. Hanson. 1996. Foreign investment, outsourcing, and relative wages. In *The Political Economy of Trade Policy: Papers in Honor of Jagdish Bhagwati* (eds R.C. Feeenstra, G.M. Grossman, and D.A. Irwin), Cambridge, MA: MIT Press, pp. 89–127.

Feenstra, Robert C., and Gordon H. Hanson. 1999. The impact of outsourcing and high-technology capital on wages: estimates for the US, 1979–1990. *Quarterly Journal of Economics* 114 (3): 907–940.

Feenstra, Robert C., and Gordon H. Hanson. 2004. Intermediaries in entrepot trade: Hong Kong re-exports of Chinese goods. *Journal of Economics and Management Strategy* 13 (1): 3–35.

Feinberg, Susan E., and Michael P. Keane. 2006. Accounting for the growth of MNC-based trade using a structural model of US MNCs. *American Economic Review* 96 (5): 1515–1558.

Feinberg, Susan E., and Michael P. Keane. 2007. Advances in logistics and the growth of intrafirm trade: the case of Canadian affiliates of US multinationals, 1984–1995. *Journal of Industrial Economics* 55 (4): 571–623.

Gordon, Roger H., and James R. Hines. 2002. International taxation. In *Handbook of Public Economics*, vol. 4 (eds Alan Auerback and Martin Feldstain), North Holand, pp. 1935–1995.

Gorg, Holger. 2000. Fragmentation and trade: US inward processing trade in the EU. *Review of World Economics* 136: 403–422.

Graham. Edward M. 2001. *Fighting the Wrong Enemy: Anti-globalization Activists and Multinational Corporations*. Washington, D.C.: Institute for International Economics.

Grossman, Gene M., and Elhanan Helpman. 2002. Integration versus outsourcing in industry equilibrium. *Quarterly Journal of Economics* 117 (1): 85–120.

Grossman, Gene M., and Elhanan Helpman. 2005. Outsourcing in a global economy. *Review of Economic Studies* 72: 135–159.

Grossman, Gene M., and Esteban Rossi-Hansberg. 2006. *Trading Tasks: A Simple Model of Outsourcing*. NBER Working Paper No. 12721. Cambridge, MA: National Bureau of Economic Research.

Gruebel, Herbert G., and Peter Lloyd. 1975. *Intra-industry Trade: The Theory and Measurement of International Trade in Differentiated Products*. London: Macmillan.

Helpman, Elhanan. 1984. A simple theory of trade with multinational corporations. *Journal of Political Economy* 92 (3): 451–471.

Helpman, Elhanan. 2006. Trade, FDI, and the organization of firms. *Journal of Economic Literature* 44 (3): 589–630.

Helpman, Elhanan and Paul R. Krugman. 1985. *Market Structure and Foreign Trade*. Cambridge, MA: MIT Press.

Helpman, Elhanan and Paul R. Krugman. 1987. *Market Structure and Foreign Trade: Increasing Returns, Imperfect Competition, and the International Economy*. Boston: MIT Press.

Helpman, Elhanan and Paul R. Krugman. 1989. *Trade Policy and Market Structure*. Cambridge, MA: MIT Press.

Helpman, Elhanan, Marc Melitz, and Stephen Yeaple. 2004. Exports versus FDI with heterogeneous firms. *American Economic Review* 94 (1): 300–316.

Hines, James R. 1999. Lessons from behavioral responses to international taxation. *National Tax Journal* 52 (2): 305–322.

Horstmann, Ignatius, and James R. Markusen. 1987. Licensing versus direct investment: a model of internalization by the multinational enterprise. *Canadian Journal of Economics* 20: 464–481.

Horstmann, Ignatius, and James R. Markusen. 1992. Endogenous market structures in international trade. *Journal of International Economics* 32 (1–2): 109–129.

Jenson, J. Bradford, and Lori Klezer. 2006. Tradable services: understanding the scope and impact of services offshoring. In *Offshoring White-Collar Work-Issues and Implications* (eds Lael Brainard and Susan M. Collins), Washington, D.C.: Brookings Institute Trade Forum 2005, pp. 75–134.

Krugman, Paul R. 1979. Increasing returns, monopolisitic competition, and international trade. *Journal of International Economics* 9 (4): 469–479.

Krugman, Paul R. 1980. Scale economies, product differentiation, and the patterns of trade. *American Economic Review* 70 (5): 950–959.

Krugman, Paul R. 1981. Intraindustry specialization and the gains from trade. *Journal of Political Economy* 89 (5): 959–973.

Markusen, James R. 1984. Multinationals, multi-plant economies, and the gains from trade. *Journal of International Economics* 16 (3–4): 205–226.

Markusen, James R. 2002. *Multinational Firms and The Theory of International Trade.* Cambridge, MA: MIT Press.

Markusen, James R., and Anthony J. Venables. 1998. Multinational firms and the new trade theory. *Journal of International Economics* 46 (2): 183–203.

Markusen, James R., and Anthony J. Venables. 2000. The theory of endowment, intraindustry, and multinational trade. *Journal of International Economics* 52 (2): 209–234.

Melitz, Marc J. 2003. The impact of trade on intra-industry reallocations and aggregate industry productivity. *Econometrica* 71 (6): 1695–25.

Narula, Rajneesh, and John H. Dunning. 2000. Industrial development, globalization, and multinational enterprises: new realities for developing countries. *Oxford Development Studies* 28(2): 141–167.

Navaretti, Giorgio Barba, and Anthony J. Venables. 2006.*Multinational Firms in the World Economy.* Princeton, New Jersey: Princeton University Press.

Organisation for Economic Co-operation and Development (OECD). 2002. Intraindustry and intrafirm trade and the internationalisation of production. *Economic Outlook*, no. 71, chap. 6, pp. 159–170.

Ranjan, Priya. 2006. Preferential trade agreements, multinational enterprises, and welfare. *Canadian Journal of Economics* 39 (2): 493–515.

United Nations Conference on Trade and Development. 2000. *World Investment Report: Cross-Border Mergers and Acquisitions and Development.* Geneva: United Nations.

United Nations Conference on Trade and Development. 2006. *World Investment Report 2006.* Geneva: United Nations.

Wilkins, Mira. 2001. The history of the multinational enterprise. In *The Oxford Handbook of International Business* (eds Alan Rugman and Thomas Brewer), Oxford: Oxford University Press, pp. 3–35.

Yi, Kei-Mu. 2003. Can vertical specialization explain the growth of world trade? *Journal of Political Economy* 111 (1): 52–102.

Notes

1. See Organisation for Economic Co-operation and Development (2002) for further discussion of these stylized facts on intra-industry trade.
2. For monopolistic competition models, see Dixit and Stigliz (1977) and Krugman (1979; 1981).

3. For oligopoly models, see Brander (1981) and Brander and Krugman (1983).
4. See Organisation for Economic Co-operation and Development (2006) for statistics on MNE activities in countries and industries.
5. For empirical studies of FDI in the trade literature, see Braconier, Norback, and Urban (2006), Brainard (1997), Caves (2007), Helpman, Melitz, and Yeaple (2004), and Markusen (2002).
6. United Nations Conference on Trade and Development (2000) provides evidence that brownfield FDI is more prominent than greenfield FDI. Discussions of brownfield investments fall under the literature on mergers and acquisitions.
7. For theoretical models that provide an integrated approach to vertical and horizontal FDI, see Markusen (2002) and Bergstrand and Egger (2007).
8. For theoretical studies of horizontal FDI, see Brainard (1997), Horstmann and Markusen (1992), Markusen (1984), and Markusen and Venables (1998; 2000).
9. See Helpman (1984) for an early theory model of vertical FDI.
10. Empirical evidence suggests that MNEs have a high value of intangible assets. For research, see Markusen (2002) and Caves (2007).
11. For research on the proximity-concentration trade-off, see Brainard (1997).
12. For studies of the effects of trade liberalization on FDI vs. trade, see Ekholm, Forslid, and Markusen (2007) and Ranjan (2006).
13. For studies of outsourcing and/or offshoring, see Feenstra and Hanson (1996; 1999; 2004), Gorg (2000), and Campa and Goldberg (1997).

Part Two

Trade Policies and Their Effects

4

Preliminaries
Trade Policy and Welfare Considerations

4.1   What Are Traditional Trade Policies?

In Part One of this book, we explored the three prominent questions of international trade theory: What are the patterns of trade? What are the gains from trade? What are the effects of protectionism versus liberalization of trade? To examine these questions, we considered the effects of moving from a state of autarky to free trade, and the effects of moving from a state of free trade to autarky. The former direction corresponds with liberalizing trade and the latter direction corresponds with adding protectionist policies. We focused on liberalization and protectionism generally, without specifying the policy instruments used to bring about these changes. In reality, countries use specific policies to affect trade. These policies are referred to by international trade economists as *trade measures* or *instruments*. When viewed together, these policies are referred to as *trade policy portfolios*.

The remainder of this book builds on Part One by considering the specific trade instruments and arrangements that have been used in practice to protect or liberalize trade. Part Two of the book considers *traditional trade policies*, which are designed to directly affect trade. Part Three considers *trade related policies*, which are designed for non-trade purposes, but affect trade as a side effect. Part Four considers *trade arrangements*, where multiple countries coordinate their trade policy portfolios.

The traditional trade policies covered in Part Two include tariffs, export subsidies, and quantitative restrictions such as import quotas, export quotas (or voluntary export restraints), and bans. We refer to these policies as "traditional" because they have a well-established history both in real-world practice and in theoretical and empirical research in international trade. We also use the term "traditional" to

Global Trade Policy: Questions and Answers, First Edition. Pamela J. Smith.
© 2014 John Wiley & Sons, Inc. Published 2014 by John Wiley & Sons, Inc.

distinguish these policies from the "trade-related" policies covered in Part Three. Trade-related policies have a much shorter history both in real-world practice and in research relative to traditional trade policies.

4.2   What Approaches Are Used to Examine Trade Policy?

The *modeling approaches* used in this book to examine *specific* trade policies and arrangements (in Parts Two, Three and Four) are distinct from the approaches used to examine *general* movements toward protectionism or liberalization (in Part One). The models presented in Part One were general equilibrium models, while the models emphasized in the remainder of the book are partial equilibrium models. *General equilibrium models* seek to explain economic behavior in a whole economy (including the global economy) where all markets interact and clear. In contrast, *partial equilibrium models* seek to explain economic behavior in a single market (including a single global market), *ceteris paribus*, where the behavior in other markets is assumed to be fixed. Partial equilibrium models provide an approach that is particularly useful for examining the effects of specific policy actions on a particular industry or group of industries. This approach allows us to examine the behavior in a market before and after a policy has been introduced or removed. Thus, the partial equilibrium approach is well suited to examining the specific trade policies and arrangements covered in the remainder of this book.

We will use the partial equilibrium approach to undertake comparative static analyses. *Comparative static analysis* compares a new equilibrium with an old one, after a disturbance such as a policy change. This approach does not consider the dynamic aspects of the way in which the new equilibrium is reached. Rather, it focuses on determining the direction in which variables will change as a consequence of the policy change. For our purposes, the variables of interest include quantities such as supply, demand, and trade (exports and imports), as well as measures that represent the well-being or "welfare" of people. For example, we will consider the welfare effects of traditional trade policies (in Part Two), trade-related policies (in Part Three), and trade arrangements (in Part Four) that result from policy changes. These "policy changes" include the adoption, elimination, or substitution of specific policy instruments or arrangements. We will examine the welfare effects that are a consequence of such policy changes.

We will explicitly examine a variety of *perspectives* in pursuing the applied welfare analysis in the remainder of this book. We will consider the well-being of consumers, producers, governments, and license holders within and across countries. We will also consider the well-being of high- and low-skilled labor and capital owners (e.g., factors of production) within and across countries. And, we will consider the aggregate well-being of countries (large and small), and their trading partners. When feasible, we will consider aggregate well-being at the global level. Finally, we will consider the well-being of groups of countries and groups of economic agents within countries under alternative arrangements for trade policy. The explicit treatment of these diverse perspectives is important because it clarifies the sometimes divergent interests surrounding policy decisions. Being explicit about perspective allows for a broader understanding that is fundamental to coordinating policies across countries, and to designing policies that balance gains and losses in economic well-being. Thus, in the remainder of the book we focus on the core questions: What are the gains (and losses) resulting from specific trade policies and arrangements? How are these gains (and losses) distributed?

These *welfare questions* are at the heart of the international trade literature. These questions are also at the heart of international debates over protection and liberalization of trade policies. Advocates of protectionist policies (which restrict trade) tend to focus on the welfare losses resulting from trade, while advocates of liberalization (which frees trade) focus on the welfare gains of trade. This debate often occurs without the explicit articulation of perspective. However, identifying the perspective of the individuals and groups of individuals who gain and lose from trade policies is a prerequisite to developing economic guidance for the policy debate. Identifying the aggregate country and global effects of trade policies and arrangements is also instructive for providing economic rationales for policies from a broader global welfare perspective.

Given the importance of these welfare questions, we discuss below what international trade economists mean by the concept of gains from trade (or trade liberalization). We discuss how this concept is illustrated in the remainder of the book.

4.3 What Are the Welfare Effects of Liberalizing Trade Policy?

The concept of *gains from trade* refers to the welfare implications of trade for the countries that engage in it. By *welfare*, economists mean the level of well-being of economic agents, whether they are consumers, producers, governments, countries, the global economy, or other groups. Economists often use the term welfare synonymously with well-being, utility, satisfaction, and happiness.

Economists also use a range of concepts to measure levels of well-being or changes in well-being. These concepts include: indifference curves, which reflect relative utility levels; producer and consumer surpluses, which reflect a net benefit or utility from production and consumption, respectively; factor prices, which reflect payments to factors of production (such as wages and rental rates paid to labor and capital); rents, which reflect an excess payment to an economic agent such as a license holder; and so forth. What these measures have in common is that they provide a means for gauging the well-being of the various agents and aggregates, which is ultimately linked to their consumption possibilities.

In the international trade literature, *country-level gains* from trade are fundamentally linked to the concept of consumption possibilities. That is, if trade results in an increase in consumption possibilities for the country, then this represents a gain from trade for that country. For example, the traditional trade theories (illustrated in Chapter 2) showed that the consumption possibilities of a country increase as a result of trade. These aggregate country-level gains are the result of efficiencies that arise from the reallocation of resources in accordance with comparative advantage. When countries specialize and trade based on comparative advantage, their joint output increases. They exchange these outputs at world prices that are preferred to autarky prices. As a consequence, countries share the increased consumption possibilities resulting from trade. These country-level gains from trade are shown in the vast majority of cases studied in the international trade literature.[1]

However, country-level gains from trade need not be similar *across countries*. The traditional trade theories (illustrated in Chapter 2) can also be applied to show that the relative sizes of the country-level gains from trade are not necessarily similar across countries. For example, if a country's autarky prices are similar to world prices with trade, then gains from trade are relatively small. That is, the country-level consumption possibilities increase but by a relatively small amount. In comparison, if a country's autarky prices are dissimilar from world prices, then gains from trade are relatively large. That is, increases in consumption possibilities are relatively large. Thus, welfare distribution issues include the relative international distribution of gains from trade across countries.

Furthermore, country-level gains from trade need not be distributed equally at the *sub-national level* to the various economic agents within a country. For example, the traditional trade theories (illustrated in Chapter 2) showed that trade results in gains and losses to different economic agents. In our examples, we focused specifically on the wages paid to labor and rental rates paid to capital and land-owners (also referred to as the prices of factors of production). We saw that gains and losses depend on economic conditions, including the mobility of the factors of production in the short and long run. For example, the Stolper-Samuelson theory showed an increase in the nominal and real prices paid to factors used intensively in a country's sector of comparative advantage and a decrease in the prices paid to factors used intensively in a country's sector of comparative disadvantage. This is a long-run result of trade. The Specific Factors model showed that gains and losses differ across mobile and immobile factors, and that the purchasing power of consumers depends on their consumption of imported versus exported goods. This is a short-run result of trade. Both theories demonstrate the distributional effects of inter-industry trade.

The New trade theory also considers the issue of gains from trade. The models in this literature emphasize the role of economies of scale (rather than comparative advantage) in determining trade and thus gains from trade. For example, the monopolistic competition model (illustrated in Chapter 3) showed that even countries that are identical in all respects can gain from trade if they specialize in industries that benefit from economics of scale. The gains arise from intra-industry trade in different varieties of similar goods. These gains include increases in consumption possibilities, as well as increases in the product variety of goods consumed. That is, if consumers have preferences for product variety, then the traditional gains from trade (associated with increased consumption possibilities) are augmented by an increase in well-being from consuming differentiated products. In both of these ways, free trade is preferred to autarky.

The gains from trade discussed above were illustrated using the general equilibrium models presented in Part One of this book.

The trade policy literature (presented in Part Two) provides yet another approach to analyzing the gains from trade and their distribution. Using partial equilibrium models, we will show that the liberalization of policies (such as tariffs, export subsidies, and quantitative restrictions) results in welfare gains at the aggregate country and global levels. We will also show that these gains from policy liberalization are distributed unequally within the trading countries. The general finding is that those who gain from liberalizing trade policies are the consumers in the countries that liberalize their policies, and the producers in the trading partners; and those who lose from liberalization are the producers in the countries that liberalize their policies, and the consumers in their trading partners. However, we will show that the magnitude of the impact on the trading partners depends on economic conditions such as the ability of a country to influence world prices. We will also show (in Part Four) that the analysis of gains from policy liberalization can be extended to cases where countries are grouped into regional and multilateral trading blocks. For example, we will show that multilateral liberalization is preferred to regional liberalization, because multilateral liberalization results in larger aggregate welfare gains globally.

The tables provided throughout this book summarize these welfare results. Taken together, they show that trade (or trade liberalization) produces gains for countries in aggregate. However, the distribution of these gains can vary considerably.

The issue of *distribution* of gains prompted international trade economists to ask the question: can gains from trade be *redistributed* such that the well-being of all agents within a country increases? Early work by Samuelson (1939) addressed this question. He showed that all consumers within a trading country are potentially better off under free trade, since those who gain can compensate those who lose while remaining better off than in autarky. Thus, trade can increase the consumption possibilities of all agents within an economy. In other words, in the presence of compensation (or the redistribution of gains from winners to losers), free trade is preferred to autarky by all economic agents because free trade results in increased consumption possibilities for everyone.

In real-world practice, much of the controversy over international trade (and trade liberalization) arises from the issues surrounding the *distribution* of welfare gains and losses from trade, and the compensation that is provided (or not) to those who lose. That is, while it is recognized that free trade raises aggregate country and global welfare, the distribution of gains and losses across countries, and across agents within countries, is a point of contention.

International trade economists and policy makers have addressed these concerns to some degree by considering how domestic and international policies can be designed to redistribute welfare, or at least to maximize net welfare gains. For example, *trade adjustment assistance* (TAA) policies are designed specifically to

support those who are adversely affected by trade or trade liberalization. TAA policies focus on compensating for the welfare losses associated with increased imports
into a country and/or shifts of domestic production to locations outside the country.
The chapter on trade and labor (Chapter 12) discusses TAA policies.

International trade economists have also considered the relative welfare effects of
alternative policy instruments. The idea is that some policies generate relatively
larger net welfare gains – they maximize gains relative to losses. For example, the
concept of *first and second best policies* is applied in trade studies. First best policies
are preferred from a welfare perspective because they generate larger net welfare
gains. In contrast, second best policies (while welfare improving) generate relatively
smaller net welfare gains, because they also introduce new distortions (inefficiencies). The concept of first and second best policies is applied in the chapter on trade
and the environment (Chapter 11) to address market failures associated with externalities. We will discuss how international trade policies can be first best policies
for addressing externalities that are international in scope, but are second best policies for externalities that are national or subnational in scope. For example, it is
possible to argue for the use of coordinated trade policies to address global warming,
but not to address local air pollution or landfills.

Finally, international trade economists have considered the concept of an optimal
policy. *Optimal policies* are preferred because they maximize net welfare gains and
minimize net welfare loses. The chapter on tariffs (Chapter 5) illustrates the concept
of an optimal tariff.

Lastly, we note that the redistribution of welfare is complicated by political
aspects of trade and policy. For example, political policy makers often place unequal
weight on the welfare of different agents within an economy. The welfare of producers is often weighted more heavily than the welfare of consumers, because of the
ability of producers to more effectively lobby for their interests. Similarly, policy
makers also often place unequal weight on the welfare of different countries within
the global economy. The welfare of countries with substantial economic and
political power is often weighted more heavily than the welfare of less influential
countries, because of the ability of politically powerful countries to lobby for their
interests. The unequal weighting of agents is discussed in Chapter 14 in the context
of trade policy arrangements. Such issues are addressed at length in the literature
on the *political economy* of trade, where the endogeneity of policies is explored.
These additional political dimensions do not create a disconnect between trade
theory and practice. Rather, trade theory provides a foundation that can be extended
to account for such political dimensions. The remainder of this book lays the foundation that is prerequisite for these extensions into subjects of political economy.

4.4   How Is Part Two Organized?

Part Two covers traditional trade policies that are designed specifically to target
trade behavior. It focuses on the effects of these policies, including their welfare

effects. Each chapter explores a distinct trade policy or set of trade policies. Chapter 5 begins by considering tariffs. We ask four core questions: What are tariffs, their types and purpose? What are the effects of tariffs? What are the effects of tariff liberalization? How protective are tariffs of the domestic industry? In answering these questions, we consider small countries that cannot influence prices in the world market as well as large countries that can influence the world market.

Chapter 6 considers export subsidies. We ask three core questions: What are export subsidies, their types and purpose? What are the effects of export subsidies? What are the effects of liberalizing export subsidies? In answering these questions, we again consider the small and large country cases. We also consider the case where an export subsidy is large enough to alter the patterns of trade. And, we consider the allocation of the burden of the export subsidy across countries and agents.

Chapter 7 covers quantitative restrictions. We ask two core questions: What are quantitative restrictions, their types and purpose? What are the effects of quantitative restrictions? In answering these questions, we consider three prominent types of quantitative restriction: (1) import quotas; (2) export quotas or voluntary export restraints; and (3) bans.

Finally, Chapter 8 provides a comparison of the above policies. We consider four core questions: What are policy equivalents, and their purpose? What are the relative effects of policy equivalents? What are the relative effects of liberalizing policies? What are the effects of substituting policies? In answering these questions, we compare the relative effects of tariffs, import quotas, export quotas (including voluntary export restraints), bans, and export subsidies. We also consider the effects of substituting policies such as converting quantitative restrictions into tariffs, and the effects of hybrid policies such as the tariff rate quota.

In each of these chapters, our ultimate goal is to illustrate the effects of these specific policies (and their liberalization) on the well-being of people. That is, to show what is at stake and for whom. Part Two provides a foundation for understanding the interests and perspectives that are often at conflict in policy dialog.

Further Reading

Anderson, James E., and Eric van Wincoop. 2004. Trade costs. *Journal of Economic Literature* 42 (3): 691–751.

Corden, W. Max. ed. 1971. *The Theory of Protection*. Oxford: Clarendon Press.

de Melo, Jaime, and David Tarr. 1992. *A General Equilibrium Analysis of US Foreign Trade Policy*. Cambridge, MA: MIT Press.

Feenstra, Robert C. 1992. How costly is protectionism? *Journal of Economics Perspectives* 6 (3): 159–178.

Hufbauer, Gary C. and Kimberly A. Elliot. 1994. *Measuring the costs of protection in the United States*. Washington, D.C.: Institute for International Economics.

Irwin, Douglas A. 1996. *Against the Tide: An Intellectual History of Free Trade*. Princeton, NJ: Princeton University Press.

Irwin, Douglas A. 2008. Antebellum tariff politics: regional coalitions and shifting economic interests. *Journal of Law and Economics* 51 (4): 715–741.

Irwin, Douglas A. 2009. *Free Trade Under Fire*. Princeton, NJ: Princeton University Press.

Krishna, Kala. 1989. Trade restrictions as facilitating practices. *Journal of International Economics* 26 (May): 251–270.

Krugman, Paul R. 1987. Is free trade passé? *Journal of Economic Perspectives* 1 (2): 131–144.

Messerlin, Patrick. 2001. *Measuring the Costs of Protection in Europe: European Commercial Policy in the 2000s*. Washington, D.C.: Institute for International Economics.

Roussland, D. and A. Auomela. 1985. *Calculating the Consumer and Net Welfare Costs of Import Relief*. US International Trade Commission Staff Research Study 15. Washington, D.C.: International Trade Commission.

Samuelson, Paul A. 1939. The gains from international trade. *Canadian Journal of Economics and Political Science* 5 (2): 195–205. Reprinted in Readings in the *Theory of International Trade*, (eds Howard S. Ellis and Lloyd A. Metzler), Philadelphia: Blakiston, 1949, 239–52.

Scott, Bradford. 2003. Paying the price: Final goods protection in OECD countries. *Review of Economics and Statistics* 85 (1): 24–37.

Vousden, Neil 1990. *The Economic Theory of Protection*. Cambridge: Cambridge University Press.

Note

1. One notable exception is the case of immizerising growth, which is discussed in Chapter 13.

5

Tariffs

5.1   What Are Tariffs, Their Types and Purpose?

The *tariff* is a tax. It is typically imposed by importing countries on goods that are imported from other countries. Tariffs are also referred to as *customs duties* because they are imposed when goods cross the border from one customs territory to another.

There are three basic types of tariffs: (1) the specific tariff; (2) the ad valorem tariff; and (3) the compound tariff. The *specific tariff* is a fixed amount of money per unit of the good imported. For example, the tax may be $100 per ton of the imported good. The *ad valorem tariff* is a percentage of the value of the good imported. For example, the tax may be 5% of the value of the import. The *compound tariff* is a combination of the specific tariff and ad valorem tariff. That is, the compound tariff is a fixed amount per unit plus a percentage of the value of the imported good. In addition to these basic tariff types, other less common types of tariffs are mixed tariffs and technical tariffs. The *mixed tariff* is a variant of the compound tariff where the tax is specific or ad valorem, depending on which is larger. *Technical tariffs* depend on the product's content of inputs, such as alcohol. In today's global economy, the ad valorem tariff is the prominent form. Countries have moved to this common form in an effort to standardize the liberalization of policies through trade agreements.

Countries establish tariff rates that are the same for all trading partners; that is, they do not discriminate between trading partners by establishing different tariffs on imports from different countries. This *non-discrimination principal* is set forth in the most favored nation (MFN) clause of the GATT and its successor, the World

Global Trade Policy: Questions and Answers, First Edition. Pamela J. Smith.
© 2014 John Wiley & Sons, Inc. Published 2014 by John Wiley & Sons, Inc.

Trade Organization (WTO). However, exceptions to the non-discrimination principal are allowed in two particular cases. Both of these exceptions allow for preferential treatment of select trading partners. The first is the case of *non-reciprocal preferences* granted by developed countries to developing countries. The second is the case of *reciprocal preferences* granted by participants in regional trade agreements to other participants.[1]

The purpose of tariffs is twofold. First, tariffs are used by governments to raise revenues. This purpose is more important for developing countries with imports that are large relative to the value of their domestic economic activities. Second, tariffs are used to protect domestic industry. Which industries? Tariffs protect industries for which the country has a comparative disadvantage.[2] That is, tariffs are used to protect the domestic suppliers of goods that the country would otherwise import under free trade conditions. Recall that tariffs are imposed by the importing country on goods that are imported. By adding a tax, the tariff allows the domestic industry in that country to compete against "imports that would have lower prices in the absence of the tariff."

In this chapter, we explore three core questions with respect to tariffs: (1) What are the effects of tariffs? (2) What are the effects of tariff liberalization? (3) How protective are tariffs of the domestic industry? In answering each of these questions, we consider the welfare effects that characterize the gains and losses associated with tariffs. That is, we consider who gains and who loses from the adoption or liberalization of tariffs.

5.2   What Are the Effects of Tariffs?

What are the effects of tariffs in both importing and exporting countries? The effects of the tariff in the *importing country* are quite intuitive. The price of the imported good goes up, as it now includes the tariff. In a competitive market, the price of the domestically produced good will equate with the tariff-inclusive price of the imports. Second, the quantity of the good supplied domestically increases as suppliers now compete against higher priced imports. At the same time, the quantity of the good demanded in the importing country decreases. This is because the price of both the domestically produced good and the imported good are higher as a result of the tariff.

The tariff also affects welfare in the importing country. Tariffs affect the welfare of consumers, producers and the government differently. Specifically, the welfare of domestic producers increases, because both the quantity of the good supplied increases and the price received increases. In contrast, the welfare of consumers decreases, because the quantity of the good demanded decreases and the price paid increases. And, the welfare of the government increases, because the government receives the revenue from the tax. If we sum together the welfare effects of these three agents, we can draw conclusions about the net welfare effects of the tariff for the importing country. We will show in the section below that the net welfare of the importing country may be either positive or negative as a result of the tariff. The direction of the net welfare effect depends on the ability of the importer to influence the price in the world market.

The effects of the tariff in the *exporting country* are more opaque. The price of the good in the *exporting country* (or *world price*) may either decrease or remain unchanged. The world price will decrease if the country imposing the tariff is large in terms of its share of the world's demand for the good. In this case, the tariff causes the quantity of world demand for the good to decrease and thus the world price decreases. The quantity of the good supplied in the exporting country decreases as suppliers now receive a lower world price for their exports. At the same time, the quantity of the good demanded in the exporting country increases, because consumers now pay a lower world price for the good.

In this case, the tariff affects welfare in the exporting country. Specifically, the welfare of domestic producers decreases, because both the quantity of the good supplied decreases and the price received decreases. In contrast, the welfare of consumers in the exporting country increases, because the quantity of the good demanded increases and the price paid decreases. And, the welfare of the government is unchanged in the exporting country, because the tariff revenues are collected by the importer. If we sum together the welfare effects of these three agents, we can draw conclusions about the net welfare effects of the tariff for the exporting country. We will show that the net welfare of the exporting country is negative as a result of the tariff, when world price changes.

Alternatively, if the country imposing the tariff is small in terms of its share of the world's demand for the good, then the world demand and thus world price remain unchanged. In this case, the quantity supplied and demanded in the exporting country remain unchanged. Similarly, consumer and producer welfare remain unchanged in the exporting country.

Below, we present a simple partial equilibrium model to illustrate these effects of a tariff. First, we develop the modeling framework. Then we consider three cases. The first case assumes that a large importer imposes a tariff. A "large country" is one that can influence the world price of the good. It is a country whose demand for the good is a large share of the world's demand for the good. The second case assumes that a small importer imposes a tariff. A "small country" is one that cannot influence the world price of the good. It is a country whose demand for the good is a small share of the world's demand for the good. The third case assumes that the exporting and importing countries differ in their responsiveness to price changes. Specifically, we consider the case where export supply is inelastic relative to import demand.

The basic assumptions of the simple partial equilibrium model are as follows. There are two countries – home and foreign. There is one good. This good is subject to a tariff. The home country is the importer of the good. The foreign country is the exporter of the good. In other words, the home country (i.e., the importer) has a comparative disadvantage in the good and the foreign country (i.e., the exporter) has a comparative advantage in the good.

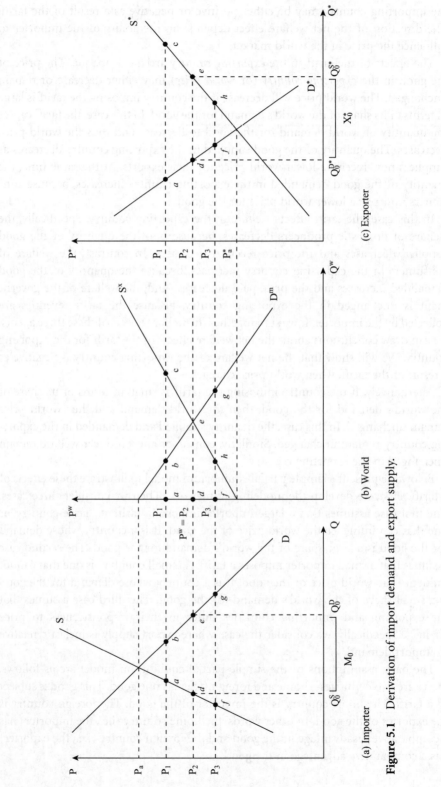

Figure 5.1 Derivation of import demand and export supply.

5.2.1   Case 1: What are the effects of a tariff imposed by a large importer?

To begin, we consider the case where the tariff is imposed by a large importer. Figure 5.1 shows the markets for the good in this large country case. Panel (a) shows the domestic supply (S) and demand (D) for the good in the home country – the importer. The equilibrium price of the good in the home country is the same as its autarky price (P_a). This is the price of the good when there is no trade. This autarky price is relatively high, reflecting the assumption that the home country has a comparative disadvantage in the good. In contrast, Panel (c) shows the domestic supply (S^*) and demand (D^*) for the good in the foreign country – the exporter. Again, the equilibrium price of the good in this foreign country is the same as its autarky price (P_a^*). This autarky price is relatively low, reflecting the assumption that the foreign country has a comparative advantage in the good.

Panel (b) then shows the supply and demand in the world market. This is the market where the home and foreign countries trade. In this middle panel, the demand is the *import demand* of the home country (D^m). The import demand in Panel (b) is derived from the behavior of the home country in Panel (a). For example, consider the home country's behavior at all possible world prices. For world prices at or above the home country's autarky price, the home country will not demand imports. Rather, its demand is satisfied by its domestic supply. However, for world prices below its autarky price, the home country will demand imports in the amount of its *excess demand*. For example, at price P_1 the home country will demand amount $\overline{ab}$ of imports. At price P_2 the home country will demand amount $\overline{de}$ in imports. And at price P_3 the home country will demand amount $\overline{fg}$ in imports. Both Panels (a) and (b) show these amounts of import demand as horizontal distances.

In contrast, the supply in the world market in Panel (b) is the *export supply* (S^x). The export supply is derived from the behavior of the foreign country in Panel (c). For example, consider the foreign country's behavior at all possible world prices. For world prices at or below its autarky price, the foreign country will not supply exports. Instead, its supply is consumed by domestic demand. However, for prices above its autarky price, the foreign country will supply exports in the amount of its *excess supply*. Specifically, at price P_1 the foreign country will supply $\overline{ac}$ in exports. At price P_2 the foreign country will supply amount $\overline{de}$ in exports. And at price P_3 the foreign country will supply amount $\overline{fh}$ in exports. Both Panels (c) and (b) show these amounts of export supply as horizontal distances.

The intersection of import demand and export supply in Panel (b) determines the equilibrium world price (P^w). The equilibrium world price is where the quantity of import demand by the home country equates with the quantity of export supply by the foreign country. At this equilibrium world price, the quantity of imports (M_0) in Panel (a) equals the quantity of exports (X_0^*) in Panel (c). The quantity of imports in Panel (a) is the excess of demand (Q_0^D) over supply (Q_0^S) at the world price. Similarly, the quantity of exports in Panel (c) is the excess of supply (Q_0^{S*}) over demand (Q_0^{D*}) at the world price.

We can also assess the welfare of producers and consumers at the equilibrium world price. Figure 5.2 illustrates welfare at the equilibrium world price. This figure mirrors Figure 5.1. Recall that *producer welfare* is typically measured as a surplus value – the area above the supply curve and below the price received by producers. Similarly, *consumer welfare* is typically measured as a surplus value – the area below the demand curve and above the price paid by consumers. In Panel (a), the importer's producer and consumer surpluses are the shaded areas labeled as PS and CS, respectively. Similarly, in Panel (c) the exporter's producer and consumer surpluses are the shared areas labeled as PS* and CS*, respectively. This is the pattern of welfare at the equilibrium world price when there are no policy barriers.

The figures described above reflect the case of the large importer. In the large country case, we assume that the home country is large in terms of its demand for the imported good in the world market. This can be seen by observing that the export supply curve has a positive elasticity – it is not infinitely elastic. What this means is that when the home country's quantity of imports demanded changes, so does the equilibrium world price.

We can now introduce a tariff into this simple framework in Panel (b). Figure 5.3 shows the effects of a tariff. (Figure 5.3 mirrors Figure 5.1 and Figure 5.2.) A tariff essentially creates a price wedge between the price of the good in the exporting country (P_t^*) and the price of the good in the importing country (P_t). The size of the tariff is the vertical distance (t) between these two prices in Panel (b). When we impose a tariff in the home country (the importer), the price of the good increases from the world price (P^w) to the tariff inclusive price (P_t) at home. This corresponds with a movement along the import demand curve and a decrease in the quantity of imports demanded by the importing country. Alternatively, from the exporters point of view, the price of the good decreases from the world price (P^w) to the new lower price after the tariff is in place (P_t^*). This corresponds with a movement along the export supply curve and a decrease in the quantity of exports supplied by the exporting country. In this case, the price effect of the tariff is shared by both the importing and exporting countries. This price sharing occurs even though the importing country alone imposes the tariff. The price change in the exporter occurs because the importing country can affect the world price.

The tariff also affects the quantities of the good supplied, demanded and traded in both the home and foreign countries (in Panels (a) and (c), respectively). The home country experiences an increase in the quantity supplied domestically (Q_0^S to Q_1^S) and a decrease in the quantity demanded domestically (Q_0^D to Q_1^D). In contrast, the foreign country experiences a decrease in the quantity supplied domestically (Q_0^{S*} to Q_1^{S*}) and an increase in the quantity demanded domestically (Q_0^{D*} to Q_1^{D*}). Consequently, both countries experience a decrease in trade. The home country's imports decrease (M_0 to M_1) and the foreign country's exports decrease (X_0^* to X_1^*).

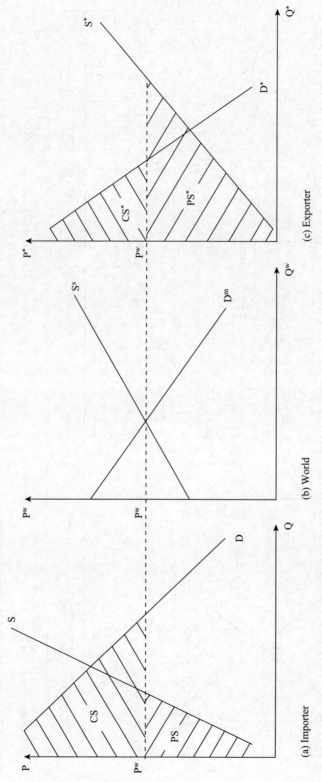

Figure 5.2 Consumer and producer welfare at equilibrium world price.

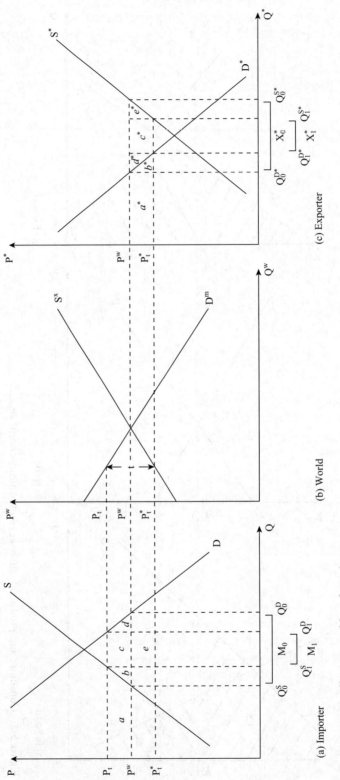

Figure 5.3 Tariff – imposed by a large importer.

Intuitively, the effects of tariffs on prices and quantities tell us a lot about the impact of tariffs on both producers and consumers. At home, producers are supplying more in their domestic market at a higher price. They have gained from the tariff in terms of revenue from sales of the good. At home, consumers are demanding less at a higher price. They have lost from the tariff in terms of the cost of the good. Alternatively, in the foreign country, producers are supplying less at a lower price. They have lost. And foreign consumers are demanding more and a lower price. They have gained.

Further, the mix of consumption of domestic versus traded goods changes as a result of the tariff. Consumers in the home country now consume more domestically produced goods and fewer imports. Consumers in the foreign market continue to consume only domestically produced goods but fewer of them.

The welfare effects of the tariff for the home and foreign countries can also be seen in Figure 5.3 and are summarized in Table 5.1. Instead of illustrating total welfare before and after the tariff is imposed, we simply illustrate the changes in welfare that result from the tariff. Panel (a) in Figure 5.1 shows the welfare effects for the importing country. As shown, the producer's welfare increases by the surplus amount $+(a)$ as a result of the tariff. The consumer's welfare decreases by the surplus amount $-(a + b + c + d)$ and the government welfare increases by the amount $+(c + e)$. This change in government welfare is the amount of the tariff revenue raised. It is the product of the quantity imported (vertically) and the value of the tariff (horizontally).

The net country welfare effect is the sum of the producer, consumer, and government welfare changes. Adding these effects together we get $+(e) - (b + d)$. Each of the areas has a distinct interpretation. Area $+(e)$ is a positive *terms of trade* effect. This is the amount by which the home country's tariff suppresses the world price of the good that it imports. Areas $-(b + d)$ are deadweight losses incurred by producers and consumers. Specifically, area $-(b)$ is a *production distortion*. This area is the loss associated with increasing the quantity of domestic supply of the good for which the home country has a comparative disadvantage. Area $-(d)$ is a *consumption distortion*. This area is the loss associated with decreasing the quantity demanded of the imported good, which had a lower price prior to the tariff. In net, the importing country is worse off as a result of the tariff if the distortions exceed the terms of trade effect, and vice versa.

Panel (c) shows the welfare effects of the tariff for the exporting country. As shown, the producer's welfare decreases by the surplus amount $-(a^* + b + c^* + d^* + e^*)$ as a result of the tariff. The consumer's welfare increases by the surplus amount $+(a^* + b^*)$. For the exporter, the government welfare does not change, as no revenue is raised. The net country welfare effect is the sum of these welfare changes. Adding these effects together we get $-(c^* + d^* + e^*)$. Area $-(c)^*$ is the *terms of trade* effect. This is the amount by which the tariff suppresses the world price of the good that is seen in the foreign country. Areas $-(d^* + e^*)$ are deadweight losses incurred by consumers and producers. Area $-(d^*)$ is a *consumption distortion*. This area is the loss associated with decreasing the quantity of domestic demand of the

Table 5.1   Welfare effects of tariffs.

Case 1 – Large country

Economic agent	Welfare effects (importer/home)	Welfare effects (exporter/foreign)
Producer	$+a$	$-(a^* + b^* + c^* + d^* + e^*)$
Consumer	$-(a + b + c + d)$	$+(a^* + b^*)$
Government	$+(c + e)$	0
Country	$+e - (b + d)$	$-(c^* + d^* + e^*)$
Country (direction)	Negative or positive	Negative

Case 2 – Small country

Economic agent	Welfare effects (importer/home)	Welfare effects (exporter/foreign)
Producer	$+a$	0
Consumer	$-(a + b + c + d)$	0
Government	$+c$	0
Country	$-(b + d)$	0
Country (direction)	Negative	None

Case 3 – Alternative elasticities

Economic agent	Welfare effects (importer/home)	Welfare effects (exporter/foreign)
Producer	$+a$	$-(a^* + b^* + c^* + d^* + e^*)$
Consumer	$-(a + b + c + d)$	$+(a^* + b^*)$
Government	$+(c + e)$	0
Country	$+e - (b + d)$	$-(c^* + d^* + e^*)$
Country (direction)	Negative or positive	Negative

Note: Case 1 and Case 3 have similar directional results but different magnitude results. In Case 1, we expect that $|e| < |b + d|$ and $|c^* + d^* + e^*|$ is relatively small. In Case 3, we expect that $|e| > |b + d|$ and $|c^* + d^* + e^*|$ is relatively large.

good for which the foreign country has a comparative advantage. Area $-(e^*)$ is a *production distortion*. This area is the loss associated with the decreasing quantity supplied of the exported good, which had a higher price prior to the importer's imposition of the tariff. In net, the exporting country is unambiguously worse off as a result of the tariff.

5.2.2   Case 2: What are the effects of a tariff imposed by a small importer?

Next, we consider the effects of a tariff under the assumption that the tariff is imposed by a small importer. In this case, we assume that the home country is small in terms of its demand for the imported good in the world market. In other words, changes in the home country's quantity of demand for the imported good does not affect the world price of the good. Rather, the importing country faces an infinitely elastic world supply of the good. The diagrams in Figure 5.3 can be altered to reflect this alternative case, as shown in Figure 5.4. Observe that the export supply curve is infinitely elastic. What this means is that when the home country's quantity of imports demanded changes, the equilibrium world price remains unchanged. In other words, the exporting country can satisfy the home country's import demand regardless of its size.

We can now introduce a tariff into this modified framework in Panel (b). As in the large country case, the tariff essentially creates a price wedge between the price of the good in the exporting country (P_t^*) and the price of the good in the importing country (P_t). The size of the tariff is the vertical distance (t) between these two prices in Panel (b). When we impose a tariff in the home country, the price of the good increases from the free-trade world price (P^w) to the tariff inclusive price (P_t) at home. This corresponds with a movement along the import demand curve and a decrease in the quantity of imports demanded by the importing country. Alternatively, from the exporter's point of view, the price of the good remains unchanged and equal to the original free-trade world price ($P^w = P_t^*$). That is, the price effect of the tariff is not shared by both the importing and exporting countries. Rather, the entire price effect of the tariff is experienced by the importing country that imposes the tariff.

The tariff also affects the quantities of the good supplied, demanded and traded in the home country (in Panel (a)). Specifically, the home country experiences an increase in the quantity supplied domestically (Q_0^D to Q_1^D) and a decrease in the quantity demanded domestically (Q_0^D to Q_1^D). In contrast, the foreign country experiences no economically significant changes. However, the trade between the importer and exporter does decrease. The home country's imports decrease (M_0 to M_1) and the foreign country's exports to the home country decrease by the same amount. This amount is economically insignificant to the exporter.

As in the previous case, the effects of tariffs on prices and quantities tell us a lot about the impact of tariffs on both producers and consumers. At home, producers are supplying more in their domestic market at a higher price. They have clearly gained from the tariff in terms of revenue from sales of the good. At home, consumers are demanding less at a higher price. They have clearly lost from the tariff in terms of the cost of the good. Further, the mix of consumption of domestic versus traded goods changes as a result of the tariff. Consumers in the home country now consume more domestically produced goods and fewer imports. In contrast, producers and consumers in the foreign country are not impacted in any economically significant way. Consumers in the foreign market continue to consume only the domestically produced good.

The welfare effects of the tariff for the home and foreign countries can also be seen in Figure 5.4 and are summarized in Table 5.1. As before, we illustrate the changes in welfare that result from the tariff. For the importing country, the

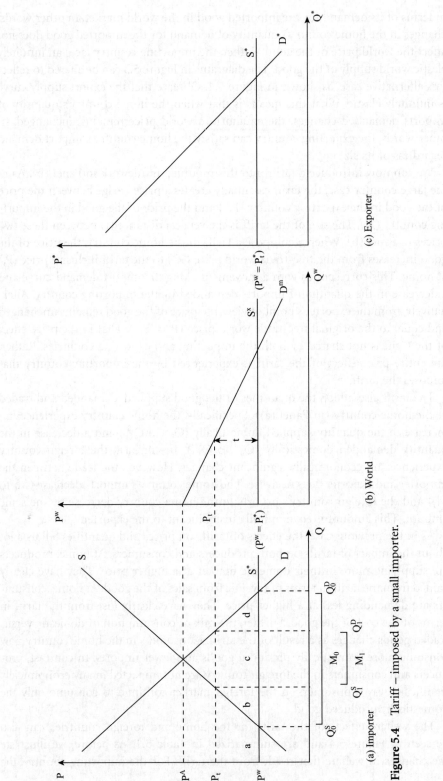

Figure 5.4 Tariff – imposed by a small importer.

producer's welfare increases by the surplus amount $+(a)$ as a result of the tariff. The consumer's welfare decreases by the surplus amount $-(a + b + c + d)$ and the government welfare increases by the amount $+(c)$. This change in government welfare is the amount of the tariff revenue raised. It is the product of the quantity imported (vertically) and the value of the tariff (horizontally).

The net country welfare effect is the sum of the producer, consumer, and government welfare changes. Adding these effects together, we get $-(b + d)$. Areas $-(b + d)$ are deadweight losses incurred by producers and consumers. Area $-(b)$ is a *production distortion* – the loss associated with increasing the quantity of domestic supply of the good for which the home country has a comparative disadvantage. Area $-(d)$ is a *consumption distortion* – the loss associated with decreasing quantity demanded of the imported good, which had a lower price prior to the tariff. It is important to note that in this small country case, there is no positive terms of trade effect from the tariff. Thus, in this case, the welfare effects for the importing country in net are unambiguously negative. For the exporting country, there are no welfare effects in this case.

5.2.3 Case 3: What are the effects of a tariff when export supply is inelastic relative to import demand?

We have considered both a large and a small importing country. First, we assumed that the large importer faced an export supply curve with a positive elasticity in the world market. Second, we assumed that the small importer faced an infinitely elastic supply curve in the world market. This next section considers one additional case – where the demand for imports is more elastic than the supply of exports. This situation can arise when the good has a relatively limited or fixed world supply. This situation can also arise when the importer's demand for the good is relatively sensitive to price.

Figure 5.5 illustrates this case. As before, the tariff essentially creates a price wedge between the price of the good in the exporting country (P_t^*) and the price of the good in the importing country (P_t). The size of the tariff is the vertical distance (t) between these two prices in Panel (b). When we impose a tariff in the home country (the importer), the price of the good increases from the free trade world price (P^w) to the tariff inclusive price (P_t) at home. This price change is relatively small. Alternatively, from the exporter's point of view, the price of the good decreases from the free-trade world price (P^w) to the new world price (P_t^*). This price change is relatively large. In other words, the price effect of the tariff is not shared equally by both the importing and exporting countries. Rather, the price effect of the tariff is experienced primarily by the exporting country. This feature of the price effect occurs because the importing country's behavior has a substantial effect on the world price of the good.

The directional effects of the tariff – on quantities of the good supplied, demanded and traded in both the home and foreign countries – are the same as those described

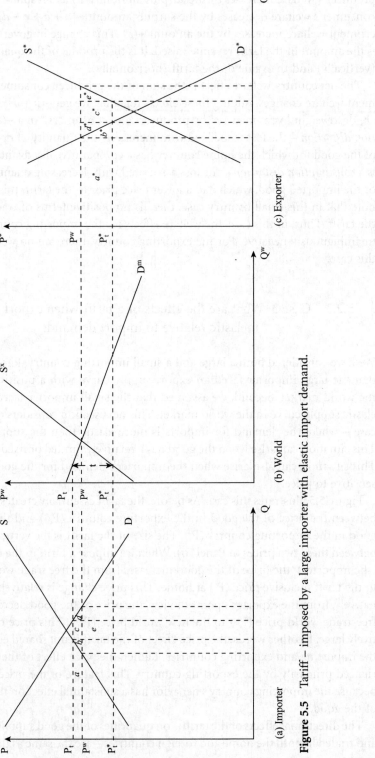

Figure 5.5 Tariff – imposed by a large importer with elastic import demand.

in Case 1. Thus, we do not repeat them here. However, the welfare effects are quite distinct in the current case because the price effect of the tariff is experienced primarily by the exporting country.

Figure 5.5 illustrates the welfare effects of the tariff for the home and foreign countries. (Table 5.1 summarizes these effects.) Panel (a) in Figure 5.5 shows the welfare effects for the importing country. As shown, the producer's welfare increases by the surplus amount $+(a)$ as a result of the tariff. The consumer's welfare decreases by the surplus amount $-(a + b + c + d)$ and the government welfare increases by the amount $+(c + e)$. The net country welfare effect is the sum of the producer, consumer, and government welfare changes. Adding these effects together, we get $+(e) - (b + d)$. As before, area $+(e)$ is a positive *terms of trade* effect. This is the amount by which the home country's tariff suppresses the world price of the good that it imports. Areas $-(b + d)$ are deadweight losses incurred by producers and consumers. Typically, the importing country is worse off in net as a result of the tariff because the distortions exceed the terms of trade effect (i.e., $(b + d) > (e)$). However, in this case the terms of trade effect is large relative to the distortions (i.e., $(b + d) < (e)$). Thus, this case illustrates an exception, where the importing country can experience an increase in net country welfare as a consequence of imposing a tariff.

This experience of the importing country is in stark contrast to the experience of the exporting country. Panel (c) shows the welfare effects of the tariff for the exporting country. As shown, the producer's welfare decreases by the surplus amount $-(a^* + b^* + c^* + d^* + e^*)$ as a result of the tariff. The consumer's welfare increases by the surplus amount $+(a^* + b^*)$. For the exporter, the government welfare does not change as no revenue is raised. The net country welfare effect is the sum of these welfare changes. Adding these effects together we get $-(c^* + d^* + e^*)$. Area $-(c)^*$ is the *terms of trade* effect. This is the amount by which the tariff suppresses the world price of the good that the foreign country exports. Areas $-(d^* + e^*)$ are deadweight losses incurred by consumers and producers. In net, the exporting country is unambiguously worse off as a result of the tariff. We can also see that the deadweight losses incurred by the exporter are large relative to the deadweight loses incurred by the importer.

In summary, the deadweight losses for the consumer and producer are relatively small in the importing country and relatively large in the exporting country. The government revenue is positive in the importing country and absent in the exporting country. And, the decrease in the world price benefits the importer of the good and hurts the exporter of the good. Essentially, the burden of the tariff is passed from the importer (who imposes the policy) to the exporter. The importing country is better off because the terms of trade effect exceeds the consumer and producer welfare losses. However, the exporting country is unambiguously worse off. Thus, while a tariff may be desirable from the national perspective of the importing country (in this case only), it is not desirable from the perspective of the exporter. The tariff is also not desirable from a global perspective since the joint welfare effect of the exporter and importer combined is negative.

5.2.4   How is the burden of the tariff allocated across countries and agents?

The price effects of the tariff are allocated in different ways across countries in the cases summarized above. This allocation of the price effects is sometimes referred to as the burden of the tariff. Furthermore, the welfare effects of the tariff are allocated in different ways within countries in the cases summarized above. This section summarizes both the *price burden* across countries and the *welfare burden* within countries that result from a tariff.

In comparing the cases, we find that the price burden of the tariff is shared between the exporter and importer when the elasticities of import demand and export supply are relatively similar. This corresponds with the large importer who can affect the world price (i.e., Case 1). For intuition, we can think of the importer as a block of countries such as Europe and the exporter as a block of countries such as North America. In such a case, the tariff policies of Europe would alter the world price experienced by North America. The absolute size of the price increase experienced in Europe can be similar to the absolute size of the price decrease experienced by North America. In this case, the price burden of the tariff is shared relatively equally. Even so, Europe would experience a relatively small welfare burden because the negative distortions associated with the tariff would be offset in some amount by the positive terms of trade improvement. At the same time, North America would experience a relatively large welfare burden because the negative distortions associated with the tariff would be augmented by the negative terms of trade deterioration.

In contrast, we find that the price burden of the tariff is experienced entirely by the importer when the export supply of the exporter is infinitely elastic. This corresponds with the small importer whose demand is completely satisfied by the exporter (i.e., Case 2). For intuition, we can think of the importer as a small country such as Haiti and the exporter as a block of countries such as South America. In such a case, the tariff policies of Haiti would likely have an economically insignificant effect on the world price of the good experienced by South America. The absolute size of the price increase experienced in Haiti can be the entire size of the tariff. In this case, the price burden of the tariff is experienced entirely by the importer. Additionally, Haiti would experience a relatively large welfare burden because the negative distortions associated with the tariff would not be offset by a positive terms of trade improvement. At the same time, South America would experience no welfare burden as this block of countries is insulated from the price effects of the tariff policies of their small trading partner.

Finally, we find that the price burden of the tariff is borne disproportionately by the exporter when export supply is inelastic relative to import demand. This corresponds with the scenario in which the good is in relatively limited export supply or the importer is relatively price responsive compared to the exporter (i.e., Case 3). For intuition, we can think of the importer as a country such as Australia, the exporter as a country such as Fiji, and the good as bottled water. In such a case, Australia's tariff on bottled water from Fiji would significantly alter the price experienced by Fiji. The absolute size of the price increase experienced in Australia would likely be small relative to the absolute size of the price decrease experienced by Fiji. In this case, the price burden of the tariff is experienced primarily by Fiji – the exporter. Furthermore, Australia would experience a relatively small welfare burden as the distortions from the tariff would be counterbalanced (at least in part) by the terms of trade improvement. At the same time, Fiji would experience a relatively large welfare burden because both the negative distortions and negative terms of trade deterioration would be large.

In summary, the price burden of the tariff would be shared in the large country case, when export demand and import supply have similar elasticities. The price burden of the tariff is experienced by the importer in the small country case, when the importer faces an infinitely elastic export supply. And the price burden of the tariff is borne by the exporter, when the export supply is inelastic relative to import demand. This last case would arise when the traded good is in limited supply or when import demand is highly price responsive. Furthermore, if we look at the welfare burden within countries, we see that in the importer the domestic consumer experiences the largest welfare loss when the country is small and faces an infinitely elastic export supply, while in the exporter the domestic producer experiences the largest welfare loss when the country's export supply is inelastic relative to the import demand of their trading partner(s).

5.3   What Are the Effects of Tariff Liberalization?

The framework discussed in the previous section illustrates the effects of imposing a tariff for both the importer and exporter. Alternatively, we could work the above examples backward to illustrate the effects of liberalizing tariffs.

In practice, there is a long history of tariff liberalization. The magnitude of tariff rates has decreased during the past seven decades. Since the 1940s, the average tariff rate decreased from between 20% and 30% to between 3% and 7% (see World Trade Organization, 2007). This liberalization occurred predominantly among developed countries. However, developing countries have also liberalized substantially since the 1980s. This decline is the result in large part of negotiations for tariff reductions under the General Agreement on Tariffs and Trade (GATT) and its successor the World Trade Organization (WTO).

The welfare effects of this liberalization can be predicted for the cases described in the previous section. Simply begin the cases with the tariff in place and then examine the effects of moving to a free trade state without the tariff. Although tariffs have not been completely eliminated in practice, the directional effects of eliminating the tariff (in the illustrations) correspond with the directional effects of reducing tariffs (in practice). Here, we summarize the results.

For *importing countries*, consumer welfare increases, producer welfare decreases, and government welfare decreases. The net country welfare increases in the small country case. The net country welfare can increase or decrease in the large country case. Specifically, net country welfare decreases from tariff liberalization if the trade distortions from the tariff are small relative to the terms of trade effect. Net country welfare increases from tariff liberalization if the trade distortions from the tariff are large relative to the terms of trade effect. This latter case more closely matches what we observe in real-world practice.

For *exporting countries*, tariff liberalization in the importer has no effect on the exporter when the importer's demand is a small share of the world demand for the good. However, in all other cases, tariff liberalization in the importer affects welfare in the exporter. Specifically, consumer welfare decreases and producer welfare increases in the exporter. However, the government experiences neither a welfare increase nor a welfare decrease, as revenue collections do not change. Further, net country welfare increases in the exporter in all cases where the importer's liberalization policies affect world prices.

Thus, from a *subnational perspective*, tariff liberalization generates distributional effects. In importers, consumers are better off from tariff liberalization and producers and government are worse off. In exporters, producers are better off and consumers are worse off. This unequal distribution of benefits from tariff liberalization helps to explain why governments impose welfare deteriorating policies such as tariffs. The explanation is that governments place different weight on the welfare of producers (and government) relative to consumers. For example, the government in the importer may place more weight on the welfare losses experienced by domestic producers than on the welfare gains experienced by domestic consumers resulting from tariff liberalization. A real-world example is the US Trade Representative (USTR), which sometimes seems to act as an advocate for industry interests, according to petitions that non-governmental organizations have signed and circulated. The lobbying power of industry groups such as the Pharmaceutical Research and Manufacturers of America (PhRMA) is particularly strong in influencing trade policy. Such issues fall under the political economy subfield of international trade.

Alternatively, from a *national perspective*, both importers and exporters experience welfare gains when tariffs are liberalized. Exporters are unambiguously better off from tariff liberalization. Importers are also better off from tariff liberalization, except in the extreme large country case (Case 1). Thus, the only economic argument in favor of tariffs and against liberalization is the case where the importer can significantly affect world prices. However, this argument is from the national perspective of the importer alone, and relies on the assumption that the importer's policies significantly affect world prices. With the exception of this unusual case, tariff liberalization is economically rational because it provides net gains to all trading countries. The sticky point then for policy makers is that of the subnational distributional issues (and related political economy issues) that need to be addressed in order to garner support for the tariff liberalization.

From a *global perspective*, tariff liberalization is also rational from an economic point of view. Tariff liberalization increases the welfare of all countries in aggregate. Thus, one's position on whether to liberalize or maintain tariffs is reflective of the hat that one wears. From a global or national perspective, tariff liberalization is economically rational. From a producer perspective in the importing country, tariff liberalization is welfare deteriorating.

Finally, it should be noted that the framework presented in this chapter is a comparatively static framework that compares two equilibrium points in time. Arguments for protection (against tariff liberalization) that are not accounted for in this framework include political economy arguments and arguments that focus on altering the patterns of comparative advantage via dynamic changes over time.

5.4 How Protective Are Tariffs of the Domestic Industry?

The partial equilibrium model set forth above showed that tariffs allow domestic producers of the import-competing good to increase the quantity they supply. In this way, tariffs protect that domestic industry. However, the effectiveness of the protection of the domestic industry is complex in practice. One reason for this is that tariffs are imposed on both final goods and intermediate inputs. For example, imagine that a country produces a good that is also imported. Imagine also that this same country imports the intermediate inputs that are used to produce this final good. If a tariff is imposed on the good but not the inputs, then the tariff is effective in protecting the domestic producer of the final good. However, if a tariff is imposed on the imported inputs but not the final good, then the tariff is not effective in protecting the domestic producer of the final good, who is actually worse off. If tariffs are imposed on both the intermediate input and final goods, then the final goods producer may be better off or worse off as a result of the tariffs.

The concept of *effective protection* provides a way to measure the net effect of tariffs on inputs and outputs. The goal is to measure the actual protection that tariffs provide to domestic producers of final goods in this complex environment. Effective protection is typically defined as the percentage difference between the industry's value added with tariffs imposed and its value added at world prices without tariffs. Value added is the difference between the value of the firm's outputs and the value of the inputs it purchases from other firms, including foreign firms.

The standard method used to model effective protection relies on a partial equilibrium model. The model assumes fixed technologies such that the combination of factor inputs is constant. The model also assumes that the intermediate inputs used to produce the final good are imported. And, the simplest case assumes a single output and single input. Given these assumptions, effective protection is measured as

$$e_j = (t_j - a_{ij}t_i)/(1 - a_{ij}) \qquad (5.1)$$

where e_j is the effective protection of output good j, t_j is the tariff rate on output j, t_i is the tariff rate on the input i, and a_{ij} is the technology coefficient under free trade conditions. This technology coefficient is the share of input i in good j.

Equation (5.1) provides intuition about the effectiveness of tariffs in protecting the domestic goods industry. As shown, effective protection increases as the output tariff increases and decreases as the input tariff increases. Further, effective protection also depends on the shares of intermediate inputs used to produce the output. Depending on these variables, effective protection can be positive or negative.

To illustrate, consider the case where the final good j is valued at $150 under free trade. This final good is produced using $100 of the intermediate input i. Value added at free trade prices is $50. Now, assume there is a 10% tariff on the final good j and a 5% tariff on the intermediate input i. These tariff rates are referred to as *nominal tariff rates*. Under this tariff structure, the value of the imported final good j becomes $165 and the value of the imported intermediate input i becomes $105. Value added with these nominal tariffs in place is $60. Thus, the difference between value added with tariffs and free trade is $10; $10 is 20% of the original value added of $50, thus, the effective rate of protection of final good j is 20%. Using Equation (5.1), this effective rate of protection can also be calculated directly as: $0.20 = (0.10 - (100/150)0.05)/(1 - (100/150))$. In this example, the effective rate of protection is positive and exceeds the nominal rate of protection of good j.

This concept and model of effective protection is used by economists to analyze the practical effects of tariffs across a wide variety of input and output industries. More complex expressions of equation (5.1) allow for its application in a wide variety of country, industry, and policy conditions.[3] Such analysis can then provide guidance for evaluating, formulating, and reforming the structure of tariffs and other trade policies. Although the usefulness of the concept of effective protection has been challenged, economists generally recognize the concept as a useful tool in empirical research.

### 5.4.1	How does tariff escalation affect the protection of the domestic industry?

One example of tariff structure that has been informed by the model of effective protection is the case of tariff escalation. *Tariff escalation* describes the structure of tariffs where nominal tariff rates increase with the degree of processing of the imported good. For example, raw materials may not be subject to tariffs, while semi-manufactured goods may be subject to moderate tariffs, and final goods may be subject to higher tariffs. This tariff escalation structure increases the effective rate of protection of final goods industries.

Tariff escalation can be measured as the difference between the nominal tariffs on goods at different stages of processing. Tariff escalation is the case where the nominal tariff on the final (more highly processed) good is greater than that on the (less processed) input good. Alternatively, tariff de-escalation is the case where the nominal tariff on the final good is less than that on the input good. In practice, the application of this measure is complicated by the task of identifying the stage of processing or processing chains of products. The application of this measure is also complicated when the final good is produced using a variety of inputs that differ in their degree of processing.

The effects of tariff escalation are complex. In theory, tariff escalation should distort the allocation of resources in both the importing and exporting countries. Specifically, we expect importing countries to have a bias toward producing more highly processed final goods with relatively higher nominal tariffs. At the same time, we expect exporting countries to have a bias toward producing less processed inputs with relatively lower nominal tariffs. In practice, it is difficult to disentangle the distortions associated with tariff escalation from other sources of distortion such as non-tariff barriers to trade.

An extension of the above argument is that tariff escalation can have an adverse effect on the environment in the exporting countries. The intuition is that their production bias toward less processed inputs, including raw materials, can lead to the over-extraction of natural resources. This bias toward raw material exports resulting from tariff escalation has been a concern raised by developing countries in multilateral trade negotiations, including the World Trade Organization's Doha Round negotiations. Escalating tariffs in industrialized countries are viewed as limiting the ability of developing countries to diversify production away from natural resources. The resulting over-extraction of natural resources is believed to generate significant environmental side effects. Chapter 11 provides further intuition on this link between trade and the environment.

5.5 Summary Remarks

What are tariffs, their types and purpose? The tariff is a tax imposed by importing countries on goods that are imported from one customs territory to another. There are several types of tariffs. The specific tariff is a fixed amount of money per unit of the good imported. The ad valorem tariff is a percentage of the value of the good imported. The compound tariff is a combination of the specific tariff and the ad valorem tariff. The mixed tariff is a variant of the compound tariff where the tax is either specific or ad valorem depending on which is larger. Technical tariffs depend on the product's content of inputs, such as alcohol. The purpose of these tariffs is to protect domestic industries for which the country has a comparative disadvantage. That is, tariffs are used to protect the domestic suppliers of goods that the country would otherwise import at lower world prices under free trade conditions.

What are the effects of tariffs? The effects of tariffs depend on the conditions in the importing and exporting countries. Specifically, the effects depend on the price responsiveness of consumers and producers in the various markets. We considered three cases in this chapter. The first was the case of a tariff imposed by a large importer who can affect the world price of the good. The second was the case of a tariff imposed by a small importer who cannot affect the world price of the good. The third was the case of a tariff imposed by an importer whose import demand was elastic relative to the exporting country's export supply. Below, we summarize the effects of tariffs in each case.

First, what are the effects of a tariff imposed by a large importer? When the importing country is large, a tariff affects the price in the importing country *and* the world price of the good. Specifically, a tariff increases the price of the good in the importer and decreases the world price of the good seen by the exporter. As a result, agents in both the importer and exporter are affected. In the importing country, producers supply more in their domestic market at a higher tariff-inclusive price. They have gained from the tariff in terms of revenue from domestic sales of the good. At the same time, consumers demand less at the higher tariff-inclusive price. They have lost from the tariff in terms of the higher cost of the good. Alternatively, in the exporting country, producers supply less to the international market at a lower world price. They have lost from the tariff in terms of revenue from international sales of the good. And consumers demand more at the lower world price. They have gained from the tariff in terms of the lower cost of the good. Furthermore, the mix of consumption of domestic versus traded goods changes as a result of the tariff. Consumers in the importing country now consume more domestically produced goods and fewer imports. Consumers in the exporting country continue to consume only domestically produced goods, but more of them.

The tariff also results in welfare changes in both the importing and exporting countries. In the importer, the producer's welfare increases, consumer's welfare decreases, and government welfare increases from tariff revenues. The net country welfare effect includes a positive terms of trade effect and negative production and consumption distortions. The importing country is worse off as a result of the tariff if the distortions exceed the terms of trade effect. This is the typical case. Alternatively, in the exporter, the producer's welfare decreases, consumer's welfare increases, and government welfare does not change. The net country welfare effect includes a negative terms of trade effect and negative production and consumption distortions. The exporting country is unambiguously worse off as a result of the tariff.

Second, what are the effects of a tariff imposed by a small importer? When the importing country is small, a tariff increases the price in the importing country but does *not* affect the world price of the good. As a result, agents in the importer are affected by the tariff; however, agents in the exporter are unaffected. In the importing country, producers supply more in their domestic market at a higher tariff-inclusive price. They have gained from the tariff in terms of revenue from domestic sales of the good. At the same time, consumers demand less at the higher tariff-inclusive price. They have lost from the tariff in terms of the higher cost of the good. Consumers in the importing country now consume more domestically produced goods and fewer imports. Alternatively, in the exporting country, producers and consumers do not alter the quantity of the supply and demand in any economically significant way. Given the size of the international market, the exporter is insulated from the policy decisions of the small importer.

The tariff also results in welfare changes in the importing country but not in the exporting country. In the importer, the producer's welfare increases, the consumer's welfare decreases, and government welfare increases from tariff revenues. The net country welfare effect includes a negative production and consumption distortion. It does not, however, include a positive terms of trade effect. This is because the small country has no effect on the world price of its imported good. The importing country is unambiguously worse off as a result of the tariff. Alternatively, in the exporter, the welfare of all agents and the country in net remains unchanged. Consumers in the exporting country continue to consume only domestically produced goods at the original world prices. The exporting country is indifferent to the tariff policies of the small importing country.

Third, what are the effects of a tariff, when export supply is inelastic relative to import demand? When the importing country faces a relatively inelastic export supply for a traded good, a tariff affects the price in the importing and exporting countries differently. Specifically, a tariff increases the price of the good in the importer by a relatively small amount and decreases the world price of the good seen by the exporter by a relatively large amount. As a result, agents in the exporter are affected relatively more than agents in the importer. That is, the price effect of the tariff is passed from the country that imposes the policy to its trading partner.

In the importing country, producers supply more in their domestic market at a higher tariff-inclusive price. They have gained from the tariff in terms of revenue from domestic sales of the good. At the same time, consumers demand less at the higher tariff-inclusive price. Consumers now consume more domestically produced goods and fewer imports. They have lost from the tariff in terms of the higher cost of the good. However, these producer gains and consumer losses are *relatively small*. Alternatively, in the exporting country, producers supply less to the international market at a lower world price. They have lost from the tariff in terms of revenue from international sales of the good. And consumers demand more at the lower world price. Consumers continue to consume only domestically produced goods, but more of them. They have gained from the tariff in terms of the lower cost of the good. These producer losses and consumer gains in the exporter are *relatively large*.

The tariff also results in welfare changes in both the importing and exporting countries. In the importer, the producer's welfare increases, consumer's welfare decreases, and government welfare increases (from tariff revenues). The net country welfare effect includes a positive terms of trade effect and negative production and consumption distortions. The importing country is worse off as a result of the tariff if the distortions exceed the terms of trade effect. However, these welfare effects in the importer are relatively small. Alternatively, in the exporter, the producer's welfare decreases, consumer's welfare increases, and government welfare does not change. The net country welfare effect includes a negative terms of trade effect and negative production and consumption distortions. The exporting country is unambiguously worse off as a result of the tariff. These welfare effects in the exporter are relatively large.

How is the burden of the tariff allocated across countries? The burden of the tariff is allocated in different ways across countries in the cases above. First, the price effects of the tariff are shared between the exporter and importer when the elasticities of import demand and export supply are relatively similar. This corresponds with the large importer who can affect the world price (i.e., Case 1). However, even when the price effects are shared, the welfare effects are not shared equally. That is, the welfare effects are mixed positive/negative for the importer and unambiguously negative for the exporter. In contrast, the price effects of the tariff are experienced entirely by the importer when the export supply is infinitely elastic. This corresponds with the small importer whose demand is completely satisfied by the exporter (i.e., Case 2). In this case, the welfare effects for the importer are unambiguously negative and relatively large, while the welfare effects for the exporter are economically insignificant. Finally, the price effects of the tariff are borne disproportionately by the exporter when the export supply is relatively inelastic compared with the import demand. This corresponds with the scenario in which the good is in relatively limited export supply or the importer is relatively price responsive (i.e., Case 3). In this case, the welfare effects for the importer are mixed positive/negative but small, while the welfare effects for the exporter are unambiguously negative and large.

What are the effects of tariff liberalization? The effects of tariff liberalization are the mirror opposite of the effects of adding tariffs. The magnitude of these effects depend on the relative elasticities of import demand and export supply. From a national perspective, both importers and exporters experience welfare gains when tariffs are liberalized. Exporters are unambiguously better off from tariff liberalization. Importers are also better off from tariff liberalization, except in the large country case where the importer can significantly affect world prices. From a subnational perspective, tariff liberalization generates distributional effects. In importers, consumers are better off from tariff liberalization and producers and governments are worse off. In exporters, producers are better off and consumers are worse off. From a global perspective, tariff liberalization increases the welfare of all countries in aggregate. Thus, a country's position on whether to liberalize tariffs reflects its perspective and the weighting of the welfare of consumers and producers.

How protective are tariffs of the domestic industry? The effectiveness of the protection of the domestic industry is complicated by the fact that tariffs are imposed on both final goods and intermediate inputs. If a tariff is imposed on the final good but not the inputs, then the tariff is effective in protecting the domestic producer of the final good. However, if a tariff is imposed on the imported inputs but not the final good, then the tariff is not effective in protecting the domestic producer of the final good, who is actually worse off. If tariffs are imposed on both the intermediate input and final good, then the final good producer can be better off or worse off as a result of the tariffs. The concept of effective protection provides a way to measure the protection that tariffs provide to domestic producers of final goods. Effective protection is typically defined as the percentage difference between the industry's value added with tariffs and without tariffs. Effective protection is positively related to the final good tariff, and is negatively related to the input tariff and the share of intermediate inputs used to produce the output.

How does tariff escalation affect the protection of the domestic industry? Tariff escalation describes the structure of tariffs where nominal tariff rates increase with the degree of processing of the imported good. This tariff escalation structure increases the effective rate of protection of final goods industries. The effects of tariff escalation are thought to distort the allocation of resources in both the importing and exporting countries. Specifically, we expect importers to have a bias toward producing more highly processed final goods with relatively higher nominal tariffs. We expect exporters to have a bias toward producing less processed inputs (e.g., raw materials) with relatively lower nominal tariffs. In practice, it is difficult to disentangle the distortions associated with tariff escalation from other sources of distortions.

Applied Problems

5.1 Examine the effect of liberalizing tariffs on prices, quantity supplied, quantity demanded, and trade in both importers and exporters. Make an assumption about whether your countries can affect the world price.

5.2 Use your knowledge of the welfare effects of tariffs to explain why policy makers interested in maximizing national and world welfare support free trade while select agents within countries (e.g., consumers, government, or producers) may not support free trade.

5.3 Consider the case where a government places unequal weight on the welfare of producers and consumers. For example, assume that the government of a country acts as an advocate for industry interests. Use your knowledge of the welfare effects of tariffs to explain why such a government may not support tariff liberalization even though the country in aggregate would gain from such liberalization.

5.4 Assume that you are a consumer advocate with an interest in maximizing consumer welfare. Furthermore, assume that your advocacy organization works to maximize consumer welfare from a global perspective. Use your knowledge of the welfare effects of tariffs to explain whether your organization would support the liberalization of tariffs.

5.5 Evaluate the effects of reducing the tariffs in all countries on the world welfare of consumers, producers and governments. Consider these effects for both the small and large country cases.

5.6 Consider the scenario where the countries of the North institute new tariffs. Examine the effects of this policy change on the welfare of the North and South. Assume that the import demand of the North is elastic relative to the export supply of the South.

5.7 Consider the scenario in which the countries of the South liberalize tariffs – that is, the South is the importer. Examine the effects of this policy change on the welfare of the North and South. Assume that the import demand of the South is inelastic relative to the export supply of the North.

5.8   Analyze how the allocation of the price effects of a tariff between the importer and exporter affects the distribution of the welfare effects between the importer and exporter.

5.9   Calculate the effective rate of protection in two alternative scenarios. First, assume that the tariff on inputs is 15%, the tariff on the final good is 20%, and the technology coefficient that describes the use of the input in the final good is 100/200. Second, assume that the tariff on inputs is 20%, the tariff on the final good is 15%, and the technology coefficient is 100/200. (a) What is the effective rate of protection in these two scenarios? (b) What does the comparison of these two scenarios tell you intuitively?

5.10   Consider the case of tariff de-escalation where tariffs on inputs are higher than tariffs on final goods. What is the effect of tariff de-escalation on effective protection?

Further Reading

Anderson, James E., and J. Peter Neary. 2007. Welfare versus market access: the implications of tariff structure for tariff reform. *Journal of International Economics* 71 (1): 187–205.

Bagwell, Kyle, and Robert W. Staiger. 1999. An economic theory of GATT. *American Economic Review* 89 (1): 215–248.

Balassa, Bela. 1965. Tariff protection in industrial countries: an evaluation. *Journal of Political Economy* 73 (6): 573–594.

Balassa, Bela, ed. 1982. *Development Strategies in Semi Industrialized Economies*. Baltimore: Johns Hopkins University Press.

Baldwin, Robert E. 1986. Toward more efficient procedures for multilateral tariff negotiations. *Aussenwirtschaft* 41 (2–3): 379–394.

Bickerdike, Charles F. 1906. The theory of incipient taxes. *Economic Journal* 16: 529–535.

Bhagwati, Jagdish. 1968. More on the equivalence of tariffs and quotas. *American Economic Review* 58 (1): 142–146.

Corden, W. Max. 1966. The structure of a tariff system and the effective protective rate. *Journal of Political Economy* 74 (3): 221–237.

Corden, W. Max. 1971. *The Theory of Protection*. Oxford: Clarendon Press.

Corden, W. Max. 1974. *Trade Policy and Economic Welfare*. Oxford: Clarendon Press.

Elamin, Nasredin, and Hansdeep Khaira. 2004. Tariff escalation in agricultural commodity markets. *FAO Commodity Market Review 2003–04*. Rome: Food and Agriculture Organization of the United Nations, pp. 101–120.

Francois, Joseph, and Will Martin. 2003. Formula approaches for market access negotiations. *World Economy* 26 (1): 1–28.

Greenaway, David, and Chris R. Milner. 1993. *Trade and Industrial Policy in Developing Countries*. London: Macmillan.

Greenaway, David, and Chris R. Milner. 2003. Effective protection, policy appraisal, and trade policy reform. *The World Economy* 26 (4): 441–456.

Hecht, Joy E. 1997. Impacts of tariff escalation on the environment: literature review and synthesis. *World Development* 25 (10): 1701–1716.

Hoda, Anwarul. 2001. *Tariff Negotiations and Renegotiations under the GATT and the WTO: Procedures and Practices*. Cambridge: Cambridge University Press.

Irwin, Douglas A. 1998. Changes in US tariffs: the role of import prices and commercial policies. *American Economic Review* 88 (4): 1015–1026.

Jean, Sebastien, David Laborde, and Will Martin. 2006. Consequences of alternative formulas for agricultural tariff cuts. In *Agricultural Trade Reform and the Doha Development Agenda* (eds Kym Anderson and Will Martin), Washington, D.C.: Palgrave Macmillan and the World Bank, pp. 81–115.

Johnson, Harry G. 1954. Optimum tariffs and retaliation. *Review of Economic Studies*: 21: 142–153.

Johnson, Harry G. 1965. The theory of tariff structure with special reference to world trade and development. *Trade and Development*. Geneva: Institut des Hautes Etudes Internationales.

Jones, Ronald W. 1971. Effective protection and substitution. *Journal of International Economics* 1 (1): 59–82.

Krueger, Anne O. 1978. *Foreign Trade Regimes and Economic Development: Liberalization Attempts and Consequences*. Cambridge, MA: Ballinger.

Lindland, Jostein 1997. *The Impact of the Uruguay Round on Tariff Escalation in Agricultural Products*. FAO Commodities and Trade Division, ESCP No. 3. Rome: FAO.

Organisation for Economic Co-operation and Development (OECD). 1999. *Post-Uruguay Round Tariff Regimes, Achievements and Outlook*. Paris: OECD.

Panagariya, Arvind. 2002. Formula approaches to reciprocal tariff liberalization. In *Development, Trade and the WTO* (eds Bernard Hoekman, Aaditya Mattoo, and Philip English), Washington, D.C.: World Bank, pp. 535–539.

United Nations Conference on Trade and Development. 2003. *Back to Basics: Market Access Issues in the Doha Agenda*. UNCTAD/DITC/TAB/Misc. 9. Geneva: UNCTAD.

United States Department of Agriculture. 2001. *Profiles of Tariffs in Global Agricultural Markets*. AER-796. Washington, D.C.: USDA.

World Trade Organization (WTO). 2007. *World Trade Report 2007: Sixty Years of the Multilateral Trading System, Achievements and Challenges*. Geneva: WTO.

World Trade Organization (WTO), ITC, and UNCTAD. 2007. *World Tariff Profiles 2006*. Geneva: WTO, ITC, and UNCTAD.

Yeats, Alexander J. 1984. On the analysis of tariff escalation. *Journal of Development Economics* 15: 77–88.

Notes

1. These exceptions are set forth in the 1979 Enabling Clause and Article XXIV of the GATT.
2. This comparative disadvantage may be explained by any of the models detailed in Part One of this book.
3. Methodologies used to analyze the effective rate of protection include the partial equilibrium model, nesting the partial equilibrium framework within the general equilibrium model, and applied general equilibrium modeling.

6

Export Subsidies

6.1　What Are Export Subsidies, Their Types and Purpose?

A subsidy is a negative tax. A production subsidy is a payment made by the government to firms that produce a specific good. There are two basic types of production subsidies. These include the domestic subsidy and the export subsidy. The *domestic subsidy* is a payment made by the government to firms that domestically produce a specific good. In contrast, an *export subsidy* is a payment to firms that produce a specific good for export. Thus, the export subsidy targets goods that cross national borders. This chapter focuses on export subsidies. For simplicity, we use the terms "export subsidy" and "subsidy" synonymously throughout the chapter.

Subsidies take a variety of forms.These forms include cash payments and the disposal of government stocks at below-market prices. They include subsidies financed by producers or processors as a result of government actions such as assessments; subsidies for marketing; and subsidies for transportation and freight. They also include subsidies for commodities contingent on their incorporation in exported products.

As with tariffs, export subsidies are typically levied on an ad valorem or specific basis. An *ad valorem export subsidy* is a percentage of the value of the good exported. For example, the subsidy can be 5% of the value of the export. A *specific export subsidy* is a fixed amount of money per unit of the good exported. For example, the subsidy can be $100 per ton of the exported good.

The purpose of export subsidies is to provide an incentive for producers to export into foreign markets. In this way, export subsidies serve to protect the domestic

Global Trade Policy: Questions and Answers, First Edition. Pamela J. Smith.

industry against competition with lower priced goods in the international market. Which industries? The answer is industries for which the country has a comparative disadvantage.[1] That is, export subsidies are used to protect the domestic suppliers of goods that the country would otherwise import (or export less of) under free trade conditions. Recall that export subsidies are imposed only on goods that are exported. By adding a negative tax, the subsidy allows the domestic industry in that country to compete in the world market against what would otherwise be lower priced goods.

In the remainder of this chapter, we explore two core questions with respect to export subsidies: (1) What are the effects of export subsidies? (2) What are the effects of liberalizing export subsidies? In answering each of these questions, we consider the welfare effects that characterize the gains and losses associated with export subsidies. That is, we consider who gains and who loses from the adoption or liberalization of export subsidies; and how the character of the trading countries affects the burden of the export subsidy across countries and across agents within countries.

6.2   What Are the Effects of Export Subsidies?

What are the effects of export subsidies in both exporting and importing countries? The effects of the export subsidy in the *exporting country* are quite intuitive. The price received by domestic producers of the exported good goes up, as it now includes the subsidy. In a competitive market, the price of the good produced for domestic consumption will equate with the subsidy-inclusive price of the exports. Thus, the price of both domestically consumed and exported goods increases. Second, the quantity of the good produced domestically increases as suppliers now receive the additional subsidy. At the same time, the quantity of the good demanded in the exporting country decreases. This is because the price of the domestically consumed good is higher as a result of the subsidy.

The export subsidy also affects welfare in the exporting country. Subsidies affect the welfare of consumers, producers, and the government differently. Specifically, the welfare of domestic producers increases, because both the quantity of the good supplied and the price received (which includes the subsidy) increase. In contrast, the welfare of consumers decreases, because the quantity of the good demanded decreases and the price paid increases. And, the welfare of the government decreases, because the government pays the subsidy. If we sum together the welfare effects of these three agents, we can draw conclusions about the net welfare effects of the export subsidy for the exporting country. We will show below that the net welfare of the exporting country is unambiguously negative as a result of the export subsidy. However, the magnitude of the net welfare effects depends on the ability of the exporter to influence the price in the world market.

The effects of the export subsidy in the *importing country* are more opaque. The price of the good in the importing country (or world price) can either decrease or remain unchanged. The world price will decrease if the country imposing the subsidy is large in terms of its share of the world's supply of the good. In this case, the subsidy causes the world supply of the good to increase and thus the world price to decrease. The quantity of the domestic good supplied in the importing country decreases, as suppliers now receive a lower world price for their goods. At the same time, the quantity of the domestic good demanded in the importing country increases, because consumers now pay a lower world price for the good.

In this case, the export subsidy affects welfare in the *importing country*. Specifically, the welfare of domestic producers decreases, because the quantity of the domestic good supplied and the price received both decrease. In contrast, the welfare of consumers in the importing country increases, because the quantity of the domestic good demanded increases and the price paid decreases. The welfare of the government is unchanged in the importing country, because the cost of the subsidy is paid by the government in the exporting country. If we sum together the welfare effects of these three agents, we can draw conclusions about the net welfare effects in the subsidy for the importing country. We will show below that the net welfare of the importing country depends on the ability of the exporting country to influence the world price of the good and on whether the subsidy reverses the patterns of trade.

Alternatively, if the country imposing the export subsidy is small in terms of its share of the world's supply of the good, then the world supply and thus world price will remain unchanged. In this case, the quantity supplied and demanded in the importing country will remain unchanged. Similarly, consumer and producer welfare will remain unchanged in the importing country.

Below, we present a simple partial equilibrium model to illustrate the effects of an export subsidy. To this end, we extend the modeling framework presented in the previous chapter on tariffs. Then we consider four cases. The first assumes that a large country imposes an export subsidy. A "large country" is one that can influence the world price of the good. It is a country whose supply of the good is a large share of the world's supply of the good. This first case also assumes that the exporter has a comparative advantage prior to the adoption of the policy. Under this assumption, the subsidy increases exports beyond what would otherwise be observed under free trade conditions. The second case extends the prior case by assuming that a small country imposes a subsidy. A "small country" is one that cannot influence the world price of the good. It is a country whose supply of the good is a small share of the world's supply of the good. Next, the third case assumes that the exporting and importing countries differ in their responsiveness to price changes. Specifically, we consider the case where the export supply is elastic relative to the import demand. Finally, the fourth case assumes that a large country has a comparative disadvantage in the good. In this case, the export subsidy reverses the patterns of trade that would otherwise be observed under free trade conditions. That is, in the absence of the subsidy the country will import the good; and in the presence of the subsidy the country will export the good. Thus, the subsidy serves to reverse the patterns of trade.

The basic assumptions of the simple partial equilibrium model are as follows. There are two countries – home and foreign. There is one good. This good is subject to an export subsidy. The home country imposes the export subsidy. In Cases 1, 2 and 3, the home country is the exporter of the good before and after the subsidy is in place. The foreign country is the importer of the good before and after the subsidy in these same cases. Alternatively, in Case 4, the subsidy reverses the patterns of trade. That is, the home country is an importer under free trade and is an exporter after the subsidy is imposed. Conversely, the foreign country is an exporter under free trade and an importer after the subsidy is imposed.

6.2.1   Case 1: What are the effects of an export subsidy imposed by a large exporter?

To begin, we consider the case where the export subsidy is imposed by a large exporter with a comparative advantage in the good. Figure 6.1 shows the markets for the good in this case. Panel (a) shows the domestic supply (S) and demand (D) for the good in the home country (the exporter). The equilibrium price of the good in the home country is the same as its autarky price. This is the price of the good when there is no trade. This autarky price is relatively low, reflecting the assumption that the home country has a comparative advantage in the good. In contrast, Panel (c) shows the domestic supply (S*) and demand (D*) for the good in the foreign country (the importer). Again, the equilibrium price of the good in this foreign country is the same as its autarky price . This autarky price is relatively high, reflecting the assumption that the foreign country has a comparative disadvantage in the good.

Panel (b) then shows the supply and demand in the world market. This is the market where the home and foreign countries trade. In this middle panel, the demand is the *import demand* of the foreign country (D^m). The import demand in Panel (b) is derived from the behavior of the foreign country in Panel (c). For example, consider the foreign country's behavior at all possible world prices. For world prices at or above the foreign country's autarky price, the foreign country will not demand imports. Rather, its demand will be satisfied by its domestic supply. However, for world prices below its autarky price, the foreign country will demand imports in the amount of its *excess demand*. For example, at price P^w the foreign country will demand in imports the amount by which its domestic demand (Q_0^{D*}) exceeds its domestic supply (Q_0^{S*}). Both Panels (b) and (c) show the amounts of import demand as horizontal distances.

In contrast, the supply in the world market in Panel (b) is the *export supply* (S^x). The export supply is derived from the behavior of the home country in Panel (a). For example, consider the home country's behavior at all possible world prices. For world prices at or below its autarky price, the home country will not supply exports. Rather, its supply will be satisfied by domestic demand. However, for prices above its autarky price, the home country will supply exports in the amount of its *excess*

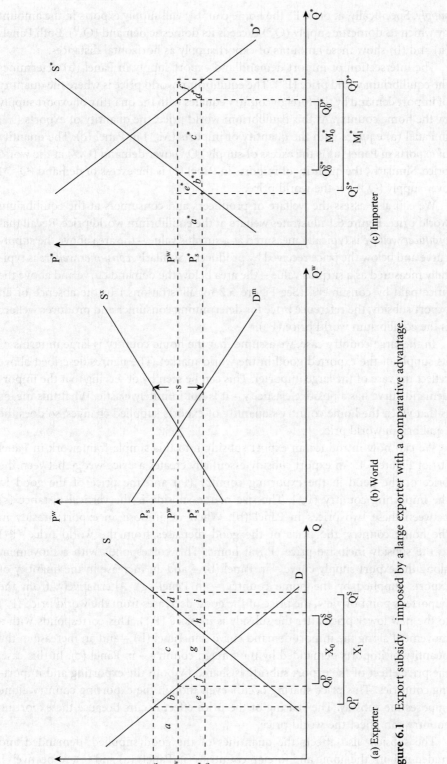

Figure 6.1 Export subsidy – imposed by a large exporter with a comparative advantage.

(a) Exporter

(b) World

(c) Importer

supply. Specifically, at price P^w the home country will supply exports in the amount by which its domestic supply (Q_0^S) exceeds its domestic demand (Q_0^D). Both Panels (a) and (b) show these amounts of export supply as horizontal distances.

The intersection of import demand and export supply in Panel (b) determines the equilibrium world price (P^w). The equilibrium world price is where the quantity of import demand by the foreign country equates with the quantity of export supply by the home country. At this equilibrium world price, the quantity of exports (X_0) in Panel (a) equates with the quantity of imports (M_0^*) in Panel (c). The quantity of exports in Panel (a) is the excess of supply (Q_0^S) over demand (Q_0^D) at the world price. Similarly, the quantity of imports in Panel (c) is the excess of demand (Q_0^{D*}) over supply (Q_0^{S*}) at the world price.

We can also assess the welfare of producers and consumers at the equilibrium world price. Figure 6.1 illustrates welfare at the equilibrium world price. Recall that *producer welfare* is typically measured as a surplus value – the area above the supply curve and below the price received by producers. Similarly, *consumer welfare* is typically measured as a surplus value – the area below the demand curve and above the price paid by consumers. (See Figure 5.2 for illustrations.) In the absence of an export subsidy, the reference price for determining consumer and producer welfare is the equilibrium world price (P^w).

In the large country case, we assume that the home country is large in terms of its supply of the exported good in the world market. The figures described above reflect the case of the large importer. This can be seen by observing that the import demand curve has a positive elasticity – it is not infinitely elastic. What this means is that when the home country's quantity of exports supplied changes, so does the equilibrium world price.

We can now introduce an export subsidy into this simple framework in Panel (b) of Figure 6.1. An export subsidy essentially creates a price wedge between the price of the good in the exporting country (P_s) and the price of the good in the importing country (P_s^*). The size of the subsidy is the vertical distance (s) between these two prices in Panel (b). When we impose an export subsidy in the home country, the price of the good increases from the world price (P^w) to the subsidy inclusive price (P_s) at home. This corresponds with a movement along the export supply curve – in Panel (b) – and an increase in the quantity of exports supplied by the home country – in Panel (a). Alternatively, from the importer's point of view, the price of the good decreases from the world price (P^w) to the new lower price after the subsidy is in place (P_s^*). This corresponds with a movement along the import demand curve – in Panel (b) – and an increase in the quantity of imports demanded by the foreign country – in Panel (c). In this case, the price effect of the export subsidy is shared by both the exporting and importing countries. This price sharing occurs even though the exporting country alone imposes the subsidy. The sharing of the price effect occurs because the exporting country can affect the world price.

The subsidy also affects the quantities of the good supplied, demanded and traded in both the home and foreign countries (in Panels (a) and (c), respectively).

The home country experiences an increase in the quantity supplied (Q_0^S to Q_1^S) and a decrease in the quantity demanded (Q_0^D to Q_1^D). In contrast, the foreign country experiences a decrease in the quantity supplied (Q_0^{S*} to Q_1^{S*}) and an increase in the quantity demanded (Q_0^{D*} to Q_1^{D*}). Consequently, both countries experience an increase in trade. The home country's exports increase (X_0 to X_1) and the foreign country's imports increase (M_0^* to M_1^*).

Intuitively, the effects of export subsidies on prices and quantities provide information about their impact on both producers and consumers. At home, producers are supplying more at a higher price. They have gained from the subsidy in terms of revenue from sales of the good. At home, consumers are demanding less at a higher price. They have lost from the subsidy in terms of the cost of the good. Alternatively, in the foreign country, producers are supplying less at a lower price. They have lost. And foreign consumers are demanding more at a lower price. They have gained. Further, the mix of production for the domestic and international markets changes as a result of the export subsidy. Producers in the home country now produce more for the export market and less for the domestic market. Producers in the foreign market continue to produce goods only for their domestic market, but fewer of them.

The welfare effects of the export subsidy for the home and foreign countries can also be seen in Figure 6.1 and are summarized in Table 6.1. Instead of illustrating total welfare before and after the subsidy is imposed, we simply illustrate the changes in welfare that result from the subsidy. Panel (a) in Figure 6.1 shows the welfare effects for the home country (exporter). As shown, the producer's welfare increases by the surplus amount $+(a + b + c)$ as a result of the subsidy. The consumer's welfare decreases by the surplus amount $-(a + b)$ as a result of the subsidy. Furthermore, the government welfare decreases by the amount $-(b + c + d + e + f + g + h + i)$ as a result of the subsidy. This change in government welfare is the cost of paying the subsidy. It is the product of the quantity exported (horizontally) and the value of the subsidy (vertically).

The net country welfare then is the sum of the producer, consumer, and government welfare changes. Adding these effects together, we get $-(b + d) - (e + f + g + h + i)$. Each of the areas has a distinct interpretation. Area $-(e + f + g + h + i)$ is a negative *terms of trade* effect. This is the amount by which the home country's subsidy suppresses the world price of the good that it exports. Areas $-(b + d)$ are deadweight losses incurred by consumers and producers. Specifically, area $-(d)$ is a *production distortion*. This area is the loss associated with increasing the quantity of domestic supply of a good above the equilibrium supply. Area $-(b)$ is a *consumption distortion*. This area is the loss associated with decreasing quantity demanded of the good, which had a lower price before the subsidy is imposed. In net, the large exporting country is worse off as a result of the subsidy, as the net welfare effect is unambiguously negative.

Panel (c) shows the welfare effects of the subsidy for the foreign country (i.e., importer). As shown, the producer's welfare decreases by the surplus amount $-(a^* + e^*)$ as a result of the subsidy. The consumer's welfare increases by the surplus

Table 6.1 Welfare effects of exports subsidies.

Case 1 – Large country

Economic agent	Welfare effects (exporter/home)	Welfare effects (importer/foreign)
Producer	$+(a + b + c)$	$-(a^* + e^*)$
Consumer	$-(a + b)$	$+(a^* + b^* + c^* + d^* + e^*)$
Government	$+(b + c + d + e + f + g + h + i)$	0
Country	$-(b + d + e + f + g + h + i)$	$+(b^* + c^* + d^*)$
Country (direction)	Negative	Positive

Case 2 – Small country

Economic agent	Welfare effects (exporter/home)	Welfare effects (importer/foreign)
Producer	$+(a + b + c)$	0
Consumer	$-(a + b)$	0
Government	$-(b + c + d)$	0
Country	$-(b + d)$	0
Country (direction)	Negative	None

Case 3 – Alternative elasticities

Economic agent	Welfare effects (exporter/home)	Welfare effects (importer/foreign)
Producer	$+(a + b + c)$	$-(a^* + e^*)$
Consumer	$-(a + b)$	$+(a^* + b^* + c^* + d^* + e^*)$
Government	$-(b + c + d + e + f + g + h + i + j)$	0
Country	$-(b + d + e + f + g + h + i + j)$	$+(b^* + c^* + d^*)$
Country (direction)	Negative	Positive

Case 4 – Large country with comparative disadvantage

Economic agent	Welfare effects (home)	Welfare effects (foreign)
Producer	$+(a + b + e)$	$-(a^* + b^* + c^* + g^* + h^* + i^*)$
Consumer	$-(a + b + c + g + h)$	$+(a^* + b^* + c^* + d^*)$
Government	$-(b + c + d + e + i)$	0
Country	$-(b + c + h + d + c + g + i)$	$+(d^*) - (g^* + h^* + i^*)$
Country (direction)	Negative	Negative or positive

Note: Cases 1 and 3 have similar directional results but different magnitude results. Case 4 extends these cases by considering a reversal in the patterns of trade resulting from the export subsidy. In Case 4, the home is an importer before the subsidy and an exporter after the subsidy; and the foreign is an exporter before the subsidy and an importer after the subsidy.

amount $+(a^* + b^* + c^* + d^* + e^*)$. For the importer, the government welfare does not change, as the subsidy is paid by the home government. The net country welfare then is the sum of the producer and consumer welfare changes. Adding these effects together we get $+(b^* + c^* + d^*)$. These areas are difficult to interpret. However, if we add and subtract e^* and f^*, then we get $+(b^* + c^* + d^* + e^* + f^*) - (e^* + f^*)$. Area $+(b^* + c^* + d^* + e^* + f^*)$ is a *terms of trade* effect. This is the amount by which the subsidy suppresses the world price of the good that the foreign country imports. Areas $-(e^* + f^*)$ are deadweight losses incurred by producers and consumers. Area $-(e^*)$ is a *production distortion*. This area is the loss associated with decreasing the quantity of domestic supply. Area $-(f^*)$ is a *consumption distortion*. This area is the loss associated with increasing quantity consumed. In net, the foreign country (i.e., importer) is better off as a result of the subsidy in the large exporter case. The foreign country is better off because its terms of trade improvement unambiguously exceeds the dead weight losses. This case, however, assumes that the country imposing the subsidy is large enough to affect the world price.

6.2.2 Case 2: What are the effects of an export subsidy imposed by a small exporter?

Next, we consider the effects of an export subsidy under the assumption that the subsidy is imposed by a small exporter. In this case, we assume that the home country is small in terms of its supply of the exported good in the world market. In other words, changes in the home country's supply of the exported good does not affect the world price of the good. Rather, the home country faces an infinitely elastic world demand of the good. Whatever the home country supplies in the world market, there is demand for it. The diagrams in Figure 6.1 can be altered to reflect this alternative case. Figure 6.2 shows this modified case. Observe that the import demand curve is infinitely elastic. What this means is that when the home country's quantity of exports supplied changes, the equilibrium world price remains unchanged.

We can now introduce a subsidy into this modified framework in Panel (b). As in the large country case, the subsidy essentially creates a price wedge between the price of the good in the exporting country (P_s) and the price of the good in the importing country (P_s^*). The size of the subsidy is the vertical distance (s) between these two prices in Panel (b). When we impose a subsidy in the home country, the price of the good increases from the free-trade world price (P^w) to the subsidy inclusive price (P_s) at home. This corresponds with a movement along the export supply curve – in Panel (b) – and an increase in the quantity of exports supplied by the home country. Alternatively, from the importer's point of view, the price of the good remains unchanged and equal to the original free-trade world price $(P^w = P_s^*)$. That is, the price effect of the subsidy is not shared by both the importing and exporting countries. Rather, the entire price effect of the subsidy is experienced by the home country that imposes the subsidy.

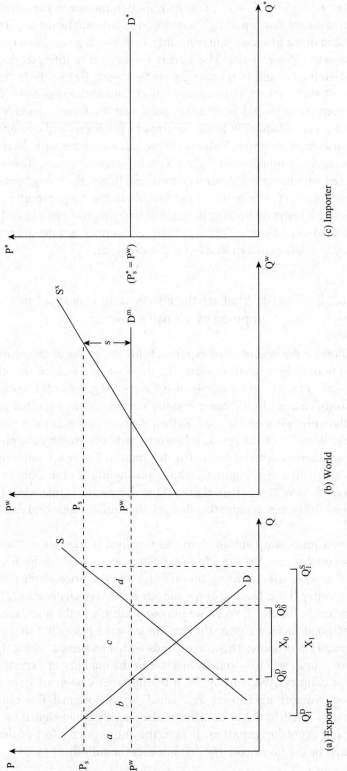

Figure 6.2 Export subsidy – imposed by a small exporter with a comparative advantage.

The subsidy also affects the quantities of the good supplied, demanded and traded in the home country, as shown in Panel (a). Specifically, the home country experiences an increase in the quantity supplied domestically (Q_0^S to Q_1^S) and a decrease in the quantity demanded domestically (Q_0^D to Q_1^D). In contrast, the foreign country experiences no economically significant changes. However, the trade between the importer and exporter does increase. The home country's exports increase (X_0 to X_1) and the foreign country's imports increase by the same amount. But this amount is economically insignificant to the importer.

As in the previous case, the effects of the subsidy on prices and quantities tell us a lot about the impact of the subsidy on both producers and consumers. At home, producers are supplying more at a higher price. They have clearly gained from the subsidy in terms of revenue from sales of the good. At home, consumers are demanding less at a higher price. They have clearly lost from the subsidy in terms of the cost of the good. Further, the mix of consumption of domestic verses traded goods changes as a result of the subsidy. Consumers in the home country now consume less of the domestically produced good as more of the good is destined for the export market. In contrast, producers and consumers in the foreign country are not impacted in any economically significant way.

The welfare effects of the subsidy for the home and foreign countries are also shown in Figure 6.2 and summarized in Table 6.1. As before, we illustrate the changes in welfare that result from the subsidy in the figure. For the home country, the producer's welfare increases by the surplus amount $+(a + b + c)$ as a result of the subsidy. The consumer's welfare decreases by the surplus amount $-(a + b)$. Furthermore, the government welfare decreases by the amount $-(b + c + d)$. This change in government welfare is the cost of the export subsidy. It is the product of the quantity exported (vertically) and the value of the subsidy (horizontally).

The net country welfare then is the sum of the producer, consumer, and government welfare changes. Adding these effects together we get $-(b + d)$. Areas $-(b + d)$ are deadweight losses incurred by producers and consumers. Area $-(d)$ is a *production distortion* – the loss associated with increasing the quantity of domestic supply of the good. Area $-(b)$ is a *consumption distortion* – the loss associated with decreasing quantity demanded of the good. It is important to note that in this small country case, there is no terms of trade effect from the subsidy. Thus, in this case, the welfare effects for the small country that imposes an export subsidy are unambiguously negative. For the foreign country, there are no welfare effects in this case.

6.2.3 Case 3: What are the effects of an export subsidy when export supply is elastic relative to import demand?

In the cases described above, we considered both a large and a small exporting country. First, we assumed that the large exporter faced an import demand curve with a positive elasticity in the world market. Second, we assumed that the small exporter faced an infinitely elastic import demand curve in the world market. This next section considers one additional case – where the supply of exports is more elastic than the demand for imports. This situation can arise when the home country is price responsive relative to the foreign country.

Figure 6.3 illustrates this case. As before, the subsidy essentially creates a price wedge between the price of the good in the exporting country (P_s) and the price of the good in the importing country (P_s^*). The size of the subsidy is the vertical distance (s) between these two prices in Panel (b). When we impose a subsidy in the home country (the exporter), the price of the good increases from the free-trade world price (P^w) to the subsidy inclusive price (P_s) at home. This price change is relatively small. Alternatively, from the importer's point of view, the price of the good decreases from the free-trade world price (P^w) to the new world price (P_s^*). This price change is relatively large. In other words, the price effect of the subsidy is not shared equally by both the exporting and importing countries. Rather, the price effect of the subsidy is experienced primarily by the importing country. This feature of the price effect occurs because the export supply is elastic relative to the import demand.

The directional effects of the subsidy – on quantities of the good supplied, demanded and traded in both the home and foreign countries – are the same as those described in Case 1. Thus, we do not repeat them here. However, the welfare effects are quite distinct in the current case because the price effect of the subsidy is experienced primarily by the importing country.

Figure 6.3 illustrates the welfare effects of the subsidy for the home and foreign countries. Table 6.1 summarizes these effects. Panel (a) in Figure 6.3 shows the welfare effects for the home country (i.e., exporter). As shown, the producer's welfare increases by the surplus amount $+(a + b + c)$ as a result of the subsidy. The consumer's welfare decreases by the surplus amount $-(a + b)$. And, the government welfare decreases by the amount $-(b + c + d + e + f + g + h + i + j)$. This change in government welfare is the cost of paying the subsidy. The net country welfare then is the sum of the producer, consumer, and government welfare changes. Adding these effects together we get $-(b + d) - (e + f + g + h + i + j)$. Area $-(e + f + g + h + i + j)$ is a negative *terms of trade* effect. This is the amount by which the home country's subsidy suppresses the world price of the good that it exports. Areas $-(b + d)$ are deadweight losses incurred by consumers and producers. As before, the home country is unambiguously worse off in net as a result of the export subsidy. However, in this case the terms of trade effect is the primary source of the welfare loss. The producer and consumer distortions are relatively small, since the price effect of the policy in the home country is small.

This experience in the exporting country is in stark contrast to the experience of the importing country. Panel (c) shows the welfare effects of the subsidy for the foreign country (i.e., the importer). As shown, the producer's welfare decreases by the surplus amount $-(a^* + e^*)$ as a result of the subsidy. The consumer's welfare increases by the surplus amount $+(a^* + b^* + c^* + d^* + e^*)$. For the importer, the government welfare does not change, as the subsidy is paid by the home government. The net country welfare then is the sum of the producer and consumer

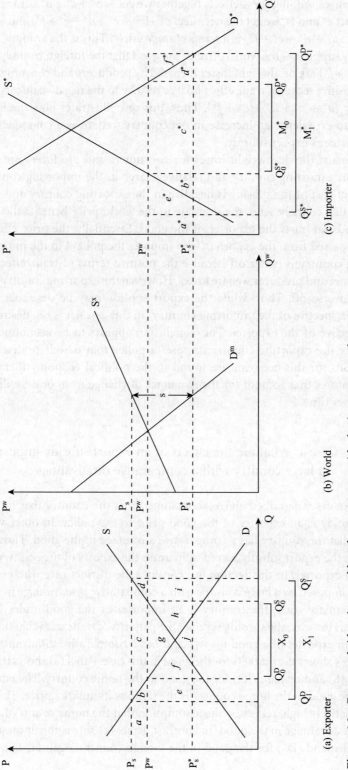

Figure 6.3 Export subsidy – imposed by a large exporter with elastic export supply.

welfare changes. Adding these effects together we get $+(b^* + c^* + d^*)$. If we then add and subtract e^* and f^*, we get the net effect of $+(b^* + c^* + d^* + e^* + f^*)$ and $-(e^* + f^*)$. Area $+(b^* + c^* + d^* + e^* + f^*)$ is a *terms of trade* effect. This is the amount by which the subsidy suppresses the world price of the good that the foreign country imports. Areas $-(e^* + f^*)$ are deadweight losses incurred by producers and consumers. In this case the positive terms of trade effect is large relative to the negative distortions (i.e., $(e^* + f^*) < (b^* + c^* + d^* + e^* + f^*)$. Thus, this case illustrates how the importing country can experience an increase in net country welfare as a consequence of its trading partner's export subsidy.

In summary, the deadweight losses for consumers and producers are relatively small in the exporting country and relatively large in the importing country. The government cost of the subsidy is negative in the exporting country and absent in the importing country. And, the decrease in the world price benefits the importer of the good and hurts the exporter of the good. Essentially, the price effect of the subsidy is passed from the exporter (who imposes the policy) to the importer. The importing country is better off because the positive terms of trade effect exceeds the consumer and producer welfare losses. However, the exporting country is unambiguously worse off. Thus, while the export subsidy may be desirable from the national perspective of the importing country (in this case), it is not desirable from the perspective of the exporter. This conclusion appears to be economically irrational since the exporting country imposes a policy that is welfare deteriorating. Explanations for this behavior are found in the political economy literature and trade literatures that account for the dynamics of change from one equilibrium to another over time.

6.2.4 Case 4: What are the effects of an export subsidy imposed by a large country with a comparative disadvantage?

In the three cases described above, we assumed that the country that imposes the export subsidy is an exporter of the good prior to the policy. In other words, we assumed that the country has a comparative advantage in the good. Thus, in these three cases the export subsidy served to increase the exports of the country that was already an exporter. In this section, we consider the distinct case where an export subsidy is imposed by a large country with a comparative *disadvantage* in the good. In this alternative case, the country is an importer of the good under free trade conditions. However, the subsidy reverses the patterns of trade such that the country becomes an exporter of a good for which it has a comparative disadvantage.

Figure 6.4 shows the markets for the good in this case. Panel (a) shows the domestic supply (S) and demand (D) for the good in the home country. The equilibrium price of the good in the home country is the same as its autarky price. This autarky price is relatively high, reflecting the assumption that the home country has a comparative *dis*advantage in the good. In contrast, Panel (c) shows the domestic supply (S*) and demand (D*) for the good in the foreign country. Again, the equilibrium

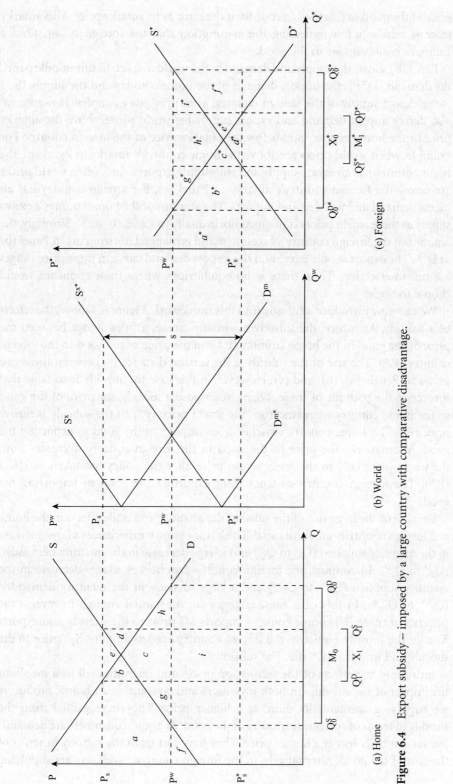

Figure 6.4 Export subsidy – imposed by a large country with comparative disadvantage.

price of the good in this foreign country is the same as its autarky price. This autarky price is relatively low, reflecting the assumption that the foreign country has a comparative advantage in the good.

Panel (b) shows the supply and demand in the world market. In this middle panel, the demand (D^m) is the import demand of the home country and the supply (S^{x*}) is the export supply of the foreign country, as in previous examples. However, we also derive import demand and export supply for world prices above the autarky price of the home country and below the autarky price of the foreign country. For example, when world prices are above the home country's autarky in Panel (a), the home country has an excess supply and will supply exports. And, when world prices are below the foreign country's autarky in Panel (c), the foreign country has an excess demand and will demand imports. The amount of the home country's excess supply at these world prices is mapped horizontally in Panel (b) as S^x. Similarly, the amount of the foreign country's excess demand is mapped horizontally in Panel (b) as D^{m*}. The export supply curve and the import demand curve in these price ranges are not intersecting. Thus, there is no equilibrium where these countries would choose to trade.

We can now introduce a subsidy into this framework. Figure 6.4 shows the effects of a subsidy. As before, the subsidy essentially creates a price wedge between the price of the good in the home country (P_s) and the price of the good in the foreign country (P_s^*). The size of the subsidy is the vertical distance (s) between these two prices in Panels (a), (b), and (c). However, in this case the subsidy is so large that it reverses the patterns of trade. When we impose a subsidy, the price of the good in the home country increases from the world price (P^w) to the subsidy inclusive price (P_s). The home country switches from importing the good to exporting the good. Alternatively, the price of the good in the foreign country decreases from the world price (P^w) to the lower world price after the policy has taken its effect (P_s^*). The foreign country switches from exporting the good to importing the good.

Because of the large size of the subsidy, the quantity and trade effects in the home and foreign countries are substantial. The home country experiences a large increase in the quantity supplied (Q_0^S to Q_1^S) and a large decrease in the quantity demanded (Q_0^D to Q_1^D). In contrast, the foreign country experiences a large decrease in the quantity supplied (Q_0^{S*} to Q_1^{S*}) and a large increase in the quantity demanded (Q_0^{D*} to Q_1^{D*}). In this case, these changes are substantial enough to reverse the patterns of trade. The home country imports M_0 prior to the subsidy and exports X_1 after the subsidy. Similarly, the foreign country exports amount X_0^* prior to the subsidy and imports M_1^* after the subsidy.

Intuitively, the effects of the subsidy on prices and quantities tell us a lot about the impact of the subsidy on both producers and consumers. At home, producers are supplying substantially more at a higher price. They have gained from the subsidy in terms of revenue from sales of the good. At home, consumers are demanding substantially less at a higher price. They have lost from the subsidy in terms of the cost of the good. Alternatively, in the foreign country, producers are supplying substantially less at a lower price. They have lost. And foreign consumers are demanding substantially more and a lower price. They have gained.

The welfare effects of the subsidy for the home and foreign countries can also be seen in Figure 6.4 and summarized in Table 6.1. Panel (a) of the figure shows the welfare effects for the home country. As shown, the producer's welfare increases by the surplus amount $+(a + b + e)$ as a result of the subsidy. The consumer's welfare decreases by the surplus amount $-(a + b + c + g + h)$. Further, the government welfare decreases by the cost of the subsidy $-(b + c + d + e + i)$. The net country welfare then is the sum of the producer, consumer, and government welfare changes. Adding these effects together we get $-(b + c + h) - (d + c + g) - (i)$. Area $-(i)$ is a negative *terms of trade* effect. Area $-(d + c + g)$ is a *production distortion*. Area $-(b + c + h)$ is a *consumption distortion*. Thus, in net the home country is unambiguously worse off as a result of the subsidy. This is the same welfare result as the previous three cases. Hence, the ability of a country to reverse the patterns of trade via an export subsidy still results in a net welfare loss for that country.

Panel (c) shows the welfare effects of the subsidy for the foreign country. As shown, the producer's welfare decreases by the surplus amount $-(a^* + b^* + c^* + g^* + h^* + i^*)$ as a result of the subsidy. The consumer's welfare increases by the surplus amount $+(a^* + b^* + c^* + d^*)$. And, the government welfare does not change, as the home government pays for the subsidy. The net country welfare then is the sum of the producer and consumer welfare changes. Adding these effects together we get $+d^* - (g^* + h^* + i^*)$. Then, adding and subtracting $(c^* + e^* + h^*)$, we get $+(c^* + d^* + e^* + h^*) - (g^* + h^* + e^*) - (c^* + h^* + i^*)$. Area $+(c^* + d^* + e^* + h^*)$ is a positive *terms of trade* effect. Area $-(g^* + h^* + e^*)$ is a *consumption distortion*. Area $-(c^* + h^* + i^*)$ is a *production distortion*. In net, the foreign country is better off if the terms of trade effect exceeds the production and consumption distortions (and vice versa). This welfare result is similar to the previous three cases. However, in this fourth case, the direction of the net effect for the foreign country depends on the relative magnitude of trade before and after the subsidy.

In summary, the four cases above provide guidance for the effects of an export subsidy on both the home country that imposes the policy and its foreign trading partners. In each large country case, the subsidy increases the welfare of producers in the home country and consumers in the foreign country. Concomitantly, the subsidy decreases the welfare of the consumers in the home country and producers in the foreign country. And, the welfare of the government decreases in the home country. If we look at the net effects, we see that the subsidy unambiguously decreases the welfare of the home country, and can increase or decrease the welfare in the foreign country. The relative magnitude of these effects depends on the extent to which the terms of trade change as a result of the subsidy. In the small country case, where world prices do not change, the effects of the subsidy apply only in the domestic country and the foreign country remains unaffected. Finally, in the case where the subsidy reverses the patterns of trade, it is possible for both the importer and exporter to be adversely affected by the export subsidy.

It is important to note, however, that all of the cases describe the comparative static effects of imposing a subsidy. They do not account for dynamic changes in behavior that occur over time. For example, it appears that the foreign country can benefit from the subsidy when consumer gains exceed producer losses in the foreign country. However, if foreign producers lose their market share in their own economies, then the country can come to rely on imports alone over time. The market structure in this situation can change particularly if there are no alternative substitutes for the good in the country's domestic market.

6.2.5   How is the burden of the export subsidy allocated across countries and agents?

The price effects of the export subsidy are allocated in different ways across countries in the cases summarized above. As discussed in the previous chapter, the allocation of the price effects is referred to as the burden of the policy. Furthermore, the welfare effects of the export subsidy are allocated in different ways within countries in the cases summarized above. This section summarizes both the *price burden* across countries and the *welfare burden* within countries that result from an export subsidy.

In comparing the cases, we find that the price burden of the subsidy is shared between the exporter and importer when the elasticities of import demand and export supply are relatively similar. This corresponds with the large exporter who can affect the world price (Case 1). For intuition, we can think of the exporter as a block of countries such as the European Union (EU) countries and the importer as a block of countries such as the North American Free Trade Area (NAFTA) countries. In such a case, the export subsidy policies of the EU would alter the world price experienced by North American countries. The absolute size of the price increase experienced by the EU countries can be similar to the absolute size of the price decrease experienced by North American countries. That is, the elasticity of the EU's export supply can be similar to the elasticity of North America's import demand. In this case, the price burden of the export subsidy is shared relatively equally. Even so, the EU would experience a relatively large welfare burden because the negative distortions associated with the subsidy are augmented by a negative terms of trade deterioration. At the same time, North America would experience a relatively small welfare burden because the negative distortions associated with the subsidy would be more than offset by the positive terms of trade improvement.

In contrast, we find that the price burden of the subsidy is experienced entirely by the exporter (who imposes the policy) when this exporter faces an infinitely elastic import demand. This corresponds with the small exporter whose supply is completely absorbed by the importer (i.e., Case 2). For intuition, we can think of the exporter as a small country such as Ghana and the importer as a block of countries such as Europe. In this case, the export subsidy policies of Ghana would likely have an economically insignificant effect on the world price of the good experienced in Europe. Additionally, Ghana would experience a relatively large welfare burden because the negative distortions associated with the subsidy would not be offset in any way. At the same time, Europe would experience no welfare burden as this block of countries is insulated from the price effects of the subsidy policies of their small trading partner.

Third, we find that the price burden of the subsidy is borne disproportionately by the importer when import demand is inelastic relative to export supply. This corresponds with the scenario where the importer is relatively price non-responsive compared to the exporter (Case 3). For intuition, we can think of the importer as a country such as Indonesia and the exporter as the rest of Asia. In such a case, Asia's export subsidy would significantly alter the price experienced by Indonesia. The absolute size of the price increase experienced in Asia would likely be small relative to the absolute size of the price decrease experienced in Indonesia. In this case, the price burden of the export subsidy is experienced primarily by Indonesia – the importer. Furthermore, Asia would experience relatively small producer and consumer distortions from the subsidy while Indonesia would experience relatively large producer and consumer distortions.

Finally, we find that the above results hold irrespectively of whether the exporter (i.e., the home country) has a comparative advantage or disadvantage in the good prior to the imposition of the export subsidy.

In summary, the price burden of the export subsidy would be shared in the large country case, when export supply and import demand have similar elasticities. The price burden of the subsidy is experienced by the exporter in the small country case, when the exporter faces an infinitely elastic import demand. And the price burden of the subsidy is borne by the importer, when the import demand is inelastic relative to the export supply. Furthermore, if we look at the welfare burden within countries, we see the following. In the exporter, the domestic consumer experiences the largest welfare losses when the country is small and faces an infinitely elastic import demand. In the importer, the domestic producer experiences the largest welfare loss when the country's import demand is inelastic relative to the export supply of its trading partner(s).

6.3 What Are the Effects of Liberalizing Export Subsidies?

The framework discussed above illustrates the effects of imposing an export subsidy for both the home and foreign countries. Alternatively, we could work the above examples backward to illustrate the effects of liberalizing export subsidies. The welfare effects of liberalizing subsidies are briefly summarized in this section.

For the country that imposes the subsidy (i.e., the home country), consumer welfare increases, producer welfare decreases, and government welfare increases. The net country welfare increases unambiguously. These patterns hold in all four cases. For the trading partner (i.e., the foreign country), subsidies have no effect when the exporter's supply is a small share of the world supply of the good.

However, in all other cases, the liberalization of subsidies in the home country affects the welfare in the foreign country. Specifically, consumer welfare decreases and producer welfare increases. However, the government experiences neither a welfare increase nor decrease, as the cost of the subsidy is paid by the government of the home country. Further, net country welfare increases in the foreign country when the benefits of eliminating the producer and consumer distortions exceed the losses from eliminating the terms of trade effect, and vice versa.

Thus, from a *sub-national perspective*, subsidy liberalization generates distributional effects. In the home country, consumers and government are better off from liberalization and producers are worse off. In the foreign country, producers are better off from liberalization and consumers are worse off. This unequal distribution of benefits from subsidy liberalization helps to explain why governments impose welfare deteriorating policies such as export subsidies. The explanation is that governments place different weight on the welfare of producers (and government) relative to consumers. As noted earlier, this issue falls under the political economy subfield in international trade.

Alternatively, from a *national perspective*, both importers and exporters can experience welfare gains when subsidies are liberalized. The home country (i.e., the exporter) is unambiguously better off from subsidy liberalization. The foreign country (i.e., the importer) experiences mixed results from subsidy liberalization. The foreign country is worse off if the terms of trade effects are large. The foreign country is unaffected if the terms of trade effects are negligible. The foreign country is better off from the liberalization of subsidies in its trading partners when the quantity of the foreign country's exports following liberalization exceeds the quantity of its imports prior to liberalization. This result can occur when subsidy liberalization reverses the patterns of trade.

Furthermore, from a *global perspective*, subsidy liberalization is rational from an economic point of view. That is, subsidy liberalization increases the welfare of all countries in aggregate. This is because the terms of trade gains experienced by one country are counterbalanced by the terms of trade losses experienced by the trading partner. What is left then are the distortions. In aggregate, liberalization eliminates the inefficiencies associated with these consumer and producer distortions. Thus, one's position on whether to liberalize or maintain subsidies is reflective of the hat that one wears. From a global perspective, subsidy liberalization is economically rational. From a producer perspective in the country that imposes the subsidy, liberalization is welfare deteriorating.

6.4   Summary Remarks

What are export subsidies, their types and purposes? An export subsidy is a payment made by the government to firms that export a specific good. The purpose of export subsidies is to provide an incentive for producers to export into foreign markets. That is, export subsidies serve to protect the domestic industry against competition with lower priced goods in the international market. Export subsidies take a variety of forms, including cash payments. Export subsidies are typically levied on an ad valorem or specific basis.

What are the effects of export subsidies? The effects of export subsidies depend on the conditions in the exporting and importing countries. We considered four cases in this chapter.

First, what are the effects of an export subsidy imposed by a large exporter? When the exporting country is large, a subsidy affects the price in the exporter and the world price of the good. Specifically, a subsidy increases the price of the good in the exporter and decreases the price of the good in the importer. As a result, agents in both the exporter and importer are affected. In the exporter, producers supply more for the international market and receive a higher subsidy-inclusive price. The export subsidy puts upward pressure on the price of the domestically consumed good such that producers are indifferent between supplying the domestic and international markets. Producers gain in terms of revenue from domestic and international sales. At the same time, consumers demand less at the higher domestic price. They lose in terms of the higher cost of the good. Consumers continue to consume only domestically produced goods, but fewer of them.

Alternatively, in the importer, producers supply less to their domestic market at the lower world price, as they must compete with the lower price imports of subsidized goods. These domestic producers in the importer lose in terms of revenue from domestic sales. And consumers in the importer demand more at the lower world price. They gain in terms of the lower cost of the good. Consumers consume more imported goods and fewer domestic goods.

The subsidy also results in welfare changes in both the exporting and importing countries. In the exporter, producer welfare increases, consumer welfare decreases, and government welfare decreases from the cost of the subsidy. The net country welfare effect includes a negative terms of trade effect and negative production and consumption distortions. The exporting country is unambiguously worse off as a result of the subsidy. Alternatively, in the importer, the producer's welfare decreases, consumer's welfare increases, and government welfare does not change. The net country welfare effect includes a positive terms of trade effect and negative production and consumption distortions. The importing country is better off as a result of the subsidy because the positive terms of trade improvement exceeds the distortions.

Second, what are the effects of an export subsidy imposed by a small exporter? When the exporter is small, the subsidy increases the price in the exporter but does *not* affect the world price of the good. As a result, agents in the exporter are affected; however, agents in the importer are unaffected. In the exporter, producers supply more at the subsidy inclusive price. They gain from the subsidy in terms of revenues from combined domestic and international sales of the good. At the same time, consumers demand less at the higher subsidy inclusive price. They lose from the subsidy in terms of the higher cost of the good. Consumers continue to consume only domestically produced goods, but fewer of them.

Alternatively, in the importer, producer and consumers do not alter the quantity of the supply and demand in any economically significant way. Given the size of the international market, the importer is insulated from the policy decisions of the small exporter.

The subsidy results in welfare changes in the exporter but not in the importer. In the exporter, producer welfare increases, consumer welfare decreases, and government welfare decreases from the cost of the subsidy. The net country effect includes a negative production and consumption distortion. It does not include a positive terms of trade effect. This is because the small country has no effect on the world price of its exported good. The exporter is unambiguously worse off as a result of the subsidy. Alternatively, in the importer, the welfare of all agents and the country in net remains unchanged. Consumers in the importer absorb the traded goods at the original world prices. The importer is indifferent to the subsidy policies of the small exporting country.

Third, what are the effects of an export subsidy when export supply is elastic relative to import demand? When the exporter faces a relatively inelastic import demand for a traded good, a subsidy affects the price in the exporter and importer differently. Specifically, a subsidy increases the price of the good in the exporter by a relatively small amount and decreases the world price of the good seen by the importer by a relatively large amount. As a result, agents in the importer are affected relatively more than agents in the exporter.

In the exporter, producers supply more at a higher subsidy inclusive price. They gain in terms of revenue from the combined domestic and international sales. At the same time, consumers demand less at the higher domestic price. They lose in terms of the higher cost of the good. However, these producer gains and consumer losses are relatively small. Alternatively, in the importer, producers supply less to their domestic market at the lower world price. They lose in terms of revenue from domestic sales of the good. And consumers demand more at the lower world price. Consumers now consume more imported goods and fewer domestically produced goods. They gain from the subsidy in terms of the lower cost of the good. These changes in the importer are relatively large.

The subsidy also results in welfare changes. In the exporter, producer welfare increases, consumer welfare decreases, and government welfare decreases from the subsidy cost. The net country welfare effect includes a negative terms of trade effect and negative production and consumption distortions. The exporter is unambiguously worse off as a result of the subsidy. However, these welfare effects for the exporter are relatively small. Alternatively, in the importer, producer welfare decreases, consumer welfare increases, and government welfare does not change. The net country welfare effects include a positive terms of trade effect and negative production and consumption distortions. The importing country is better off as a result of the subsidy because the positive terms of trade improvement exceeds the distortions. These welfare effects for the importer are relatively large.

Fourth, what are the effects of an export subsidy imposed by large country with a comparative disadvantage? In the three cases of subsidies summarized above, we assumed that the country that imposes the subsidy has a comparative advantage in the good prior to adopting the subsidy. That is, the country is already an exporter of the good prior to the subsidy policy. In these cases, the subsidy serves to increase the volume of the exports above the free trade levels. In reality, we cannot observe whether a country has a comparative advantage or disadvantage in the absence of subsidies. However, the adoption of a protectionist policy (such as export subsidies) suggests that in the absence of the policy, the country would have difficulty competing with lower priced goods in the international market. Thus, we considered a fourth case where a large country with a comparative disadvantage adopts an export subsidy. The results of this case mirror those of the previous cases. The primary difference is that the home country is an importer prior to the policy and an exporter after the policy. Similarly, the foreign country is an exporter prior to the policy and an importer after the policy. Furthermore, in this case it is possible for both the importer and exporter to be adversely affected by the export subsidy which reverses the patterns of trade.

How is the burden of the export subsidy allocated across countries and agents? The price effect of the subsidy is allocated in different ways across countries in the cases above. The price effects of the subsidy are shared between the exporter and importer when the elasticities of export supply and import demand are relatively similar. This corresponds with the large exporter who can affect the world price, but faces an importer who is similarly price responsive (i.e., Case 1). However, even when the price effects are shared, the welfare effects are not shared equally. The welfare effects are unambiguously negative for the exporter and are positive for the importer. In contrast, the price effects of the subsidy are experienced entirely by the exporter when the exporter faces an infinitely elastic import demand. This corresponds with the small exporter whose supply is completely absorbed by the importer (i.e., Case 2). In this case, the welfare effects for the exporter are unambiguously negative and relatively large, while the welfare effects for the importer are economically insignificant. Finally, the price effects of the subsidy are borne disproportionately by the importer when the import demand is inelastic compared with the export supply. This corresponds with the scenario in which the importer is relatively price non-responsive (i.e., Case 3). In this case, the negative terms of trade effect for the exporter is small, while the positive terms of trade effect for the importer is large.

What are the effects of liberalizing export subsidies? The effects of subsidy liberalization are the mirror opposites of the effects of adopting subsidies. The magnitude of these effects depends on the relative elasticities of import demand and export supply. From a national perspective, both exporters and importers can experience welfare gains when subsidies are liberalized. Exporters are unambiguously better off from subsidy liberalization. In contrast, importers can be better off or worse off from liberalization. Importers can be better off from liberalization in the case where liberalization of subsidies reverses the patterns of trade. In this case, the importer becomes an exporter of the good after liberalization. From a subnational perspective, subsidy liberalization generates distributional effects. In exporters, consumers and government are better off from subsidy liberalization, and producers are worse off. In importers, producers are better off and consumers are worse off. From a global perspective, subsidy liberalization increases the welfare of all countries in aggregate. Thus, alternative positions on whether to liberalize subsidies reflect the various perspectives. In the country with subsidies in place, consumers have an incentive to support liberalization while producers have an incentive to resist liberalization.

Applied Problems

6.1   Examine the effects of liberalizing export subsidies on prices, quantities supplied, quantities demanded, and trade in both importers and exporters. Make an assumption about whether your countries can affect the world price.

6.2   Use your knowledge of the welfare effects of export subsidies to explain why policy makers interested in maximizing national and world welfare support free trade while select agents within countries (e.g., consumers, government, or producers) may not support free trade.

6.3   Assume that you are a producer advocate with an interest in maximizing producer welfare. Furthermore, assume that your advocacy organization works to maximize producer welfare from a global perspective. Use your knowledge of welfare effects to explain whether your organization would support the liberalization of export subsidies worldwide.

6.4   Evaluate the effects of reducing the export subsidies in all countries on world welfare of consumers, producers and governments. Consider these effects for both the small and large country cases.

6.5   Examine the effects of an export subsidy on the welfare of the importer. What conclusions can you draw about the interests of the importer in the liberalization of its trading partner's policies?

6.6   Consider the scenario in which the countries of the North eliminate export subsidies. Examine the effects of this policy change on the welfare of the North and South. Assume that the export supply of the North is elastic relative to the import demand of the South.

6.7   Assume that the Dominican Republic has a comparative advantage in milk and the EU countries have a comparative disadvantage in milk. Further, assume that the EU countries impose a substantial export subsidy on milk that reverses the pattern of trade between the EU and Dominican Republic. Examine the effects of this export subsidy on producers and consumers in the Dominican Republic and in the EU.

6.8   Assume that South Africa has a comparative advantage in sugar and the EU countries have a comparative disadvantage in sugar. Assume that the supply and demand for sugar in the EU is elastic relative to the supply and demand for sugar in South Africa. Furthermore, assume that the EU is large enough to affect the world price of sugar. Assume that the EU countries impose a substantial export subsidy on sugar that reverses the pattern of trade between the EU and South Africa. Examine the effects of the export subsidy on prices in the EU and South Africa.

Further Reading

Anderson, K. Ed. 2008. *Distortions to Agricultural Incentives: Global Perspectives.* London: Palgrave Macmillan.

Anderson, K., W. Martin, and D. Van der Mensbrugghe. 2006. Distortions to world trade: impacts on agricultural markets and farm incomes. *Review of Agricultural Economics* 28 (2): 168–194.

Anderson, K., and E. Valenzuela. 2007. Do global trade distortions still harm developing country farmers? *Review of World Economics* 143 (1): 108–139.

Brander, James A and Barbara J. Spencer. 1985. Export subsidies and international market share rivalry. *Journal of International Economics* 16: 83–100.

Collie, David. 1991. Export subsidies and countervailing tariffs. *Journal of International Economics* 31 (November): 309–324.

Coleman, William, Wyn Grant, and Timothy Josling. 2004. *Agriculture in the New Global Economy.* Cheltenham, UK: Edward Elgar.

Haberler, G. 1958. *Trends in International Trade: A Report by a Panel of Experts.* Geneva: GATT.

Josling, Timothy E., Stefan Tangermann, and Thorald K. Warley. 1996. *Agriculture in the GATT.* Basingstoke, UK: Macmillan.

Krueger, Anne O., M. Schiff, and A. Valdes. 1988. Agricultural incentives in developing countries: measuring the effect of sectoral and economywide policies. *World Bank Economic Review* 2 (3): 255–272.

Krueger, Anne O., M. Schiff, and A. Valdes. 1991. *The Political Economy of Agricultural Pricing Policy.* Baltimore: Johns Hopkins University Press for the World Bank.

Lindert, P. 1991. Historical patterns of agricultural protection. In *Agriculture and the State* (ed. P. Timmer). Ithaca: Cornell University Press.

Organisation for Economic Co-operation and Development (OECD). 2001. *The Uruguay Round Agreement on Agriculture: An Evaluation of its Implementation in OECD Countries.* Paris: OECD.

Organisation for Economic Co-operation and Development (OECD). 2006. *Producer Support Estimates* and *Consumer Support Estimates,* OECD Database 1986–2004. Paris: OECD.

Sumner, Daniel A. and Stefan Tangermann. 2002. International trade policy and negotiations. In *Handbook of Agricultural Economics,* vol. 2B, *Agricultural and Food Policy* (eds Bruce L. Gardner and Gordon C. Rausser), Amsterdam, Netherlands: North Holland Press, pp. 1999–2055.

World Trade Organization (WTO). 1996. *The Results of the Uruguay Round of Multilateral Trade Negotiations: The Legal Texts.* Geneva: WTO.

World Trade Organization (WTO). 2000. *Export Subsidies.* Background Paper by the Secretariat. G/AG/NG/S/5 (11 May). Geneva: WTO.

Note

1. This comparative disadvantage may be explained by any of the models detailed in Part One of this book.

7

Quantitative Restrictions

7.1   What Are Quantitative Restrictions, Their Types and Purpose?

Quantitative restrictions are limitations on the amount of a good that is either exported from or imported into a country during a specific period of time, typically a year. Quantitative restrictions differ from tariffs and export subsidies, which alter the price of a good via a positive or negative tax. In contrast, quantitative restrictions establish a maximum total value or quantity of a good that is traded. Such quantitative restrictions can be adopted to restrict trade between specific trading partners, or to restrict trade globally.

Types of quantitative restrictions include import quotas, export quotas, voluntary export restraints, and bans. An *import quota* is a restriction on the quantity of a good imported. Import quotas are imposed by the importing country. These quotas are usually imposed for a pre-specified period of time. Typically, the government of the importing country issues licenses or permits among importing firms. The distribution of these licenses is often determined by the amounts that these importing firms imported in a selected base year, although other methods have also been applied. An example of the use of import quotas is the US restrictions on imports of petroleum during the 1960s and early 1970s.

An *export quota* is a restriction on the quantity of a good exported. Export quotas are imposed by the exporting country for a specified period of time. Typically, the government of the exporting country issues licenses or permits among exporting firms. An example of the use of export quotas by a group of countries is the restrictions on exports of petroleum by the Organization of the Petroleum Exporting Countries (OPEC).

Global Trade Policy: Questions and Answers, First Edition. Pamela J. Smith.
© 2014 John Wiley & Sons, Inc. Published 2014 by John Wiley & Sons, Inc.

A *voluntary export restraint* (VER) is an export quota that is imposed at the request of the importing country; that is, a VER is voluntarily applied by the exporting country on shipments of a particular good to a particular importing country at that country's request. VERs are typically the result of negotiations between the exporting and importing countries in cases where the importer wants to protect a domestic industry but cannot do so without violating an existing international trade agreement. In such cases, the exporter may voluntarily agree to restrict exports to this country in order to prevent future trade retaliation by the importer. An example of the use of VERs is Japan's restrictions on exports of automobiles to the United States in the 1980s. An example of a VER that includes multiple countries is the Multi-Fiber Arrangement (MFA), which limited textile exports from 22 countries until 2005. This broader type of VER is referred to as an orderly marketing agreement.

A *ban* or *embargo* is the extreme version of these policies, where either the exporter or importer restricts the quantity of trade in a good to zero. Bans are typically applied to a specific good or specific country. Examples of specific goods that have been banned include products originating from endangered species, weapons, and radioactive materials. Examples of the use of bans on specific countries include the United Nations embargo on trade with South Africa during apartheid.

The purpose or goal of each of these types of quantitative restrictions is somewhat distinct. The purpose of *import quotas* is to protect domestic producers from import competition (i.e., the need to compete with lower priced imports) and thereby encourage domestic production. In addition to this purpose, import quotas have also been used as a means to address the balance of payments problems of countries. That is, import quotas have been used to restrict the outflow of international reserves from countries with large balance of payments deficits.

The purpose of *export quotas* is to restrict the supply of the good in the international market. Such restrictions serve to stabilize and/or sustain the world price of the good at a high level, such as in the case of restricted OPEC exports of petroleum. Export quotas have also been used to retain greater supplies of a product for domestic use and/or to keep the domestic prices of these goods below the world market prices.

In contrast, the purpose of *voluntary export restraints* is typically to forestall an official protective action (i.e., retaliation) by an importing country. To preempt retaliation, the exporting country agrees voluntarily to restrict its exports to the particular importer in a specific good. VERs allow the importing countries to protect their domestic industries without themselves imposing policy restrictions that may be prohibited under existing international trade agreements.

Quantitative restrictions create a rent associated with the traded good. The *rent* is the product of the markup in the price of the restricted good and the quantity of the good traded. This rent goes to the holder of the license rights to the traded good. The holder of the license rights purchases the good at the lower world price and then sells the good at the higher price that results from restricting the quantity of the good traded. This markup in price applies to each unit of the good that is traded. The holders of the license rights may be domestic firms, foreign firms, or governments. The nationality of the license holders is important because it affects which country benefits from the rents. That is, the rents to license holders are included in the calculation of the national welfare effects of the policy. In the case of import quotas, the licenses are allocated by the governments of importers, while in the case of export quotas and voluntary export restraints, the licenses are allocated by the governments of exporters.

The methods that have been used to allocate the rights to import or export under a quota system are many. These methods include: allocations on a first-come, first-served basis; allocations based on trade shares during a specified base year; allocations in proportion to the domestic production of firms; allocations determined by political decisions; and the auctioning of quotas to the highest bidders, among others. Of these methods, the trade shares approach has been prominent. Under this method, the shares of the quota are allocated among traders based on their volumes of trade in a previous base period. For example, if a firm imported 8% of the total imports of the good in the base period, then this firm would be allocated 8% of imports under the import quota.

In practice, the use of quotas has decreased over time as trade has been liberalized under the GATT and WTO agreements. However, understanding quantitative restrictions remains relevant today as non-tariff trade instruments (including quantitative restrictions) are converted into tariffs through the process known as tariffication. This conversion process sometimes makes use of a policy instrument referred to as the *tariff rate quota* (TRQ). TRQs set quantitative restrictions on imports that can enter a country at a low tariff rate. Imports above the restricted amount (i.e., above the quota) are subject to a higher tariff rate. If this higher tariff rate is sufficiently high, then the TRQ functions just like an import quota. (See Chapter 8 for further discussion.) This hybrid policy instrument is used to harmonize external trade barriers in regional trade agreements, to implement preferences for developing countries, and to provide a system of safeguards against import surges. It is also used to facilitate the process of converting quotas and bans into tariffs, particularly important in the agricultural sector.

In this chapter, we explore the effects of quantitative restrictions under a variety of conditions. We consider three core questions: (1) What are the effects of an import quota imposed by a large importer? (2) What are the effects of an export quota or voluntary export restriction imposed by a large exporter? (3) What are the effects of a ban imposed between two large countries? In answering each of these questions, we consider the welfare effects that characterize the gains and losses associated with quantitative restrictions; that is, we consider who gains and who loses from the adoption of quantitative restrictions.

7.2   What Are the Effects of Quantitative Restrictions?

The effects of quantitative restrictions can be viewed from multiple perspectives including that of the nation (importer and exporter), subnational agents (consumers, producers, and governments), and globally.

The effects of *quantitative restrictions* on the *importing country* are quite intuitive. The price of the imported good goes up, as the quantity of the good in the domestic market is now restricted. In a competitive market, the price of the domestically produced good will equate with the higher price of the restricted imports. Second, the quantity of the good supplied domestically increases as suppliers now compete against higher priced imports. At the same time, the quantity of the good demanded in the importing country decreases. This is because the prices of both the domestically produced good and the imported good are higher as a result of the quantitative restriction.

The quantitative restriction also affects welfare in the importing country. Quantitative restrictions affect the welfare of consumers, producers and the government differently. Specifically, the welfare of domestic producers increases, because both the quantity of the good supplied increases and the price received increases. In contrast, the welfare of consumers decreases, because the quantity of the good demanded decreases and the price paid increases. And, the welfare of the government is unchanged (in economic terms) as there is no revenue or cost associated with the quota. If we sum together the welfare effects of these three agents, we can draw conclusions about the net welfare effects of the quantitative restriction for the importing country. We will show in the section below that the net welfare of the importing country can be either positive or negative as a result of a restriction. The direction of the net welfare effects depends on the ability of the importer to influence the price in the world market. It also depends on the nationality of the holders of the licenses for rights to trade the restricted good. In the case of the import quota, these rents tend to go to firms in the importing country. In the case of the export quota or VER, these rents tend to go to firms in the exporting country. In the case of bans, the rents are zero as the good is not traded.

The effects of a quantitative restriction on the *exporting country* are more opaque. The price of the good in the exporting country (or world price) may either decrease or remain unchanged. The world price will decrease if either the exporter or importer is large in terms of its share of the world supply or demand for the good. In the large country case, the restriction causes the quantity of the good supplied/demanded in the world market to decrease and thus the world price decreases. Consequently, the quantity of the good supplied in the exporting country decreases as suppliers now receive a lower world price for their exports. At the same time, the quantity of the good demanded in the exporting country increases, because consumers now pay a lower world price for the good in their domestic market.

In this large country case, the quantitative restriction also affects welfare in the *exporting country*. Specifically, the welfare of domestic producers decreases, because both the quantity of the good supplied decreases and the price received decreases. In contrast, the welfare of consumers in the exporting country increases, because the quantity of the good demanded increases and the price paid decreases. And, the welfare of the government is unchanged in the exporting country (in economic terms). If we sum together the welfare effects of these three agents, we can draw conclusions about the net welfare effects of the restriction for the exporting country. We will show in the section below that the direction of the net welfare effects depends on the ability of the trading partners to influence the world price of the good. It also depends on the nationality of the holders of the licenses for rights to trade the restricted good.

Alternatively, if the countries imposing the restriction are small in terms of their supply and/or demand shares of the world market for the good, then the world price will remain unchanged. For example, if the country imposing the import quota is small in terms of its share of world demand, the price of the good will remain unchanged in the exporting countries. And, if the country imposing an export quota is small in terms of its share of world supply, the price of the good will remain unchanged in the importing country. Similarly, consumer and producer welfare will remain unchanged in the partner country.

Below, we present a simple partial equilibrium model to illustrate the effects of quantitative restrictions. We consider three cases. The first case assumes that a large country imposes an import quota. The second case assumes that a large country imposes an export quota or VER. The third case assumes that a complete ban on trade is imposed between two large countries. In each case, a "large country" is one that can influence the world price of the good. We do not consider the "small country" case here, but encourage the reader to do this on their own.

The assumptions of the simple partial equilibrium model are as follows. There are two countries – home and foreign. There is one good. This good is subject to a quantitative restriction. The home country is the importer of the good. The foreign country is the exporter of the good.

7.2.1 Case 1: What are the effects of an import quota imposed by a large importer?

In this section we consider the case where the import quota is imposed by a large country. Figure 7.1 shows the markets for the good in this large country case. Panel (a) shows the domestic supply (S) and demand (D) for the good in the home country – the importer. The equilibrium price of the good in the home country is the same as its autarky price (P_a). This is the price of the good when there is no trade. This autarky price is relatively high, reflecting the assumption that the home country has a comparative disadvantage in the good. In contrast, Panel (c) shows the domestic supply (S^*) and demand (D^*) for the good in the foreign country – the exporter. Again, the equilibrium price of the good in this foreign country is the same as its autarky price. This autarky price is relatively low, reflecting the assumption that the foreign country has a comparative advantage in the good.

Panel (b) then shows the supply and demand in the world market. This is the market where the home and foreign countries trade. In this middle panel, the demand is the *import demand* of the home country (D^m). The import demand in Panel (b) is derived from the behavior of the home country in Panel (a). For

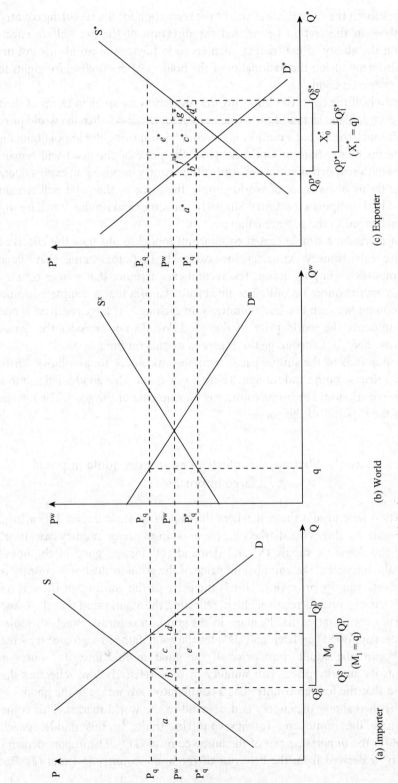

Figure 7.1 Quantitative restrictions – imposed by a large country.

example, consider the home country's behavior at all possible world prices. For world prices at or above the home country's autarky price, the home country will not demand imports. Rather, its demand is satisfied by its domestic supply. However, for world prices below its autarky price, the home country will demand imports in the amount of its *excess demand*.

In contrast, the supply in the world market in Panel (b) is the *export supply* (S^x). The export supply is derived from the behavior of the foreign country in Panel (c). For example, consider the foreign country's behavior at all possible world prices. For world prices at or below its autarky price, the foreign country will not supply exports. Rather, its supply is satisfied by domestic demand. However, for prices above its autarky price, the foreign country will supply exports in the amount of its *excess supply*.

The intersection of import demand and export supply in Panel (b) determines the equilibrium world price (P^w). The equilibrium world price is where the quantity of import demand by the home country equates with the quantity of export supply by the foreign country. At this equilibrium world price, the quantity of imports (M_0) in Panel (a) equates with the quantity of exports (X_0^*) in Panel (c). The quantity of imports in Panel (a) is the excess of demand (Q_0^D) over supply (Q_0^D) at the world price. Similarly, the quantity of exports in Panel (c) is the excess of supply (Q_0^{S*}) over demand (Q_0^{S*}) at the world price.

We can now introduce an import quota into this simple framework in Panel (b) of Figure 7.1. An import quota essentially creates a "quantity limit" on the good supplied and demanded in the international market. The size of the quota is the horizontal distance (q) in Panel (b). When we impose a quota in the home country, the price of the good increases from the world price (P^w) to a higher price (P_q) on the restricted good. This corresponds with a movement along the import demand curve and a decrease in the quantity of imports demanded by the importing country. From the exporter's point of view, the price of the good decreases from the world price (P^w) to the new lower price after the quota is in place (P_q^*). This corresponds with a movement along the export supply curve and a decrease in the quantity of exports supplied by the exporting country. In this case, the price effect of the quota is shared by both the importing and exporting countries. This price sharing occurs even though the importing country alone imposes the quota. The sharing of the price effect occurs because the importing country can affect the world price.

The import quota also affects the quantities of the good supplied, demanded and traded in both the home and foreign countries (in Panels (a) and (c), respectively). The home country experiences an increase in the quantity supplied domestically (Q_0^S to Q_1^S) and a decrease in the quantity demanded domestically (Q_0^D to Q_1^D). In contrast, the foreign country experiences a decrease in the quantity supplied domestically (Q_0^{S*} to Q_1^{S*}) and an increase in the quantity demanded domestically (Q_0^{D*} to Q_1^{D*}). Consequently, both countries experience a decrease in trade. The home country's imports decrease (M_0 to M_1) and the foreign country's exports decrease (X_0^* to X_1^*) to the quantity q.

Intuitively, the effects of an import quota on prices and quantities tell us about the impact on both producers and consumers. At home, producers are supplying more in their domestic market at a higher price. They have gained from the quota in terms of revenue from sales of the good. At home, consumers are demanding less at a higher price. They have lost from the quota in terms of the cost of the good. Alternatively, in the foreign country, producers are supplying less at a lower price. They have lost. And foreign consumers are demanding more and a lower price. They have gained. Further, the mix of consumption of domestic and traded goods changes as a result of the quota. Consumers in the home country now consume more domestically produced goods and fewer imports. Consumers in the foreign market continue to consume only domestically produced goods, but more of them.

The welfare effects of the quota for the home and foreign countries can also be seen in Figure 7.1 and are summarized in Table 7.1 (Case 1). Instead of illustrating

Table 7.1 Welfare effects of quantitative restrictions.

Case 1 – Import quota

Economic agent	Welfare effects (importer/home)	Welfare effects (exporter/foreign)
Producer	$+a$	$-(a^* + b^* + c^* + f^* + g^*)$
Consumer	$-(a + b + c + d)$	$+(a^* + b^*)$
License holders	$+(c + e)$	0
Country	$+e - (b + d)$	$-(c^* + f^* + g^*)$
Country (direction)	Negative or positive	Negative

Case 2 – VER/export quota

Economic agent	Welfare effects (importer/home)	Welfare effects (exporter/foreign)
Producer	$+a$	$-(a^* + b^* + c^* + f^* + g^*)$
Consumer	$-(a + b + c + d)$	$+(a^* + b^*)$
Licence holders	0	$+(c^* + e^*)$
Country	$-(b + c + d)$	$+e^* - (f^* + g^*)$
Country (direction)	Negative	Negative or positive

Case 3 – Ban

Economic agent	Welfare effects (importer/home)	Welfare effects (exporter/foreign)
Producer	$+a$	$-(a^* + b^* + c^* + d^*)$
Consumer	$-(a + b + c)$	$+(a^* + b^*)$
Country	$-(b + c)$	$-(c^* + d^*)$
Country (direction)	Negative	Negative

Notes: Case 1 assumes that import quota licenses are held by domestic agents of the importer. Case 2 assumes that export quota licences are held by domestic agents of the exporter.

total welfare before and after the quota is imposed, we simply illustrate the changes in welfare that result from the quota in the figure. Panel (a) shows the welfare effects for the importing country. As shown, the producer's welfare increases by the surplus amount $+(a)$ as a result of the quota. The consumer's welfare decreases by the surplus amount $-(a + b + c + d)$. Furthermore, the welfare of license holders increases by the amount $+(c + e)$. This quota rent is the quantity of the quota times the price effect from the quota. It is the product of the quantity imported (horizontally) and the price markup (vertically). That is, the quota rent is $(M_0 \times (P_q - P_q^*))$.

The net country welfare then is the sum of the producer, consumer, and license holder welfare changes. If we assume that the license holders to the quota rents are firms or the government of the importer, then we can include the quota rent in our calculation of the home country's welfare. Adding these effects together, we get $+(e) - (b + d)$. Area $+(e)$ is a positive *net transfer* of quota rents from the exporting country to the importing country. This transfer is net of the terms of trade effect. Areas $-(b + d)$ are deadweight losses incurred by producers and consumers. Specifically, area $-(b)$ is a *production distortion* and area $-(d)$ is a *consumption distortion*. In net, the importing country is worse off as a result of the quota if the distortions exceed the net transfer of quota rents, and vice versa.

Panel (c) shows the welfare effects of the quota for the exporting country. As shown, the producer's welfare decreases by the surplus amount $-(a^* + b^* + c^* + f^* + g^*)$ as a result of the quota. The consumer's welfare increases by the surplus amount $+(a^* + b^*)$. The net country welfare then is the sum of the producer and consumer welfare changes. Adding these effects together we get $-(c^* + f^* + g^*)$. Area $-(c)^*$ is a *terms of trade* effect. Areas $-(f^* + g^*)$ are deadweight losses incurred by consumers and producers. Area $-(f^*)$ is a *consumption distortion* and area $-(g^*)$ is a *production distortion*. In net, the exporting country is unambiguously worse off as a result of the quota.

7.2.2 Case 2: What are the effects of an export quota (or voluntary export restriction) imposed by a large exporter?

In this section we consider the case where the *export quota* or *VER* is imposed by a large country. This case is nearly identical to the preceding one. The prominent difference is that the exporter, rather than the importer, imposes the restriction. The other prominent difference is that the license holders to the rents tend to be the firms or government of the exporting country, rather than the importing country. Thus, the welfare effects of the policy are altered by the nationality of the license holders.

Figure 7.1 can be used again to illustrate the markets for the good in the large country case. We can introduce an export quota or VER into this simple framework in Panel (b) of Figure 7.1. This export restriction essentially creates a "quantity limit" on the good supplied and demanded in the international market in the same way as the import quota. The size of the export quota or VER is the horizontal distance q in Panel (b). All of the price and quantity effects of the previous case apply as a result of this export restriction, so we do not repeat them here.

The welfare effects of the export quota or VER for the home and foreign countries can also be seen in Figure 7.1 and are summarized in Table 7.1 (Case 2). Panel (a) of Figure 1 shows the welfare effects for the importing country. As shown, the producer's welfare increases by the surplus amount $+(a)$ as a result of the export quota or VER. The consumer's welfare decreases by the surplus amount $-(a + b + c + d)$. The net country welfare then is the sum of the producer, consumer, and license holder welfare changes. If we assume that the license holders to the rents are foreign firms or the government of the exporter, then we cannot include the rent in our calculation of the home country's welfare. Rather, the net welfare effect for the home country is $-(b + d + c)$. Area $-(c)$ is a welfare transfer from the importing country to the exporting country. Areas $-(b + d)$ are deadweight losses incurred by producers and consumers. Area $-(b)$ is a *production distortion* and area $-(d)$ is a *consumption distortion*. In net, the importing country is unambiguously worse off as a result of the export quota or VER.

Panel (c) shows the welfare effects of the export quota or VER for the exporting country. As shown, the producer's welfare decreases by the surplus amount $-(a^* + b^* + c^* + f^* + g^*)$ as a result of the restriction. The consumer's welfare increases by the surplus amount $+(a^* + b^*)$. Assuming that license holders are of foreign nationality, then the rents are $+(c^* + e^*)$. The net country welfare then is the sum of the producer, consumer, and license holder welfare changes. Adding these effects together, we get $+(e^*) - (f^* + g^*)$. Area $+(e^*)$ is a *net transfer* of license rents from the importer to the exporter. This transfer is net of the terms of trade effect. Areas $-(f^* + g^*)$ are deadweight losses incurred by consumers and producers. Area $-(f^*)$ is a *consumption distortion* and area $-(g^*)$ is a *production distortion*. As shown, the exporting country is worse off as a result of the restriction if the distortions exceed the net transfer from the importer to the exporter, and vice versa.

7.2.3   Case 3: What are the effects of a ban imposed between two large countries?

In this section, we consider the case where a ban or embargo is imposed between two large countries. Figure 7.2 shows the markets for the good in this large country case.

As before, the intersection of import demand and export supply in Panel (b) determines the equilibrium world price (P^w). The equilibrium world price is where the quantity of import demand by the home country equates with the quantity of export supply by the foreign country. At this equilibrium world price, the quantity of imports (M_0) in Panel (a) equates with the quantity of exports (X_0^*) in Panel (c). The quantity of imports in Panel (a) is the excess of demand (Q_0^D) over supply (Q_0^S) at the world price. Similarly, the quantity of exports in Panel (c) is the excess of supply (Q_0^{S*}) over demand (Q_0^{D*}) at the world price.

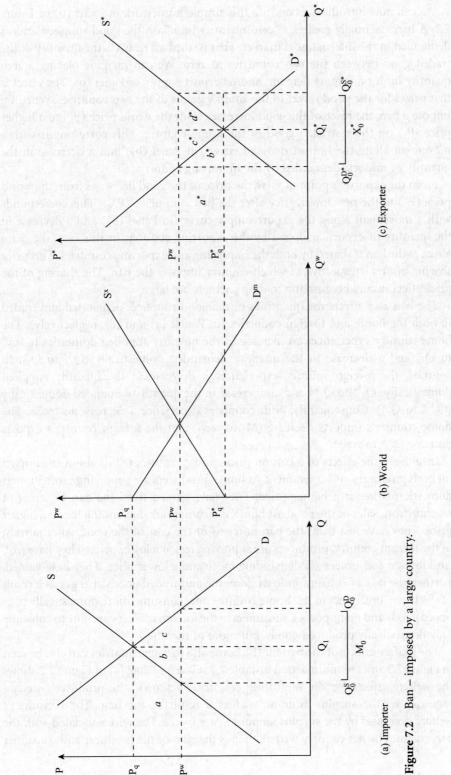

Figure 7.2 Ban – imposed by a large country.

(a) Importer

(b) World

(c) Exporter

We can now introduce a ban into this simple framework in Panel (b) of Figure 7.2. A ban essentially creates a "zero quantity limit" on the good supplied and/or demanded in the international market. That is, the ban restricts the quantity of the traded good between the two countries to zero. We can imagine placing a zero quantity limit on import demand and/or export supply in Panel (b). The effect is that prices for the good revert to the autarky prices of the two countries. When we impose a ban, the price of the good increases from the world price (P^w) to a higher price (P_q) on the restricted good in the home country. This corresponds with a movement along the import demand curve (in Panel (b)) and a decrease in the quantity of imports demanded by the importing country.

From the exporter's point of view, the price of the good decreases from the world price (P^w) to the new lower price after the ban is in place (P^*_q). This corresponds with a movement along the export supply curve (in Panel (b)) and a decrease in the quantity of exports supplied by the exporting country. In this case, the price effect of the ban is shared by both the importing and exporting countries. This price sharing occurs irrespective of which country imposes the ban. The sharing of the price effect occurs because the trading partners are large.

The ban also affects the quantities of the good supplied, demanded and traded in both the home and foreign countries (in Panels (a) and (c), respectively). The home country experiences an increase in the quantity supplied domestically (Q_0^S to Q_1) and a decrease in the quantity demanded domestically (Q_0^D to Q_1). In contrast, the foreign country experiences a decrease in the quantity supplied domestically (Q_0^{S*} to Q_1^*) and an increase in the quantity demanded domestically (Q_0^{D*} to Q_1^*). Consequently, both countries experience a decrease in trade. The home country's imports decrease (M_0 to zero) and the foreign country's exports decrease (X_0^* to zero).

Intuitively, the effects of a ban on prices and quantities tell us about the impact on both producers and consumers. At home, producers are supplying more in their domestic market at a higher price. They have gained from the ban in terms of revenue from sales of the good. At home, consumers are demanding less at a higher price. They have lost the ban in terms of the cost of the good. Alternatively, in the foreign country, producers are supplying less at a lower price. They have lost. And foreign consumers are demanding more and a lower price. They have gained. Further, the mix of consumption of domestic and traded goods changes as a result of the ban. Consumers in the home country now consume more domestically produced goods and no imports. Consumers in the foreign market continue to consume only domestically produced goods, but more of them.

The welfare effects of the ban for the home and foreign countries can also be seen in Figure 7.2 and are summarized in Table 7.1 (Case 3). Panel (a) of Figure 7.2 shows the welfare effects for the importing country. As shown, the producer's welfare increases by the surplus amount $+(a)$ as a result of the ban. The consumer's welfare decreases by the surplus amount $-(a + b + c)$. The rent associated with the ban is zero. The net country welfare then is the sum of the producer and consumer welfare changes. Adding these effects together we get $-(b + c)$. These areas are deadweight losses incurred by producers and consumers. Area $-(b)$ is a *production distortion* and area $-(c)$ is a *consumption distortion*. In net, the importing country is unambiguously worse off as a result of the ban.

Panel (c) shows the welfare effects of the ban for the exporting country. As shown, the producer's welfare decreases by the surplus amount $-(a^* + b^* + c^* + d^*)$ as a result of a ban. The consumer's welfare increases by the surplus amount $+(a^* + b^*)$. The net country welfare then is the sum of the producer and consumer welfare changes. Adding these effects together we get $-(c^* + d^*)$, where area $-(d^*)$ is a *consumption distortion* and area $-(d^*)$ is a *production distortion*. In net, the exporting country is unambiguously worse off as a result of the ban.

7.3 Summary Remarks

What are quantitative restrictions, their types and purpose? Quantitative restrictions are limitations on the amount of a good that is either exported from or imported into a country. Quantitative restrictions include import quotas, export quotas, voluntary export restraints, and bans. An import quota is a restriction imposed by the importer on the quantity of a good imported. The purpose of this policy is to restrict the purchase of goods from foreign origins in order to protect domestic producers. An export quota is a restriction imposed by the exporter on the quantity of a good exported. The primary purpose of this policy is to restrict the supply of the good in the international market in order to stabilize the world price of the good. A voluntary export restraint is a variant of the export quota, where the policy is imposed by the exporter at the request of the importer. The purpose of this policy is to forestall an official protective action by the importer. A *ban* or *embargo* is the extreme version of these policies, where either the exporter or importer restricts the quantity of trade in a good to zero. Quantitative restrictions create a rent associated with the traded good. The rent is the product of the markup in the price of the restricted good and the quantity of the good traded. This rent goes to the holder of the license rights to the traded good. In the case of a ban or embargo, the rent is zero.

What are the effects of quantitative restrictions? The effects of quantitative restrictions depend on the conditions in the importing and exporting countries. They also depend on the type of quantitative restriction. We considered three cases in this chapter. The first was the case of an import quota imposed by a large country that can affect the world price of the good. The second was the case of an export quota or VER imposed by a large country that can affect the world price of the good. The third was the case of a complete ban or embargo on trade imposed between two large countries. Below, we summarize the effects of the policies in each case.

First, what are the effects of an import quota imposed by a large importer? When the importing country is large, an import quota affects the price in the importing country and the world price of the good. Specifically, an import quota increases the price of the good in the importer and decreases the price of the good in the exporter. As a result, agents in both the importer and exporter are affected. In the importing country, producers supply more in their domestic market at a higher quota-induced price. They have gained from the import quota in terms of revenue from domestic sales of the good. At the same time, consumers demand less at the higher quota-induced price. They have lost from the quota in terms of the higher cost of the good. Alternatively, in the exporting country, producers supply less to the international market at a lower world price. They have lost from the quota in terms of revenue from international sales of the good. And consumers demand more at the lower world price. They have gained from the quota in terms of the lower cost of the good. Furthermore, the mix of consumption of domestic and traded goods changes as a result of the quota. Consumers in the importing country now consume more domestically produced goods and fewer imports. Consumers in the exporting country continue to consume only domestically produced goods, but more of them.

The import quota also results in welfare changes in both the importing and exporting countries. In the importer, the producer's welfare increases, the consumer's welfare decreases, and the license holder captures a rent. If we assume that the license holders are domestic in the case of an import quota, then we can include this rent in the welfare calculation for the importer. Consequently, the net country welfare includes a positive net rent and negative production and consumption distortions. The importing country is worse off as a result of the import quota if the distortions exceed the positive net rent, and vice versa. Alternatively, in the exporter, the producer's welfare decreases and the consumer's welfare increases. The net country welfare effect includes a negative net rent transfer to the importer and negative production and consumption distortions. The exporting country is unambiguously worse off as a result of the import quota.

Second, what are the effects of an export quota (or VER) imposed by a large exporter? The effects of an export quota or VER imposed by a large country are nearly identical to the case of the import quota. All of the price and quantity effects are the same. The prominent economic difference is that the exporter, rather than the importer, imposes an export quota or VER. Furthermore, in the case of an export restriction, the license holders to the rents tend to be the firms or government of the exporting country, rather than the importing country. Thus, the welfare effects of the policy are altered by the nationality of the license holders.

The export restrictions result in welfare changes in both the importing and exporting countries. In the exporter, the producer's welfare decreases, the consumer's welfare increases, and license holders to export receive the rent. The net country welfare effect includes a positive net rent and negative production and consumption distortions. The exporting country is worse off as a result of the export restriction if the negative distortions exceed the positive net rent, and vice versa. Alternatively, in the importer, the producer's welfare increases and the consumer's welfare decreases. The net country welfare effect includes a negative net rent transfer and negative production and consumption distortions. The importing country is unambiguously worse off as a result of the export restriction.

Third, what are the effects of a ban imposed between two large countries? The effects of a ban or embargo imposed between two large countries are an extreme version of the previous cases. The ban (or embargo) restricts the quantity of the traded good between the two countries to zero. The effect is that prices for the good revert to the autarky prices of the two countries. Specifically, the ban increases the price of the good in the importer and decreases the price of the good in the exporter. As a result, agents in both the importer and exporter are affected. This price sharing occurs irrespective of which country imposes the ban. In the importing country, producers supply more in their domestic market at the higher autarky price. They have gained from the ban in terms of revenue from domestic sales of the good. At the same time, consumers demand less at the higher autarky price. They have lost from the ban in terms of the higher cost of the good. Alternatively, in the exporting country, producers no longer supply to the international market. They have lost from the ban in terms of revenues from international sales of the good. And, consumers demand more at the lower autarky prices in the exporter. They have gained from the ban in terms of the lower cost of the good. Further, the mix of consumption of domestic and traded goods changes as a result of the ban. Consumers in the home country now consume more domestically produced goods and no imports. Consumers in the foreign market continue to consume only domestically produced goods, but more of them.

The ban also results in welfare changes in both the importing and exporting countries. In the importer, the producer's welfare increases and consumer's welfare decreases. The net country welfare effect includes negative production and consumption distortions. The importing country is unambiguously worse off as a result of the ban. Alternatively, in the exporter, the producer's welfare decreases and the consumer's welfare increases. The net country welfare effect includes negative production and consumption distortions. The importing country is also unambiguously worse off as a result of the ban. Further, given that trade is reduced to zero, there is neither a rent nor a terms of trade effect to counterbalance the negative distortions. Thus, bans are welfare deteriorating in economic terms from national and global perspectives.

This chapter did not consider several aspects of quantitative restrictions. We did not assess the implications of the small country case where the country imposing the restriction cannot affect the world price. We did not assess the implications of alternative elasticities of export supply and import demand. And, we did not assess the implications of liberalizing quantitative restrictions. We encourage the reader to do this independently, using the tools developed in the previous chapters. Furthermore, we did not account for political and non-economic explanations for bans or embargos as a policy tool. These aspects fall under the topic of the political economy of trade policy. Finally, we did not discuss the effects of the hybrid policy known as tariff rate quotas. This topic is discussed in the following Chapter 8 in the context of policy comparisons.

Applied Problems

7.1 Examine the effects of liberalizing import quotas on prices, quantities supplied, quantity demanded, and trade in both importers and exporters. Make an assumption about whether your countries can affect the world price.

7.2 Use your knowledge of the welfare effects of import quotas to explain why policy makers interested in maximizing national and world welfare support free trade while select agents within countries (e.g., consumers, government, or producers) may not support free trade.

7.3 Assume that you are an advocate for producers and license holders with an interest in maximizing rents to license holders and producer welfare. Furthermore, assume that your advocacy organization works to maximize rents and producer welfare from a global perspective. Explain whether your organization would support the liberalization of import quotas worldwide.

7.4 Evaluate the effects of reducing import quotas in all countries on world welfare of consumers, producers and governments. Consider these effects for both the small and large country cases.

7.5 Compare the welfare effects of an import quota and voluntary export restriction in both the importing and exporting countries. Which policy is preferred from the importer's point of view? Which policy is preferred from the exporter's point of view? Why?

7.6 Evaluate the effects of a voluntary export restraint on the welfare of producers in the exporting country. Assume the large country case. Discuss why the exporting country may be willing to impose such a policy.

7.7 Consider the case of a ban on the trade of a particular good. Who wins and who loses from such a policy in both the importing and exporting countries?

7.8 Consider the case where a country imposes a complete ban on all trade (imports and exports). Examine the effect of this ban on the welfare of that country.

Further Reading

Anderson, James E. 1988. *The Relative Inefficiency of Quotas*. Cambridge, MA: MIT Press.

Bergstrand, C. Fred, Kimberley A. Elliot, Jeffrey Schott, and Wendy E. Takacs. 1987. *Auction Quotas and US Trade Policy*. Washington, D.C.: Institute for International Economics.

Bhagwati, Jagdish. 1968. More on the equivalence of tariffs and quotas. *American Economic Review* 58 (1): 142–146.

Eaton, Jonathan, and Maxim Engers. 1992. *Sanctions. Journal of Political Economy* 100 (5): 899–928.

de Gorter, Harry, and Erika Kliauga. 2006. Reducing tariffs versus expanding tariff rate quotas. In *Agricultural Trade Reform and the Doha Development Agenda* (eds Kym Anderson and Will Martin), Washington, D.C.: World Bank and Palgrave Macmillan, pp. 117–160.

Hamilton, Carl. 1988. ASEAN systems for allocation of export licenses under VERs. In *The Political Economy of Manufacturing Protection: Experiences of ASEAN and Australia* (eds Christopher Findlay and Ross Garnaut), London: Allen and Unwin, pp. 235–247.

Hranaiova, Jana, Harry de Gorter, and James Falk. 2006. The economics of administering import quotas with licenses-on-demand in agriculture. *American Journal of Agricultural Economics* 88 (2): 3318–3350.

Hufbauer, Gary C., Jeffrey J. Schott, and Kimberly A. Elliott. 1990. *Economic Sanctions Reconsidered: History and Current Policy*, 2nd edn. Washington, D.C.: Institute for International Economics.

Krueger, Anne O. 1974. The political economy of the rent-seeking society. *American Economic Review* 64 (3): 291–303.

McCulloch, Rachel, and Harry G. Johnson. 1973. A note on proportionally distributed quotas. *American Economic Review* 63 (4): 726–732.

de Melo, Jaime, and David Tarr. 1992. *A General Equilibrium Analysis of US Foreign Trade Policy*. Cambridge, MA: MIT Press.

Rom, Michael. 1979. *The Role of Tariff Quotas in Commercial Policy*. New York: Holmes and Meier.

Skully, David W. 2001. *Economics of Tariff-Rate Quota Administration*. US Department of Agriculture, Economic Research Service, Technical Bulletin Number 1893 (April). Washington, D.C.: USDA.

Vousden, N. 1990. *The Economic Theory of Protection*. Cambridge: Cambridge University Press.

World Trade Organization (WTO). 1997. *European Communities-Regime for the Importation, Sale, and Distribution of Bananas*. Report of the Appellate Body (September 9). Geneva: WTO.

World Trade Organization (WTO). 2006. *Tariff Quota Administration Methods and Tariff Quota Fill*. Committee on Agricuture Background Paper TN/AG/S/22 (April 27). Geneva: WTO.

8
Policy Comparisons

8.1   What Are Policy Equivalents, and Their Purpose?

This chapter summarizes and compares the effects of the policies discussed in the previous chapters, including tariffs, export subsidies, import quotas, voluntary export restraints (VERs), and bans. To this end, we compare *policy equivalents* when possible. By this we mean policies that produce quantity, price, and welfare effects that are similar in magnitude.

The purpose of comparing policies is to consider their relative effects. Such analysis is insightful in three key ways. First, we can determine who wins and who loses when alternative policies are adopted or liberalized. We will show that certain agents (governments and license holders in particular) are not neutral when it comes to the choice of policy instruments (such as tariffs versus quotas). We will also show that countries are not neutral when it comes to the choice of policies that generate rents (such as quotas versus VERs). Second, we can determine the implications of substituting one policy type for another, such as replacing import quotas with tariffs. This understanding is important in assessing the process of tariffication and in assessing hybrid policy instruments such as tariff rate quotas. Third, we can analyze the effects of alternative policies from a global perspective. That is, we can assess whether some policy instruments are better at raising the aggregate global welfare than others. Insights from these three analyses help explain why different groups within countries and within the global economy tend to support the use of different policy instruments.

Analysis of policy equivalents dates back to early research by Bhagwati (1965 and 1968). It is still relevant today as policy makers search for solutions for liberalizing

Global Trade Policy: Questions and Answers, First Edition. Pamela J. Smith.
© 2014 John Wiley & Sons, Inc. Published 2014 by John Wiley & Sons, Inc.

trade barriers, particularly those that are difficult to quantify and/or compare across countries. For example, the Uruguay Round Agreement on Agriculture supported the adoption of tariff rate quotas on commodities that were previously subject to non-tariff protections. The tariff rate quota is a hybrid of the two policy instruments. One of the goals of this policy instrument is to ensure that those developing countries that export agricultural commodities have access to the markets of developed countries. The hybrid policy provides a means for simultaneously converting non-tariff barriers into tariffs and using "quotas" to ensure market access in the process of liberalizing agricultural trade. In this chapter, we discuss the relative effects of policy equivalent tariffs and quotas, and illustrate the effects of substituting the quota with a tariff. We also discuss the effects of the hybrid policy instrument – the tariff rate quota. The latter is particularly important since the use of this instrument continues to evolve in real world practice.

This chapter is organized as follows. First, we compare the effects of adopting policies that reduce trade. These policies include tariffs, import quotas, and VERs. In each case, we consider the large country case where the world price is affected by the policy adoption. We also compare these trade-reducing policies to bans and export subsidies. Specifically, we consider how the effects of bans and export subsidies compare *relative* to the effects of tariffs, quotas, and VERs. Second, we consider the relative effects of liberalizing these policies. Third, we consider the effects of substituting policies. In particular, we evaluate the effects of substituting a quantitative restriction such as an import quota with a tariff, and the effects of tariff rate quotas. Throughout, we consider the effects of policy adoption and liberalization from multiple perspectives including global, national and subnational (i.e., consumers, producers, and government) perspectives.

8.2   What Are the Relative Effects of Policy Equivalents?

8.2.1   What are the relative effects of tariffs, quotas, and VERs?

What are the effects of imposing equivalent trade-reducing policies? We begin by considering tariffs, quotas, and VERs, as these policies can be directly compared. This comparison builds on the materials covered in Chapters 5 and 7.

Figure 8.1 illustrates the effects of equivalent policies imposed by large countries. To begin, we introduce an equivalent tariff, import quota and VER (or export quota) into Panel (b). The quota and VER are both quantitative restrictions and are measured on the horizontal axis. The tariff is a value restriction and is measured on the vertical axis. A quantitative restriction in the amount of q produces a price effect that is equivalent to the magnitude of a tariff of the value t. Similarly, a tariff of the value t produces a quantity effect that is equivalent to the magnitude of the quantitative restriction q.

These equivalent policies produce the price and quantity effects that are detailed in previous chapters. To review briefly, these policies each increase the price seen in

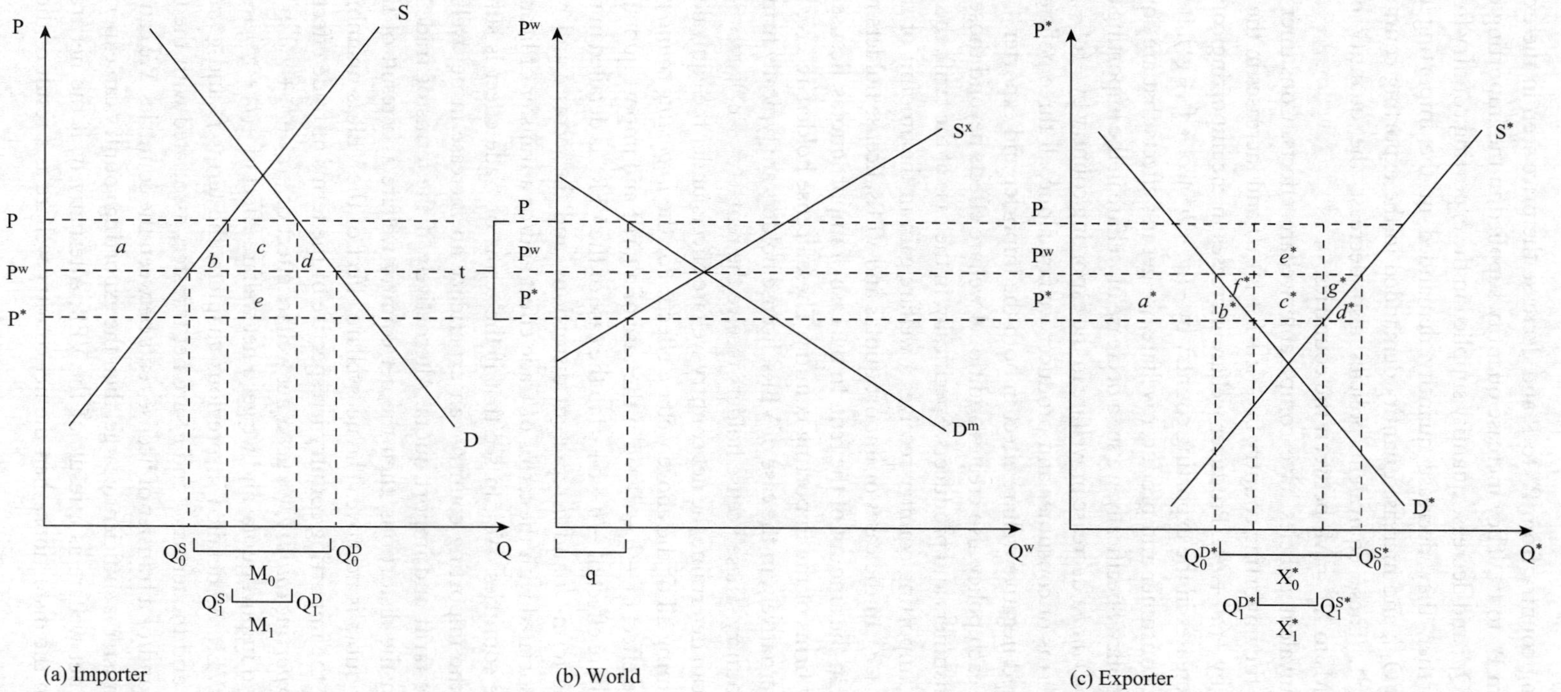

(a) Importer

S
D
P
P^w
P^*
t
a b c d e
Q_0^S Q_1^S Q_1^D Q_0^D
M_0
M_1
Q

(b) World

P^w
P
P^w
P^*
S^x
D^m
q
Q^w

(c) Exporter

S^*
D^*
P^*
P
P^w
P^*
a^* b^* c^* d^* e^* f g
$Q_0^{D^*}$ $Q_1^{D^*}$ $Q_1^{S^*}$ $Q_0^{S^*}$
X_0^*
X_1^*
Q^*

Figure 8.1 Policy equivalents – imposed by a large country.

the importing country from P^w to P and decrease the price seen in the exporting country from P^w to P^*. They increase quantity supplied in the importing country from Q_0^S to Q_1^S; and decrease quantity supplied in the exporting country from Q_0^{S*} to Q_1^{S*}. Further, they decrease quantity demanded in the importing country from Q_0^D to Q_1^D; and increase quantity demanded in the exporting country from Q_0^{D*} to Q_1^{D*}. These equivalent policies also decrease the quantity of trade from $X_0^* = M_0$ to $X_1^* = M_1$ between the countries.

These equivalent policies have comparable welfare effects. Consumer welfare decreases in the importing country by $-(a + b + c + d)$ and increases in the exporting country by $+(a^* + b^*)$. Producer welfare increases in the importing country by $+(a)$ and decreases in the exporting country by $-(a^* + b^* + c^* + f^* + g^*)$. If we sum together the consumer and producer welfare, we get net effects that are equivalent under each policy. Specifically, we see a decrease in welfare in the importing country by $-(b + c + d)$ *and* a decrease in welfare in the exporting country by $-(c^* + f^* + g^*)$. That is, in terms of consumer and producer welfare alone, all three policies result in a combined negative welfare effect in both the importer and exporter.

However, each policy also creates additional welfare effects beyond those experienced by consumers and producers. Specifically, in the case of the tariff, the government in the importing country receives a welfare gain in the amount of the tariff revenue $+(c + e)$. In the cases of import quotas and VERs, license holders receive a welfare gain in the amount of the rent. In the case of import quotas, license holders are typically firms of the importing country. These license holders receive the rent $+(c + e)$. Alternatively, in the case of VERs, license holders are typically firms in the exporting country. These license holders receive the rent $+(c^* + e^*)$.

Now, we can determine the net country welfare effects under the equivalent policies by summing all of the above welfare effects. For the *importing country*, we get a net welfare effect of $-(b + d) + e$ in the case of a tariff and import quota; and we get a net welfare effect of $-(b + c + d)$ in the case of the VER. As detailed in previous chapters, the terms b and d represent distortions, and the terms c and e are net transfers associated with the terms of trade effect and/or a transfer of license rents between the countries. We can see that if the terms of trade effect is sufficiently large, then the importing country can experience an increase in net welfare as a result of the tariff and import quota. Alternatively, if the terms of trade effect is smaller than the distortions, then the net country welfare as a result of the tariff and import quota is negative. The net welfare effect of the VER is unambiguously negative for the importing country irrespective of the terms of trade effect.

For the *exporting country*, we get a net welfare effect of $-(c^* + f^* + g^*)$ in the case of a tariff and import quota; and we get a net welfare effect of $-(f^* + g^*) + e^*$ in the case of the VER. As detailed in previous chapters, the terms f^* and g^* represent distortions; and the terms c^* and e^* are net transfers associated with the terms of trade effect and/or a transfer of license rents between the countries. We can see that if the net transfer is sufficiently large, then the exporting country can experience an increase in net welfare as a result of the VER. Alternatively, if the net transfer is smaller than the distortions, then the net country welfare as a result of the VER is

Table 8.1 Welfare effects of policy equivalents.

(a) Importer

Economic agent	Welfare effects of tariff	Welfare effects of import quota	Welfare effects of VER/ export quota
Producer	$+a$	$+a$	$+a$
Consumer	$-(a+b+c+d)$	$-(a+b+c+d)$	$-(a+b+c+d)$
Government	$+(c+e)$	0	0
License holders	0	$+(c+e)$	0
Country	$-(b+d)+e$	$-(b+d)+e$	$-(b+c+d)$
Country (direction)	Negative or positive	Negative or positive	Negative

(b) Exporter

Economic agent	Welfare effects of tariff	Welfare effects of import quota	Welfare effects of VER/ export quota
Producer	$-(a^*+b^*+c^*$ $+f^*+g^*)$	$-(a^*+b^*+c^*$ $+f^*+g^*)$	$-(a^*+b^*+c^*$ $+f^*+g^*)$
Consumer	$+(a^*+b^*)$	$+(a^*+b^*)$	$+(a^*+b^*)$
Government	0	0	
License holders	0	0	$+(c^*+e^*)$
Country	$-(c^*+f^*+g^*)$	$-(c^*+f^*+g^*)$	$-(f^*+g^*)+e^*$
Country (direction)	Negative	Negative	Negative or positive

Note: These cases assume that import quota licenses are held by domestics of the importer, and VER (or export quota) licenses are held by domestics of the exporter.

negative. In contrast, the net welfare effect in the exporting country of the tariff and import quota is unambiguously negative.

These welfare effects allow us to examine the interests of the various economic agents in both trading partners. Table 8.1 summarizes the welfare effects of policy equivalents. From a subnational perspective, producers in the importing country will support a tariff, quota, or VER; while producers in the exporting country will not support these policies. Alternatively, consumers in the exporting country will support a tariff, quota, or VER; while consumers in the importing country will not support these policies. Further, license holders associated with the importer will support an import quota; while license holders associated with an exporter will support a VER. And, government in the importing country will support a tariff to raise revenues. From a broader national perspective, the importing country will prefer a tariff and import quota over a VER; while the exporting country will prefer a VER over a tariff or import quota. Finally, from a global perspective, the transfer across the countries associated with the terms of trade effects and/or license rents counterbalance each other. They wash each other out in aggregate. What remains are the producer and consumer distortions in both the importing and exporting countries. Thus, from a global perspective none of the policies are preferred as they are welfare deteriorating for the countries in aggregate, and thus for the global economy.

8.2.2   What are the relative effects of bans?

A ban is an extreme version of the policy equivalents described above. Specifically, a ban is equivalent to a quantitative restriction such as an import quota or VER of zero, or a value restriction such as a tariff that drives trade to zero. Chapter 7 details the effects of a ban, so we will not repeat these effects here. Rather, we will summarize the effects in relation to the policies described above.

The price and quantity effects of a ban are identical to the above policies in terms of their direction. However, because a ban eliminates trade in a particular good, the magnitude of the price and quantity effects is larger. Furthermore, because the countries stop trading with each other, the terms of trade effect of the policy becomes irrelevant. Recall that the terms of trade describes the price of the good imported, relative to the price of the good exported. When a ban is imposed, imports and exports cease and both countries revert to their autarky prices for the particular good.

The welfare effects of a ban are also comparable to the effects of the tariff, quota, and VER. That is, the consumer and producer welfare changes are similar in direction to the policies described above. However, the magnitude of the effects on consumers and producers is larger. Further, in contrast to the tariff, quota, and VER, a ban produces no revenues or rents. Thus, the net country effects of the ban are large consumer and producer distortions alone. In net, both the importer and exporter experience an unambiguously negative welfare loss as a result of a ban.

8.2.3   What are the relative effects of export subsidies?

It is not possible to compare an export subsidy that is equivalent to the policies described above. This is because export subsidies are trade augmenting, whereas tariffs, quotas, VERs, and bans are trade reducing. Furthermore, export subsidies (if sufficiently large) can reverse the patterns of trade such that an importer of a good becomes an exporter of that good. Chapter 6 details the effects of export subsidies, so we will not repeat these effects here. Rather, we will summarize the direction of the effects in relation to the trade-reducing policies.

The price and quantity effects of an export subsidy are the mirror opposites of the effects of trade-reducing policies. For example, trade-reducing policies increase the price in the importing country and can decrease the price in the exporting country. In contrast, export subsidies increase the price in the exporting country and decrease the price in the importing country. The implications for quantities supplied and demanded are also mirror images. Trade-reducing policies increase the quantity supplied and decrease the quantity demanded in the importing countries; and they decrease the quantity supplied and increase the quantity demanded in the exporting countries. In contrast, export subsidies increase the quantity supplied and decrease the quantity demanded in the exporting countries; and they decrease the quantity supplied and increase the quantity demanded in the importing countries. Furthermore, while trade-reducing policies decrease trade (exports and imports), export subsidies increase trade (exports and imports).

The welfare effects of an export subsidy are related to the trade-reducing policies in a mirror-opposite way. The export subsidy can most directly be compared to the tariff, as they both impact the welfare of the government and neither produces a rent to license holders. Whereas tariffs decrease the welfare of consumers and increase the welfare of producers in the importing country, export subsidies increase the welfare of consumers and decrease the welfare of producers in the importing country. Conversely, whereas tariffs increase the welfare of consumers and decrease the welfare of producers in the exporting country, export subsidies decrease the welfare of consumers and increase the welfare of producers in the exporting country. Finally, whereas tariffs generate a revenue for the government, export subsidies generate a cost for the government. In both cases, the size of the revenue or cost is the volume of trade times the price magnitude of the policy (tariff or subsidy). Essentially, an export subsidy can be viewed as a negative import tariff.

Thus, from a subnational perspective, producers in the exporting country will support a subsidy, while producers in the importing country will support a tariff, quota, or VER. Alternatively, consumers in the importing country will support a subsidy, while consumers in the exporting country will support a tariff, quota, or VER. Further, government in the exporting country will not support a subsidy in terms of the cost of the subsidy; while government in the importing country will support a tariff in terms of the revenues generated. From a broader national perspective, the exporting country will prefer none of the policies as they are all welfare deteriorating in net (except possibly the VER), while the importing country will prefer the policy that generates the largest terms of trade improvement. Finally, from a global perspective, the transfers across the countries associated with the terms of trade effects counterbalance one another. They wash each other out in aggregate. What remains are the producer and consumer distortions in both the importing and exporting countries. Thus, from a global perspective none of the policies (including export subsidies) are preferred as they are welfare deteriorating for the countries in aggregate, and thus for the global economy.

8.2.4 How do the policies compare?

The effects of trade-reducing and trade-augmenting policies are clearly related. These policies differ primarily in the distribution of welfare effects. Table 8.2 and Table 8.3 provide a summary of these effects. Table 8.2 summarizes the *price*

Table 8.2 Price and quantity effects of adopting policies.

(a) Importer

Variable	Tariff[a]	Quota[a]	VER[b]	Ban[c]	Export subsidy[b]
Price	Increase	Increase	Increase	Increase	Decrease
Quantity supplied	Increase	Increase	Increase	Increase	Decrease
Quantity demanded	Decrease	Decrease	Decrease	Decrease	Increase
Trade (imports)	Decrease	Decrease	Decrease	Decrease	Increase

(b) Exporter

Variable	Tariff[a]	Quota[a]	VER[b]	Ban[c]	Export subsidy[b]
Price	Decrease	Decrease	Decrease	Decrease	Increase
Quantity supplied	Decrease	Decrease	Decrease	Decrease	Increase
Quantity demanded	Increase	Increase	Increase	Increase	Decrease
Trade (Exports)	Decrease	Decrease	Decrease	Decrease	Increase

[a] Policies are imposed by the importing country; these are the "home" countries in the related figures.
[b] Policies are imposed by the exporting country; these are the "home" countries in the related figures.
[c] Policies are imposed by either the importing or exporting countries.

and quantity effects of adopting a tariff, quota, VER, ban, and/or export subsidy in the importing and exporting countries. Table 8.3 summarizes the *welfare effects* of these same policies. These tables provide the national and subnational perspectives. (See Table 8.6 for a summary of the welfare effects of adopting these policies from a global perspective.)

Several insightful patterns emerge from these tables. First, we can see from Table 8.3 that a welfare increase for an agent in one country is mirrored by a welfare decrease for another agent in that same country. Similarly, a welfare increase for an agent in one country is mirrored by a welfare decrease by a similar agent in its trading partner. Thus, the policies produce welfare transfers both within countries and across countries. Furthermore, if we consider country welfare in aggregate, we see that *both importers and exporters experience a decrease in welfare under all of the policies considered.* The only exceptions are the cases where the terms of trade effects are large. In these exceptional cases, only one of the two trading partners experiences an increase in country welfare.

These findings are relevant to policy debate. They help explain the widely diverging views about the preservation or liberalization of trade policies. Stated in general terms, those who gain from these trade policies are the producers and rent recipients in the country that imposes the policy. For example, producers in the importing country gain in the case of trade-reducing policies (e.g., tariffs and quotas), and producers in the exporting country gain in the case of trade-increasing policies (e.g., export subsidies). In contrast, those who lose from these policies are the consumers

Table 8.3 Welfare effects of adopting policies.

(a) Importer welfare

Economic agent	Tariff[a]	Quota[a]	VER[b]	Ban[c]	Export subsidy[b]
Consumer	Decrease	Decrease	Decrease	Decrease	Increase
Producer	Increase	Increase	Increase	Increase	Decrease
Government	Increase				
License holder		Increase			
Net country (terms of trade effect > distortions)	Increase	Increase	Decrease		Increase
Net country (distortions > terms of trade effect)	Decrease	Decrease	Decrease	Decrease	Increase or decrease[d]

(b) Exporter welfare

Economic agent	Tariff[a]	Quota[a]	VER[b]	Ban[c]	Export subsidy[b]
Consumer	Increase	Increase	Increase	Increase	Decrease
Producer	Decrease	Decrease	Decrease	Decrease	Increase
Government					Decrease
License holder			Increase		
Net country (terms of trade effect > distortions)	Decrease	Decrease	Increase		Decrease
Net country (distortions > terms of trade effect)	Decrease	Decrease	Decrease	Decrease	Decrease

[a] Policies are imposed by the importing country; these are the "home" countries in the related figures.
[b] Policies are imposed by the exporting country; these are the "home" countries in the related figures.
[c] Policies are imposed by either the importing or exporting countries.
[d] Net country welfare can decrease in one specific case: when an export subsidy reverses the direction of trade *and* distortions are greater than the terms of trade effect.

in the country that imposes the policy. For example, consumers in the importing country lose in the case of trade-reducing policies (e.g., tariffs and quotas), and consumers in the exporting country lose in the case of trade-increasing policies (e.g., export subsidies).

Thus, whether one supports these policies depends on one's perspective. When evaluating policy it is important to be explicit about this perspective. Is your perspective that of a producer, a consumer, a government, or a license holder? Is your perspective that of an importer or an exporter? Is your perspective that of a policy maker who seeks to maximize national welfare or a policy maker who seeks to maximize global welfare? Within a country, there are clearly diverging interests in adopting trade policies. At the national level, the adoption of these trade policies decreases national welfare except where the policy brings about an improvement in the country's terms of trade. And, at the global level, the adoption of these trade policies decreases global welfare.

8.3   What Are the Relative Effects of Liberalizing Policies?

The relative effects of liberalizing policies are summarized in Tables 8.4 and 8.5. Table 8.4 summarizes the *price and quantity effects* of liberalizing a tariff, quota, VER, ban, and/or export subsidy in the importing and exporting countries. Table 8.5 summarizes the *welfare effects* of liberalizing these same policies. These effects are the mirror opposites of those found in Tables 8.2 and 8.3. We include them here for the purpose of direct reference. These tables provide the national and subnational perspectives. (See Table 8.6 for a summary of the welfare effects of liberalizing these policies from a global perspective.)

Furthermore, we could use all of the figures presented in previous chapters to analyze liberalization of trade policies. We would simply work all of the analyses backward. That is, instead of adding a policy (in Panel (b) of the figures), we would consider the case where the policy is already in place and we would remove the policy or reduce its magnitude. In the case of complete liberalization, we would see a reversion to free trade world prices (P^w). In the case of partial policy liberalization, we would see a movement toward the free trade world price (P^w). In this partial liberalization case, the absolute magnitude of the price, quantity and welfare effects described in previous chapters would be reduced.

Table 8.4   Price and quantity effects of liberalizing policies.

(a) Importer

Variable	Tariff[a]	Quota[a]	VER[b]	Ban[c]	Export subsidy[b]
Price	Decrease	Decrease	Decrease	Decrease	Increase
Quantity supplied	Decrease	Decrease	Decrease	Decrease	Increase
Quantity demanded	Increase	Increase	Increase	Increase	Decrease
Trade (imports)	Increase	Increase	Increase	Increase	Decrease

(b) Exporter

Variable	Tariff[a]	Quota[a]	VER[b]	Ban[c]	Export subsidy[b]
Price	Increase	Increase	Increase	Increase	Decrease
Quantity supplied	Increase	Increase	Increase	Increase	Decrease
Quantity demanded	Decrease	Decrease	Decrease	Decrease	Increase
Trade (exports)	Increase	Increase	Increase	Increase	Decrease

[a] Policies are imposed by the importing country; these are the "home" countries in the related figures.
[b] Policies are imposed by the exporting country; these are the "home" countries in the related figures.
[c] Policies are imposed by either the importing or exporting countries.

Table 8.5 Welfare effects of liberalizing policies.

(a) Importer welfare

Economic agent	Tariff[a]	Quota[a]	VER[b]	Ban[c]	Export subsidy[b]
Consumer	Increase	Increase	Increase	Increase	Decrease
Producer	Decrease	Decrease	Decrease	Decrease	Increase
Government	Decrease				
License holder		Decrease			
Net country (terms of trade effect > distortions)	Decrease	Decrease	Increase		Decrease
Net country (distortions > terms of trade effect)	Increase	Increase	Increase	Increase	Decrease or increase[d]

(b) Exporter welfare

Economic agent	Tariff[a]	Quota[a]	VER[b]	Ban[c]	Export subsidy[b]
Consumer	Decrease	Decrease	Decrease	Decrease	Increase
Producer	Increase	Increase	Increase	Increase	Decrease
Government					Increase
License holder			Decrease		
Net country (terms of trade effect > distortions)	Increase	Increase	Decrease		Increase
Net country (distortions > terms of trade effect)	Increase	Increase	Increase	Increase	Increase

[a] Policies are imposed by the importing country; these are the "home" countries in the related figures.
[b] Policies are imposed by the exporting country; these are the "home" countries in the related figures.
[c] Policies are imposed by either the importing or exporting countries.
[d] Net country welfare can increase in one specific case: when liberalizing an export subsidy reverses the direction of trade *and* distortions eliminated are greater than the terms of trade effect eliminated.

The patterns that emerge from analysis of policy liberalization are as follow. First, the liberalization of policies produces welfare transfers both within countries and across countries. At the national level, we see that *both importers and exporters experience an increase in welfare when any of the policies considered are liberalized.* The only exceptions are where the terms of trade effects are large. In these exceptional cases, only one of the two trading partners may experience an increase in country welfare.

These findings are again relevant to policy debate. They help explain the widely diverging views about the preservation or liberalization of trade policies. Stated in general terms, those who gain from liberalizing trade policies tend to be the

Table 8.6 Global effects of policy adoption and liberalization.

(a) Policy adoption

Variables	Tariff[a]	Quota[a]	VER[b]	Ban[c]	Export subsidy[b]
Trade (imports and exports)	Decrease	Decrease	Decrease	Decrease	Increase
Joint welfare of importer and exporter (distortions > terms of trade effects)	Decrease	Decrease	Decrease	Decrease	Decrease

(b) Policy liberalization

Variables	Tariff[a]	Quota[a]	VER[b]	Ban[c]	Export subsidy[b]
Trade (imports and exports)	Increase	Increase	Increase	Increase	Decrease
Joint welfare of importer and exporter (distortions > terms of trade effects)	Increase	Increase	Increase	Increase	Increase

[a] Policies are imposed by the importing country; these are the "home" countries in the related figures.
[b] Policies are imposed by the exporting country; these are the "home" countries in the related figures.
[c] Policies are imposed by either the importing or exporting countries.

consumers in the country that liberalizes the policy. For example, consumers in the importing country gain in the case of liberalizing trade-reducing policies (e.g., tariffs and quota), and consumers in the exporting country gain in the case of liberalizing trade-increasing policies (e.g., export subsidies). In contrast, those who lose from liberalizing these policies tend to be the producers in the country that liberalizes the policy. For example, producers in the importing country lose in the case of liberalizing trade-reducing policies (e.g., tariffs and quotas), and producers in the exporting country lose in the case of liberalizing trade-increasing policies (e.g., export subsidies).

Again, whether one supports the liberalization of policies depends on one's perspective, as discussed previously. Within a country, there are clearly diverging interests in liberalization of trade policies. At the national level, the liberalization of these trade policies increases national welfare, except where the policy brings about a large deterioration in the country's terms of trade. And, at the global level, the liberalization of these trade policies increases global welfare.

8.4   What Are the Effects of Substituting Policies?

The reason for considering policy substitution is a practical one. Policy substitution can provide a means for moving from a position of restricted trade toward liberalization of trade barriers. For example, policies that produce large welfare losses can be converted into substitute policies that achieve similar objectives but are less welfare deteriorating. Additionally, policies that are opaque and/or difficult to monitor can be converted into substitute policies that are more transparent and easily monitored.

In practice, efforts to liberalize trade have included the conversion of non-tariff barriers into tariffs, followed by the liberalization of the tariffs. This is because tariffs are viewed to be more transparent, more easily monitored, and less welfare distorting, relative to other non-tariff barriers. *Tariffication* refers to the process of converting non-tariff barriers into tariff equivalents. As discussed earlier in this chapter, tariff equivalents are tariff rates that produce price and quantity effects that are equivalent to the policy being replaced.

Below, we consider the case of converting an import quota into a tariff equivalent. We consider this case as a first step toward understanding the more complex instrument referred to as tariff rate quotas, which are used in practice to facilitate the conversion of quotas (and other non-tariff barriers) into tariffs. We revisit Figure 8.1 to assess the effects of converting an import quota into a tariff equivalent. Recall that the quota in amount q produces price effects that are equivalent to a tariff in the amount t. Thus, tariff t is the policy equivalent to quota q.

What are the price and quantity effects of converting a quota into a tariff equivalent? The answer is that there are no price and quantity effects if the policies are indeed equivalent. The price seen in the importer is P before and after the policy substitution. And, the price seen in the exporter is P* before and after the policy substitution.

What are the welfare effects of converting a quota into a tariff equivalent? The answer is that consumer and producer welfare remains unchanged in both the importing and exporting countries. This is because both policies produce the same welfare effects for consumers and producers. In the importing country, consumers gain $+(a + b + c + d)$ from removing the quota but then lose the same amount by adding the tariff. Similarly producers lose $-(a)$ from removing the quota but then gain the same amount by adding the tariff. This same intuition applies to consumers and producers in the exporting country.

The primary impact of the policy conversion is on the government and license holders in the importing country. Specifically, the license holders lose their rents $-(c + e)$ when the quota is removed; and the government gains the tariff revenues $+(c + e)$ when the tariff is substituted. Thus, the policy conversion results in a transfer from license holders to the government, where the quota rents lost equate with the tariff revenues gained. Because these transfers are equivalent, the national welfare of the country remains unchanged by the conversion.

There is one exception to this pattern. This is the case where the license holders to the quotas are foreign firms of the exporter rather than domestic firms of the importer. In this case, the loss in quota rents would be incurred by the exporter while the gain in tariff revenue would be incurred by the importer. That is, the policy conversion would result in a welfare transfer from the exporter in the amount $+(c^* + e^*)$ to the importer in amount $+(c + e)$. Jointly, however, their aggregate welfare would remain unchanged since $(c^* + e^*) = (c + e)$.

The above discussion of policy conversion helps to inform our understanding of the hybrid policy instrument known as the *tariff rate quota* (TRQ). The tariff rate quota is currently used in agriculture to facilitate the conversion of import bans and quotas into tariffs. So, the discussion of policy conversion above provides a jumping off point for understanding this more complex policy instrument. The TRQ differs from a typical quota because it does not establish a maximum quantity of imports. Rather, it establishes a quantity of imports (a "quota") that can enter a country at a lower tariff rate. This lower tariff rate is referred to as the *in-quota tariff*. Imports in excess of that quantity are subject to a higher tariff rate. This higher rate is referred to as the *over-quota tariff*. If the over-quota tariff is high enough to prohibit imports, then the TRQ mirrors the case of a quota-tariff equivalent.

We can use Figure 8.1 as a foundation for examining the TRQ.[1] In Figure 8.1, we can think of the quantity q and tariff t as policy equivalents. In the case of the TRQ, we can think of the tariff rate t as the in-quota tariff. Under this instrument, imports that enter this country in quantity q are subject to the tariff t (i.e., the in-quota tariff). Any imports in excess of q are subject to a higher tariff t' (i.e., the over-quota tariff). These imports would occur, for example, if the import demand curve were to be shifted right. For simplicity, the over-quota tariff is not illustrated in Figure 8.1, but we can envision it as any tariff that exceeds t that is applied to imports in excess of q. If the over-quota tariff (t') is sufficiently high, then the quantity of imports will effectively be limited to the quota (q), which is policy equivalent to the in-quota tariff (t). In practice, the quantity q can be set to ensure a minimum market access of exporters into the importer's market.

Under certain scenarios, this policy instrument can generate a rent to license holders in addition to the tariff revenues. In practice, the methods used to allocate licenses and therefore rents are varied. Methods identified by the World Trade Organization (2006) include: (a) applied tariffs, where no licenses are allocated; (b) licenses-on-demand, where firms request licenses that are then prorated based on total requests; (c) historical imports, where licenses are allocated based on past imports; (d) first-come, first-served, where licenses are allocated based on the timing of requests; (e) state trading enterprises, where licenses are controlled by these enterprises; and (f) auctioning, where licenses are allocated to the highest bidders. These methods have differing effects on the distribution of the rents both within and across countries.

Finally, the liberalization of TRQs can be accomplished by either decreasing the higher over-quota tariff (t') or expanding the quota q that is subject to the lower in-quota tariff (t). In practice, the decision about how to liberalize TRQs is still an issue of policy debate.

8.5   Summary Remarks

What are policy equivalents and their purpose? This chapter summarized and com-pared the effects of the policies discussed in the previous chapters. When possible, we compared *policy equivalents* that produce quantity and price effects that are similar in magnitude. Our purpose was to determine the relative effects of policies including price, quantity and welfare effects. Such analysis helps explain why different groups within countries and within the global economy prefer alternative policy instruments.

What are the relative effects of policy equivalents? We considered four comparisons of policies. *First, what are the relative effects of tariffs, quotas, and VERs?* To answer this question, we directly compared the effects of policy equivalents. We illustrated that these policy equivalents produce similar price and quantity effects. Specifically, these policies each increase the price seen in the importer and decrease the price seen in the exporter. Consequently, these policies have identical effects on the quantity demanded and supplied, and trade. These equivalent policies also have some comparable welfare effects. Consumer welfare decreases in the importer and increases in the exporter. Producer welfare increases in the importer and decreases in the exporter. In terms of consumer and producer welfare alone, all three policies result in an identical combined negative welfare effect in both the importer and exporter.

However, the tariff, quota, and VER differ in their welfare effects beyond those experienced by consumers and producers. In the case of the tariff, the government in the importer receives a welfare gain in the amount of the tariff revenue. In the cases of import quotas and VERs, license holders receive a welfare gain in the amount of the rent. Because of these additional welfare effects, the net country welfare effects differ under the equivalent policies. The *importing country* can experience an increase or decrease in net welfare as a result of the tariff and import quota. The direction of the effect depends on the size of the terms of trade effect relative to the distortions. Alternatively, the net welfare effect of the VER is unambiguously negative for the importing country irrespective of the terms of trade effect. Alternatively, the *exporting country* can experience an increase or decrease in net welfare as a result of the VER. The direction of the effect depends on the size of the transfer associated with the license rents relative to the distortions. Alternatively, the net welfare effects of the tariff and import quota are unambiguously negative for the exporting country.

Thus, from a subnational perspective, producers and consumers are indifferent among the three policy equivalents. However, license holders associated with the importer will support an import quota, while license holders associated with an exporter will support a VER. And, the government in the importing country will support a tariff. From a national perspective, the importer will prefer a tariff and import quota over a VER; while the exporting country will prefer a VER over a tariff or import quota. Finally, from a global perspective, the transfers across countries associated with the terms of trade effects and/or license rents counterbalance each other. What remains are the producer and consumer distortions in both the importer and exporter. Thus, from a global perspective none of the policies are preferred as they are welfare deteriorating for the global economy.

Second, what are the relative effects of bans? A ban is an extreme version of the policy equivalents described above. Specifically, a ban is equivalent to a tariff, quota, or VER that results in zero trade. The price and quantity effects of a ban are identical to the above policies in terms of their direction. However, the magnitude of the price and quantity effects is larger under a ban. Furthermore, because the countries eliminate trade in the good, the terms of trade effect is irrelevant. When a ban is imposed, imports and exports cease and both countries revert to their autarky prices. Further, the welfare effects of a ban are comparable to the effects of an extreme tariff, quota and VER. The consumer and producer welfare changes are similar in direction to the policies described above. However, the magnitude of the effects on consumers and producers is larger. Also, in contrast to the tariff, quota, and VER, a ban produces no revenues or rents. Thus, the net country effects of the ban are large consumer and producer distortions alone. In net, both the importer and exporter experience an unambiguously negative welfare loss as a result of a ban.

Third, what are the relative effects of export subsidies? It is not possible to compare an export subsidy that is equivalent to the above described policies directly, because export subsidies are trade augmenting whereas tariffs, quotas, VERs and bans are trade reducing. Indeed, an export subsidy can be viewed as a negative tariff.

As a result, the price and quantity effects of an export subsidy are the mirror opposites of the effects of the trade-reducing policies. For example, trade-reducing policies increase the price in the importer and can decrease the price in the exporter. In contrast, export subsidies increase the price in the exporter and can decrease the price in the importer. Consequently, the implications for quantities supplied and demanded are mirror images. Further, while trade-reducing policies decrease trade, export subsidies increase trade.

The welfare effects of an export subsidy can be most directly compared to the tariff as they both impact the welfare of the government, and neither produces a rent to license holders. Whereas tariffs decrease the welfare of consumers and increase the welfare of producers in the importer, export subsidies increase the welfare of consumers and decrease the welfare of producers in the importer. Conversely, whereas tariffs increase the welfare of consumers and decrease the welfare of producers in the exporter, export subsidies decrease the welfare of consumers and increase the welfare of producers in the exporter. Finally, whereas tariffs generate a revenue for the government, export subsidies generate a cost for the government. The size of the revenue or cost is the volume of trade times the price magnitude of the policy.

Thus, from a subnational perspective, producers in the exporter will support a subsidy, while producers in the importer will support a tariff, quota, or VER. Alternatively, consumers in the importer will support a subsidy, while consumers in the exporter will support a tariff, quota, or VER. Further, government in the exporter will not support a subsidy in terms of the cost of the subsidy, while government in the importer will support a tariff in terms of the revenues generated. From a national perspective, the exporter will prefer none of the policies as they are all welfare deteriorating in net, while the importer will prefer the policy that generates the largest terms of trade improvement. Finally, from a global perspective, the transfers across the countries associated with the terms of trade effects counterbalance each other. What remains are the producer and consumer distortions. Thus, none of the policies (including export subsidies) are preferred, as they are welfare deteriorating for the global economy in aggregate.

Fourth, how do the policies compare? The effects of trade-reducing policies (i.e., tariffs and quantitative restrictions) and trade-augmenting policies (i.e., export subsidies) are clearly related. These policies differ primarily in the distribution of welfare effects. Several insightful patterns emerge for all these policies. First, a welfare increase for an agent in one country is mirrored by a welfare decrease for another agent in that same country. Similarly, a welfare increase for an agent in one country is mirrored by a welfare decrease by a similar agent in its trading partner. Thus, the policies produce welfare transfers both within countries and across countries. Further, if we consider country welfare in aggregate, we see that both importers and exporters experience a decrease in welfare under all of the policies considered. The only exceptions are where the terms of trade effect is large. In these exceptional cases, only one of the two trading partners experiences an increase in country welfare.

These findings are relevant to policy debate in that they explain the widely diverging views about the preservation or liberalization of trade policies. Those who gain from these trade policies are the producers and rent recipients in the country that imposes the policy. Those who lose from these policies are the consumers in the country that imposes the policy. Thus, whether one supports these policies depends on one's perspective. Within a country, there are clearly diverging interests in adopting trade policies. At the national level, the adoption of these trade policies decreases national welfare except where the policy brings about an improvement in the country's terms of trade. And, at the global level, the adoption of these trade policies decreases global welfare.

What are the relative effects of liberalizing policies? The effects of liberalizing policies (i.e., tariffs, quantitative restriction, export subsidies) are the mirror opposites of the effects of adopting the policies. We can simply work all of the analyses backward. That is, instead of adding a policy, we consider the case where the policy is already in place and we remove it or reduce its magnitude. In the case of complete liberalization, we see a reversion to free trade world prices. In the case of partial policy liberalization, we see a movement toward the free trade world price. In this partial liberalization case, the absolute magnitude of the price, quantity and welfare effects described in the preceding section and previous chapters would be reduced.

The general patterns that emerge from analysis of policy liberalization are as follows. Those who gain from liberalizing trade policies are the consumers in the country that liberalizes the policies. In contrast, those who lose from liberalizing these policies are the producers in the country that liberalizes the policy. Thus, whether one supports the liberalization of policies depends on one's perspective. Within a country, there are clearly diverging interests in liberalization of trade policies. At the national level, the liberalization of these trade policies increases national welfare (except where the policy brings about a deterioration in the country's terms of trade). At the global level, the liberalization of these trade policies increases global welfare.

What are the effects of substituting policies? Tariffication is the process of converting non-tariff measures into tariff equivalents. In this chapter, we considered the case of converting an import quota into a tariff equivalent. We showed that there are no price and quantity effects from substitution if the policies are indeed equivalent. Further, we showed that consumer and producer welfare remains unchanged because both policies produce the same welfare effects for consumers and producers. The primary impact of the policy conversion is on the government and license holders in the importing country. Specifically, the license holders lose their rents when the quota is removed, and the government gains the tariff revenues when the tariff is substituted. Thus, the policy conversion results in a transfer from license holders to the government. Because these transfers are equivalent, the national welfare of the countries remains unchanged by the conversion.

There is one exception to this pattern. This is the case where the license holders to the quotas are foreign firms of the exporter rather than domestic firms of the importer. In this case, the loss in quota rents would be incurred by the exporter while the gain in tariff revenue would be incurred by the importer. That is, the policy conversion would result in a welfare transfer from the exporter to the importer. Jointly, however, their aggregate welfare would remain unchanged as a consequence of policy substitution.

Finally, this welfare analysis can be used to inform hybrid policies, such as the tariff rate quota, which are used to facilitate the conversion of bans and quotas into tariffs to advance the process of liberalization.

Applied Problems

8.1   Choose two countries and one industry that you are interested in examining. Using these countries and industry, consider trade policies including tariffs, export subsidies, quotas, bans, and voluntary export restraints. Examine and compare the effects of eliminating each of these policies on prices, quantities supplied, quantities demanded, and trade. Make an assumption about whether your countries can affect the world price.

8.2   Choose two countries and one industry that you are interested in examining. Using these countries and industry, and your knowledge of the welfare effects of the trade policies, to explain why policy makers interested in maximizing national and world welfare support free trade, while select agents within countries (e.g., consumers, government, producers) may not support free trade. Consider and compare policies including tariffs, export subsidies, quotas, bans, and voluntary export restraints.

8.3   International agreements to liberalize trade often convert non-tariff barriers to trade into tariffs and then establish a schedule for tariff reductions over time. Consider a large importing country that has agreed to replace its quotas with tariffs. Evaluate the effects of replacing a quota with a tariff on welfare in the importing country.

8.4   Examine the effects of tariffs and import quotas (that are policy equivalent) on the welfare of the exporter. What conclusions can you draw about the interests of the exporter in the liberalization of its trading partner's policies?

8.5   Consider a case where the EU simultaneously imposes two policies: (a) an export subsidy on sugar; and (b) an import tariff on sugar. Examine the impact of these simultaneous policies from a national and global perspective.

8.6   Consider the case where Ghana liberalizes its subsidies, tariffs, and quotas in the poultry and maize sectors. Consider the impact of this liberalization on producer welfare in Ghana. Now, consider the case where the EU maintains export subsidies on poultry and maize at the same time that Ghana liberalizes trade in these sectors. Examine the effects of these simultaneous policies on producer welfare in Ghana.

8.7   Consider the case where Spain subsidizes exports of tomatoes. Furthermore, assume that Morocco imposes an import quota on imports of Spanish tomatoes. Examine the effects of these simultaneous policies on consumer welfare in both countries.

8.8   Policies to liberalize trade have succeeded at reducing tariffs and a variety of non-tariff barriers to trade. As a by-product, new more subtle barriers to trade arise. Consider a trade barrier called a voluntary export tax (VET). Assume that the VET is identical to a tariff except that it is imposed by the exporting country. (a) Evaluate the welfare effects of a VET on the importing and exporting countries. (b) Compare the welfare effects of a VET with a tariff.

8.9   Consider the case where the United States imports electronics from Japan and these imports are subject to a tariff. Assume that the United States is large in terms of the market for electronics. (a) What is the effect on US consumption of domestic versus foreign electronics of eliminating this tariff? Now, suppose that in exchange for the US tariff reduction, Japan agrees to adopt a voluntary export restraint on its exports of electronics to the United States. Assume that the VER is a policy equivalent with the original tariff. (b) What is the effect of adopting the VER on US consumption of domestic versus foreign electronics?

8.10 Consider a government that is interested in maximizing government welfare only; that is, this government places no weight on the welfare of consumers, producers, or license holders of any kind. This government has a choice between a variety of policies, including tariffs, import quotas, bans, VERs, and export subsidies. From a government welfare perspective, rank these policies in order from best to worst. Support your conclusion.

8.11 Use the journal articles listed under "further reading" at the end of this chapter to consider the policy instrument referred to as the tariff rate quota.

Illustrate and discuss the implications of the following scenarios: (a) the demand for imports is less than the quota; (b) the demand for imports exceeds the quota and the quota is enforced; (c) the demand for imports exceeds the quota and the quota is not enforced; and (d) the over-quota tariff is sufficiently high such that no imports occur after the quota is satisfied.

8.12   Use the journal articles to consider the liberalization of tariff rate quotas. Explore the debate over liberalization of tariff rate quotas via increasing the quota, versus liberalization of tariff rate quotas via decreasing the over-quota tariff.

Further Reading

Bhagwati, Jagdish. 1965. On the equivalence of tariffs and quotas. In *Trade, Growth, and the Balance of Payments* (eds Robert E. Baldwin, *et al.*). Chicago: Rand McNally.

Bhagwati, Jagdish. 1968. More on the equivalence of tariffs and quotas. *American Economic Review* 58 (1): 142–146.

de Gorter, Harry, and Erika Kliauga. 2006. Reducing tariffs versus expanding tariff rate quotas. In *Agricultural Trade Reform and the Doha Development Agenda* (eds Kym Anderson and Will Martin), Washington, D.C.: World Bank and Palgrave Macmillan, pp. 117–160.

Hranaiova, Jana, Harry de Gorter, and James Falk. 2006. The economics of administering import quotas with licenses-on-demand in agriculture. *American Journal of Agricultural Economics* 88 (2): 3318–3350.

Rom, Michael. 1979. *The Role of Tariff Quotas in Commercial Policy*. New York: Holmes and Meier.

Skully, David W. 2001. *Economics of Tariff-Rate Quota Administration*. US Department of Agriculture, Economic Research Service, Technical Bulletin Number 1893 (April). Washington, D.C.: USDA.

Vousden, N. 1990. *The Economic Theory of Protection*. Cambridge: Cambridge University Press.

World Trade Organization (WTO). 1997. *European Communities-Regime for the Importation, Sale, and Distribution of Bananas*. Report of the Appellate Body (September 9). Geneva: WTO.

World Trade Organization (WTO). 2006. *Tariff Quota Administration Methods and Tariff Quota Fill*. Committee on Agricure Background Paper TN/AG/S/22 (April 27). Geneva: WTO.

Note

1. For detailed illustrations of tariff rate quotas under a variety of scenarios, see de Gorter and Kliauga (2006), Skully (2001), and World Trade Organization (2006; 1997).

Part Three
Trade-Related Policies

9

Preliminaries
Trade-Related Policies and
Trade in Services

9.1 What Are Trade-Related Policies?

In Part Two of this book, we considered the effects of traditional trade policies including tariffs, export subsidies, and quantitative restrictions. These *traditional trade policies* are policies that are specifically targeted to affect trade. In Part Three, we turn to trade-related policies. *Trade-related policies* are policies designed for non-trade purposes that affect trade as a side effect. Prominent trade-related policies include intellectual property rights, environmental policies, labor policies, and growth and development policies, among others.

Trade-related policies differ from traditional trade policies in several key ways. They tend to be less *transparent* in terms of their effects on prices, trade, and welfare. Trade-related policies also tend to be more *discriminatory* against a particular country or group of countries, or against a particular good or group of goods. And, trade-related policies tend to be more *discretionary* in that government authorities have more control over the application of these policies.

The relative importance of trade-related policies in trade negotiations has increased during the past decade. Their economic significance has become more evident as traditional trade policies have been liberalized. The emergence of trade-related policies is in part due to efforts to seek new forms of protection in the absence of traditional forms of protection.

These characteristics of trade-related policies have implications for the character of research. The literature on trade-related policies is more nascent and opaque than is the literature on traditional trade policies. In contrast to studies of traditional trade policies, few models can be held up as classic illustrations of the effects of trade-related policies. Areas of consensus among economists continue to evolve in

Global Trade Policy: Questions and Answers, First Edition. Pamela J. Smith.
© 2014 John Wiley & Sons, Inc. Published 2014 by John Wiley & Sons, Inc.

response to ongoing changes in real-world practice. Further, since trade-related policies affect trade as a side effect, it is more problematic to assume a single direction of causality where the trade policy is exogenous. For example, environmental policies can affect trade, and trade policies can affect the environment. Thus, trade policy is not necessarily exogenous with respect to environmental policy, and vice versa.

Given these features, we take a descriptive approach to examining trade-related policies and their effects in Part Three. When possible, we apply methods from the traditional trade literature to examine effects. Furthermore, we extend our analysis by considering the alternative approach that reverses the direction of causality. For example, we consider the effects of environmental and labor policies on trade in addition to considering the effects of trade policy on the environment and on labor. And, we consider the effects of growth and development in the presence of trade, in addition to considering the effects of trade policy on development and growth. As in Part Two of the book, Part Three examines these policies one at a time. Part Four then considers the institutional arrangements within which these trade policies are negotiated and managed.

Before turning to our analysis of trade-related policies, we briefly summarize a selection of changes that have occurred in real-world practice to bring these trade-related policies to the forefront of policy dialog. That is, we ask the question: How have trade-related policies evolved over time in practice? We also consider the growing role of services trade and ask: How have trade policies toward services evolved over time in practice?

9.2   How Have Trade-Related Policies Evolved over Time in Practice?

The importance of trade-related policies became evident in policy dialog beginning in the 1980s during the Uruguay Round of negotiations of the General Agreement on Tariffs and Trade (GATT). This new dialog emerged in the wake of strong pressures for protectionism in the late 1970s and early 1980s. To counter these pressures, efforts were initiated among GATT members to extend the scope of subjects negotiated under the GATT. New areas of emphasis in the Uruguay Round included consideration of sector-specific policies for agricultural trade, and textile and clothing trade; and consideration of newly recognized trade-related policies such as intellectual property rights, investment measures and rules for services trade, among others.

The Uruguay Round of negotiations of the GATT was contentious and lasted nine years (from 1986 to 1994). However, these negotiations brought about substantial changes in the application of traditional trade policies and the scope of trade-related policies under multilateral management. Prominent changes in *traditional trade policies* include: (1) commitments for reductions in agricultural support including reductions in domestic and *export subsidies*; (2) liberalization of *quantitative restrictions* in textiles and clothing; (3) an agreement on rules related to safeguards[1] banning the use of *voluntary export restraints*; and (4) reductions in *tariffs* beyond those achieved in previous rounds of negotiations. Prominent changes in the scope of trade-related policies include: (5) beginning commitments for liberalizing trade in services; (6) articulation of standards for intellectual property rights; (7) new rules for product standards; and (8) new rules for trade-related investment measures, among others.

The Uruguay Round also brought about substantial changes in the institutional arrangements for managing these traditional and trade-related policies. Most significantly, the Uruguay Round agreement resulted in the establishment of the World Trade Organization (WTO) in 1995, as the successor of the GATT; and the creation of a dispute settlement mechanism that would provide a more neutral and binding means for resolving disputes. These changes in the scope and management of trade policies are the most economically significant changes in the multilateral management of trade policies to date.

The content of the Uruguay Round includes 60 agreements, annexes, decisions and understandings. However, six main agreements create the core structure. One is the umbrella agreement establishing the WTO; a second is the agreement on dispute settlement; a third is the agreement on reviews of the trade policies of governments; and the three other prominent agreements cover broad subjects of trade including goods, services, and intellectual property rights. The basic principles covering these subjects are articulated in the General Agreement on Tariffs and Trade (GATT), the General Agreement on Trade in Services (GATS), and the Agreement on Trade-Related Aspects of Intellectual Property Rights (TRIPS), respectively. The additional 50-plus agreements and annexes address special requirements relevant to select industries or select issues. Lastly, the agreement includes lists of commitments by individual countries concerning access to their markets for specific goods and services.

Part Three covers a sampling of the trade-related issues that have been controversial and/or have experienced significant changes in the wake of the WTO agreement. These issues include intellectual property rights, the environment, and labor. Part Three also considers growth and development policies because these policies are intimately connected to trade, and help us to understand the sometimes contrasting perspectives of developed and developing countries in trade negotiations. We make no attempt to be complete in our coverage of trade-related policies. There are 60 agreements, annexes, decisions and understandings of the WTO agreement alone. Rather, our goal is to provide a framework for thinking about a selection of economically significant issues that are and will continue to be on the policy frontier for the coming decade.

One issue that is not covered in Part Three is particularly noteworthy. This issue is trade in services. As noted at the beginning of this book, international flows include movements of goods, services, and factors of production. Of these categories, trade in services has grown most dramatically since the 1980s. Hence, the rules governing international trade have broadened in recent agreements to cover these newer forms of international flows. Thus, before proceeding, we briefly summarize how trade policies toward services have evolved over time in practice.

9.3   How Have Trade Policies Toward Services Evolved over Time in Practice?

Trade in *services* includes international transactions in non-tangibles. These include functions and tasks performed for which there is demand and thus a price determined in the market. Services are typically non-transferable in that they cannot be purchased and then resold at a different price. These types of transactions go beyond the traditional definition of trade in goods that physically cross national borders. Examples of trade in non-tangible services include international transactions in business, communication, construction, distribution, education, environment, finance, health and social-related functions, tourism and travel, recreation, culture, and sporting and transportation.

The importance of trade in services became apparent beginning in the 1980s. Since then, trade in services has grown rapidly.[2] The data on services transactions between the residents and non-residents of countries show a 15% annual increase in services trade since 1980. This growth rate exceeds that of other components of trade. Services trade is now believed to contribute more than 20% of the total value of world trade in goods and services. The United States and the European Union are leaders in services trade, accounting for more than 60% of world services exports. However, there are also a number of developing countries with rapidly growing exports of services. These include Brazil, China, and India, among others. The rapid expansion of trade in services is due in large part to advances in information technologies.

The character of trade in services is similar to the character of trade in goods.[3] For example, trade in services includes *inter-industry trade* where there is two-way trade between countries in dissimilar services. Trade in services also includes *intra-industry trade* where countries trade different varieties of similar services with each other. Trade in services also includes *intra-firm trade* where trade across countries occurs within the same firm – such as between a parent firm and affiliates, or between different firms under a multinational umbrella. This intra-firm trade includes foreign direct investment, and offshoring of services. Explanations for these patterns of trade include the sources of comparative advantage (covered in Chapter 2), and economies of scale (covered in Chapter 3), among others.

Barriers to trade in services are distinct from barriers to trade in goods.[4] Barriers to trade in services tend to arise from domestic regulations that focus on non-trade concerns. For example, the domestic regulation of services tends to focus on correcting for market failures, as well as protecting domestic producers from international competition. This protection of services comes primarily in the form of *quantitative restrictions*. For example, restrictions are used to limit the participation of foreign producers in supplying a service domestically, to limit the number of foreign suppliers in select service sectors, to limit foreign ownership in firms providing services domestically, and to limit the movement of service-providing labor. Given this difference in the character of barriers, the liberalization of trade in services is quite distinct from the liberalization of trade in goods. Arrangements for liberalizing services trade tend to focus on the concept of non-discrimination and the reform of domestic regulations.

The effects of liberalizing services trade include welfare gains similar to those from liberalizing goods trade. The gains from trade in services refer to the welfare implications of services trade for the countries that participate in it. These gains include increased consumption opportunities for countries that trade services. The gains also include increases in the variety (including quality) of services consumed. However, the liberalization of services trade results in winners and losers, just as does the liberalization of trade in goods. Thus, liberalizing services trade requires attention to policies that support the reallocation of factors of production (including labor) out of sectors of comparative disadvantage and into sectors of comparative advantage. The liberalization of services trade also requires attention to policies that address welfare distribution. Finally, services are somewhat unique in the sense that services outputs are often used as inputs in the production of other goods and/ or services. Thus, the liberalization of trade in service inputs is intimately linked to the prices of final goods and services.

In practice, the most significant liberalization of services trade has occurred through the General Agreement on Trade in Services (GATS) – the 1995 agreement resulting from the Uruguay Round of negotiations of the GATT. GATS contains the first multilateral rules for trade in services. This agreement has provided a first step toward creating a multilateral rules-based environment for managing international services trade.[5]

The coverage of services included under the GATS is broad, including essentially all measures that affect trade in services. Examples are listed at the beginning of this section. GATS also defines the modes for services trade broadly. These modes include transactions that involve: (1) *cross-border* flows, where services supplied from one country flow into the territory of another country; (2) *consumption abroad*, where services supplied in one country are consumed in another; (3) *commercial presence*, where services of a firm of one country are supplied in the territory of another country; and (4) *presence of natural persons*, where the services of nationals of one country are supplied in the territory of another country.[6] The inclusion of the last two modes in the GATS agreement represents a significant broadening of the multilateral management of concerns that were previously managed predominantly by national governments.

The rules of the GATS fall into two broad categories: the general rules affecting trade in services that apply to all members and all service sector; and the commitments made by specific member countries for liberalizing services trade in specific sectors. One important component of the general rules is the most favored nation (MFN) obligation of GATS. The MFN obligation requires that members of the agreement grant to each other treatment that is as favorable as they extend to any other member regarding the application of the GATS rules. Certain exemptions to this obligation are allowed in specific sensitive service sectors, however. Departure from the MFN obligation is also permitted in the context of regional trade arrangements that liberalize trade in services beyond the obligations of GATS. Exception from the MFN rule is also permitted for the movement of natural persons in the context of agreements designed to integrate labor markets across countries.

In contrast to these general principals, the commitments made by specific member countries for liberalizing services trade in specific sectors focus on market access and national treatment. The *market access* rules provide limits on the use of restrictions that create barriers to trade in services. These rules focus primarily on the quantitative restrictions described at the beginning of this section as barriers to trade. The rules provide limitations on the use of quantitative restrictions that create barriers to services via any of the modes described previously. Further, the *national treatment* rules require that members of the agreement grant – to the services and service suppliers of any member – treatment that is as favorable as they extend to their own services and service suppliers. This principle is designed to reduce discrimination against the entry and operation of foreign service providers. The specific country commitments made in the GATS agreement specify the service sectors to be subject to these principles, and specify the exceptions to these rules for specific service sectors and modes of service trade. It should be noted that many of these rules for services were modeled on those of the GATT agreement that provides coverage for trade in goods.

These commitments made under the GATS agreement have created a rules-based environment for the multilateral management of trade in services. However, in practice the liberalization of trade in services is still in early stages.

9.4   How Is Part Three Organized?

Part Three covers trade-related policies and their effects. As noted earlier, trade-related policies are policies designed for non-trade purposes that affect trade as a side effect. This part includes four component chapters, each covering distinct policy concerns.

Chapter 10 covers intellectual property rights. We ask four core questions: What are intellectual property rights, their types, and purpose? What are the effects of intellectual property rights? How have intellectual property rights evolved over time in practice? What are the intellectual property rights issues on the policy frontier? In examining the effects of intellectual property rights, we take three alternative perspectives. First, we consider the domestic effects of intellectual property rights. Second, we consider the effects of country differences in intellectual property rights. Third, we consider the relative effects of intellectual property rights on trade, foreign direct investment, and licensing.

Chapter 11 covers environmental policies. We consider four core questions: What are trade-related environmental policies, their types, and purpose? What are the effects of trade policy on the environment? What are the effects of environmental policy on trade? What are the implications of using trade policy to address environmental externalities? In answering the latter question, we consider the effects of using a variety of trade policies to correct for externalities in an open economy setting where countries trade. These externalities include a negative production externality in a small exporter, and a negative consumption externality in a small importer. Such externalities include pollution and other forms of environmental damage.

Chapter 12 covers labor policies. We consider four core questions: What are trade-related labor policies, their types, and purpose? What are the effects of trade policy on labor? How can the gains and losses from trade be redistributed within countries? What are the effects of labor policy on trade? In considering the effects of trade policy on labor, we explore both the long-run and short-run effects of trade on wages.

Finally, Chapter 13 covers growth and development policies. We consider three core questions: What are trade-related development and growth policies, their types, and purpose? What are the effects of trade on development and growth? What are the effects of growth on development in the presence of trade?

In each of these chapters, we consider the effects of trade and trade-related policies on welfare and the distribution of welfare. As throughout the book, we seek to identify the diverse perspectives contributing to the policy dialog, and to highlight what is at stake and for whom.

Further Reading

Deardorff, Alan V., and Robert M. Stern. 2007. Empirical analysis of barriers to international services transactions and the consequences of liberalization. In *Handbook of Services Trade* (eds Aaditya Mattoo, Robert M. Stern, and Gianni Zanini), Oxford: Oxford University Press, pp. 169–220.

Feketekuty, Geza. 1988. *International Trade in Services: An Overview and Blueprint for Negotiations.* Cambridge, MA: Ballinger.

Hindley, Brian, and Alasdair Smith. 1984. Comparative advantage and trade in service. *World Economy* 7 (4): 369–390.

Hoekman, Bernard. 1996. Assessing the General Agreement on Trade and Services. In *The Uruguay Round and the Developing Countries* (eds Will Martin and L. Alan Winters), Cambridge: Cambridge University Press, pp. 88–124.

Hoekman, Bernard. 2006. *Liberalizing Trade in Services: A Survey.* World Bank Policy Research Working Paper No. 4030, Washington, D.C.: World Bank.

Maskus, Keith E., and John S. Wilson, eds. 2001. *Quantifying the Impact of Technical Barriers to Trade: Can It Be Done?* Ann Arbor: University of Michigan Press.

Mattoo, Aaditya. 2005. Services in a development round: three goals and three proposals. *Journal of World Trade* 39 (6): 1223–1238.

Mattoo, Aaditya, Robert M. Stern, and Gianni Zanini, eds. 2007. *Handbook of Services Trade.* Oxford: Oxford Unversity Press.

Winters, L. Alan, T. L. Wlamsley, Z. K. Wang, R. Grynberg. 2003. Liberalizing temporary movement of national persons: an agenda for the development round. *World Economy* 26 (8): 1137–1161.

Notes

1. Safeguards are a form of contingent protection, where a country can reimpose a barrier to imports in order to protect their domestic industries from injury caused by import competition.
2. See Hoekman (2006) and Mattoo, Stern, and Zanini (2007) for comprehensive studies of trade in services.
3. See Hindley and Smith (1984) for an early study of comparative advantage in services trade.
4. See Deardorff and Stern (2007) for discussion of barriers to trade in services and their liberalization.
5. See Feketekuty (1988), Hoekman (1996) and Mattoo (2005) for discussions of the GATS agreement.
6. See Winters, *et al.* (2003) for empirical evidence on the "natural persons" immigration issue.

10

Intellectual Property Rights

10.1   What Are Intellectual Property Rights, Their Types, and Purpose?

Intellectual property refers to creations of the mind including inventions, literary and artistic works, and symbols, names, images and designs used in commerce. These creations of the mind have two distinctive characteristics typically associated with public goods. They are non-rivalrous and non-excludable. The *non-rival* characteristic means that the use of the intellectual property does not reduce its availability for use by others. Indeed, once created, the marginal cost of access to intellectual property is small. The *non-excludable* characteristic means that the use of intellectual property by others is difficult to limit in the private market. That is, in the absence of legal protections, it is difficult to restrict the use of intellectual property.

Intellectual property rights (IPRs) are laws regarding the protection of intellectual property. These laws describe the ways in which the creators of intellectual property can control its use. They are provided to create a private market for what would otherwise be a public good with non-rivalrous and non-excludable characteristics.

The primary *forms of IPRs*, include patents, copyrights, trademarks and service-marks, plant breeders' rights, *sui generis rights*, and trade secrets. These various forms of IPR protect different types of creations of the mind. Below, we briefly summarize each of these types of IPRs.

Patents are the form of IPRs that protects inventions. Patents are issued by the Patent and Trademark Office of a country. The term of a new patent is usually 20

Global Trade Policy: Questions and Answers, First Edition. Pamela J. Smith.
© 2014 John Wiley & Sons, Inc. Published 2014 by John Wiley & Sons, Inc.

years. Patents are effective only within the country and sometimes its territories and possessions. The rights conferred by a patent grant are the rights to exclude others from making, using, offering for sale or selling the invention in the country, or importing the invention into the country. In order to qualify for protection via a patent, the invention must be novel. This novelty requirement applies to both products and processes. For example, patents can be used to protect a novel chemical invention as well as a novel method for producing the chemical.

Utility models provide an alternative to patents to protect inventions in some countries. Utility models differ from patents in several significant ways. First, although they cover inventions as do patents, the inventions covered tend to be less technically complex. Second, the requirements for qualifying for a utility model are less stringent than that for a patent. Third, the length of protection tends to be shorter for utility models than for patents.

Industrial designs also provide a variant to patent protection. Industrial designs protect features of a product that are produced by industrial means. These features can be ornamental or aesthetic, such as the shape, pattern or color of the product.

Copyrights are the form of IPRs that protects original works of authorship including literary, dramatic, musical, artistic and certain other technology-based works such as computer programs, electronic databases, and multimedia productions. Copyrights apply to both published and unpublished original work. The term of a copyright is usually 50 to 70 years after the death of the author, or 95 years from publication if the work is of corporate authorship. Copyrights are effective in the country where they are registered. They generally give the owner of the copyright the exclusive right to reproduce the copyrighted work, to prepare derivative works, to distribute copies or phonorecords of the copyrighted work, to perform the copyrighted work publicly, or to display the copyrighted work publicly. The copyright protects the form of expression rather than the subject matter of the writing. For example, a description of a trade model could be copyrighted, but this would only prevent others from copying the description. It would not prevent others from writing a description of their own or using the model.

Trademarks are the form of IPRs that protects a word, name, symbol or device. These marks are used to indicate the source of a good and to distinguish it from other goods. *Servicemarks* are similar to trademarks except that they identify and distinguish the source of a service rather than a product. Examples of services include financial services, insurance services, and technical support services, among others. In recent decades, trade in services has grown dramatically, along with the importance of servicemarks. Trademarks and servicemarks are registered with the Patent and Trademark Office of a country. They are used to prevent others from using an identical mark, but not to prevent others from making the same goods or services, or from selling the same goods or services under a clearly different mark.

Geographical indications are a variant of trademarks and servicemarks. Geographical indications are signs on a good associated with the origin of the good. They indicate that the good is from the particular location or that it has a quality or reputation due to its location of origin. For example, signs are included on wine and other food products to indicate the location of origin and quality.

Plant breeders' rights (PBRs), also known as *plant variety rights* (PVRs), are rights granted to the breeder of a new variety of plant or to another person or entity that can claim title in the new plant variety. These laws typically grant the plant breeder control of the propagating material (including seeds, cuttings, divisions, and tissue cultures) and harvested material (including cut flowers, fruit, and foliage) of a new variety for a number of years. With these rights, the breeder can choose to become the exclusive marketer of the variety, or to license the variety to others. In order to qualify for protection by PBRs, a variety must be new, distinct, uniform and stable. A variety is *new* if it has not been commercialized for more than one year in the country of protection. A variety is *distinct* if it differs from all other known varieties by one or more botanical characteristic, such as height, maturity, or color. A variety is *uniform* if the plant characteristics are consistent from plant to plant within the variety. A variety is *stable* if the plant characteristics are genetically fixed and therefore remain the same from generation to generation, or after a cycle of reproduction in the case of hybrid varieties. The breeder must give the variety a "denomination", which becomes its generic name and must be used by anyone who markets the variety.

Sui generis rights provide protection to forms of intellectual property that do not fit into the standard categories of intellectual property provided by a country. Sui generis rights usually apply to new types of intellectual property arising from advances in technology. Examples of intellectual property covered by sui generis rights include the electronic transmission of databases or broadcasts, computer software, and layout design of integrated circuits. Sui generis rights also apply to types of intellectual property that are not covered by other forms of protection. For example, sui generis protections cover plant breeders' rights in countries without such rights.

Trade secrets protect confidential business information that provides a firm with a competitive edge. The subject matter of trade secrets includes industrial property such as advertising strategies, consumer profiles, distribution methods, lists of suppliers and clients, manufacturing processes such as secret ingredients, and sales methods. The unauthorized use or disclosure of such information is regarded as an unfair practice and a violation of the trade secret. Depending on the legal system, the protection of trade secrets is part of the protection against unfair competition, or is part of provisions or case law regarding the protection of confidential information. Trade secrets have no period of time attached to them. Rather, trade secrets expire when the information becomes part of the public domain through legal means such as reverse engineering or disclosures of the information on public documents. Trade secrets are sometimes used as an alternative to the previously discussed forms of IPRs, because these other forms require reporting of technical information in pubic documents whereas trade secrets do not have such a requirement.

The *purpose* of the forms of IPRs described above is to create an incentive for the creation of intellectual property. This incentive is created by ensuring a return on the investments required for the creation to take place. That is, IPRs give the owner of the intellectual property the right to exclude others from using the intellectual property for a set period of time. In this way, IPRs confer a monopoly power to the owner of the intellectual property for a period of time. During this time, the owner of the intellectual property can earn a return to cover their investments in the creation of the intellectual property. Investments can include, for example, monies spent on research and development, and time invested in writing a book. Without IPRs, the intellectual property may be used or copied by individuals or firms other than the creator of the intellectual property. If this occurs, the creator may not be able to cover the costs associated with the creation and has little incentive to create. With IPRs, the creator is able to cover the costs of creation and thus has an incentive to create.

10.2   What Are the Effects of Intellectual Property Rights?

This section considers the effects of IPRs. We consider three specific questions: (1) What are the domestic effects of IPRs? (2) What are the effects of country differences in IPRs? (3) What are the relative effects of IPRs on trade, foreign direct investment, and licensing? The reason we address these three separate questions is twofold. First, domestic and international policies governing IPRs differ. This is because IPRs are national laws and countries vary in the character and enforcement of their national laws. Second, intellectual property (i.e., a creation of the mind) is exposed to infringement in a variety of ways. International flows of intellectual property occur via a variety of channels including trade, foreign direct investment, and licensing contracts with unaffiliated foreign firms. IPRs can have differential effects on these alternative channels of intellectual property flow.

10.2.1   What are the domestic effects of intellectual property rights?

We begin by considering the domestic effects of IPR policies because IPRs are national in scope. That is, laws governing the protection of intellectual property are national laws. The protection provided by these national laws extends only to the geographic boundaries of the country, and sometimes its territories or possessions.

There is a tradeoff associated with the strength of national laws governing IPRs. On one hand, IPRs provide incentives for the development of creations of the mind by providing higher profits to the holders of the intellectual property. This can have a positive welfare effect on society by increasing innovation. Also, the disclosure of information via the patent application can foster the development of derivative technologies. Assuming that these technologies do not infringe on the protected intellectual property, the creation of these new technologies can also have a positive effect on social welfare. On the other hand, IPRs confer a temporary monopoly over the creation. Such monopoly power can result in higher prices and lower economic efficiency. This temporary monopoly can also restrict the diffusion and access to the knowledge. This can have a negative welfare effect on society by temporarily limiting public access to new creations.

The concept of *optimal IPRs* is related to the strength of protection provided by the laws, and the tradeoff discussed above. The strength of protection has two dimensions. The first is the *scope* of the creations that are covered. For example, basic inventions with many applications are not typically covered by patents. However, narrower applications may be covered. The reason is that granting patents to basic inventions would grant monopoly power over too broad a range of activities. The second dimension of strength is the *length* of protection of creations. For example, the owner may be granted exclusive rights for 20 years or 50 years. This length of protection varies depending on the form of protection (e.g., patents, copyrights). After the period ends, the intellectual property goes into the public domain.

The *optimal strength* of IPRs is that strength (i.e., scope and length) that maximizes welfare. The optimal strength induces incentives for creation without conferring excess monopoly power. IPRs that are too strong result in excessive monopoly over the creation. In this case, output is restricted in order to sell goods at higher monopoly prices. This lowers welfare. Alternatively, IPRs that are too weak result in underinvestment in creations of the mind. Free access to knowledge can create welfare gains in the short run. However, free access creates a disincentive to the creation of new forms of intellectual property in the long run. This lowers welfare.

10.2.2 What are the effects of country differences in intellectual property rights?

The effects of IPRs are even more complex at the international level. As mentioned earlier, IPRs are national in geographic scope. This means that firms need to apply for IPRs in all countries where they want protection. The protections provided in different countries, however, are not equivalent. Furthermore, the enforcement of IPRs varies widely across countries. This variation tends to be correlated with the level of development of countries. That is, developed countries tend to have stronger IPRs than do developing countries.

This variation can affect the way that goods, services and the factors of production move across countries. This is because intellectual property is embodied in goods, services and the factors of production. More specifically, intellectual property can move across national borders via trade, foreign direct investment, or licensing arrangements. With trade, the intellectual property is embodied in the goods and services that physically move across countries. With foreign direct investment, the intellectual property is moved to a new or existing affiliated foreign subsidiary and used to produce the good or service in the foreign location. With licensing, the intellectual property is transferred to an unaffiliated foreign firm who then produces the good or service. Each of these forms of movement of intellectual property internationally can be affected by cross-country differences in laws affecting the protection of intellectual property.

The effects of IPRs on international flows of intellectual property can be understood by considering the incentives for countries that are abundant in intellectual property versus countries that are scarce in intellectual property. Countries abundant in intellectual property tend to be the sources of intellectual property embodied either in goods, services or factors of production. Countries scarce in intellectual property tend to be recipients of embodied intellectual property. What then are the effects of country differences in IPRs on the incentives to move intellectual property between source countries and recipient countries?

The current research suggests that there is an ambiguous relationship between IPRs and international flows of intellectual property.[1] From the source country's perspective, this ambiguity arises because there are two countervailing effects. On the one hand, source firms have incentives to transfer their intellectual property to markets where IPRs are relatively strong. This is because the source firm can apply for protection in the foreign market and reduce the risk that its creations will be copied. The need for intellectual property protection is particularly relevant when domestic firms in the recipient market have the ability to imitate the intellectual property. In this case, there is a positive relationship between the strength of IPRs in a recipient country and the source firm's incentives to transfer intellectual property to its market. (As noted earlier, this transfer can occur via trade, FDI, or licensing). This effect is referred to as the *market expansion effect* of IPRs since stronger IPRs expand international flows of intellectual property in this case.

On the other hand, source firms also have incentives to restrict their transfer of intellectual property to markets where IPRs are relatively strong. This is because the firms can apply for protection in the foreign market and decrease their exports to extract monopoly prices. This situation is particularly relevant when the source firm is servicing foreign markets where few close substitutes are available, where imitative abilities are weak, and/or where there are few competing domestic firms. In this case, there is a negative relationship between the strength of protection in the recipient country and the source firm's incentives to transfer intellectual property to their market. This effect is referred to as the *monopoly power effect* of IPRs since stronger IPRs reduce international flows of intellectual property by supporting monopoly behavior.

The net effect of IPRs on the source firms' incentives to transfer intellectual property into foreign markets depends on the relative dominance of the market expansion and monopoly power effects. However, despite this ambiguity, the country that is the source of the intellectual property prefers that recipient countries have strong intellectual property protections, either to reduce risk of imitation or allow for monopoly behavior in the recipient countries' markets. As noted earlier, developed countries tend to be sources of intellectual property whereas developing countries tend to be recipients of intellectual property that flow in the international market. The effects described above help to explain why developed countries with strong IPRs prefer that recipient countries adopt equally strong IPRs such that there are gains either via market expansion or monopoly power.

From the recipient country's perspective, the incentives for protecting intellectual property are mixed. On the one hand, countries that are recipients of intellectual property have a disincentive to strengthen intellectual property laws. This is because adopting stronger IPRs can induce both static and dynamic costs. Static costs include: higher monopoly prices of goods, services, and factors of production that embody the intellectual property; the transfer of rents associated with intellectual property outside the recipient country to the source country monopolies; and the loss of competitiveness of domestic firms in the recipient country that rely on imitated intellectual property as inputs. These costs are associated with the monopoly power effect of IPRs. Further, dynamic costs include reduced spillovers associated with the imitation of intellectual property. If such spillovers contribute to economic growth, then adopting stronger IPRs can have a negative effect on growth in the recipient country.

Alternatively, countries that are recipients of intellectual property also have an incentive to strengthen their own IPRs. This perspective is based on the assumption of dynamic welfare gains from stronger protection. The argument is that stronger IPRs facilitate (rather than restrict) the diffusion of intellectual property in recipient countries by increasing transactions with countries that are the sources of intellectual property. The diffusion of this intellectual property can contribute to growth. This perspective relies on the market expansion effect of IPRs. Furthermore, dynamic welfare gains can also be achieved if stronger IPRs create an incentive for domestic firms in recipient countries to innovate and seek protection for their own intellectual property. However, these welfare gains require that the country has the ability to produce or reproduce the intellectual property, such as via innovation, imitation, or reverse engineering.

Thus, the incentives for the recipient country to adopt relatively strong IPRs depend on whether the costs of the protections outweigh the benefits. In the former case, the recipient of intellectual property prefers to adopt relatively weak intellectual property protections to allow for domestic imitation and prevent monopoly behavior in their market. In the latter case, the recipient of intellectual property prefers to adopt relatively strong intellectual property protections to facilitate technology transfer and provide domestic incentives for innovation. These mixed incentives help explain why developing countries (who are recipients of intellectual property) have resisted strengthening their intellectual property laws, despite the strong pressure from developed countries (who are sources of intellectual property). The view of most developing countries is that the costs associated with adopting strong IPRs outweigh the benefits.

10.2.3   What are the relative effects of intellectual property rights on trade, foreign direct investment, and licensing?

In the section above, we described the effects of IPRs on international flows of intellectual property. We considered the incentives of both the source and recipient countries of the intellectual property. This discussion[3] applies to all forms of international flow of intellectual property, regardless of the means. Next, we step back and ask whether IPRs have differential effects on the means by which intellectual property flows across countries; that is, what are the relative effects of IPRs on the alternative means of servicing markets?[2]

Firms can transfer intellectual property to foreign markets in several ways. A source firm can transfer intellectual property embodied in goods and services to the foreign market via trade. A source firm can transfer intellectual property via foreign direct investment, whereby the firm establishes a subsidiary in the foreign market and transfers its intellectual property to this subsidiary. Or, a source firm can transfer intellectual property via a licensing arrangement, whereby the firm transfers its intellectual property to an unaffiliated firm in the recipient market. Thus, intellectual property can be transferred internationally via trade, FDI, and/or licensing. The source firms of the intellectual property can choose between these alternative means of servicing.

The relationship between IPRs and these servicing decisions is complex and not well understood. This is because intellectual property is transferred via a variety of mechanisms. For example, intellectual property can be transferred via trade if firms in the recipient country are able to imitate the technology by reverse engineering either the traded products that embody the intellectual property or the process such as production methods. Intellectual property can be transferred via FDI as a result of the diffusion of the intellectual property from the subsidiary to a domestic firm in the recipient country. This can occur from the movement of factors of production (such as labor) between firms and from externalities such as knowledge spillovers. Intellectual property can also be transferred via licensing arrangements that include contractual agreements to transfer rights to unaffiliated foreign firms, including the rights to use intellectual property. Intellectual property laws require that the user of the intellectual property – acquired by these various means – compensate the creator or source of the intellectual property.

The literature provides some guidance on the relative effects of IPRs on these alternative means of transferring intellectual property and servicing foreign markets. In this literature, the Ownership-Location-Internalization (OLI) framework developed by Dunning (1973) is applied to examine the relationship between IPRs and firms' decisions about servicing foreign markets.[3] According to this framework (which was discussed in Chapter 3), a firm's ownership, location, and internalization advantages affect its decisions about whether and how to service foreign markets. The ownership advantage helps to explain whether a firm will service a foreign market at all. The location and internalization advantages help explain the relative magnitudes of trade versus FDI versus licensing as means of servicing foreign markets. These advantages describe a firm's ability to control its assets – including knowledge assets – and are thus linked to intellectual property.

First, an *ownership advantage* is required for a firm to service a foreign market at all. This is because the firm has a disadvantage relative to domestic firms in that foreign market, at least on initial entry. Thus, in order to compete in that foreign market, a firm must have firm-specific assets that confer a cost advantage. These firm-specific assets can include intellectual property (also referred to as knowledge assets).

The ability to control access to these knowledge assets via IPRs becomes important when servicing foreign markets where the knowledge assets can be imitated. Strong IPRs support the ownership advantage of the source firm in the foreign market by providing legal recourse against violations of its knowledge assets. That is, strong IPRs in the foreign market increase the cost of imitation of the knowledge assets by other firms in that market. This protection allows the source firm to control its knowledge assets and reap a return on its investments in the creation of these assets.

Although strong IPRs enhance a firm's ownership advantage (and provide conditions for entry), a strong ownership advantage can translate into increased or decreased servicing of the foreign market. This is because of the two countervailing effects of IPRs (discussed previously). The market expansion effect predicts that strong IPRs will increase servicing of the foreign market. Alternatively, the monopoly power effect predicts that strong IPRs will decrease servicing of the foreign market. Thus, although strong IPRs increase a firm's ownership advantage over its knowledge assets, this ownership advantage can result in increased or decreased servicing of the foreign market via trade, FDI and licensing. The direction depends on the relative dominance of the market expansion or market power effects.

Once a firm has an ownership advantage in the foreign market, it then decides the means by which it will service that market. The location and internalization advantages help explain that decision. A *location advantage* is required for a firm to service the foreign market via FDI rather than trade. In other words, there must be a cost advantage to engaging in FDI rather than trade. Sources of such cost advantages of locating production in the foreign market include the ability to skirt tariff barriers, access to lower cost inputs, weaker standards and regulations, and closer proximity to the final consumer. Concomitantly, an *internalization advantage* is required for a firm to service the foreign market via trade and FDI rather than licensing to location firms in the foreign market. In other words, an internalization advantage arises when there is a cost *dis*advantage to externalizing the transaction through licensing. One significant cost disadvantage of licensing is the costs associated with preventing the violation of the licensing contract.

The ability to control access to knowledge assets via IPRs becomes important when servicing foreign markets via FDI and licensing rather than trade. This is because the decision to engage in FDI (rather than trade) means that the source firm will transfer production, and knowledge assets, outside of the source country. The decision to engage in licensing (rather than FDI or trade) means that the source firm will transfer production, and knowledge assets, both outside the source country and outside the source firm. In the former case, strong IPRs can reduce costs associated with preventing violations of knowledge assets of the subsidiary located in the foreign market. In the latter case, strong IPRs can reduce costs associated with licensing contracts including the costs associated with monitoring compliance.

Thus, in order to assess the impact of IPRs on servicing decisions, we need to understand the risk associated with violations of the intellectual property in each case. The literature suggests that the risk that knowledge assets will be violated is higher when the knowledge assets are transferred outside the source country via FDI and licensing (rather than trade). The literature is less definitive on whether the risk that knowledge assets will be violated is higher when the knowledge assets are transferred outside the source firm to a foreign firm via licensing (rather than FDI and trade). However, there is some evidence to suggest that this is indeed to the case.[4]

10.3   How Have Intellectual Property Rights Evolved over Time in Practice?

In practice, there is a strong policy interest in arrangements that govern IPRs. IPRs are of interest to individuals and firms who wish to create, buy or sell intellectual property. IPRs are also of interest to country governments since these laws can affect economy-wide behavior including innovation, technology transfer, growth, trade, foreign direct investment, and licensing.

The earliest international arrangements governing IPRs are the Paris Convention for the Protection of Industrial Property of 1883, and the Berne Convention for the Protection of Literary and Artistic Works of 1886. The *Paris Convention* was the first international treaty designed to help individuals in one country obtain protection in other countries. The forms of these early protections included patents, trademarks and industrial designs. The original treaty was signed by 14 member states, which established an international bureau to coordinate the administration of the treaty. The *Berne Convention* extended this treaty to provide protections in the form of copyrights for literary and artistic works. This second treaty was designed to help individuals in the member states to obtain international protection of their rights to control, and receive payment for, the use of their creative works. This treaty also established an international bureau for administrative purposes.

In 1893, these two organizations combined to form an international organization referred to as the *United International Bureaux for the Protection of Intellectual Property* (BIRPI). These arrangements established a system by which creators of intellectual property could seek protection in other countries that would be as favorable as the protection provided to domestic nationals. In other words, one could seek protection of intellectual property by filing for a patent, trademark, industrial design, or copyright in the desired country and would be subject to the same protection as that provided to domestic residents seeking similar protection in their own country.

Interests in protecting intellectual property have evolved since these early arrangements in two prominent ways. First, new forms of IPR have been developed to protect technologies that did not fit well with the existing forms of protection. Examples of newer forms of protection include plant breeders' rights, geographical indicators, and sui generis protections. Second, controversy over country differences in legal protection of IPRs has increased along with trends toward globalization. For example, controversy has increased as countries have become increasingly integrated via international trade, foreign direct investment and international licensing arrangements.

Much of the current and ongoing policy debate over IPRs reflects a tension between the interests of the North (developed countries) and the South (developing countries). This is due to the fact that resources required for innovation that generates intellectual property are concentrated in a relatively small number of developed countries. These developed countries tend to be the sources of intellectual property in the international market, whereas developing countries tend to be the recipients of intellectual property via international inflows.

The firms and governments of the North have pushed for stronger IPRs internationally in an effort to protect their increasingly large international outflows of intellectual property. These flows occur through trade, FDI, and licensing arrangements. They also occur through the activities of multinational enterprises (MNEs) that move knowledge assets to multiple locations of production around the globe. As discussed earlier, the incentives of the North are unambiguous. Strong IPRs confer monopoly power and market expansion effects that both benefit the source of the intellectual property. As a consequence, the countries (and industries) of the North have put a substantial amount of pressure on the countries of the South to reform and strengthen their intellectual property regimes. This effort was advanced by a broad cross-industry alliance from the North with interests in trading in intellectual property intensive industries.

The firms and governments of the South have begun to reform their IPR systems, but with resistence. As discussed earlier, their interests in adopting stronger IPRs are mixed. On the positive side, strong IPRs can protect and encourage the innovations of domestic firms that produce products tailored to the domestic market. Strong IPRs can also encourage inward flows of intellectual property and thus encourage technology transfer from the North to South. On the negative side, strong IPRs can create the conditions for monopoly behavior of the Northern firms servicing their market. This can result in higher monopoly prices, transfer of monopoly rents to Northern firms, the loss of competitiveness of Southern firms, and reductions in technology transfers from North to South. Despite these mixed incentives, the South has made efforts to reform its IPR systems in part, as a tradeoff for other concessions from the North in other policy areas. In other words, the South has agreed to reforms in the context of negotiation over a portfolio of policy reforms of the North and South.

Institutional arrangements for protecting intellectual property have evolved along with these tensions. Current protections are found in treaties and agreements at the bilateral, regional, and international levels. One prominent international organization is the *World Intellectual Property Organization* (WIPO), which is the successor of BIRPI. WIPO was established in 1970 by the Convention of 1967. In 1974, WIPO became a specialized agency of the United Nations. This convention mandates that member states promote the international protection of intellectual property through cooperation between countries and in collaboration with other international organizations. The objective of WIPO is to support a balanced and accessible international intellectual property system, which rewards creativity, stimulates innovations and contributes to economic development while safeguarding the public interest. The mission and mandate of WIPO continue to evolve. Membership now includes approximately 184 countries.

The Agreement on Trade-Related Aspects of Intellectual Property Rights (TRIPs) is the most significant multilateral arrangement on IPRs to date. This agreement is a product of the Uruguay Round negotiations of the General Agreement on Tariffs and Trade (GATT) that produced the 1995 agreements including the establishment of the World Trade Organization (WTO). Signatories of the agreements include approximately 153 countries to date. The TRIPs agreement was and continues to be highly controversial.

The TRIPs agreement is distinct from previous arrangements in several ways. First, it establishes minimum standards of intellectual property protection that are similar to or stronger than the standards of many industrialized countries. Second, TRIPs covers all of the prominent forms of protection (e.g,. patents, copyrights, trademarks) in a single agreement, and incorporates provisions of previous arrangements including the major WIPO conventions. Third, TRIPs is one of a package of agreements adopted in 1995. Countries cannot be members of the WTO without also adopting TRIPs. Thus, TRIPs was negotiated within the context of a broader policy portfolio. In this context, the South provided concessions on IPRs in exchange for concessions in textiles and agriculture by the North. Fourth, the 1995 agreements established a dispute settlement mechanism whereby TRIPs disputes are settled. This mechanism provides a dispute settlement process that is more binding than had existed in any previous arrangement. For these reasons, TRIPs is the most economically significant multilateral arrangement in the area of intellectual property to date.

The primary goal of the TRIPs agreement – as stated in the preamble – is to strike a balance between the need to promote effective and adequate protection of IPRs and the need of national governments to promote public policy objectives, including technological development. The preamble also links trade to IPRs by recognizing the need for a multilateral framework to address trade in counterfeit goods.

Key provisions of the agreement address issues including national treatment, the most favored nation principle, and human health. For example, Article 3 requires that the National Treatment Principle be applied with respect to IPRs. This means that IPRs must be applied in a nondiscriminatory manner whereby nationals (individuals and firms) of all WTO signatories are treated in the same manner as the domestic nationals of a given country. Article 4 requires that the Most Favored Nation Principle be applied with respect to IPRs. This means that concessions granted by one member country to another member country must also be extended to all WTO signatories. This principle requires a consistency of treatment across all signatory countries. Article 8.1 links IPRs to *human health*. This article states that members "adopt measures necessary to protect human health and nutrition, and to promote the public interest in sectors of vital importance to their socio-economic and technological development."

The key provisions of the agreement also address the issues of coverage and compliance. For example, Part II addresses the *coverage* of intellectual property including patents, copyrights, trademarks, geographic designs, layout-designs of integrated circuits, protection of undisclosed information, and control of anti-competitive practices in contractual licenses. This coverage includes, by reference, provisions of the Paris Convention on the Protection of Industrial Property and the Berne Convention of Literary and Artistic Works. All WTO signatories are required to adopt these provisions, irrespective of whether they were signatories to these earlier conventions.

Finally, the TRIPs agreement articulates compliance requirements. The agreement established a phase-in process of varying lengths for countries at different levels of development. Specifically, industrialized countries were required to comply with TRIPs within one year of the agreement coming into force, or by January 1, 1996. Developing countries and transition economies were required to comply within five years, or by January 1, 2000. Developing countries that did not previously have intellectual property protections in all of the coverage areas were provided an extension period of five additional years, or by January 1, 2005. Least developed countries (LDCs) were required to comply within 11 years, or by January 1, 2006. The LDCs have subsequently secured a seven-and-a-half year extension for compliance, or by July 1, 2013. These phase-in periods are applied to all original signatories and continue to be applied to countries that have since acceded to the WTO.

For these countries, the TRIPs agreement requires national enforcement mechanisms and provides the dispute settlement mechanism to resolve disputes. To manage the ongoing evolution of policy toward IPRs, the agreement provides for oversight by the Council for Trade-Related Intellectual Property Rights. This council is mandated to review the implementation of TRIPs every two years, including issues of compliance, consultations, and dispute settlement procedures.

Finally, in addition to TRIPs, bilateral and regional agreements play an important role in the arena of IPRs. In recent years, some of these agreements have included TRIPs-plus provisions for IPRs. The term *TRIPs-plus* refers to provisions that add to the requirements of the 1995 TRIPs agreement. Examples include provisions that extend the term of a patent beyond the 20-year minimum, limit the use of compulsory licenses, and/or restrict competition in generic drugs. Developed countries (such as the United States and European countries) have used such arrangements to advance intellectual property protections in developing countries who concede in order to improve their access to the developed world's markets. The issues of contention are whether developed countries are using TRIPs-plus provisions to circumvent the flexibilities granted to developing countries in the original TRIPs agreement, and whether the stronger protections provided in TRIPs-plus provisions are appropriate to the needs of developing countries. In this context, the provisions are sometimes referred to as "TRIPs-minus" due to their potential negative effects.

10.4   What Are the Intellectual Property Rights Issues on the Policy Frontier?

There are numerous pending IPRs issues on the policy frontier. Several contentious areas of discussion include compulsory licensing, parallel trade, and the protection of traditional knowledge and biological diversity.

Compulsory licensing is an arrangement where the laws in a country require that a foreign patent holder must license their intellectual property to a domestic firm as a condition of obtaining the patent protection. This also can apply to other forms of protection beyond patents. The purpose of compulsory licensing is to transfer technology from foreign firms in industrialized countries to domestic firms in developing countries. International policy toward compulsory licensing is included in the TRIPs agreement of the World Trade Organization. This agreement allows for compulsory licensing in situations such as those that pertain to public health (e.g., access to medicines). The public health ramifications of IPRs continue to be an issue of controversy. The core of the discussion is that strong intellectual property agreements like TRIPs can raise the price of pharmaceuticals in developing countries. Compulsory licensing provides one means for transferring the technologies associated with pharmaceuticals to domestic firms in developing countries.

A second frontier issue is parallel trade. *Parallel trade* occurs when a good is exported to a market where IPRs are relatively strong and protections have been obtained (e.g., patents filed), and then the good is re-exported to another market where IPRs are relatively weak and/or protections have not been obtained. Specifically, parallel trade occurs when the good is re-traded into a second country without the authorization of the intellectual property owner.

The primary incentive for parallel trade is related to price discrimination across countries. That is, parallel trade arises when there are price differences across countries in a good. Such price differences can arise across countries at different income levels due to differences in demand elasticities. The monopoly power behavior associated with IPRs supports the environment for price discrimination across countries. However, these price differences create an incentive for international arbitrage behavior. If transportation costs are low, then an independent trader can profit by selling the good in the country with the highest price, without respect for the intellectual property protections in that country. Thus, parallel trade is a form of arbitrage behavior which then reduces or eliminates the ability of a firm to price discriminate across countries. Alternatively, banning parallel trade has the opposite effect of allowing for price discrimination.

Policy toward parallel trade is in its infancy. At the international level, parallel trade is not prohibited via the TRIPs agreement of the World Trade Organization. Rather, each country is allowed to establish its own regime with respect to parallel trade. At the national level, the legality of parallel trade depends on whether intellectual property protections are confined to the country where the good is first sold or extended to subsequent markets where the good may be re-traded. Countries are free to choose the geographical area within which the IPRs are "exhausted" after the first sale of the good. Under the *international exhaustion* regime, the protection is confined to the country where the good is originally sold. That is, the protection of IPRs is exhausted internationally. The result is that a firm cannot control the international distribution of a good once it has been first sold in a given country. Parallel imports are legal in this case. Alternatively, under the *national exhaustion regime*, the owners of the intellectual property can legally exclude parallel imports. Finally, under the *regional exhaustion* regime, parallel imports are legal when the good originates within a member country of the region. The United States has adopted a national exhaustion regime, whereas other industrialized countries such as Australia, New Zealand and Japan have adopted an international exhaustion regime. The European Union has adopted a regional exhaustion regime.

The primary policy debate concerns the legality of parallel trade. Those who support the legality of parallel trade argue that restricting parallel trade would constitute a nontariff barrier to trade that is inconsistent with the WTO principles. Those who support the illegality of parallel trade argue that the owner of the intellectual property should have exclusive rights to control the distribution of the good internationally. A primary motive behind a firm's interest in restricting parallel trade is that it supports its ability to price discriminate across countries. Given the link between price discrimination and parallel trade, parallel trade can be viewed as a competition policy issue as well as a trade policy issue.

A third frontier issue is the protection of traditional knowledge and biological diversity. *Traditional knowledge* refers to the long-standing traditions that are specific to countries, regions, indigenous peoples, and/or local communities. The expressions of these traditions can be thought of as a form of intellectual property. *Biological diversity* (or "biodiversity") refers to the variety of life forms (including plants, animals, and their genes) in a particular habitat or ecosystem, or more broadly in the planet. Controversial issues in this area include whether IPRs should cover these forms of intellectual property (i.e., traditional knowledge and life forms) and whether such protections support the piracy of traditional knowledge and genetic materials across countries. Another controversial issue is whether intellectual property protection of life forms (such as genetically modified organisms) extends to subsequent generations of the life form (such as saved seeds). This is only a small sampling of the numerous issues related to IPRs at the international level that are on the policy frontier.

10.5   Summary Remarks

What are intellectual property rights, their types, and purpose? Intellectual property refers to creations of the mind. These creations have public goods characteristics in that they are non-rivalrous and non-excludable. The non-rival characteristic means that the use of the intellectual property does not reduce its availability for use by others. The non-excludable characteristic means that the use of intellectual property by others is difficult to limit in the private market. Intellectual property rights are laws regarding the protection of intellectual property. These laws describe the ways in which the creators of intellectual property can control its use. The primary forms of IPRs include patents, copyrights, trademarks and servicemarks, plant breeders' rights, sui generis rights, and trade secrets. These forms protect different types of creations of the mind. Patents protect inventions. Copyrights protect literary and artistic works. Trademarks and servicemarks protect symbols, names, images, and designs associated with products and services. Plant breeders' rights protect plant varieties. Trade secrets protect intellectual property held within the boundaries of a firm. The purpose of these protections is to create an incentive for the creation of intellectual property by ensuring a return on the investments required for the creation to take place.

What are the effects of intellectual property rights? We considered three effects of IPRs – domestic effects, international effects, and relative effects on flows of intellectual property via trade, foreign direct investment, and licensing.

What are the domestic effects of intellectual property rights? There is a tradeoff associated with the strength of national laws governing IPRs. IPRs provide incentives for the development of creations of the mind by providing higher profits to the holders of the intellectual property. This can have a positive welfare effect on an economy by increasing innovation. Alternatively, IPRs confer a temporary monopoly over the creation. This can have a negative welfare effect on an economy by temporarily limiting public access to new creations and the associated knowledge. The optimal strength of IPRs is that strength (i.e., scope and length) that maximizes welfare by inducing incentives for creation without conferring excess monopoly power.

What are the effects of country differences in intellectual property rights? The protection and enforcement of IPRs vary widely across countries. This variation can affect the way that goods, services and the factors of production move across countries. This is because intellectual property is embodied in goods, services and the factors of production. The current research suggests that there is an ambiguous relationship between IPRs and international flows of intellectual property. From the source country's perspective, this ambiguity arises because there are two countervailing effects. On one hand, source firms have incentives to transfer their intellectual property to markets where IPRs are strong because they can apply for protection and reduce the risk of imitation. In this case, stronger IPRs expand international flows of intellectual property – the market expansion effect. Alternatively, source firms also have incentives to restrict their transfers of intellectual property to markets where IPRs are strong because they can apply for protection and decrease their exports to extract monopoly prices. In this case, stronger IPRs reduce international flows of intellectual property by supporting monopoly behavior – the monopoly power effect. The net effect depends on the relative dominance of these two effects.

Despite this ambiguity, the country that is the source of the intellectual property prefers that recipient countries have strong intellectual property protections, either to reduce the risk of imitation or to allow for monopoly behavior in the recipient countries' markets. In contrast, from the recipient country's perspective, the incentives for protecting intellectual property are mixed. The recipient of intellectual property prefers to adopt relatively weak intellectual property protections to allow for domestic imitation and prevent monopoly behavior in their market. Alternatively, the recipient prefers to adopt relatively strong intellectual property protections to facilitate technology transfer and provide domestic incentives for innovation. These mixed incentives help explain why developing countries (i.e., recipients of intellectual property) have resisted adopting strong intellectual property laws, despite the pressure of industrialized countries. The view of many developing countries is that the costs of adopting strong IPRs outweigh the benefits.

What are the relative effects of intellectual property rights on trade, foreign direct investment, and licensing? Firms transfer intellectual property to foreign markets via trade, foreign direct investment, and licensing. The literature provides some guidance on the relative effects of IPRs on these alternative transmission channels. Specifically, the Ownership-Location-Internalization framework helps explain the effects of IPRs. An ownership advantage is required for a firm to service a foreign market at all. An ownership advantage arises when a firm has firm-specific assets (such as intellectual property) that confer a cost advantage in the foreign market relative to other domestic firms. Strong IPRs support the ownership advantage of the source firm in the foreign market by providing legal recourse against violations of their knowledge assets.

Once a firm has an ownership advantage, it then decides the means by which it will service that market. The location and internalization advantages help explain that decision. A location advantage arises when there is a cost advantage to engaging in FDI rather than trade. Strong IPRs can reduce costs associated with preventing violations of knowledge assets of the subsidiary located in the foreign market. An internalization advantage arises when there is a cost *dis*advantage to externalizing the transaction through licensing. Strong IPRs can reduce costs associated with licensing contracts, including the costs associated with monitoring compliance.

Thus, servicing decisions depend on the risk associated with violations of intellectual property in each case. The literature suggests that the risk that knowledge assets will be violated is higher when intellectual property is transferred outside the source country via FDI and licensing. The literature is less definitive on whether the risk of violation is higher when the knowledge assets are transferred outside the source firm to a foreign firm via licensing. However, there is some evidence to suggest that this is the case.

How have intellectual property rights evolved over time in practice? The earliest international arrangements governing IPRs are the Paris Convention for the Protection of Industrial Property of 1883, and the Berne Convention for the Protection of Literary and Artistic Works of 1886. In 1893, these two organizations combined to form BIRPI. These arrangements established a system by which creators of intellectual property could seek protection in other countries that would be as favorable as the protections provided to domestic nationals. In 1970, the World Intellectual Property Organization (WIPO) was established as the successor to BIRPI. In 1974, WIPO became a specialized agency of the UN. This convention mandated that members promote the international protection of intellectual property through cooperation between countries and in collaboration with other international organizations.

Interests in protecting intellectual property have evolved since these early arrangements. Developed countries have pushed for stronger rights in an effort to protect their growing international outflows of intellectual property. The incentives of developed countries are unambiguous. Strong rights confer monopoly power and market expansion effects that benefit the developed countries – the source of most intellectual property. Concomitantly, the interests of developing countries are more mixed. Strong protections can promote their domestic innovation, can encourage inward flows of intellectual property (via the market expansion effect), and can result in inward technology transfer. However, strong protections can also result in higher monopoly prices domestically (via the monopoly power effect), the transfer of monopoly rents to developed countries, the loss of competitiveness of developing country firms, and reductions in inward technology transfers. Despite these mixed incentives, the South has begun to reform its protections in the context of negotiations over a portfolio of policy reforms.

The most economically significant multilateral arrangement for these reforms is the 1995 agreement of the WTO, the Agreement on Trade-Related Aspects of Intellectual Property Rights (TRIPs). TRIPs establishes minimum standards of intellectual property protection, covers all of the prominent forms of protection in a single agreement, and incorporates provisions of previous arrangements including WIPO conventions. Countries cannot join the WTO without also signing up to TRIPs. The WTO also established a dispute settlement mechanism whereby disputes over the enforcement of IPRs are settled. This mechanism provides a process for dispute settlement that is more binding than previous arrangements. Finally, in addition to the TRIPs agreement, bilateral and regional agreements have played an important role in recent years. Many of these agreements include "TRIPs-plus" provisions that provide stronger protections than does TRIPs. Developed countries have used such arrangements to advance intellectual property protections in developing countries that concede in this area in order to improve their access to the developed world's market.

What are the issues on the policy frontier of intellectual property rights? There are numerous pending IPRs issues on the policy frontier including compulsory licensing, parallel trade, and the protection of traditional knowledge and biodiversity, among others. Compulsory licensing is an arrangement where the laws in a country require that a foreign intellectual property holder must license their intellectual property to a domestic firm as a condition of obtaining the protection. International policy allows for compulsory licensing in situations such as those that pertain to public health (e.g., access to medicines). Parallel trade occurs when a good is exported to a market where intellectual property protections have been obtained (e.g., patents filed) and then re-exported to another market where protections have not been obtained, without the authorization of the intellectual property owner. The legality of parallel trade depends on whether intellectual property protections are confined to the country where the good is first sold or extended to subsequent markets where the good may be re-traded. Countries choose the geographical area within which the IPRs are "exhausted". Finally, traditional knowledge refers to the long-standing traditions that are specific to countries, regions, indigenous peoples, and/or local communities. Biological diversity refers to the variety of life forms (including plants, animals, and their genes) in a particular habitat or ecosystem, or more broadly in the planet. Issues of controversy include whether IPRs should cover these forms of intellectual property; whether such protections support the piracy of traditional knowledge and of genetic materials across countries; and whether intellectual property protection of life forms (such as GMOs) should extend to subsequent generations (such as saved seeds).

Applied Problems

10.1   The forms of intellectual property rights (IPRs) include: (a) patents, (b) utility models, (c) industrial designs, (d) copyright, (e) trademarks, (f) serv-icemarks, (g) geographic indications, (h) plant breeders' rights, (i) *sui generis* protections, and (j) trade secrets. Briefly describe the type of creation that each of these forms of IPRs protects.

10.2   Briefly answer the following questions: (a) What is the purpose of IPRs? (b) What is the geographic scope of IPRs? (c) What is the optimal strength of IPRs? (d) What are the effects of country differences in IPRs? (e) What are the relative effects of IPRs on trade, foreign direct investment, and licensing? (f) How does the Ownership-Location-Internalization (OLI) framework help explain these relative effects?

10.3   Why do countries in the North and South have different interests in adopting strong IPRs? Consider the market expansion and market power effects of IPRs as a starting point for analyzing this question.

10.4   Consider the following issues on the policy frontier of IPRs. (a) What is compulsory licensing and its purpose? (b) What is parallel trade? Why does it occur? What are the possible exhaustion regimes? (c) What is traditional knowledge and biological diversity? What are the implications of IPRs in these areas?

10.5   Consider the case of the salmon that has been genetically modified to be super-sized. Briefly answer the following questions: (a) Assume that the creators of this super-sized salmon file for patent protection. What is the purpose of this patent protection? (b) Assume that patents are filed and awarded only in countries with strong patent right laws. What is the geographic scope of this patent protection? (c) Assume that the super-sized salmon escape into international waters and cannot be contained from crossing national boundaries. What are the effects of country differences in patent protection? (d) What are the arguments in favor of and against patenting of genetically modified life forms such as super-sized salmon? (e) Use the OLI framework to reassess the arguments above.

10.6 Consider the case of crops such as canola that have been genetically modified to have traits such as pest resistance. Briefly answer the following questions: (a) Assume that the creators of genetically modified canola (such as Monsanto) file for patent protection. What is the purpose of this patent protection? (b) Assume that patents are filed and awarded only in countries with strong patent laws. What is the geographic scope of this patent protection? (c) Assume that the genetically modified seed blows across a national border (such as the US-Mexican border). Assume that one country has stronger patent laws than the other (e.g., the United States has stronger patent laws than does Mexico). What are the effects of such country differences in patent protection?

Further Reading

Branstetter, L., R. Fisman, and C. Foley. 2006. Do stronger intellectual property rights increase international technology transfer? Empirical evidence from US firm-level panel data. *Quarterly Journal of Economics* 121, 321–349.

Chen, Yongmin, and Thitima Puttitanun. 2005. Intellectual property rights and innovation in developing countries. *Journal of Development Economics* 78 (2): 474–493.

Finger, J. Michael, and Philip Schuler. 2003. *Poor People's Knowledge: Promoting Intellectual Properties in Developing Countries*. Washington, D.C.: World Bank and Oxford University Press.

Fink, Carsten, and Keith E. Maskus, eds. 2005. *Intellectual Property and Development: Lessons from Recent Economic Research*. Washington, D.C.: World Bank and Oxford University Press.

Ginarte, Juan Carlos, and Walter G. Park. 1997. Determinants of patent rights: a cross-national study. *Research Policy* 26 (3): 283–301.

Glass, Amy J., and K. Saggi. 2002. Intellectual property rights and foreign direct investment. *Journal of International Economics* 56 (2): 387–410.

Glass, Amy J., and S. Wu. 2007. Intellectual property rights and quality improvement. *Journal of Development Economics* 82 (2): 393–415.

Helpman, Elhanan. 1993. Innovation, imitation, and intellectual property rights. *Econometrica* 61 (6): 1247–1280.

Invus, Olena. 2010. Do stronger patent rights raise high-tech exports to the developing world? *Journal of International Economics* 81 (1): 38–47.

Lee, Jeong-Yeon, and Edwin Mansfield. 1996. Intellectual property protection and US foreign direct investment. *The Review of Economics and Statistics* 78 (2): 181–186.

Li, Changying, and Keith E. Maskus. 2006. The impact of parallel imports on investments in cost-reducing research and development. *Journal of International Economic* 68: 443–455.

Malueg, David, and Marius Schwartz. 1994. Parallel imports, demand dispersion, and international price fiscriminations. *Journal of International Economics* 37 (3–4): 167–195.

Mansfield, Edwin. 1994. *Intellectual Property Protection, Foreign Direct Investment, and Technology Transfer*. Discussion Paper No. 19. Washington, D.C.: International Finance Corporation.

Maskus, Keith E. 2000. *Intellectual Property Rights in the Global Economy*. Washington, D.C.: Institute for International Economics.

Maskus, Keith E. 2000. Parallel imports. *World Economy* 23 (9): 269–284.

Maskus, Keith E., Kamal Saggi, and Thitima Puttitanun. 2005. Patent rights and international technology transfer through direct investment and licensing. In *International Public Goods and Transfer of Technology under a Globalized Intellectual Property Regime* (eds Keith E. Maskus and Jerome H. Reichman), Cambridge: Cambridge University Press, pp. 265–281.

Matthews, Duncan. 2002. *Globalizing Intellectual Property Rights: The TRIPS Agreement*. London: Routledge.

May, Christopher. 2007. *The World Intellectual Property Organization: Resurgence and the Development Agenda*. London: Routledge.

Owen, Lippert. 1999. *Competitive Strategies for the Protection of Intellectual Property*. Vancouver, Canada: Fraser Institute.

Park, Walter G. 2008. International patent protection: 1960–2005. *Research Policy* 37, 761–766.

Primo Braga, Carlos A., and Carsten Fink. 1998. The relationship between intellectual property rights and foreign direct investment. *Duke Journal of Comparative and International Law* 9: 163–187.

Raff, Horst, and Nicolas Schmitt. 2007. Why parallel imports may raise producers' profits. *Journal of International Economics* 71 (2): 434–447.

Rapp, Richard, and Richard Rozek. 1990. Benefits and costs of intellectual property protection in developing countries. *Journal of World Trade* 24: 75–102.

Ryan, Michael P. 1998. *Knowledge Diplomacy: Global Competition and the Politics of Intellectual Property*. Washington, D.C.: Brookings Institution Press.

Sell, Susan K. 2003. *Private Power, Public Law: The Globalization of Intellectual Property Rights*. Cambridge: Cambridge University Press.

Smarzynska, Beata. 2004. The composition of foreign direct investment and protection of intellectual property rights: evidence from transition economies. *European Economic Review* 48: 39–62.

Smith, Pamela J. 1999. Are weak patent rights a barrier to US exports? *Journal of International Economics* 48: 151–177.

Smith, Pamela J. 2001. How do foreign patent rights affect US exports, affiliate sales, and licenses? *Journal of International Economics* 55: 411–440.

Smith, Pamela J. 2002. Patent rights and trade: analysis of biological products, medicinals and botanicals, and pharmaceuticals. *American Journal of Agricultural Economics* 84 (2): 498–512.

Smith, Pamela J., Omar B. Da'ar, Kevin H. Monroe, *et al.*, 2009. How do copyrights affect economic development and international trade? *Journal of World Intellectual Property* 12 (3): 198–218.

United Nations Conference on Trade and Development, and International Center for Trade and Sustainable Development. 2003. *Intellectual Property Rights: Implications for Development.* Geneva: UNCTAD-ICTSD.

United Nations Conference on Trade and Development, and International Center for Trade and Sustainable Development. 2005. *Resource Book on TRIPs and Development.* Cambridge: Cambridge University Press.

Watal, Jayashree. 2001. *Intellectual Property Rights in the WTO and Developing Countries.* New Delhi: Oxford University Press.

World Bank. 2001. *Global Economic Prospects and the Developing Countries 2002: Making Trade Work for the World's Poor.* Washington, D.C.: World Bank, Chapter 5.

Yang, Guifand, and Keith E. Maskus. 2001. Intellectual property rights, licensing, and innovation in an endogenous product-cycle model. *Journal of International Economics* 53: 169–187.

Notes

1. Early studies in the ecronomics literature on the relationship between IPRs and trade include Maskus and Penubarti (1995) and Smith (1999).
2. Early studies of the relationship between IPRs and multinationals behavior include Lee and Mansfield (1996) and Horstman and Markusen (1987).
3. Ethier and Markusen (1996) provide early work on the link between knowledge assets and firms' decisions about how to service foreign markets. Other early theory studies in this area include Glass (2000), and Helpman (1993). Early empirical studies in this area include Maskus (1998), Ferrantino (1993), Smarzynsky (2004), and Smith (2001).
4. See Horstmann and Markusen (1987), Lee and Mansfield (1996), Maskus, Saggi, and Puttitanun (2005), Primo Braga and Fink (1998), Smarzynska (2004), Smith (2001), Yang and Maskus (2001).

11

Environmental Policies

11.1 What Are Trade-Related Environmental Policies, Their Types and Purpose?

Environmental policies include a vast array of national and international laws to protect the environment. These cover a wide range of concerns including air and water pollution, global warming, the exhaustion of renewable and non-renewable resources, the extinction of endangered species, the loss of natural habitats, and the use of genetically modified organisms (GMOs).

The relationship between trade and the environment is complex. Laws adopted to protect the environment can affect trade. Similarly, laws adopted to restrict or liberalize trade can affect the environment. Thus, environmental policies are related to trade, and trade policies are related to the environment. This relationship was recognized in the Uruguay Round discussions of the GATT that lead to the establishment of the WTO in 1995. This agreement sought to strengthen international rules regarding the extent to which national laws can affect international trade, including national environmental laws. One of the implications is that the dispute settlement mechanism of the WTO can rule on cases where national environmental standards are believed to unreasonably limit international trade flows.

The relationship between trade and the environment can be observed generally in global trends over the past two decades. International trade has grown rapidly, while international policy restrictions on trade have fallen. During the same time period, environmental trends have been both positive and negative. On the positive side, trends suggest improvements in urban environmental air and water quality. On the negative side, trends show a worsening of global environment pollution (e.g.,

Global Trade Policy: Questions and Answers, First Edition. Pamela J. Smith.

carbon dioxide) and a worsening of rural environmental quality with respect to natural forests and other habitats, along with a loss of species and increase in global warming. Thus, urban environmental conditions have improved while rural and global environmental conditions have worsened, during a period of trade liberalization.

These environmental changes differ in their *geographic scope* – urban versus rural versus global. The scope of environmental impact is important to consider when designing policy responses that maximize welfare. For example, a global environmental issue such as global warming is best addressed using coordinated global policies, while a national environmental issue such as water quality is best addressed using national level policies. In these examples, the scope of the policy matches the scope of the environmental concern. Such policy responses are efficient in the sense that they do not create new distortions as a side effect. In contrast, if the scope of the policy doesn't match the scope of the environmental problem, then new distortions are generated. For example, we will show in this chapter that using *international* trade policy to address *national* environmental issues can correct the environmental problem, but also introduces new distortions. We will show that this policy response is not optimal from a welfare point of view.

This chapter explores how environmental and trade policies are related. The chapter is organized around three key questions: (1) What are the effects of trade policy on the environment? (2) What are the effects of environmental policy on trade? (3) What are the implications of using trade policy to address environmental externalities?

11.2   What Are the Effects of Trade Policy on the Environment?

This section considers the effects of trade policy on the environment. Specifically, we consider whether trade, or the liberalization of trade policy, leads to an improvement or worsening of environmental quality. Research in this area suggests that there are four prominent effects of trade (or trade liberalization) on the environment.[1] These include: the composition effect; the growth effect; the scale effect; and the technique effect. Research also suggests that there is a relationship between the income of an economy and environmental quality. This research focuses on explaining the well-known Environmental Kuznets Curve. The relationship described by this curve can be linked to trade. These bodies of research have theoretical foundations in the models discussed in other chapters of this book. We summarize the prominent findings of this research below and reference the related chapters.

First, the *composition effect* refers to the changes in the composition of outputs that occur as a consequence of trade. These composition changes occur as countries specialize in their sectors of comparative advantage. Countries with a comparative advantage in dirty industries will shift the composition of their outputs toward these industries when trade is liberalized. Similarly, countries with a comparative advantage in clean industries will shift their outputs toward these industries when trade is liberalized. Much of the research assumes that dirty industries are intensive in the use of capital and/or natural resources as inputs; and clean industries are intensive in the use of human capital as inputs. Under these assumptions, trade liberalization leads to the following results. Countries that are capital and/or natural resource abundant experience an increase in environmental damage (e.g., pollution, resource degradation, deforestation) and countries that are human capital abundant experience a decrease in environmental damage. (See the Heckscher-Ohlin model in Chapter 2 for the underlying theory foundations for this composition effect.)

Second, the *growth effect* refers to an increase in the rate of economic growth as a consequence of trade, which then generates environmental impacts as a by-product. There is a large body of research that links trade to economic growth (see Chapter 13). The logic for the growth effect of trade is that growth may outpace changes in environmental policies and institutions. In this case, rapid growth can lead to increased environmental damage. In other words, a country experiencing rapid growth may be less able to adapt its environmental policies and institutions fast enough to protect the environment well and may thus experience greater environmental damage relative to a country with slower economic growth. Conversely, a country experiencing more moderate growth may be able to adapt its policies and institutions fast enough to address the environmental side effects of trade and growth.

Third, the *scale effect* refers to an increase in the scale of production as a consequence of trade, which then generates environmental impacts (e.g., pollution) as a by-product. One of the results of trade liberalization is that producers have increased access to a larger global market. Thus, the scale of production increases as countries specialize in their sectors of comparative advantage. In theory, global output and consumption increases as a consequence of this specialization and trade (see Chapter 3). The scale effect results in an increase in the forms of environmental impact (e.g., pollution) that are by-products of the expanded production. The scale effect also results in an increase in the forms of environmental impact associated with the movement of the traded goods over longer distances (e.g., transportation-related environmental impact).

Fourth, the *technique effect* refers to the reduction in the intensity of pollution per unit of output as a consequence of trade. The intuition for this effect is as follows. Trade can lead to an increase in income. This increase in income can then lead to an increase in the demand for environmental quality, assuming environmental quality is a normal good. This increase in demand for environmental quality can then lead to stricter environmental regulations, assuming a responsive government. The stricter environmental regulations can then lead to a reduction in environment impact per unit of output.

These four effects (composition, growth, scale, and technique) highlight the complexity of relationship between trade and the environment. When we consider the effects together, the net effect of trade (or trade liberalization) on the environment is ambiguous. That is, in some cases trade has a positive effect on the environment and in other cases it has a negative effect. For example, the composition effect suggests that trade has a *positive* effect on the environment in those countries with a comparative advantage in clean industries and a *negative* effect in those countries with a comparative advantage in dirty industries. The growth effect suggests that trade has a *negative* effect in those countries that are slow to adapt their environmental policies. The scale effect suggests that trade has a *negative* effect on the environment of all countries that increase their scale of production. This change leads to negative environmental impacts as a direct consequence, and also as an indirect consequence of increased reliance on the transport of goods over longer distances. Finally, the technique effect suggests that trade has a *positive* effect on the environment, assuming that environmental quality is a normal good and policy bodies are responsive.

The ambiguity of the effect of trade on the environment arises at all geographic levels, whether rural, urban, national, or global. That is, trade can have a positive effect on the environment if a region has a comparative advantage in clean industries (composition effect); and if environmental quality is a normal good and policy makers are responsive to demand for environment quality (technique effect). Alternatively, trade can have a negative effect on the environment if a region has a comparative advantage in dirty industries (composition effect); if growth outpaces changes in environmental policy (growth effect); and if the increased scale of production and increased distance of transport results in environmental damage (scale effect). Thus, the net effect depends on which of these effects is dominant for the given region.

Another prominent body of research that links trade and the environment focuses on the income or level of development of an economy. This relationship is characterized in the *Environmental Kuznets Curve*, which describes an inverted U-shaped relationship between income per capita (or income) and environmental damage (or pollution). Figure 11.1 illustrates the Environmental Kuznets Curve. Initially, an increase in income per capital (Y/N) is associated with an increase in environmental damage (ED), between points *a* and *b*. Then, there is a turning point where further increases in income per capita are associated with a decrease in environmental damage, between points *b* and *c*. In practice, this relationship is observed across countries at different stages of development. It is also observed across time as a given country progresses through different stages of development.

International trade is related to this Environmental Kuznets Curve. There are two prominent explanations for how trade factors into this relationship between income per capita and environmental quality. First, in the initial phase (between *a* and *b*), international trade (or trade liberalization) leads to an increase in the scale of production or in economic growth. These changes lead to an increase in income and an increase in environmental damage consistent with the growth and scale effects (discussed earlier). Then there is a turning point (*b*) where an increase in income leads to an increase in demand for environmental quality as well as stronger environmental regulation. This occurs when the preferences for environmental quality dominate preferences for consumption. This change leads to a decrease in environmental damage consistent with the technique effect (between *b* and *c*). The demand

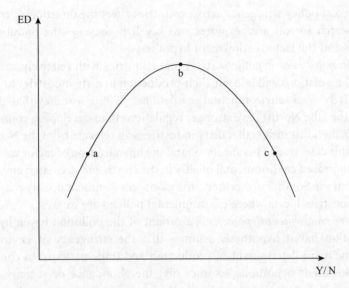

Figure 11.1 Environmental Kuznets Curve.

and policy responses to the income changes occur with a lag, resulting in an inverted U-shaped relationship between income per capita and environmental damage.

Another prominent explanation links the Environmental Kuznets Curve to changes in endowments over time. The intuition is that as countries develop, their accumulation of endowments evolves. At early development stages, countries tend to be abundant in physical capital, which is used intensively in dirty industries. At later stages of development, countries accumulate larger stocks of human capital (or knowledge capital), which is used intensively in clean industries. Thus, the patterns of comparative advantage and trade evolve over time with the stages of country development. At early development stages, income is low and environmental damage is high (e.g., points *a* to *b*). At later stages of development, income is high and environmental damage is low (e.g., points *b* to *c*). These patterns are consistent with the composition effect of trade on the environment, where the composition of international trade changes over time with development.

What then are the effects of trade policy on the environment? The Environmental Kuznets Curve suggests that at lower income levels and early stages of development, the liberalization of trade policy would lead to an increase in environmental damage. Concomitantly, at higher income levels and latter stages of development, the liberalization of trade policy would lead to a decrease in environmental damage.

11.3 What Are the Effects of Environmental Policy on Trade?

Next, we consider the effects of environmental policies on trade. That is, we reverse the direction of causality. Our specific question is whether differences in environmental policy stringency across countries affect the direction of trade. Economic research in this area explores two key hypotheses – the pollution haven hypothesis and the factor endowment hypothesis.

The *pollution haven hypothesis* states that countries with relatively strong environmental regulations will relocate their production in dirty industries to countries with relatively weak environmental regulations.[2] If one assumes that developed countries (i.e., the North) have stronger regulations than developing countries (i.e., the South), then this means that dirty industries will relocate from the North to the South. In this case, trade liberalization (and the liberalization of factor movements) results in increased environmental quality in the North and decreased environmental quality in the South. Furthermore, the global environment quality may decrease as dirty industries locate where environmental policies are weakest.

The *factor endowment hypothesis* is a variant of the pollution haven hypothesis. The pollution haven hypothesis assumes that the stringency of environmental policy is the main determinant of production and trade patterns. In contrast, the factor endowment hypothesis assumes that the abundance or scarcity of factor endowments *and* environment policy both determine the patterns of production and trade, and thus environmental quality. (See Chapter 2 for theory foundations.) The intuition is as follows. With trade, dirty industries will locate in countries that are abundant in the factor endowments that are used intensively in these industries. If environmental policies are strong in these countries, then trade will result in a decrease in environmental damage. Alternatively, if environmental policies are weak in these countries, then trade will result in an increase in environmental damage. Furthermore, if country differences in environmental policies are large, these differences may diminish or reverse the patterns of comparative advantage based on endowment differences.

For example, consider a scenario where capital is used intensively in dirty industries, developed countries are abundant in capital, and developed countries have strong environmental policies. In this case, dirty industries will locate in the North, based on comparative advantage, and the strong environmental policies will reduce environmental damage from these industries. In contrast, consider the scenario where labor or natural resources are used intensively in dirty industries, developing countries are abundant in these factors, and developing countries have weak environmental policies. In this case, dirty industries will locate in the South based on comparative advantage, and the weak environmental policies will increase the environmental damage from these industries. The first scenario is consistent with the pollution haven result but the second scenario is not.

Finally, it is possible that the differences in strength of environmental regulations are large enough to reverse the patterns of comparative advantage based on endowments. In this case, the pollution haven effect dominates the endowments effect. That is, strong environmental policies can diminish the cost advantage that a country may have, based on an abundance of the factor input that is used intensively in the industry. For example, if the North has a comparative advantage in dirty industries as a consequence of an abundance of capital that is used intensively in dirty industries, then this comparative advantage can be eliminated if the costs associated with compliance with strong environmental regulations are sufficiently high (e.g., pollution abatement costs). Alternatively, if the South has a comparative advantage in dirty industries as a consequence of an abundance of labor or natural resources that are used intensively in dirty industries, then this comparative advantage can be eliminated if the costs associated with strengthening environmental regulations are high.

11.4   What Are the Implications of Using Trade Policy to Address Environmental Externalities?

In this section, we consider the use of trade policy to achieve environmental objectives. To this end, we explore externalities in an open economy setting. Externalities include environmental damage such as pollution. When externalities are present, there is a market failure and the government can intervene to correct the market failure. The government can choose domestic national policies or international trade policies as a way to correct a market failure. This raises the question of whether trade policy is the preferred choice to address domestic environmental externalities.[3]

In order to answer this question, we will explore the scope of government intervention to address environmental damage. In particular, we will demonstrate that environmental externalities that are national in scope are best treated using domestic national policies. Similarly, environmental externalities that are global in scope (e.g., global warming) are best treated using coordinated global policies; and environmental externalities that are subnational in scope (e.g., local landfills) are best treated using subnational policies.

Before turning to this analysis, we introduce the concept of externalities. Environmental damage is a classic example of an externality that can arise as a by-product of both production and consumption. *Externalities* arise when the act of production or consumption results in a side effect on an external agent in an economy. This side effect impacts someone other than the original producer or consumer; that is, the side effect impacts society as a whole or a subset of society. The affected agents can be other producers or consumers. For example, an externality can increase or decrease the production of affected producers, or the utility of the affected consumers. In other words, an externality is a social benefit or cost that is incurred by agents other than the original producer or consumer. Externalities arise when there are no economic markets. The nonexistence of markets tends to occur for intangibles that are socially beneficial (environmental quality) or socially costly (environmental damage).

Externalities can be positive or negative and can affect consumers or producers. A *negative production externality* occurs when the process of production generates a negative effect on an external agent. Environmental damage to air or water quality are examples of negative production externalities. For example, an upstream manufacturing plant that pollutes a river can have a negative effect on fishing production downstream. It can also have a negative health effect on the utility of individuals living in downstream communities. Similarly, a *negative consumption externality* occurs when the process of consuming generates a negative effect on an external agent. Environmental damage associated with the elimination of consumer goods is an example of a negative consumption externality. For example, consumption of goods that contain toxic materials or are packaged in nonrecyclable containers generates waste that contributes to local landfills and toxic materials that create damage to environment quality and/or consumer health.

Externalities such as environmental damage are a classic case of market failure. *Market failure* describes the situation where private markets do not generate the socially optimal levels of production and/or consumption. Firms tend to overproduce goods that generate negative externalities because they do not take into account the social cost of their production. Similarly, consumers tend to overconsume goods that generate negative externalities because they do not take into account the social cost of their consumption. The private production and consumption are in excess of the socially optimal levels of production and consumption. *Socially optimal* levels take into account the externalities.

The role of government in the case of a market failure is to adopt policies that provide incentives for producers and/or consumers to produce and consume the socially optimal levels of the good associated with the externality. Typically that means adopting policies that legally require the producer and/or consumer to incur the cost of the externality. Examples include government policies that require producers to pay fees (up front) to cover the cost of disposing of environmentally damaging goods after they have served their purpose. Examples also include government policies that require consumers to pay fees for disposing of goods. The former policies create incentives for producers to decrease the quantity of their supply of environmentally damaging goods. The latter policies create incentives for consumers to decrease the quantity of their demand for environmentally damaging goods.

What then are the optimal policies for addressing environmental concerns? The answer is, it depends. The socially optimal policy depends on the scope of the externality – that is, the scope of the market failure that needs correction. *First-best policies* are policies for which the scope of the policy matches with the scope of the externality. Such policies correct the market failure without introducing new distortions into the market. For example, domestic policy is optimal policy for correcting a domestic market failure. Domestic policy corrects the domestic market failure without introducing new distortions. Alternatively, *second-best policies* are policies for which the scope of the policy does not match with the scope of the externality. Such policies correct the market failure, but simultaneously introduce new distortions. For example, international policy is the second-best policy for correcting a domestic market failure. International policy corrects the domestic market failure but simultaneously introduces new distortions.

So, when are trade policies the optimal policy choice? Trade policies can be used to correct for externalities by altering production and/or consumption incentives to the socially optimal levels. However, we need to consider whether trade policies are first-best or second-best policies. If the externality is international in scope, then a case can be made that coordinated international trade policies are a first-best policy for correcting the market failure. However, if the externality is smaller in scope (national or subnational), then trade policies are second-best for correcting the market failure.

To illustrate this intuition, we consider two alternative cases of externalities and policy responses. In the first case, we consider a negative production externality that arises within a small exporting country. In the second case, we consider a negative consumption externality that arises within a small importing country. In each case, we assume that the scope of the externality is national. We explore the welfare effects of first-best and second-best policies. We consider whether trade policy is a first- or second-best policy response to a national externality.

The modeling approach builds on the partial equilibrium framework presented in Part Two of this book. Specifically, we explore the use of trade policies such as tariffs and quantitative restrictions as a means for correcting market failures. However, we extend the framework from Part Two in one important way, in that we consider the socially optimal levels of production and consumption in the presence of externalities. To this end, we add social supply and social demand curves to the previous framework. The slopes of the social supply and social demand curves reflect the marginal social costs of production and consumption. These costs are attributed to society but not directly to producers or consumers.

11.4.1   Case 1: Can trade policy correct a negative production externality in a small exporter?

In the first case, we consider a negative production externality that arises within a small exporting country. Thus, the externality is generated through the process of production and the externality is contained in scope within the exporting country.

Further, we assume that this country is not large enough to affect the world price of the good. In other words, the country is small in terms of its contributions to the world supply of the good. We refer to the externality as environmental damage. We refer to the good as a dirty good.

One implication of these assumptions is that the social cost of producing the dirty good is greater than the private cost of producing the dirty good. In the absence of government intervention, the private sector will overproduce the dirty good and create environmental damage as a by-product.

Figure 11.2 illustrates these implications. At each price, the private supply (S_P) exceeds the social supply (S_S) for the country. The difference between the two supply curves reflects the negative production externality. We can see this by comparing the private and social producer surpluses at a world price such as P^W. The private producer surplus is the area represented by $(a + b + c)$. In contrast, the social producer surplus is the area represented by a. The area $(b + c)$ represents the difference.

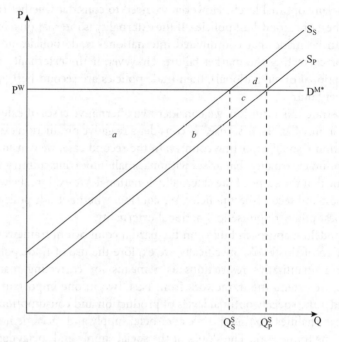

Figure 11.2 Negative production externality.

In the absence of government intervention, the private sector will produce output of the dirty good in the amount Q_P^S. In contrast, the socially optimal supply of the dirty good at price P^W is Q_S^S. Thus, areas c and d represent the social welfare loss from overproducing the good.

The first-best policy response is a domestic policy because the externality is assumed to be domestic in scope. A domestic production tax is a domestic policy that would create a disincentive to production.

Figure 11.3 illustrates the effects of this first-best policy response to the negative production externality. Prior to the policy, the small exporter faces an infinitely elastic import demand (D^{M*}) for the dirty good from the rest of the world (ROW) at price P^W. At this price, domestic consumers demand Q_0^D of the dirty good and domestic producers supply Q_0^S of the dirty good. The excess of supply over demand is the amount of exports (X_0) of the dirty good to the international market or ROW. The area $+(e + f)$ represents that social welfare loss from overproducing the dirty good.

Now consider the effects of imposing a production tax in amount t. This tax is set to equate with the difference between the private and social supply curves that decreases production to the socially optimal amount of Q_1^S. The tax decreases the price received by private producers from P^W to P^t and consequently decreases quantity supplied from Q_0^S to Q_1^S. The tax also has the effect of decreasing exports from X_0 to X_1.

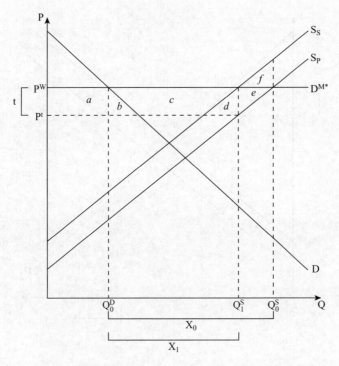

Figure 11.3 Negative production externality – first-best policy of a small exporter.

In terms of welfare, the production tax has the following effects. The private producer's welfare decreases by the surplus amount $-(a + b + c + d + e)$. The government welfare increases by the amount $+(a + b + c + d)$. This change in government welfare is the amount of tax revenue raised. It is the product of the quantity of the good supplied and the value of the tax. Further, social welfare increases by the amount $+(e + f)$. This social welfare change is the amount of the negative externality that is eliminated as a consequence of decreasing production. It is positive as it represents a decrease in environmental damage. Finally, the consumer welfare does not change as the producer alone experiences the price effect of the tax.

The net country welfare effect is the sum of the consumer, producer, government, and social welfare changes. Adding these together we get a welfare gain in the amount $+(f)$ for the country in aggregate. As noted above, the reduction in environmental damage is $+(f + e)$. Area $+e$ is a transfer from the private producer to society resulting from the policy. Area f is a net country gain from the policy. In this illustration, the externality is corrected by the production tax, without introducing a new distortion.

The second-best policy response is an international trade policy. An export tax is a policy that would create a disincentive to production. However, this international trade policy does not match the scope of the externality which is domestic in scope.

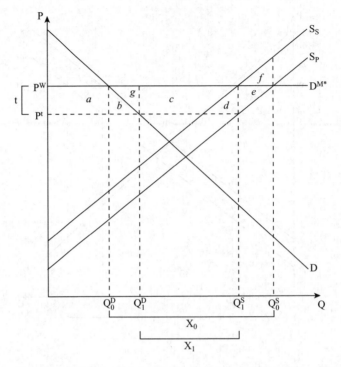

Figure 11.4 Negative production externality – second-best policy of a small exporter.

Figure 11.4 illustrates the effects of this second-best policy response to the negative production externality. As before, the small exporter faces an infinitely elastic import demand (D^{M*}) for the dirty good from the rest of the world (ROW) at price P^W. At this price, domestic consumers demand Q_0^D of the dirty good and domestic producers supply Q_0^S of the dirty good. The excess of domestic supply over demand is the amount of exports (X_0) of the dirty good to the international market or the ROW. As before, the area $+(e + f)$ represents that social welfare loss from overproducing the dirty good.

Now consider the effects of imposing an export tax in amount t. This tax is set to equate with the difference between the private and social supply curves that decreases production to the socially optimal amount of Q_1^S. The tax decreases the price received by private producers from P^W to P^t and consequently decreases quantity supplied from Q_0^S to Q_1^S. However, the tax is imposed only on exports. In order for producers to be indifferent between supplying the domestic and export markets, the price on goods sold domestically must equate with the lower tax inclusive price. This means that consumers in the exporter will face the lower domestic price of P^t. Further, the export tax has the effect of decreasing exports from X_0 to X_1. This change in exports is larger in the case of an export tax relative to the case of the production tax.

In terms of welfare, the export tax has the following effects. The private producer's welfare decreases by the surplus amount $-(a + b + c + d + e + g)$. The government welfare increases by the amount $+(c + d)$. This change in government welfare is the amount of tax revenue raised on exports alone. It is the product of the quantity of the good exported and the value of the export tax. Further, social welfare increases by the amount $+(e + f)$. This social welfare change is the amount of the negative externality that is eliminated as a consequence of decreasing production. It is positive as it represents a decrease in environmental damage. Finally, consumer welfare increases by the surplus amount $+(a + b)$ as they now face a lower price on the domestically produced good.

The net country welfare effect is the sum of the consumer, producer, government, and social welfare changes. Adding these together we get a welfare change in the amount $+(f) - (g)$ for the country in aggregate. As noted above, the reduction in environmental damage is $+(f + e)$. Area $+e$ is a transfer from the private producer to society resulting from the policy. The area $-(g)$ represents a dead weight loss associated with a new consumption distortion that is introduced.

Table 11.1 summarizes the welfare effects of first- and second-best policies to address a negative production externality (Case 1). When we compare the welfare effects of the first- and second-best policies, we see that both policies result in a net gain from the reduction in environmental damage to society. However, the second-best policy also introduces a new distortion. This distortion arises because the scope of the policy does not match the scope of the externality. In our specific example,

Table 11.1 Welfare effects of first and second best policies.

Case 1 – Negative production externality in small exporter

Economic agent	Welfare effects of first best policy (production tax)	Welfare effects of second best policy (export tax)
Private producer	$-(a + b + c + d + e)$	$-(a + b + c + d + e + g)$
Government	$+(a + b + c + d)$	$+(c + d)$
Society	$+(e + f)$	$+(e + f)$
Consumer	0	$+(a + b)$
Country	$+f$	$+f - g$
Country (direction)	Positive	Positive or negative

Case 2 – Negative consumption externality in small importer

Economic agent	Welfare effects of first best policy (consumption tax)	Welfare effects of second best policy (tariff/import tax)
Private consumer	$-(c + d + g + h)$	$-(c + k + d + g + h)$
Government	$+(c + d + g)$	$+(d + g)$
Society	$+(h + i)$	$+(h + i)$
Producer	0	$+c$
Country	$+i$	$+i - k$
Country (direction)	Positive	Positive or negative

the scope of the production externality is national. In this case, a national policy (i.e., production tax) is the first-best policy to address the environmental concern and an international trade policy (i.e., export tax) is the second-best policy. Both policies correct the externality. However, the latter introduces new economic inefficiencies.

11.4.2   Case 2: Can trade policy correct a negative consumption externality in a small importer?

In the second case, we consider a negative consumption externality that arises within a small importing country. Thus, the externality is generated through the process of consumption and the externality is contained in scope within the importing country. Further, this country is not large enough to affect the world price of the good. In other words, the country is small in terms of its contributions to the world demand of the good. As before, we will refer to the externality as environmental damage. We will refer to the good as a dirty good.

One implication of these assumptions is that the social cost of consuming the dirty good is greater than the private cost of consuming the dirty good. In the absence of government intervention, the private sector will overconsume the dirty good and create environmental damage as a by-product.

Figure 11.5 illustrates these implications. At each price, the private demand (D_P) exceeds the social demand (D_S) in the country. The difference between the two demand curves reflects the negative consumption externality. We can see this by comparing the private and social consumer surpluses at a world price such as P^W. The private consumer surplus is the area represented by *(a + b + c)*. In contrast, the social consumer surplus is the area represented by *a*. The area *(b + c)* represents the difference. Further, in the absence of government intervention, the private sector will consume output of the dirty good in the amount Q_P^D. In contrast, the socially optimal consumption of the dirty good at price P^W is Q_S^D. Thus, areas *(c + d)* represent the social welfare loss from overconsuming the good.

The first-best policy response is a national policy because the externality is assumed to be national in scope. A consumption tax is a national-level policy that would create a disincentive to consumption.

Figure 11.6 illustrates the effects of this first-best policy response to the negative consumption externality. Prior to the policy, the small importer faces an infinitely elastic export supply (S^{S*}) for the dirty good from the rest of the world (ROW) at price P^W. At this price, domestic consumers in the importer demand Q_0^D of the dirty good and domestic producers supply Q_0^S of the dirty good. The excess of domestic demand over supply is the amount of imports (M_0) of the dirty good from the international market or the ROW. The area $+(h + i)$ represents that social welfare loss from overconsuming the dirty good.

Now consider the effects of imposing a domestic consumption tax in amount *t*. This tax is set to equate with the difference between the private and social demand

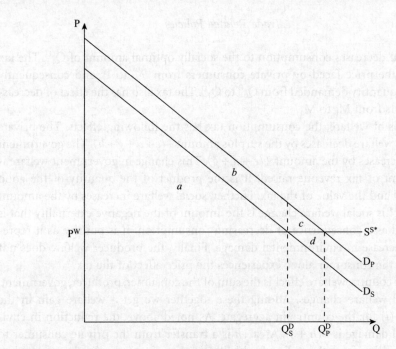

Figure 11.5 Negative consumption externality.

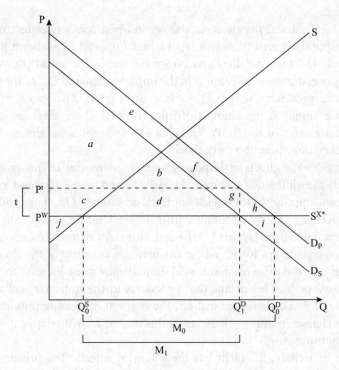

Figure 11.6 Negative consumption externality – first-best policy of a small importer.

curves that decreases consumption to the socially optimal amount of Q_1^D. The tax increases the price faced by private consumers from P^W to P^t and consequently decreases quantity demanded from Q_0^D to Q_1^D. The tax also has the effect of decreasing imports from M_0 to M_1.

In terms of welfare, the consumption tax has the following effects. The private consumer welfare decreases by the surplus amount $-(c + d + g + h)$. The government welfare increases by the amount $+(c + d + g)$. This change in government welfare is the amount of tax revenue raised. It is the product of the quantity of the good consumed and the value of the tax. Further, social welfare increases by the amount $+(h + i)$. This social welfare change is the amount of the negative externality that is eliminated as a consequence of decreasing consumption. It is positive as it represents a decrease in environmental damage. Finally, the producer welfare does not change as the consumer alone experiences the price effect of the tax.

The net country welfare effect is the sum of the consumer, producer, government, and social welfare changes. Adding these together we get a welfare gain in the amount $+(i)$ for the country in aggregate. As noted above, the reduction in environmental damage is $+(h + i)$. Area $+h$ is a transfer from the private consumer to society resulting from the policy. In this illustration, the externality is corrected by the consumption tax, without introducing a new distortion.

The second-best policy response is an international trade policy. Such a policy does not match the scope of the externality, which we have assumed to be national in scope. An import tax (or tariff) is a policy that would create a disincentive to consumption.

Figure 11.7 illustrates the effects of this second-best policy response to the negative consumption externality. As before, the small importer faces an infinitely elastic export supply (S^{S*}) for the dirty good from the rest of the world (ROW) at price P^W. At this price, domestic consumers in the importer demand Q_0^D of the dirty good and domestic producers supply Q_0^S of the dirty good. The excess of domestic demand over supply is the amount of imports (M_0) of the dirty good from the international market or the ROW. The area $+(h + i)$ represents that social welfare loss from overconsuming the dirty good.

Now consider the effects of imposing a tariff in amount t. This tariff is set to equate with the difference between the private and social demand curves that decreases consumption to the socially optimal amount of Q_1^D. The tariff increases the price faced by private consumers from P^W to P^t and consequently decreases quantity demanded from Q_0^D to Q_1^D. However, the tariff is imposed only on imports. In order for consumers to be indifferent between consuming the domestic and imported goods, the price on goods sold domestically must increase to the higher tariff inclusive price. This means that producers in the importer will receive the higher price of P^t. Further, the tariff has the effect of decreasing imports from M_0 to M_1. This change in imports is larger in this case of a tariff relative to the case of the consumption tax.

In terms of welfare, the tariff has the following effects. The private consumer welfare decreases by the surplus amount $-(c + k + d + g + h)$. The government

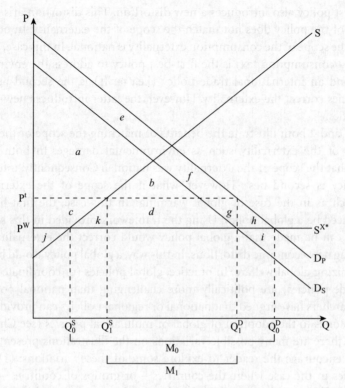

Figure 11.7 Negative consumption externality – second-best policy of a small importer.

welfare increases by the amount $+(d + g)$. This change in government welfare is the amount of tax revenue raised on imports. It is the product of the quantity of the good imported and the value of the tariff. Further, social welfare increases by the amount $+(h + i)$. This social welfare change is the amount of the negative externality that is eliminated as a consequence of decreasing consumption. It is positive as it represents a decrease in environmental damage. Finally, the producer welfare increases by the surplus amount $+(c)$ as they now face a higher price on the domestically consumed good.

The net country welfare effect is the sum of the consumer, producer, government, and social welfare changes. Adding these together we get a welfare change in the amount $+(i) - (k)$ for the country in aggregate. As noted above, the reduction in environmental damage is $+(h + i)$. Area $+h$ is a transfer from the private consumer to society resulting from the policy. The area $-(k)$ represents a dead weight loss associated with a new production distortion that is introduced.

Table 11.1 summarizes the welfare effects of first- and second-best policies to address a negative consumption externality (Case 2). When we compare the welfare effects of the first- and second-best policies, we see that both policies result in a net gain from the reduction in environmental damage to society. However, the second-best policy also introduces a new distortion. This distortion arises because the scope of the policy does not match the scope of the externality. In our specific example, the scope of the consumption externality is national. In this case, a national policy (i.e., consumption tax) is the first-best policy to address the environmental concern and an international trade policy (i.e., tariff) is the second-best policy. Both policies correct the externality. However, the latter introduces new economic inefficiencies.

Cases 1 and 2 both illustrate the benefits of matching the scope of the policy to the scope of the externality such as environmental damage. In both cases, we assumed that the scope of the externality was national. Consequently, international trade policy is second best. However, what if the scope of the externality was global, such as in the case of global warming? In this case, the first-best policy would indeed be a global policy. Using the framework provided in this section, an argument can be made that a global policy would correct the externality without introducing new economic distortions. In this way, a global policy would be optimal for maximizing global welfare. In practice, global policies (or coordinated international trade policies) are politically more challenging than national policies, but some researchers have argued that national or regional policies can provide political stepping stones to the adoption of global or multilateral policies (see Chapter 14).

Finally, there are many possible variations on the illustrations presented in this chapter. I encourage the reader to explore some of these variations: (1) consider externalities in the case where the countries – or groups of countries – are large enough to affect world prices; (2) consider the first- and second-best policies to address subnational externalities (such as local pollution); (3) consider the first- and second-best policies to address global externalities (such as global warming); (4) consider policy responses to positive environmental externalities (such as tree planting); (5) consider the case where optimal policy is designed to maximize global welfare, rather than national welfare, in the presence of externalities with various scopes. See the applied exercises for a starting point for these extensions.

11.5 Summary Remarks

What are trade-related environmental policies, their types and purpose? Environmental policies include a vast array of laws to protect the environment against concerns such as air and water pollution, global warming, the exhaustion of renewable and non-renewable resources, the extinction of endangered species, the loss of natural habitats, and the use of genetically modified organisms (GMOs). Environmental policies are "trade-related" because environmental policies affect trade and trade policies affect the environment. However, the relationship between trade and the environment is complex. Trends in trade policy and environmental quality suggest that the liberalization of trade policy corresponds with a period of improvement in urban environmental quality, and deterioration in global and rural environmental quality. These trends may be explained by political factors as well as difficulties associated with matching the scope of a policy with the scope of the environmental impact, such as addressing global environmental concerns with national policies.

What are the effects of trade policy on the environment? That is, does trade (or trade liberalization) lead to an improvement or worsening of environmental quality? Research suggests four prominent effects. The composition effect refers to changes in the composition of outputs as a consequence of trade, which generate an environmental impact. Specifically, countries with a comparative advantage in dirty industries shift their output composition toward dirty industries, and countries with a comparative advantage in clean industries shift their output composition toward clean industries. Second, the growth effect refers to an increase in the rate of economic growth as a consequence of trade, which then generates environmental impacts as a by-product. This impact arises when trade-induced growth outpaces changes in environmental policies and institutions. Third, the scale effect refers to an increase in the scale of production as a consequence of trade, which then generates environmental impacts as a by-product. That is, global output increases as a consequence of trade, resulting in larger environmental impacts from production scale and from the transport of goods over longer distances. Finally, the technique effect refers to the reduction in the intensity of environmental damage per unit of output as a consequence of trade. Specifically, trade leads to an increase in income, which results in an increase in the demand for environmental quality, stricter environmental regulations, and thus a decrease in environment damage per unit of output.

Combining these four effects, we see that the net effect of trade (or trade liberalization) on the environment is ambiguous. That is, trade can have a positive effect on the environment if a country has a comparative advantage in clean industries (composition effect); and if environmental quality is a normal good and policy makers are responsive to demand for environment quality (technique effect). Alternatively, trade can have a negative effect on the environment if a region has a comparative advantage in dirty industries (composition effect); if growth outpaces changes in environmental policy (growth effect); and if the increased scale of production and increased distance of transport results in environmental damage (scale effect). The net effect depends on which of these effects is dominant.

The effects of trade policy on the environment are also explored in research on the Environmental Kuznets Curve. This curve describes an inverted U-shaped relationship between income and environmental damage. There are two prominent explanations for how trade factors into this inverted U-shaped relationship. First, in the initial phase, trade leads to an increase in the scale of production and/or in economic growth. These changes lead to an increase in income and environmental damage consistent with the growth and scale effects. Then there is a turning point where an increase in income leads to an increase in demand for environmental quality and for environmental regulation. This change leads to a decrease in environmental damage consistent with the technique effect. The demand and policy responses to the income changes occur with a lag, resulting in an inverted U-shaped relationship between income and environment damage.

Another prominent explanation links the Environmental Kuznets Curve to changes in endowments over time. At early development stages, countries tend to be abundant in physical capital, which is used intensively in dirty industries. At later stages of development, countries accumulate larger stocks of human capital, which is used intensively in clean industries. This pattern is consistent with the composition effect of trade on the environment, where the composition of international trade changes over time with development. This explanation suggests that at lower income levels and early stages of development, trade liberalization leads to an increase in environmental damage. Concomitantly, at higher income levels and later stages of development, the trade liberalization leads to a decrease in environmental damage.

What are the effects of environmental policy on trade? Economic research in this area explores two key hypotheses. The pollution haven hypothesis states that countries with relatively strong environmental regulations will relocate their production in dirty industries to countries with relatively weak regulations. In this case, trade liberalization results in increased environmental quality in countries with strong regulations and decreased environmental quality in countries with weak regulations. Further, global environment quality may decrease as dirty industries locate where environmental policies are weakest. The factor endowment hypothesis is a variant of the pollution haven hypothesis that assumes that the abundance of endowments *and* environment policy both determine the patterns of production and trade, and thus environmental quality. In this case, dirty industries locate in countries that are abundant in endowments used intensively in dirty industries. If environmental policies are strong in these countries, then trade will result in a decrease in environmental damage. Alternatively, if environmental policies are weak in these countries, then trade will result in an increase in environmental damage. The first scenario is consistent with the pollution haven result but the second scenario is not. Further, if country differences in environmental policies are large, these differences may reverse the patterns of comparative advantage based on endowments. In this case, the pollution haven effect dominates the endowments effect.

What are the implications of using trade policy to address environmental externalities? To answer this question, we explored externalities in an open economy setting. Externalities arise when the act of production or consumption results in a side effect on an external agent in an economy (e.g., society). A negative production externality occurs when the process of production generates a negative effect on society. A negative consumption externality occurs when the process of consuming generates a negative effect on society. Environmental damage is an example of a negative externality that can arise from production and/or consumption. Such externalities result in a failure of the private market. Market failure is the situation where private markets do not generate the socially optimal levels of production and/or consumption. That is, firms overproduce goods that generate negative externalities because they do not take into account the social cost of their production; and consumers overconsume goods that generate negative externalities because they do not take into account the social cost of their consumption. The socially optimal levels of production and consumption take into account the externalities.

When externalities are present, the government can intervene to correct the market failure by adopting policies that provide incentives for producers and/or consumers to produce and/or consume the socially optimal levels of the good. However, the socially optimal policy depends on the scope of the externality. First-best policies are policies for which the scope of the policy matches with the scope of the externality. Such policies correct the market failure without introducing a new distortion. Alternatively, second-best policies are policies for which the scope of the policy does not match with the scope of the externality. Such policies correct the market failure, but simultaneously introduce a new distortion.

Trade policies can be first- or second-best policies depending on the scope of the externality. In this chapter, we considered two illustrative cases to demonstrate this point. First, we considered a negative production externality that arises within a small exporting country. In this case, private producers in the exporter overproduce the dirty good because they do not take into account the effect of the externality on the domestic society. A first-best policy response is a domestic production tax. This tax alters the production incentives to decrease supply. It has the effect of correcting the externality without introducing a new distortion in the market. In contrast, the second-best policy response is an export tax. This export tax also alters the production incentives to decrease supply as above. However, it has the effect of correcting the production externality and introducing a new consumption distortion.

Second, we considered a negative consumption externality that arises within a small importing country. In this case, private consumers in the importer overconsume the dirty good because they do not take into account the effect of their externality on the domestic society. A first-best policy response is a domestic consumption tax. This tax alters the consumption incentives to decrease demand. It has the effect of correcting the externality without introducing a new distortion in the market. In contrast, the second-best policy response is a tariff. This tariff also alters the consumption incentives to decrease demand. However, it has the effect of correcting the consumption externality and introducing a new production distortion.

These two illustrations show that it is desirable (from an economic welfare perspective) to match the scope of the policy to the scope of the environmental externality. That is, environmental externalities that are national in scope are best treated using national policies. This same intuition applies to other regional definitions. That is, environmental externalities that are global in scope (e.g., global warming) are best treated using coordinated global policies; and environmental externalities that are subnational in scope (e.g., local landfills) are best treated using subnational policies.

Applied Problems

11.1   Consider the externalities listed below. What are the first- and second-best policies for addressing these externalities? Examine the welfare effects of these first- and second-best policies for the following two cases: (a) negative production externality in a small exporter; (b) negative consumption externality in a small importer.

11.2   Consider a scenario where the production of GMO crops creates a negative production externality in a small exporting country. This externality could be the unwanted contamination of nearby land with GMO seeds blown by the wind. Examine the first- and second-best policies for correcting this externality. Examine the effects of these policies on the welfare of the exporter of GMO crops (such as the United States) including the welfare of society.

11.3   Consider a scenario where the production of GMO crops creates a positive production externality. This externality could be the improved traits of crops experienced by farmers with nearby land where GMO seeds are blown by the wind. Examine the first-and second-best policies for correcting this externality. Examine the effects of these policies on the welfare of an exporter of GMO crops (such as the United States), including the welfare of society.

11.4   Consider a scenario where consumers purchase goods packaged in #3 plastic (also known as polyvinyl chloride or PVC). This is often used in plastic wraps and salad dressing bottles; it is not typically recyclable and thus ends up in domestic landfills. Assume that the consumption of these goods creates a negative consumption externality in a small importing country. Examine the first- and second-best policies for correcting this externality. Examine the effects of these policies on the welfare of the importer, including the welfare of society.

11.5   Consider a scenario where the consumption of goods packaged in clamshell packaging creates a negative consumption externality in a small exporting country. For example, the act of consumption could contribute to domestic landfill and/or the Pacific Gyre if the packaging is disposed of in waterways. Propose and analyze a first- and second-best policy for correcting this externality. Examine the effects of these policies on the welfare of the exporter, including the welfare of society.

11.6   Analyze the questions above for a large country that can affect the world price. Be sure to make assumptions about the relative elasticities of supply and demand in the trading countries.

11.7   Use your knowledge to analyze the following questions: (a) How does trade policy affect the environment? For example, what are the environmental consequences of trade liberalization? (b) How does environmental policy affect trade? For example, what are the trade consequences of cross-country differences in environmental policies? (c) What are the implications of using trade policy to address environmental externalities?

11.8   Suppose that all of the importing countries in the world pursue a second-best policy to reduce drug consumption (which generates negative consumption externalities such as crime and HIV/AIDS). Use your knowledge of welfare effects to determine who would support this policy in the importing countries. Would any agents in the exporting countries support this policy? How does your answer depend on the market size of the countries involved? How does your answer depend on elasticities of export supply and import demand?

11.9 Consider a goods market with a negative consumption externality (e.g., alcohol or cigarette consumption). Assume a small country produces and imports the good. Evaluate the effects of replacing a first-best policy with a second-best policy on welfare in the importing country.

11.10 Consider the scenario where the production of trees in large tree farms creates a positive production externality (i.e., a positive impact on the environment). Assume a small country produces and imports trees. Evaluate the effects of both a first-best policy and a second-best policy on welfare in the importing country.

11.11 Consider the scenario where the production of cheap consumption goods creates a negative production externality. This externality could be the negative health effects experienced by employees who are exposed to hazardous materials in their working environments. Examine the second-best policy for correcting this externality. Examine the effects of this policy on the welfare of an exporter of cheap consumption goods (such as China).

11.12 Suppose that all of the countries in the world (importers and exporters) pursue a second-best policy to reduce drug consumption (which generates negative consumption externalities such as crime and HIV/AIDS). Evaluate the effects of such policies on: (a) world producer welfare; (b) world consumer welfare; (c) world government welfare; (d) world social welfare; and (e) world welfare of any other agents involved. Assume that the importing and exporting countries are large enough to affect the world price.

Further Reading

Antweiler, Werner, Brian R. Copeland, and M. Scott Taylor. 2001. Is free trade good for the environment? *American Economics Review* 91 (4): 877–908.

Brack, Duncan, and Kevin Gray. 2003. *Multilateral Environmental Agreements and the WTO.* London: The Royal Institute of International Affairs. Sustainable Development Program Report, September.

Brander, James A., and M. Scott Taylor. 1997. International trade and open access renewable resources: the small open economy case. *Canadian Journal of Economics* 30 (3): 526–552.

Brander, James A., and M. Scott Taylor. 1998. Open access renewable resources: trade and trade policy in a two-country world. *Journal of International Economics* 44 (2): 181–210.

Chichinisky, Graciela. 1994. North-south trade and the global environment. *American Economic Review* 84 (4): 851–874.

Copeland, Brian R., and Sumeet Gulati. 2006. Trade and the environment in developing
    countries. In *Economic Development and Environmental Sustainability* (eds R. Lopez and
    M. Toman), Oxford: Oxford University Press, pp. 178–216.
Copeland, Brian R., and M. Scott Taylor. 1994. North-south trade and the global environ-
    ment. *Quarterly Journal of Economics* 109: 755–787.
Copeland, Brian R., and M. Scott Taylor. 1999. Trade, spatial separation, and the environ-
    ment. *Journal of International Economics* 47 (1): 137–168.
Copeland, Brian R., and M. Scott Taylor. 2003. *Trade and the Environment: Theory and Evi-
    dence.* Princeton University Press, Princeton.
Copeland, Brian R., and M. Scott Taylor. 2004. Trade, growth and the environment. *Journal
    of Economic Literature* (March): 7–71.
Copeland, Brian R., and M. Scott Taylor. 2009. Trade, tragedy, and the commons. *American
    Economic Review* 99 (3): 725–749.
Eckersley, Robyn. 2004. The big chill: the WTO and multilateral environmental agreements.
    Global Environmental Politics 4 (2): 24–50.
Gallagher, Kevin P., ed. 2009. *Handbook on Trade and the Environment.* Cheltenham, United
    Kingdom: Edward Elgar Publishing.
Grossman, Gene M., and A.B. Krueger. 1994. Environmental impacts of a North American
    free trade agreement. In *The US-Mexico Free Trade Agreement* (ed P. Gaber), Cambridge,
    MA: MIT Press.
Johnson, Pierre Marc, and Andre Beaulieu. 1996. *The Environment and NAFTA: Understand-
    ing and Implementing the New Continental Law.* Washington, D.C.: Island Press.
Lopez, Ramon. 1997. Environmental externalities in traditional agriculture and the impact
    of trade liberalization: the case of Ghana. *Journal of Development Economics* 53 (1):
    17–39.
Lopez, Ramon, and Gregmar I. Galinato. 2005. Deforestation and forest-induced carbon
    dioxide emissions in tropical countries: how do governance and trade openness affect
    the forest-income relationship? *Journal of Environment and Development* 14 (1): 73–100.
McAusland, Carol. 2008. Trade, politics, and the environment: tailpipie vs. smokestack.
    Journal of Environmental Economics and Management 55 (1): 52–71.
Runge, C. Ford. 2001. A global environment organization (GEO) and the world trading
    system. *Journal of World Trade* 35 (4): 399–426.
World Trade Organization Committee on Trade and Environment (CTE). 2000. *The Rela-
    tionship between the Provisions of the Multilateral Trading System and Multilateral Envi-
    ronmental Agreements (MEAs).* Submission by Switzerland , June 8 (WT/CTE/W/139).
    Geneva: WTO.

Notes

1. For background on these effects of trade on the environment, see Antweiler, Copeland
   and Taylor (2001); Copeland and Taylor (2003); Lopez (1997); and Lopez and Galinato
   (2005).
2. For analysis of the pollution haven hypothesis, see Chichinisky (1994) and Copeland and
   Gulati (2006).
3. The question of whether trade policy should be used to address environmental concerns
   is addressed at length in Copeland and Taylor (2004).

12

Labor Policies

12.1 What Are Trade-Related Labor Policies, Their Types, and Purpose?

Labor policies include a vast array of national and international laws concerning labor standards that directly affect workers. The economics literature on labor standards defines two prominent types – core standards and outcome standards. *Core labor standards* are those that regulate the labor market process to ensure basic human rights. The International Labor Organization (ILO) identifies four such core standards. These include: rights to free association and collective bargaining; prohibition against forced labor; abolition of exploitative child labor; and elimination of exploitative child labor. In contrast, *outcome labor standards* are those that regulate characteristics of labor contracts. These characteristics include the number of hours worked, wage rates, occupational health and safety, among others.

Labor policies and trade policies are related. Laws adopted to address labor concerns can affect trade. Similarly, laws adopted to address trade can affect labor. Thus, labor policies are related to trade, and trade policies are related to labor. Policy arrangements on labor standards are found in national laws and international trade agreements. Individual countries establish their own national laws for protecting labor. International trade agreements link trade to these national labor policies and seek to provide some limited coordination of labor policies across trading partners. *International labor standards* refer to those policies that coordinate labor practices at the international level.

In practice, the treatment of labor standards in international trade agreements is limited. Within the General Agreement on Tariffs and Trade (GATT), and its

Global Trade Policy: Questions and Answers, First Edition. Pamela J. Smith.

successor the World Trade Organization (WTO), Article XXIII provides some limited grounds for the international coordination of national labor standards. This article articulates a nullification and impairment clause. The implication of this clause is that WTO members are expected to provide a degree of market access to their trading partners. If labor policies limit market access, then the affected country can file a complaint. The nullification and impairment clause provides a means by which the affected country can be compensated by its trading partner. Article XX(e) of the WTO Agreement also provides some limited grounds for the international coordination of labor standards. This article allows WTO members to limit imports of goods that are produced using prison labor. Efforts to extend this article to include other labor practices have not been successful.

The ILO was established in 1919 and became part of the United Nations in 1946. It currently serves as the prominent body responsible for establishing and monitoring labor standards internationally. It puts forth recommendations and conventions, and provides technical assistance for the purpose of raising labor standards. However, compliance by ILO member governments with these initiatives is voluntary.

The relationship between trade and labor is complex and continues to pose unresolved puzzles for economists. Research on the relationship between trade and labor has a long history. The models presented earlier in this book demonstrate that trade (or trade liberalization) increases a country's welfare in aggregate. However, these same models show that trade (or trade liberalization) creates winners and losers within a country. Everyone within a country can be made better off only if the winners compensate the losers (see Chapter 4). Winners and losers include labor at different skill levels; that is, with trade, some types of labor win and others lose in terms of their wage changes. In practice, compensation does not often occur between these winners and losers, and when it does occur, its impact is modest at best (see section 12.3). Thus, trade can contribute to income inequality within countries.

The Stolper-Samuelson theory (presented in Chapter 2) provides the best-known explanation of the effects of trade on wages paid to labor. This theory shows that trade leads to an increased return to the factors of production that are used intensively in the export sectors and leads to a decreased return to the factors of production that are used intensively in the import-competing sectors. Thus, in countries that are abundant in skilled labor (such as in the North), we expect an increase in the relative wage of *skilled-to-unskilled labor*; and in countries that are abundant in unskilled labor (such as in the South), we expect an increase in the relative wage of *unskilled-to-skilled labor*. These changes would produce an *increase* in income inequality within countries abundant in skilled labor (the North) and a *decrease* in income inequality within countries abundant in relatively unskilled labor (the South). That is, we expect trade to produce asymmetric changes in wage inequality in the North versus the South.

This theoretical result does not explain well the growing global trends in income and wage inequality within both developed *and* developing countries, which poses a puzzle to international trade economists. The empirical evidence motivating the puzzle has appeared in global trends over the past two decades. During this period, international trade has grown rapidly, while international policy restrictions on trade have decreased. During this same period, relative wages have changed across developed and developing countries, as well as within countries. Since the 1970s and 1980s, wage inequality has increased dramatically within many developed countries including Australia, Belgium, Canada, Denmark, Germany, Italy, Japan, and the United States. Wage inequality has also increased in many developing countries, including the Latin American countries among others. These patterns are seen in the dramatic increases in wage inequality between labor with different skills levels as measured by education, experience, and occupation.[1]

This evidence appears to be inconsistent with the predictions of trade theory (in Chapter 2). Traditional trade theory predicts increasing wage inequality in developed countries and decreasing wage inequality in developing countries. The empirical evidence, however, shows increasing wage inequality in both developed and developing countries. As a consequence of this inconsistency, many trade economists have doubts about the role of trade in causing wage (and income) inequality. The puzzle – the contraction between trade theory and wage changes in practice – is one of the core issues illustrated in this chapter. We do not resolve the puzzle, but rather provide the foundations for understanding it.[2]

There are two prominent bodies of economic literature on the relationship between trade and labor. One focuses on the relationship between trade and wages (as described above). The second literature focuses on trade and labor standards. This chapter explores the key findings in these two literatures. The chapter is organized around three key questions. First, what are the effects of trade policy on labor, in the short run and long run? Second, how can the gains and losses from trade be redistributed within countries? Third, what are the effects of labor policy on trade?

12.2 What Are the Effects of Trade Policy on Labor?

We begin by considering the effects of trade policy on labor. Specifically, we consider the effects of trade (or trade liberalization) on the relative wages paid to labor (or the distribution of income across skilled and unskilled labor). We will illustrate the long-run effects using the Heckscher-Ohlin model, and we will illustrate the short-run (or transition) effects using the Specific Factors model. We present a specific application of these models where we define endowments to include skilled and unskilled labor. This application allows us to consider the differential effects of trade on wages paid to skilled and unskilled labor within and across countries. Our conception of skilled and unskilled labor is a *relative* one. In practice, there is a continuum of levels of skill that varies based on education, experience, and occupation. In our application, skilled labor can be viewed as being relatively more educated or experienced, or employed in skills-intensive industries such as a high-technology industry. This application is a variation on the models in Chapter 2.

12.2.1   What are the long-run effects of trade on wages?

The long-run effects of trade on wages can be predicted using the Heckscher-Ohlin (HO) model. Several prominent theories emerge from the HO model that explain the income distribution effects of trade within a country and across trading countries. The *Stolper-Samuelson theory* says that trade (and the associated price changes) leads to increased returns to a country's abundant endowments and decreased returns to a country's scarce endowments. These returns include wages paid to labor. Thus, this theory links the price changes associated with trade to wages paid to abundant and scarce labor within countries. For example, this theory predicts that countries abundant in skilled labor will experience an increase in the relative wage paid to skilled labor, and countries abundant in unskilled labor will experience an increase in the relative wage paid to unskilled labor. The *Factor-Price Equalization theory* says that factor prices (including wages paid to labor) are equalized across countries as a result of trade. Thus, this theory links trade with wages paid to similarly skilled labor across countries. For example, this theory predicts that the wages paid to skilled labor in different countries will converge as a consequence of trade, and the wages paid to unskilled labor in different countries will also converge across countries.

The key assumption of the HO model is that endowments differ across countries. For our application, we make the following assumptions. There are two countries – home and foreign. To illustrate, we define home to include all developed countries, and foreign to include all developing countries. For simplicity, we will refer to the developed countries as the North and the developing countries as the South. There are two goods – x and y. There are two endowments – skilled labor and unskilled labor. Skilled and unskilled labor are immobile across countries, but mobile across industries within a country. This mobility/immobility assumption is the key feature that makes the model appropriate for a long-run analysis. That is, we assume that in the long run, skilled and unskilled labor can be retrained to be employed in either industry.

Furthermore, we maintain the standard assumptions discussed in Chapter 2. That is, the market structure is perfect competition. There are constant returns to scale. The technology is such that both endowments are used in the production of both goods. There is a fixed coefficients technology such that only one combination of the endowments can be used to produce each good.

The *fixed coefficients technology* is shown in the unit input requirements. *Unit input requirements* express the amount of an endowment required to produce a unit of the output. We define k_x as the amount of skilled labor required to produce one unit of good x; l_x is the amount of unskilled labor required to produce one unit of good x; k_y is the amount of skilled labor required to produce one unit of good y; and l_y is the amount of unskilled labor required to produce one unit of good y. We use the notation k to denote skilled labor, as such labor is often referred to by economists as *human capital*. These unit input requirements differ across industries, yet they are the same across countries.

In our example, we will assume that good x is intensive in skilled labor and good y is intensive in unskilled labor. This means that good x is produced using a relatively higher ratio of skilled-to-unskilled labor; and good y is produced using a relatively higher ratio of unskilled-to-skilled labor. We can think of good x as a high-skill intensive good, and good y as a low-skill intensive good. In practice, skill intensity is often linked to the technical intensity of an industry. As such, we can also think of the high-skill intensive good x as a high-tech good, and the low-skill intensive good y as a low-tech good.

The assumption of skill intensity above can be written as

$$k_x/l_x > k_y/l_y, \text{ or} \tag{12.1}$$

$$k_x/k_y > l_x/l_y$$

We can now determine the production possibilities of a country using our knowledge of relative abundance of endowments and factor intensities. In our example, the production possibilities frontier (PPF) shows the tradeoff between the outputs of good x (Q_x) and good y (Q_y) given the factor intensities of each good and the factor endowments of the country. The production possibilities are constrained by the factor endowments available in the country as follows:

$$k_x Q_x + k_y Q_y \leq K \tag{12.2}$$

$$l_x Q_x + l_y Q_y \leq L \tag{12.3}$$

Equation (12.2) shows that the amount of skilled labor used to produce output of good x plus good y must be less than or equal to the supply of skilled labor (K) within the country. Similarly, equation (12.3) shows that the amount of unskilled labor used to produce output of good x plus good y must be less than or equal to the supply of unskilled labor (L) within the country. Assuming that all of the skilled and unskilled labor is employed within the country (i.e., no unemployment), then equations (12.2) and (12.3) hold with equality.

Figure 12.1 shows these production possibilities for good x and good y for the country. This is a simple diagrammatic plotting of equations (12.2) and (12.3) that we derive by rearranging the equations as follows:

$$Q_x = K/k_x - (k_y/k_x)Q_y \tag{12.4}$$

$$Q_x = L/l_x - (l_y/l_x)Q_y \tag{12.5}$$

The diagram shows the tradeoff between producing good x and good y, given the relative factor intensities of the two goods reflected in the slopes of the production constraints (k_y/k_x and l_y/l_x). Given that both resource constraints must hold

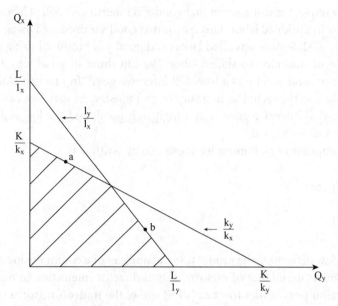

Figure 12.1 Heckscher Ohlin model – production possibilities.

simultaneously, the production possibilities set is the shaded area where both equations (12.4) and (12.5) hold.

Intuitively, the slope of each constraint reflects the opportunity cost of producing good x in terms of good y foregone, and vice versa. Because there are two endowments (skilled and unskilled labor), the opportunity cost differs at various points along the PPF. In this simple version, the frontier is kinked and has two slopes.

Next, we illustrate the Stolper-Samuelson theory – the relationship between goods prices and factor prices. The factor prices in our application are the wages paid to skilled and unskilled labor. To illustrate the Stolper-Samuelson theory, we must examine equilibrium in the factor market for skilled and unskilled labor. Given the HO model assumption of perfect competition, we know that goods prices equal the sum of factor prices in each sector in equilibrium. In our example, this equilibrium condition is

$$P_x = k_x w_s + l_x w_u \tag{12.6}$$

$$P_y = k_y w_s + l_y w_u$$

where w_s is the wage paid to skilled labor, w_u is the wage paid to unskilled labor, and P_x and P_y are the prices of goods x and y, respectively.

To plot these equations, we simply rearrange equations (12.6) to get

$$w_s = P_x / k_x - (l_x / k_x) w_u \tag{12.7}$$

$$w_s = P_y / k_y - (l_y / k_y) w_u$$

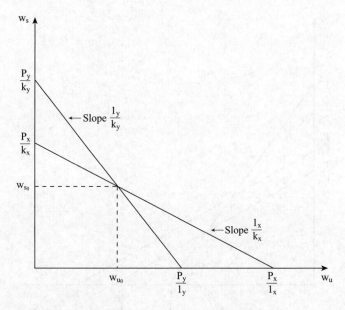

Figure 12.2 Heckscher Ohlin model – factor market equilibrium.

Furthermore, we need to apply our knowledge of factor intensities. As discussed earlier, good x is intensive in skilled labor and good y is intensive in unskilled labor. Figure 12.2 shows the labor market equilibrium under this assumption. That is, this figure shows equations (12.7) with the factor intensity assumption in equation (12.1). The equilibrium factor prices (i.e., wages paid to labor) are w_{s0} and w_{u0}.

We can now illustrate the Stolper-Samuelson theory. Figure 12.3 shows the effects of changes in goods prices on wages. Specifically, the figure shows the effect of an increase in the price of good x (from P_{x0} to P_{x1}) on the wages paid to skilled and unskilled labor. We can see that this change leads to an increase in the wage paid to skilled labor (w_{s0} to w_{s1}) and a decrease in the wage paid to unskilled labor (w_{u0} to w_{u1}). Alternatively, we could have shown that an increase in the price of good y leads to an increase in the wage paid to unskilled labor and a decrease in the wage paid to skilled labor. These are changes in *nominal wages* paid to skilled and unskilled labor.

We can also examine the effect of changes in goods prices on *real wages* paid to labor to determine the impact on purchasing power. To do this, we need to look at wages relative to goods prices. For example, the real wages paid to skilled labor in terms of goods x and y are w_s/P_x and w_s/P_y, respectively. Similarly, the real wages paid to unskilled labor in terms of good x and y are w_u/P_x and w_u/P_y, respectively. Thus, to determine changes in real wages, we need to consider changes in wages relative to changes in goods prices. In Figure 12.3, we see that the changes in the wages paid to skilled and unskilled labor are larger than the change in the price of good x. The change in the price of good x is the vertical distance corresponding with the price change (i.e., $P_{x1} - P_{x0}$).

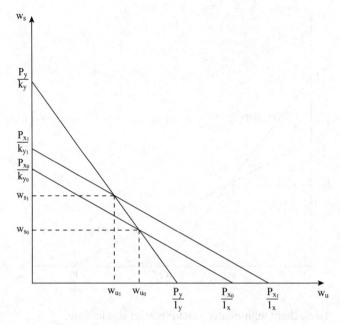

Figure 12.3 Heckscher Ohlin model – Stolper-Samuelson effect.

That is

$$|(w_{s1} - w_{s0})| > |(P_{x1} - P_{x0})|$$ (12.8)

$$|(w_{u1} - w_{u0})| > |(P_{x1} - P_{x0})|$$

Thus, the real wage paid to skilled labor increases in terms of good x and the real wage paid to unskilled labor decreases in terms of good x. Also, since the price of good y does not change in our example, the real and the nominal changes in wages paid to skilled and unskilled labor are the same in terms of good y.

We can draw two general conclusions from this application of the Stolper-Samuelson theorem. First, an increase in the price of a good leads to an increase in the nominal and real wages paid to labor that is used intensively in the production of that good. This is a cross-time effect. In this case, the changes shown in Figure 12.3 represent two points in time, such as a move from autarky to free trade for one country. Second, when goods prices differ across countries, the nominal and real wages will also differ across countries. This is the cross-country effect. In this case, the differences shown in the figure may represent two countries in a state of autarky.

Furthermore, there is a *magnification effect*. That is, the magnitude of the changes/differences in nominal wages exceeds the magnitude of changes in goods prices. Consequently, both real and nominal wages move in the same direction as a result of changes in goods prices.

We can now extend this application to examine the effects of trade (or trade liberalization) on wages paid to skilled and unskilled labor in the North versus the South. To illustrate, assume that the North and the South have identical technologies such that

$$(k_x/l_x) = (k_x*/l_x*) \tag{12.9}$$

$$(k_y/l_y) = (k_y*/l_y*)$$

where asteriks denote the South. However, the technologies differ across industries in both the North and the South as shown in equation (12.1) such that

$$(k_x/l_x) > (k_y/l_y) \tag{12.10}$$

$$(k_x*/l_x*) > (k_y*/l_y*)$$

where good x is intensive in skilled labor and good y is intensive in unskilled labor.

Further, assume that the North and South differ in their relative abundance of endowments. Specifically, the North is abundant in skilled labor and the South is abundant in unskilled labor. Thus, the production constraints differ across the North and South such that

$$K/L > K*/L* \tag{12.11}$$

where K/L is the skilled-to-unskilled labor endowment ratio of the North and K*/L* is the skilled-to-unskilled labor endowment ratio of the South.

We can illustrate these differences by plotting production possibility frontiers for the North and South. Figure 12.4 shows the PPFs for the (a) North and (b) South under these conditions. As shown, the skilled labor constraint for the North is further from the origin, reflecting the North's abundance in skilled labor. Similarly, the unskilled labor constraint for the South is further from the origin, reflecting the South's abundance of unskilled labor. However, the slopes of the constraints are identical across the two countries, reflecting their identical technologies. The shaded areas show the production possibilities. We can see that the outputs of the North and South are biased toward the sectors that use the abundant endowment intensively in production. That is, the frontier of the North is biased toward good x and the frontier of the South is biased toward good y.

The production and consumption of the North and South in autarky may be any point along the PPFs. The specific point depends on preferences. We can envision indifference curves tangent to the possibilities frontiers such as i and i*. These are the indifference curves that would maximize utility given the constraint that both the North and South can only consume what they produce in a state of autarky. In this case, the North will produce and consume along the portion of the frontier

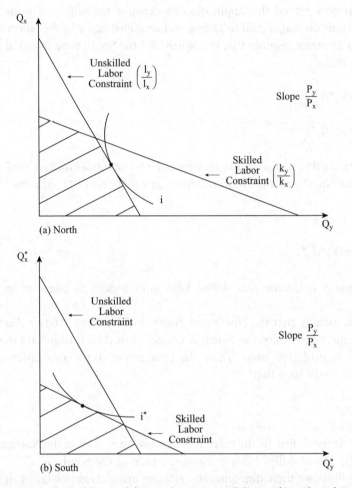

Figure 12.4 Heckscher Ohlin model – production possibilities of North and South.

with slope l_y/l_x; and the South will produce and consume along the portion of the frontier with slope k_y/k_x.

As shown in the figure, goods prices differ across the countries in autarky. Goods prices are determined by the technologies and are reflected in the slopes of the PPFs. The price of the skilled-labor-intensive good (x) is relatively low in the North and the price of the unskilled-labor-intensive good (y) is relatively low in the South; that is, $P_y/P_x > P_y^*/P_x^*$.

What then is the relative price of goods at which trade will occur in the world market? The intuitive answer is that the North and South will only trade at prices that are more favorable than the prices in autarky. That is, the North and South are willing to export goods at higher prices and import goods at lower prices, relative to autarky prices. To illustrate these prices, we must look at the world market for goods x and y. Given our simple model of two groups of countries (North and

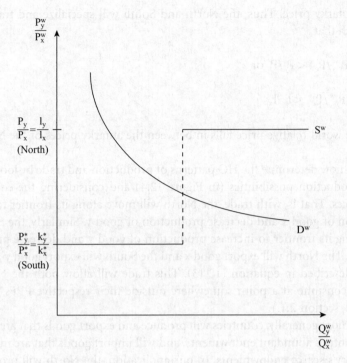

Figure 12.5 Heckscher Ohlin model – world relative supply and demand.

South), the world quantities of goods x and y are the sums of the quantities of the North and South. Thus

$$Q_x^w = Q_x + Q_x^* \tag{12.12}$$

$$Q_y^w = Q_y + Q_y^*$$

where Q_x^w is the world output of good x and Q_y^w is the world output of good y.

Figure 12.5 illustrates the determination of world prices. This figure plots the world relative supply S^w and demand D^w curves for goods x and y. The relative demand curve shows that the relative world demand for good y increases as the relative price of good y falls. The relative supply curve is discontinuous. We know that the North's autarky price corresponds with the slope of the unskilled labor constraint ($P_y/P_x = l_y/l_x$) and the South's autarky price corresponds with the slope of the skilled constraint ($P_y^*/P_x^* = k_y^*/k_x^*$). Intuitively, this reflects that the North is unskilled-labor-scarce and the South is skilled-labor-scarce. Thus, the equilibrium world price must fall in between the autarky prices of the North and South. In this range, the North will specialize in good x because the world relative price of good x is higher than the North's autarky relative price. Similarly, the South will specialize in good y because the world relative price of good y is higher than the South's

relative autarky price. Thus, the North and South will specialize and trade for all
prices such that

$$P_y^*/P_x^* < P_y^w/P_x^w < P_y/P_x \text{ or} \qquad\qquad\qquad (12.13)$$

$$k_y^*/k_x^* < P_y^w/P_x^w < l_y/l_x$$

where the world relative price falls in between the autarky prices of the North and
South.

We can now determine the HO patterns of production and trade by looking back
at our production possibilities (in Figure 12.4) and considering the equilibrium
world prices. That is, with trade, the North will move along its frontier to increase
production of good x and decrease production of good y. Similarly, the South will
move along its frontier to increase production of good y and decrease production
of good x. The North will export good x and the South will export good y at a world
price as described in equation (12.13). This trade will allow both the North and
South to consume at a point somewhere outside their respective PPFs. (See also
Chapter 2, section 2.1.)

Stated more generally, countries will produce and export goods that are intensive
in the country's abundant endowments, and will import goods that are intensive in
the country's scarce endowments. In our application, the North will produce and
export skilled-labor-intensive goods, and import unskilled-labor-intensive goods;
and the South will produce and export unskilled-labor-intensive goods, and import
skilled-labor-intensive goods.

What are the effects of this trade? Table 12.1 (a) summarizes the gains from trade
illustrated in this application of the HO model. At the aggregate level, we know that
both the North and South gain from trade because their consumption possibilities
increase as a result of specialization and trade. Specifically, at equilibrium world
prices, both the North and South can consume on an indifference curve that is
outside their respective PPFs (shown in Figure 12.4). The aggregate utility of both
the North and South increases with trade.

We can also observe the distribution of wages within countries. To this end, we
revisit our labor market constraints. We consider the effects on wages of changes in
goods prices resulting from trade. Figure 12.5 and equations (12.13) describe the
changes in prices that result when the North and South move from autarky to trade
(or liberalize trade). Specifically, we know that the North will experience an increase
in the relative price of good x and the South will experience an increase in the relative price of good y, as a result of trade.

What are the effects of these goods price changes on wages paid to skilled and
unskilled labor in each country? Figure 12.6 illustrates these effects. For the (a)
North, the price of good x rises relative to good y. We show this relative change by
increasing the price of good x and leaving the price of good y unchanged. The results
include an increase in the nominal wage paid to skilled labor (w_s) as well as an
increase in the real wages paid to skilled labor (w_s/P_x and w_s/P_y). The results also
include a decrease in the nominal wage paid to unskilled labor (w_u) and real wages

Table 12.1 Welfare effects in North and South.

(a) Heckscher-Ohlin model

North/South	Welfare effects
Aggregate gains	Increase consumption possibilities and utility in North and South.
Distribution within North and South	North: Increase in nominal and real wage paid to skilled labor, and decrease in nominal and real wage paid to unskilled labor.
	South: Increase in nominal and real wage paid to unskilled labor, and decrease in nominal and real wage paid to skilled labor.
Distribution across North and South	Wage paid to skilled labor increases in the North and decreases in the South until these wages are equalized across the North and South. Wages paid to unskilled labor increases in the South and decreases in the North until these wages are equalized across the North and South.

(b) Specific Factors model

North/South	Welfare effects
Aggregate gains	Increase consumption possibilities and utility in North and South.
Distribution within North and South (immobile labor)	North: Increase in real wage paid to skilled labor and decrease in real wage paid to unskilled labor.
	South: Increase in real wage paid to unskilled labor and decrease in real wage paid to skilled labor.
Distribution within North and South (mobile capital)	Increase nominal rent paid to capital. Increase real rent paid to capital in terms of purchasing power of the imported good. Decrease real rent paid to capital in terms of the purchasing power of the exported good.

Notes: Case (a) assumes that the North is abundant in skilled labor and the South is abundant in unskilled labor. Further, skilled and unskilled labor are *mobile* across industries.

Case (b) assumes that the North is abundant in skilled labor and the South is abundant in unskilled labor. Further, skilled and unskilled labor are *immobile* across industries. The North and South are similarly endowed in capital, which is *mobile* across industries.

to unskilled labor (w_u/P_x and w_u/P_y). That is, skilled labor gains in terms of its purchasing power of both goods x and y, and unskilled labor loses in terms of its purchasing power of both goods x and y in the North.

In contrast, for the (b) South, the price of good y rises relative to good x as a result of trade. We show this relative change by increasing the price of good y and leaving the price of good x unchanged. The results include a decrease in the nominal wage to skilled labor (w_s^*) as well as a decrease in the real wages to skilled labor (w_s^*/P_x^* and w_s^*/P_y^*). The results also include an increase in the nominal wage

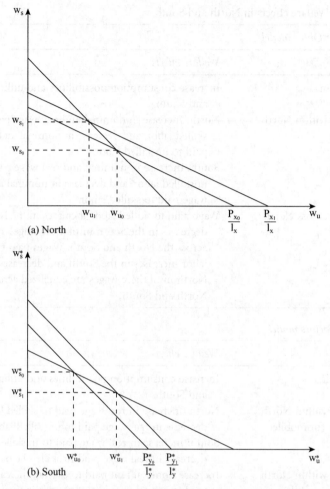

Figure 12.6 Heckscher Ohlin model – comparison of autarky and trade for North and South.

paid to unskilled labor (w_u^*) and real wages paid to unskilled labor (w_u^*/P_x^* and w_u^*/P_y^*). That is, skilled labor loses in terms of its purchasing power of both goods x and y and unskilled labor gains in terms of its purchasing power of both goods x and y in the South.

Finally, we can describe the effects of trade in terms of relative wages across countries. Specifically, the *Factor-Price Equalization Theory* says that factor prices (or wages) are equalized across countries as a result of trade. This is the consequence of the changes in goods prices that result from trade, as shown in Figure 12.5. These changes in goods prices lead to changes in wages, as shown in Figure 12.6. In our example, the skilled-labor-abundant North has a relatively low wage paid to skilled labor and a relatively high wage paid to unskilled labor in autarky (compared to the South). As the North opens to trade and specializes in the skilled-labor-intensive good x, the wage paid to skilled labor rises and the wage paid to unskilled labor falls (in real and nominal terms). Similarly, the unskilled-labor-abundant South has a relatively low wage paid to unskilled labor and a relatively high wage paid to skilled labor in autarky (compared to the North). As the South opens to trade and specializes in the unskilled-labor-intensive good y, the wage paid to unskilled labor rises and the wage paid to skilled labor falls (in real and nominal terms). Through this process, the high- and low-skilled labor wages of the two countries continue to change until they are equalized across the North and South. With trade, the world equilibrium prices are

$$P_x^w = w_u^w l_x + w_s^w k_x \qquad\qquad (12.14)$$

$$P_y^w = w_u^w l_y + w_s^w k_y$$

where world wages paid to skilled and unskilled labor equal the wages paid to skilled and unskilled labor in the North and South (i.e., $w_s^w = w_s = w_s^*$ and $w_u^w = w_u = w_u^*$).

This application of the HO model helps us to evaluate the wage effects from trade when we move from a hypothetical state of autarky to free trade (or vice versa). The model also provides guidance for understanding what happens if we move closer to autarky or closer to free trade by changing policies. Several basic conclusions emerge.

In the North, where skilled labor is abundant, skilled labor experiences an increase in wages as a result of trade, and unskilled labor experiences a wage decrease. Conversely, in the South, where unskilled labor is abundant, unskilled labor experiences an increase in wages as a result of trade, and skilled labor experiences a wage decrease. Given the magnification effect, these changes apply to both nominal and real wages. In theory, these wage changes continue until wages equalize across countries. That is, the wage paid to skilled labor increases in the North and decreases in the South until these wages are equalized; and the wage paid to unskilled labor increases in the South and decreases in the North until these wages are equalized.

Further, the model predicts a widening gap in income distribution in the North and a narrowing gap in income distribution in the South as a consequence of trade. In the North, the wage paid to skilled labor increases and the wage paid to unskilled labor decreases. Consequently, the internal difference $(w_s - w_u)$ increases. In the South, the wage paid to skilled labor decreases and the wage paid to unskilled labor increases. Consequently, the internal difference $(w_s^* - w_u^*)$ decreases.

These are the well-known results of the Stolper-Samuelson and Factor-Price Equalization theories, applied to the case of skilled and unskilled labor. The wage effects within countries are asymmetric in that one type of labor is better off and the other is worse off as a consequence of trade or trade liberalization. The income distribution effects of trade are also asymmetric as one group of countries experiences a widening of their internal wage gap while the other experiences a narrowing of their internal wage gap. This result contributes to the puzzle introduced at the beginning of this chapter. These results correspond with the *long run*, where skilled and unskilled labor moves between the industries to specialize their production for trade.

12.2.2   What are the short-run effects of trade on wages?

Next, we use the Specific Factors model to illustrate the short-run effects of trade on wages. The source of comparative advantage in the specific factors model is country differences in endowments of specific factors. *Specific Factors* are immobile across industries; that is, they are "specific" to a particular industry. For our application, we will assume that skilled labor is specific to one industry and unskilled labor is specific to another industry. The immobility assumption reflects a short-run situation where skilled and unskilled labor cannot move effortlessly in and out of the two industries. Rather, a time lag is required for retraining and/or reallocation. We can think of the Specific Factors model as a short-run extension of the HO model, where the assumption that all factors of production are mobile across industries is relaxed.

Below we present a simple expression of the specific factors model as applied to skilled and unskilled labor. The assumptions of this expression are as follows. There are two countries – home and foreign. Again, we will refer to home as the North (or all developed countries) and foreign as the South (or all developing countries). There are two goods – good x and good y. There are three factor endowments – skilled labor (L_s), unskilled labor (L_u), and physical capital (K). These factor endowments differ in their mobility across industries. Specifically, we assume that capital is mobile across industries, and skilled and unskilled labor are immobile across industries. Furthermore, we assume that the immobile factors are specific to different industries; that is, skilled labor is specific to good x; and unskilled labor is specific to good y.

Now, we can determine the production possibilities for a given country in the Specific Factors model. We determine the production possibilities using our knowledge of the country's endowments of both mobile and immobile factors. To begin, we need to determine the constraint on the use of the mobile factor in each industry. In our example, this is the amount of capital that can be divided between the production of goods x and y. We also need to determine the production functions of the two industries, given their mobile and immobile factor endowments. In our example, this is the amount of output of goods x and y that can be produced given the country's resources of capital, skilled labor, and unskilled labor.

Figure 12.7 shows the derivation of the production possibilities for goods x and y for the country.

The capital constraint is

$$K_x + K_y \leq K \tag{12.15}$$

where K_x is capital used in good x, K_y is capital used in good y, and K is the total capital supply of the country. Assuming no unemployment of capital, this constraint

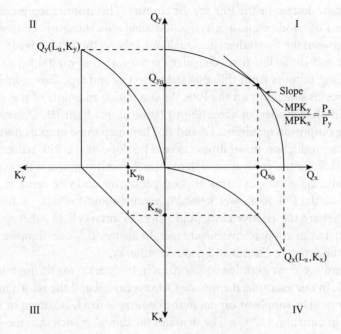

Figure 12.7 Specific factors model – production possibilities.

holds with equality. Quadrant III in Figure 12.7 shows a plotting of this capital constraint. Intuitively, this constraint shows that the capital used in goods x and y must be less than or equal to the total capital supply. This total capital supply can be allocated in various ways across the two industries. An increase in the use of capital in good x corresponds with a decrease in the use of capital in good y, and vice versa.

Figure 12.7 also shows the production functions. Quadrants II and IV show the production functions for goods y and x, respectively. The production functions show how much output of goods x and y the country can produce given the country's endowments. These endowments include skilled labor, which is specific to good x; unskilled labor, which is specific to good y; and capital, which can move between the industries. The production function in quadrant IV plots the relationship between the mobile capital input (K_x) and output of good x (Q_x), given a fixed amount of immobile skilled labor (L_s). Similarly, the production function in quadrant II plots the relationship between the mobile capital input (K_y) and output of good y (Q_y), given fixed amounts of immobile unskilled labor (L_u).

The slopes of each production function show the marginal product of capital (MPK) in each industry. The MPK is the additional output generated by adding one unit of capital. The concave shape reflects the diminishing MPK. That is, each additional unit of capital adds less output, given that the specific immobile input is held constant. This concept of diminishing MPK is important as it will help us to assess the gains from trade shortly.

We can now determine the PPF for the country. This frontier represents the possible outputs of goods x and y, given all possible allocations of the mobile factor (capital) between the two industries. Quadrant I shows the PPF derived from quadrants II, III and IV. To illustrate, consider the allocation of capital K_{x0} and K_{y0}. The corresponding outputs from this allocation are Q_{x0} and Q_{y0}. This combination of outputs gives us one point on the PPF. We can derive all points of the PPF in this manner. Simply consider an allocation of labor in quadrant III. Observe the corresponding outputs in quadrants IV and II. Then map these outputs into quadrant I to plot the production possibilities curve. The slope of the PPF reflects the ratio of MPK_y/MPK_x for the given allocation of capital. Intuitively, this is the opportunity cost of producing good x in terms of good y foregone and vice versa.

We can use the PPF to answer several questions about the state of autarky. Specifically, what are the relative costs (and prices in autarky)? In other words, what are the patterns of comparative advantage? To answer this question, we first need to look at the prices of factors and goods in autarky.

To this end, we must examine equilibrium in the market for the mobile factor of production. In our example, the mobile factor is capital and the return to capital is the rental rate. The supply of capital in the country is fixed, as shown in the capital constraint in equation (12.15). The demand for capital is such that the rental rate equals the value of the MPK. Intuitively, capital is demanded at the point where the value of the additional unit of capital equals the cost of the additional unit of capital. This relationship can be written as

$$r_x = P_x MPK_x \tag{12.16}$$

$$r_y = P_y MPK_y$$

where r_x and r_y are the rental rates in sectors x and y; and P_x and P_y are the autarky prices of good x and y.

Further, we know that capital is mobile across industries in our example. Thus, the rental rates in the two industries must be equal in equilibrium. For example, if the rental rate were higher in industry x, then capital would have an incentive to move out of industry y and into industry x. This movement of capital would put downward pressure on the rental rate paid to capital owners in industry x and upward pressure on the rental rate paid to capital in industry y, until the two rental rates equate. Thus, in equilibrium the rental rates in goods x and y equate as

$$r = r_x = r_y \tag{12.17}$$

Figure 12.8 illustrates this equilibrium in the market for the mobile factor. The horizontal width of the figure represents the fixed supply of capital (K) that can be allocated between the two industries, as shown in equation (12.15). The amount of capital employed in good x is measured from left to right, and the amount of capital employed in good y is measured from right to left. The vertical axis of the figure represents the rental rate, which equals the value of the marginal product of capital

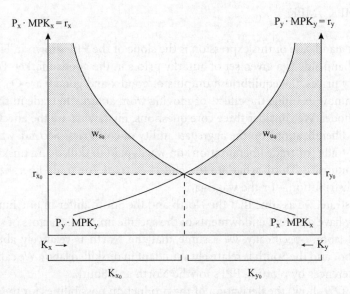

Figure 12.8 Specific factors model – factor market equilibrium.

(VMPK), as shown in equation (12.16). The two curves represent rental rates paid to capital owners in industries x and y given alternative allocations of capital between the two industries. (The two curves are plotted together in a side-by-side fashion with the rental rate curve for good y flipped horizontally.) Both curves are convex to their respective origins. The convex shape of the curves reflects the diminishing MPK; that is, as more capital is employed in an industry, the value of the MPK decreases, but at a decreasing rate.

The equilibrium price of the mobile factor (capital) in Figure 12.8 is where the rental rates in the two industries equate at $r_{x0} = r_{y0}$, as shown in equation (12.17). This intersection determines the equilibrium rental rates in both sectors. The corresponding allocation of capital is such that K_{x0} is the amount of capital employed to produce good x and K_{y0} is the amount of capital employed to produce good y.

Figure 12.8 also provides information about the real returns to the immobile factors of production that are specific to each industry. These returns include the wage paid to skilled labor (w_s) and the wage paid to unskilled labor (w_u). Recall that skilled labor is specific to good x. Thus, the real return to skilled labor is the shaded area below the VMPK curve for good x (i.e., $P_x^* MPK_x$) and above the equilibrium rental rate (r_{x0}). Also recall that unskilled labor is specific to good y. Thus, the real return to unskilled labor is the shaded area below the VMPK curve for good y (i.e., $P_y^* MPK_y$) and above the equilibrium rental rate (r_{y0}). Intuitively, these returns represent the surplus of the VMPK above the equilibrium rental rate for each unit of capital employed in that industry.

Finally, we can now return to Figure 12.7 to observe the equilibrium outputs in the goods market in autarky. To this end, we combine the equilibrium conditions in equations (12.16) and (12.17) to show that

$P_x/P_y = MPK_y/MPK_x$ (12.18)

The right-hand side of this expression is the slope of the PPF shown in Figure 12.7. The left-hand side is a given set of autarky prices in the goods market. For this set of autarky prices, the equilibrium outputs of good x and good y are Q_{x0} and Q_{y0}.

We can now examine the effects of moving from autarky to trade in the Specific Factors model. We consider three core questions. First, what are the effects of trade (or trade liberalization) on the aggregate utility of countries? Second, what are the effects of trade (or trade liberalization) on wages paid to skilled and unskilled labor within countries? Third, what are the effects of trade (or trade liberalization) on income distribution – or the wage gap?

To illustrate, we assume that the North and the South differ in one fundamental way. They have different endowments of the specific immobile factors of skilled and unskilled labor. Specifically, we assume that the North is relatively abundant in skilled labor and the South is relatively abundant in unskilled labor. We can illustrate these differences by plotting PPFs for the North and South.

Figure 12.9 shows the derivation of the production possibilities for the (a) North and (b) South under these conditions. As shown, the production functions in quadrants II and IV differ between the North and South. For the North, the MPK in good x is relatively high given the North's relatively large skilled labor endowment. Conversely, for the South, the MPL in good y is relatively high given the South's relatively large unskilled labor endowment. Thus, when we derive the PPF for the North and South in quadrant I, the slope reflects these differences in marginal productivities. As shown, the outputs of the North and South are biased toward the sectors that use the abundant specific factor intensively in production. This is a similar result as in the HO model.

The production and consumption of the North and South in autarky can be any point along their PPFs. The specific point depends on preferences. Assuming that the North and South have identical preferences, we can envision an indifference curve tangent to each PPF such as i and i*. This is the indifference curve that would maximize utility given the constraint that each group of countries can only consume what they produce in autarky. In this case, the North will produce and consume the combination of goods x and y where $c_0 = p_0$. Similarly, the South will produce and consume the combination of goods x and y where $c_0^* = p_0^*$.

We can then see that goods prices differ across the North and South in autarky. The goods prices are reflected in the slopes of the PPFs at the production point. As shown, in autarky the relative price of good x is low in the North and the relative price of good y is low in the South. That is, in autarky $P_x/P_y < P_x^*/P_y^*$.

What then is the relative price of goods where trade will occur in the world market? As in the previous models, the intuitive answer is that the North and South will only trade at prices that are more favorable than their prices in autarky. That is, they are willing to export goods at higher prices and import goods at lower prices, relative to autarky prices. To illustrate these prices, we must look at the world market

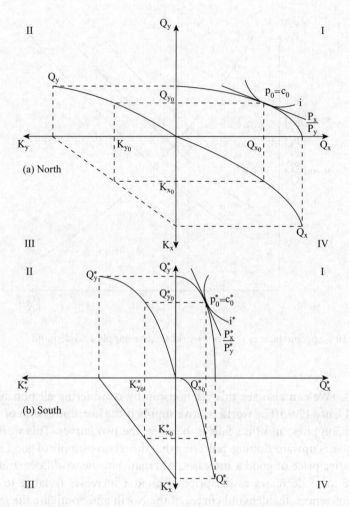

Figure 12.9 Specific factors model – autarky for North and South.

for good x and good y. Given our application, the world quantities of goods x and y are the sums of the quantities in the North and South or

$$Q_x^w = Q_x + Q_x^* \qquad\qquad (12.19)$$

$$Q_y^w = Q_y + Q_y^*$$

where Q_x^w is the world output of good x and Q_y^w is the world output of good y.

Figure 12.10 illustrates the determination of world prices. This figure plots the relative supply curves for the North (S), South (S*), and world (S\^w). As shown, for each relative price, the North's supply of good x (relative to good y) exceeds that of

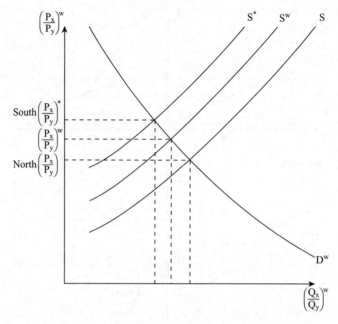

Figure 12.10 Specific factors model – world relative supply and demand.

the South. (We can also see this relationship by considering all possible relative prices in Figure 12.9.) The world relative supply is the horizontal sum of the North and South supplies, and thus falls in between the two curves. This world relative supply curve is upward sloping. reflecting that the relative supply of good x increases as the relative price of good x increases. Alternatively, the world demand for good x (relative to y) decreases as the price of good x increases (relative to y). Given similar preferences, the demand curves of the North and South are the same as the world demand curve.

Figure 12.10 shows that the equilibrium world price falls in between the equilibrium autarky prices in the two countries. For such world prices, the North will specialize in good x because the world relative price of good x is higher than the North's autarky relative price. Similarly, the South will specialize in good y because the world relative price of good y is higher than the South's relative autarky price. Thus, the North and South both have an incentive to specialize and trade for all world prices such that

$$P_x/P_y < P_x^w/P_y^w < P_x^*/P_y^* \qquad\qquad (12.20)$$

What are the effects of trade (or trade liberalization) on the aggregate utility of countries? Table 12.1 (b) summarizes the gains from trade illustrated in this application of the Specific Factors model. We know that both the North and South gain from trade because their consumption possibilities increase as a result of specialization and trade. Specifically, at equilibrium world prices, both can consume on indifference curves that are outside of their respective PPFs.

Second, what are the effects of trade (or trade liberalization) on wages paid to skilled and unskilled labor within countries (and rental rates paid to capital owners)? To answer this question, we revisit our labor market figures. We consider the effects of changes in goods prices resulting from trade on changes in wages. Figure 12.10 and equation (2.20) describe the changes in goods prices that result when the North and South move from autarky to trade. Specifically, we know that the North will experience an increase in the relative price of good x and the South will experience an increase in the relative price of good y, as a result of trade. What then are the effects of these goods price changes on the wage paid to skilled labor and unskilled labor, and the rental rates paid to capital owners in the North and South?

Figure 12.11 illustrates the effects of trade for the (a) North and (b) South. For the North, the price of good x rises relative to good y. We show this relative change

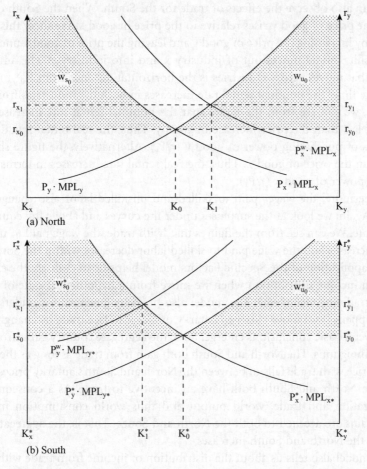

Figure 12.11 Specific factors model – gains from trade for North and South, within regions.

by increasing the price of good x and leaving the price of good y unchanged. As a result of this change, capital moves out of industry y and into industry x. The amount of capital that moves across industries is the horizontal distance from K_0 to K_1. At the same time, the nominal rental rate paid to capital owners increases in both industries x and y. The amount of the nominal rental rate increase is r_0 to r_1. But, we can see from Figure 12.11 that the nominal rental rate increases by an amount less than the price increase in good x. Thus, the real rental rate decreases in terms of purchasing power of good x (r/P_x). Alternatively, since there is no change in the price of good y, the real rental rate increases in terms of purchasing power of good y (r/P_y).

Furthermore, the wages paid to skilled and unskilled labor also change. Recall that the wage paid to skilled labor is the surplus of the value of the MPK in good x above the equilibrium rental rate; and, the wage paid to unskilled labor is the surplus of the value of the MPK in good y above the equilibrium rental rate. We can see from the figures that, with trade, the wage paid to skilled labor increases and the wage paid to unskilled labor decreases for the North.

We can also observe the effects of trade for the South. When the South opens to trade, the price of good y rises relative to the price of good x. We show this relative change by increasing the price of good y and leaving the price of good x unchanged. As a result, capital moves out of industry x and into industry y. The amount of capital that moves across industries is the horizontal distance from K_0^* to K_1^*. At the same time, the nominal rental rate increases in both the industries from r_0^* to r_1^*. But, we can see from the figure that the nominal rental rate increases by an amount less than the price increase in good y. Thus, the real rental rate decreases in terms of purchasing power of good y (r/P_y). Alternatively, the figure shows no change in the price of good x. Thus, the real rental rate increases in terms of purchasing power of good x (r/P_x).

Furthermore, the wages paid to skilled and unskilled labor also change in the South. Again, we look at the surpluses under the curves and above the equilibrium rental rate. We can see from the figures that, with trade, the wage paid to unskilled labor increases and the wage paid to skilled labor decreases within the South.

This application of the Specific Factors model helps us to evaluate the effects of trade on income distribution when we move from a hypothetical state of autarky to free trade (or vice versa). The model also provides guidance for understanding what happens if we move closer to autarky or closer to free trade by changing policies. Several basic conclusions emerge. First, the aggregate country gains from trade are unambiguous. The North and South both gain from trade as long as the relative world price with trade falls in between the North and South's autarky prices. In this case, the North and South both have an incentive to trade. As a consequence of specialization and trade, world output and thus world consumption increases. These gains are accrued to both the North and South. That is, the aggregate utility of both the North and South increases.

The model also tells us about the distribution of income from trade within both the North and South. In our application, capital owners gain in terms of their nominal rental rate. However, in real terms, capital owners lose in terms of their purchasing power of the good that is exported and gain in terms of their purchasing power of the good that is imported. The model also shows gains and losses in the wages paid to skilled and unskilled labor. That is, those that gain from trade are the abundant immobile factors; and those that lose from trade are the scarce immobile factors. The abundant immobile factors are those used in the export sector and the scarce immobile factors are those used in the import sector. Thus, skilled labor gains in the North and unskilled labor gains in the South. These are the effects of trade or trade liberalization in the short run.

If we compare the income distribution effects in the HO and Specific Factors models, we see a consistency of results across the short and long run (see Table 12.1). In both cases, the abundant factor endowment gains from trade and the scarce factor endowment loses from trade. In our application, skilled labor experienced a wage increase and unskilled labor experienced a wage decrease in the North. Conversely, unskilled labor experienced a wage increase and skilled labor experience a wage decrease in the South. These changes apply to both the short and long run. In the long run, however, some of the labor that is hurt by trade moves out of the import sector and into the export sector.

The primary point of contrast between the two models is the effect on the mobile endowment in the short run; that is, the Specific Factors model demonstrates that such an endowment may be better off or worse off in real terms depending on the consumption shares of the imported good versus the exported good. In our application, we assumed that capital was the mobile endowment in the short run. Thus, this ambiguous result applies to the rental rate paid to capital owners in the short run.

What are the effects of trade (or trade liberalization) on income distribution – or the wage gap? The Factor-Price Equalization theory extends the above results one step further to answer this question. This theory suggests that the wages paid to endowments (such as labor) will continue to change as a consequence of trade until they are equalized across countries. In our application, this means that wages paid to unskilled labor in the South (which are initially low) will increase; and wages paid to unskilled labor in the North (which are initially high) will decrease. These changes will continue to occur until the wages paid to unskilled labor in the North and South equate. This same result also applies to skilled labor. In theory, these wage changes from trade or trade liberalization lead to changes in income inequality (i.e., the wage gap). Specifically, the wage changes result in an increase in the wage gap in the North (as w_s increases and w_u decreases) and a decrease in the wage gap in the South (as $w_u{}^*$ increases and $w_s{}^*$ decreases).

The Stolper-Samuelson and Factor-Price Equalization theories have provided a long-standing foundation for research on the effects of trade and trade liberalization on wages. However, as mentioned earlier the results are at odds with the observed evidence of increasing wage gaps in *both* the developed and developing countries. Newer lines of research have attempted to explain this puzzle. Some of this research focuses on explaining deviations from these core findings by altering underlying assumptions and considering special cases. Other lines of research consider whether wage differentials across countries are better explained by technology changes rather than trade. Extensions of the literature on trade and multinationals (in Chapter 3) also consider the role of outsourcing in explaining the relationship between trade and wages. This literature has not reached a consensus and continues to evolve. The readings at the end of this chapter cover these extended considerations.

12.3   How can the Gains and Losses from Trade Be Redistributed within Countries?

In section 12.2, we showed that the gains from trade (or trade liberalization) are distributed unequally across different types of labor within a country. To address this unequal distribution, countries sometimes adopt policies referred to as *trade adjustment assistance* (TAA) programs. These are national-level programs designed to support those who are adversely affected by international trade. In practice, TAA programs typically focus on compensating for the damages associated with increased imports into a country and/or shifts of domestic production to locations outside the country.

The purpose of TAA programs is to reduce the impacts of trade (or trade liberalization) on those who lose within countries. These programs do so by facilitating the reallocation of factors of production (such as labor) out of sectors of comparative disadvantage and into sectors of comparative advantage, or by improving the productivity of those factors of production (including labor) that are adversely affected.

Although programs differ by country, those receiving support typically include workers, farmers, fisherman, firms, and/or communities. For example, support to *workers* includes job retraining, employment search services, and income and insurance assistance. The process for seeking assistance typically involves filing a petition that indicates that the workers have lost their jobs or experienced reduced hours and/or wages as a consequence of international trade. Support for *firms* includes financial and technical assistance to improve the competitiveness of the domestic firms. The firm's process for seeking assistance typically includes filing a petition that indicates that the firm has experienced a decrease in sales and employment as a consequence of import competition. Support for *farmers* and *fisherman* includes payments to agricultural producers who have experienced a decrease in their commodity prices as a consequence of imports. Support for *communities* includes assistance for responding to plant closures.

TAA programs are national programs. However, some programs are also provided under regional trade arrangements, such as the North American Free Trade Agreement. In this case, assistance may be provided to workers who are affected by imports or by a shift in the production of their firm to a country within the regional trade arrangement of which the country is a member; that is, assistance is provided to compensate for adverse effects that arise as a result of the regional agreement.

12.4   What Are the Effects of Labor Policy on Trade?

In this section, we focus specifically on the effects of labor standards on trade, goods prices, and wages.

There are two primary channels by which labor standards affect trade, goods prices, and wages. The first is via *production*. Specifically, country differences in labor standards affect production costs and consequently affect both the patterns of trade (who exports and imports what) and the terms of trade (the relative prices of exports and imports). These changes in turn affect factor prices, including wages. For example, weak labor standards can increase a country's supply of unskilled labor (or decrease the cost of unskilled labor). For example, the use of child labor or "sweatshop labor" can increase the effective supply (or decrease the cost) of labor in a country with weak standards. If the country is relatively abundant in unskilled labor, it will have a comparative advantage in exporting goods that are produced with technologies that are intensive in unskilled labor. The increased supply of unskilled-labor-intensive goods in the world market results in a decrease in the price of these goods and a decrease in wages paid to unskilled labor.

Conversely, strong labor standards can decrease a country's supply of unskilled labor (or increase the cost of that unskilled labor). This can diminish a country's comparative advantage in exporting goods that are produced with unskilled-labor-intensive technologies. The decreased supply of unskilled-labor-intensive goods in the world market results in an increase in the price of these goods and an increase in wages paid to unskilled labor. In these examples, labor standards affect production, which in turn affects trade, goods prices, and wages.

Labor standards can also affect trade through *consumption*. For example, weak labor standards in countries can result in a decrease in consumer demand for imports from such countries. A prominent example is when the weak labor standards are associated with inhumane labor practices. Consumers in importing countries may have preferences against the consumption of goods produced with such practices. For example, consumers may prefer not to consume goods that have been produced using "unfair trade" practices, or using "sweatshop labor". The decreased demand for those goods in the world market results in a decrease in the price of the goods and a decrease in wages paid to the unskilled labor that is used intensively to produce the goods.

Conversely, strengthening labor standards in such countries can result in an increase in consumer demand for imports from these countries. This increased demand occurs when consumers have preferences for goods produced with more humane practices. The increased demand for the goods in the world market results in an increase in the price of these goods and an increase in wages paid to unskilled labor that is used intensively to produce the goods.

In these examples, labor standards affect consumption, which in turn affects trade, goods prices, and wages.

These effects provide the basis for several prominent arguments in favor and against strengthening labor standards. The *race to the bottom* is a prominent argument against weak labor standards, or in favor of stronger labor standards. This argument tends to focus on weak labor standards in unskilled-labor-abundant countries (e.g., the South) and their negative effects on the wages and standards of unskilled-labor-scarce countries (e.g., the North). The intuition is that there can be a race to the bottom in labor standards as countries attempt to compete internationally in goods that are intensive in unskilled labor. For example, a country (in the North) that imports unskilled-labor-intensive goods may simultaneously lower labor standards and lower barriers to trade, such as tariffs. The lower labor standards may allow the importing country (in the North) to compete more effectively with the imports (from the South). In this case, the exporter (in the South) may experience no gains in market access to the importers (in the North), despite the trade liberalization. And, the importer (in the North) that lowers its labor standards can experience a decrease in wages paid to its scarce unskilled labor.

An extension of this "race to the bottom" argument focuses on the effects of labor standards on the terms of trade. Recall that the terms of trade are defined as the price of a country's exports relative to its imports. A rise in the relative price of exports is an improvement in a country's terms of trade; and a decrease in the relative price of exports is a deterioration in a country's terms of trade. In the case of a race to the bottom, where countries (in the North and South) adopt weaker labor standards, the effective world supply of unskilled labor would increase. For example, the weaker standards may allow for the use of child labor and prisoners in the labor market. As a result, the relative price of unskilled-labor-intensive goods would decrease. This change would correspond with a deterioration in the terms of trade of unskilled labor abundant countries (e.g., the South) and a decrease in wages paid to unskilled labor in these countries. This terms-of-trade effect could provide an incentive for such countries to strengthen their labor standards.

The flip side of this argument is that stronger labor standards decrease the supply of unskilled labor, but increase wages paid to this unskilled labor. This argument posits that stronger standards decrease the number of jobs for unskilled labor, but that this effect is outweighed by the increased wages of those employed. This argument tends to be supported by developed countries (i.e., the North).

The prominent argument against stronger international labor standards (or in favor of existing weaker standards) focuses on whether requiring higher labor standards creates a *barrier to trade*. This argument tends to focus on the effects of strengthening labor standards in unskilled-labor abundant countries (in the South) and the negative effects on the ability of these countries to export to unskilled-labor-scarce countries (in the North). The argument is that if labor standards are set at levels that cannot be met by developing countries (in the South), then this would effectively limit the market access of developing countries to the markets of the developed world (in the North). This argument also raises concerns about using international trade policy to address domestic labor market issues. Such concerns include the effects of trade policy in undermining national sovereignty. The argument that stronger labor standards create a barrier to trade tends to be a concern raised by developing countries.

The effects of labor standards on trade, goods prices, and factor prices can be illustrated using the frameworks developed in this chapter (i.e., the HO model and specific factors model) and in Chapter 2. We encourage the reader to explore these applications using the foundations provided in this chapter.

12.5   Summary Remarks

What are trade-related labor policies, their types, and purpose? Labor policies include national and international laws concerning labor standards. Core labor standards regulate the labor market process to ensure basic human rights. Outcome labor standards regulate characteristics of labor contracts. These labor policies can affect trade, and trade policy can affect labor. However, the relationship between trade and labor is complex and continues to pose unresolved puzzles for economists. Research on the relationship has a long history. The Stolper-Samuelson theory provides the best-known explanation of the effects of trade on wages paid to labor. However, the results of this theory do not explain well the growing global trends in wage inequality within both developed *and* developing countries. As a consequence of this inconsistency, many trade economists have doubts about the role of trade in causing wage inequality. We do not resolve the puzzle in this chapter, but rather provide the foundations for understanding the puzzle.

What are the long-run effects of trade on wages? We illustrate the long-run effects of trade on wages using the Heckscher-Ohlin (HO) model. Prominent theories associated with the HO model explain the income distribution effects of trade. The Stolper-Samuelson theory says that trade (and the associated price changes) leads to an increased return to a country's abundant endowments and a decreased return to a country's scarce endowments. This theory links trade with returns (including wages) within countries. The Factor-Price Equalization theory says that factor prices are equalized across countries as a result of trade. This theory links trade with factor prices (including wages) across trading partners.

To assess long-run wage effects, we apply these theories to the case of the North and South, where the North is abundant in skilled labor and the South is abundant in unskilled labor. We assume that skilled and unskilled labor can move across industries within the North, or within the South, in the long run. Further, we assume two types of goods: a skilled-labor-intensive good and an unskilled-labor-intensive good. We assume that the North and South use similar technologies to produce these goods.

Several basic results emerge from this framework. First, in the North where skilled labor is relatively abundant, skilled labor experiences an increase in wages as a result of trade, and unskilled labor experiences a wage decrease. Conversely, in the South where unskilled labor is relatively abundant, unskilled labor experiences an increase in wages as a result of trade, and skilled labor experiences a wage decrease. These changes apply to both nominal and real wages. Thus, the wage effects within countries of the North and South are asymmetric in that one type of labor is better off and the other is worse off as a consequence of trade or trade liberalization.

Second, these wage changes continue until wages equalize across countries. The wage paid to skilled labor increases in the North and decreases in the South until these wages are equalized; and the wage paid to unskilled labor increases in the South and decreases in the North until these wages are equalized. Thus, trade results in an equalization (or movement toward equalization) of wages across the North and South for labor with similar skill levels.

Third, the model predicts a widening gap in income distribution in the North and a narrowing gap in income distribution in the South as a consequence of trade. In the North, the wage paid to skilled labor increases and the wage paid to unskilled labor decreases such that the internal wage gap increases. In the South, the wage paid to skilled labor decreases and the wage paid to unskilled labor increases such that the internal wage gap decreases. Thus, the income distribution effects of trade are also asymmetric in that the North experiences a widening wage gap while the South experiences a narrowing wage gap. This result poses a puzzle because it is inconsistent with the observed increases in wage inequality in both the North and South in practice.

What are the short-run effects of trade on wages? We use the Specific Factors model to illustrate the short-run effects of trade on wages. We apply the model to the case of the North and South, where the North is abundant in skilled labor and the South is abundant in unskilled labor. We assume that skilled and unskilled labor are specific factors that are immobile across industries. This immobility reflects the short run where skilled and unskilled labor cannot move effortlessly across industries. We also assume a third endowment of physical capital that is mobile across the industries.

Several basic results emerge from this model. First, we find both gains and losses in the wages paid to skilled and unskilled labor. Those who gain from trade are the abundant immobile factors, and those who lose are the scarce immobile factors. Specifically, in the North where skilled labor is relatively abundant, skilled labor experiences an increase in wages as a result of trade, and unskilled labor experiences a wage decrease. Conversely, in the South where unskilled labor is relatively abundant, unskilled labor experiences an increase in wages as a result of trade, and skilled labor experiences a wage decrease. The effects of trade on the rental rates paid to capital owners are more ambiguous. Capital owners gain in terms of their nominal rental rate; however, they lose in terms of their purchasing power of the exported good and gain in terms of their purchasing power of the imported good.

The Specific Factors model is a short-run variation of the HO model. The conclusions from these models depend on whether we assume that labor is mobile or immobile across industries. In the Specific Factors model, we assumed that both skilled and unskilled labor are immobile. In this case, we see a consistency of results across the short and long run. The abundant endowment (or specific factor) gains from trade and the scarce endowment (or specific factor) loses from trade.

The point of contrast between the models is the effect of trade on the mobile endowment in the short run. The Specific Factors model demonstrates that such an endowment may be better off or worse off in real terms, depending on their consumption of imported versus exported goods. In our application, we assumed that capital was the mobile endowment in the short run. Thus, this ambiguous result applies to the rental rate paid to capital owners in the short run. If we had assumed that skilled labor (for example) was a mobile endowment in the short run, then the ambiguous result would apply to skilled labor.

These models and theorems provide a long-standing foundation for research on the effects of trade on wages. However, they also pose puzzles that remain unresolved. The prominent puzzle is why wage inequality is increasing in both developed *and* developing countries in practice.

How can the gains and losses from trade be redistributed within countries? Countries sometimes adopt policies to address the unequal distribution of gains and losses from trade. Trade adjustment assistance (TAA) programs seek to compensate for damages associated with increased imports into a country or shifts of domestic production to locations outside a country. The purpose of TAA programs is to reduce the impacts of trade on those who lose within countries. TAA programs do so by facilitating the reallocation of factors of production (such as labor) out of sectors of comparative disadvantage and into sectors of comparative advantage, or by improving the productivity of those factors (including labor) that are adversely affected. TAA programs are national-level programs. However, programs are also provided under some regional trade arrangements.

What are the effects of labor policy on trade? There are two primary channels by which labor standards affect trade: via production and via consumption. On the production side, country differences in labor standards affect production costs and consequently affect trade and wages. For example, weak labor standards in the South can increase the South's supply of unskilled labor. If the South is relatively abundant in unskilled labor, then the South will have a comparative advantage in exporting goods that are intensive in unskilled labor. The increased supply of unskilled labor results in increased exports of unskilled-labor-intensive goods into the world market. This in turn results in a decrease in the price of those goods and wages paid to unskilled labor.

On the consumption side, country differences in labor standards affect consumer demand and consequently affect trade and wages. For example, weak labor standards in the South can decrease the North's consumer demand for imports if the North's consumers have preferences against goods produced with inhumane practices. The decreased import demand for these goods in the world market results in a decrease in their price and in wages paid to the unskilled labor used to produce those goods.

These effects provide the basis for several prominent arguments in favor and against strengthening labor standards. The "race to the bottom" is an argument against weak labor standards. The intuition is that weak standards result in a race to the bottom in standards as countries attempt to compete internationally in goods intensive in unskilled labor. For example, lowering standards in unskilled-labor-scarce countries in the North allows these countries to compete more effectively with imports from the unskilled-labor-abundant countries in the South. The lower standards result in an increase in the effective world supply of unskilled labor. Consequently, the relative price of unskilled-labor-intensive goods decreases. This change results in a deterioration in the terms of trade of the South and a decrease in wages paid to unskilled labor. The race to the bottom tends to be a concern raised by the North.

In contrast, the "barrier to trade" argument is an argument against strengthening labor standards. The intuition is that if labor standards are set at levels that cannot be met by the South, then this effectively limits the access of the South to the markets of the North. This argument also raises concerns about using international trade policy to address domestic labor market issues. Such concerns include the effects of trade policy in undermining national sovereignty. The argument that stronger labor standards create a barrier to trade tends to be a concern raised by the South.

Applied Problems

12.1 Consider two groups of countries (the North and South), two industries (manufacturing and agriculture), and two endowments (skilled labor and unskilled labor). Assume that manufacturing is intensive in skilled labor, and agriculture is intensive in unskilled labor. Further, assume that the North is relatively abundant in skilled labor and the South is relatively abundant in unskilled labor. Use the Heckscher-Ohlin model and Stolper-Samuelson theory to examine the long-run effects of trade (or trade liberalization) on wages in the North and South.

12.2 Consider two groups of countries (the North and South), two industries (manufacturing and agriculture), and three endowments (skilled labor, unskilled labor, and capital). Assume that skilled labor is specific to manufacturing, unskilled labor is specific to agriculture, and capital is mobile between the two industries. Further, assume that the North is relatively abundant in skilled labor and the South is relatively abundant in unskilled labor. Apply the Specific Factors model to examine the short-run effects of trade (or trade liberalization) on wages in the North and South.

12.3 The General Agreement on Tariffs and Trade (GATT) and World Trade Organization (WTO) have lead to substantial liberalization of world trade through multilateral agreement. Use your knowledge to evaluate the short-run and long-run effects on income inequality of going from a world with restricted trade to a world with free trade, both within countries and across countries.

12.4 Politicians sometimes argue in favor of restricting trade. Use your knowledge to evaluate the effects of imposing protectionist policies on: (a) wages paid to skilled and unskilled labor in the short run; and (b) wages paid to skilled and unskilled labor in the long run. Consider these wage effects both within countries and across countries. Consider these effects for two countries and two industries of interest to you. Be sure to articulate the assumptions that underlie your analysis.

12.5 Analyze the impact of trade on wages when: (a) labor is mobile across industries and immobile across countries; (b) labor is immobile across industries and immobile across countries; and (c) labor is mobile across industries and mobile across countries.

12.6 Consider the effects of labor standards on *production*, trade, goods prices, and wages. (a) Specifically, consider the effects of increasing the effective supply of unskilled labor in the short run using the Specific Factors model. (b) Then consider the effects of increasing the effective supply of unskilled labor in the long run using the Heckscher-Ohlin model. Be sure to articulate any underlying assumptions.

12.7 Consider the effect of labor standards on *consumption*, trade, goods price, and wages. Specifically, consider the case where the North has relatively strong preferences against goods produced with unskilled labor in countries with weak labor standards.

Further Reading

Acemoglu, Daron 2003. Patterns of skill premia. *Review of Economic Studies* 70 (2): 231–251.

Basu, Kaushik, Henrik Horn, Lisa Roman, and Judith Shapiro, eds. 2003. *International Labor Standards*. Malden, MA: Blackwell.

Brown, Drusilla K. 2001. Labor standards: where do they belong on the international trade agenda? *Journal of Economic Perspectives* 15 (3): 89–112.

Davis, Donald. 1996. *Trade Liberalization and Income Distribution*. NBER Working Paper No. 5693. Cambridge, MA: National Bureau of Economic Research.

Elliott, Kimberly A. 2001. *Can Labor Standards Improve under Globalization?* Washington, D.C.: Institute for International Economics.

Feenstra, Robert C. 2010. *Offshoring in the Global Economy: Microeconomic Structure and Macroeconomic Implications*. Cambridge, MA: MIT Press.

Feenstra, Robert C., and Gordon H. Hanson. 1996. Foreign investment, outsourcing, and relative wages. In *The Political Economy of Trade Policy: Papers in Honor of Jagdish Bhagwati* (eds R.C. Feeenstra, G.M. Grossman, and D.A. Irwin), Cambridge, MA: MIT Press, pp. 89–127.

Jones, Ronald W., and Stanley Engerman. 1996. Trade, technology, and wages: a tale of two countries. *American Economic Review* 86: 35–40.

Jones Ronald W., and Sugata Marjit. 1985. A simple production model with Stolper-Samuelson property. *International Economic Review* 26 (3): 565–567.

Jones, Ronald W., and Sugata Marjit. 2003. Economic development, trade, and wages. *German Economic Review* 4: 1–17.

Jones Ronald W., and Jose Scheinkman. 1977. The relevance of the two-sector production model in trade theory. *Journal of Political Economy* 85: 909–935.

Krugman, Paul. 2000. Technology, trade, and factor prices. *Journal of International Economics* 50 (1): 51–71.

Leamer, Edward. 2000. What's the use of factor contents? *Journal of International Economics* 50 (1): 73–90.

Magee, Christopher. 2001. Administered protection for workers: an analysis of the trade adjustment assistance program. *Journal of International Economics* 53 (1): 105–125.

Marjit, Sugata, and Rajat Acharyya. 2003. *International Trade, Wage Inequality, and the Developing Economy: A General Equilibrium Approach*. Heidelberg: Physica/Springer Verlag.

Marjit, Sugata, and Rajat Acharyya. 2006. Trade liberalization, skill-linked intermediate production, and two-sided wage gap. *Journal of Policy Reform* 9 (3): 203–217.

Marjit, Sugata, Hamid Beladi, and Avik Chakrabarti. 2003. Trade and wage inequality in developing countries. *Economic Inquiry* 42 (92): 295–303.

Robbins, Donald. 1995. *Trade, Trade Liberalization, and Inequality in Latin America and East Asia: Synthesis of Seven Country Studies*. Mimeo, Harvard Institute of International Development.

Samuelson, Paul A. 1953. Prices of factors and goods in general equilibrium. *Review of Economic Studies* 21: 1–20.

Wood, Adrian. 1997. Openness and wage inequality in developing countries: the Latin American challenges to East Asian conventional wisdom. *World Bank Research Observer* 11 (1): 33–57.

Xu, Bin. 2003. Trade liberalization, wage inequality, and endogenously determined non-traded goods. *Journal of International Economics* 60 (2): 417–431.

Notes

1. For examples of studies of trade and wage inequality, see Acemoglu (2003); Davis (1996); Feenstra (2010), Feenstra and Hanson (1996); Jones and Marjit (2003, 1985); Leamer (2000), Marjit and Acharyya (2006, 2003); Marjit, Beladi, and Chakrabarti (2003); Robbins (1995), Wood (1997) and Xu (2003).

2. For examples of studies that focus on this ongoing puzzle, see Feenstra and Hanson (1996), Jones and Engerman (1996), Krugman (2000), Lawrence (1995), Leamer (2000), and Richardson (1995).

13

Growth and Development Policies

13.1 What Are Trade-Related Development and Growth Policies, Their Types, and Purpose?

Economic development refers to the process of raising the standard of living or welfare of a population, including that of a country. Thus, policies designed to promote economic development aim to improve the economic and social well-being of people. Such economic development policies are vast in scope. They include efforts to foster the development of human capital, raise literacy, and reduce poverty. They also include efforts to advance the competitiveness of a country (or regions) in the global market. Such efforts to raise national competitiveness include trade policy.

In contrast, *economic growth* refers to the increase in the value of output of a country (or regions). Economic growth is typically measured as the percentage change over time in gross domestic product or gross national product. Economic growth is also sometimes measured in per capita terms. This alternative measure seeks to gauge changes in the standard of living of the population of a country (or a region). Thus, economic growth provides an indicator of economic development over time.

However, economic development and economic growth are not synonymous concepts. Economic growth is one means by which economic development can occur. It is possible for a country to experience economic growth without experiencing economic development in the form of an improved standard of living. Thus, research on economic development examines economic growth as well as issues that may not be alleviated by economic growth. Such issues include the distribution of income within an economy, and poverty concerns.

Global Trade Policy: Questions and Answers, First Edition. Pamela J. Smith.
© 2014 John Wiley & Sons, Inc. Published 2014 by John Wiley & Sons, Inc.

The development and growth policies of *developing countries* have been concerned with two primary objectives: promoting industrialization, and addressing income distribution concerns. Government policies to promote industrialization are often based on the infant industry argument, which is that domestic industries need a period of time during which they are protected (e.g., via trade policy) from international competition. During this time, the infant industry matures until it is able to compete without protection in the international market. This need for temporary protection is justified by the argument that in the absence of protection, the industry will not produce at socially optimal levels due to market failure. Sources of market failure relevant to developing countries include the inability to appropriate the returns to knowledge (i.e., intellectual property) and imperfections in capital markets. Prominent trade policies used to support infant industry development and industrialization include import substitution and export promotion policies.

Import substitution policies are measures used by governments to promote the substitution of goods and services that the country imports with goods and services that are produced domestically. These measures include: industrial policies that strategically promote the domestic production of targeted substitutes for imports; trade policies that restrict imports in industries targeted for development and alter the terms of trade against exports of primary goods; and monetary and exchange rate policies that promote the use of foreign exchange for imports of noncompetitive intermediate and capital goods.

Export promotion policies are measures used by governments to promote exports and/or the production of exported goods and services. There are two basic types of export promotion policies. The first includes measures that create incentives for exporting or production in export industries, such as export subsidies. This approach to export promotion involves government intervention policies that specifically target incentives to export. The second includes the removal of barriers that restrict trade in order to allow for market-led increases in exports, such as the removal of tariffs and quantitative restrictions.

The relationship between trade and economic development and growth is complex. The economics literature on trade and growth, and on trade and development, has a long history. This literature includes macro-level studies that focus on countries in aggregate, microeconomic studies that focus on the channels through which trade affects growth and/or development, and historical country studies. Despite the long history of this literature, conclusions about the relationship between trade, economic development, and growth remain opaque.

In this chapter, we focus on select dimensions of this literature. The chapter is organized around several key questions. First, what are the effects of trade on development and growth? We consider three dimensions of this relationship, specifically: (1) What are the effects of trade on country welfare? (2) What are the effects of trade on growth? (3) What are the effects of trade on income distribution? We then consider an alternative perspective, that is: What are the effects of growth on development (or welfare) in the presence of trade?

13.2   What Are the Effects of Trade on Development and Growth?

This first section considers the effects of trade (or trade liberalization) on development and growth. Specifically, we consider the effects of trade on country: (1) welfare; (2) growth rates in income over time; and (3) distribution of income. In our illustrations, we use the concept of utility or welfare to gauge the standard of living or level of development. Thus, we use the terms *welfare* and *utility* interchangeably to refer to the level of economic development. We use the term *growth* to refer to changes over time in production possibilities or income. Further, we use the term *distribution of income* to refer to the allocation of income (or development benefits) across groups within an economy. The two prominent allocation issues concern poverty and wage differences across labor with different skill levels.

13.2.1   What are the effects of trade on country welfare?

Research on the effects of trade on welfare (measured as income or income per capita or real gross domestic product) of countries shows a positive relationship;[1] that is, trade or trade liberalization increases the level of income of countries. This positive effect occurs through several channels. One is that trade (and trade liberalization) allows for specialization based on comparative advantage, and this results in gains in efficiency and consequently in welfare. A second is that trade (and trade liberalization) exposes domestic firms to international competition. This can result in a decrease in the monopoly behavior of inefficient domestic firms that must now compete with foreign firms. A third is that trade (and trade liberalization) can result in consumer access to a larger variety of goods, which can raise consumer utility. The research also shows that the positive effect of trade on income levels of countries is related to institutions. That is, trade (and trade liberalization) has a positive effect on institutions, which in turn has a positive effect on income. Although the details of these approaches vary, there is a consensus on the positive relationship between trade and income in static studies in the international economics literature.

Below, we use a simple model to illustrate the first channel, where trade results in gains in efficiency that raise country welfare. The approach builds on the general equilibrium models presented in Part One of this book. Specifically, we build on the production-side models (e.g., Ricardian and Heckscher-Ohlin) that explain trade in terms of comparative advantage. We extend these models here in one important way, in that we consider the consumption side in addition to the production side. The framework we present is sometimes referred to as the *Standard Trade model*. It is not a specific model, but rather a consumption-side extension of production-side models of trade.

We will focus our attention on changes in welfare that result from changes in a country's terms of trade. Recall that the *terms of trade* refer to the price of a country's exports relative to its imports. An increase in the price of exports relative to imports represents an improvement in a country's terms of trade. Conversely, a decrease in the price of exports relative to imports represents a deterioration in a country's terms of trade. We will examine the effects of such price movements on welfare, for countries that trade.

For illustrative purposes, we present a simple expression of the Standard Trade model; but keep in mind that this expression can be extended to more complicated scenarios by relaxing underlying assumptions. The basic expression presented here assumes the following. There are two countries – home and foreign. We will refer to the home as the developed countries (e.g., the North) and foreign as developing countries (e.g., the South). There are two goods – x and y. (If desired, one can think of good x as a manufactured good and good y as a primary good such as agriculture.) The market structure is perfect competition, such that goods are priced at the cost of production. The mobility of factors of production is such that they are immobile across countries, but mobile across industries within a country. The mobility of factors across industries is consistent with a long-run scenario, where factors such as labor can be retrained for use in other industries. Further, the technology is such that the inputs in production are imperfect substitutes. The implication is that there are diminishing marginal products with respect to these inputs. These assumptions mirror those of the Heckscher-Ohlin model in Part One of this book.

The production possibilities for a country under these assumptions is shown in Figure 13.1. The familiar frontier represents the tradeoff between producing goods

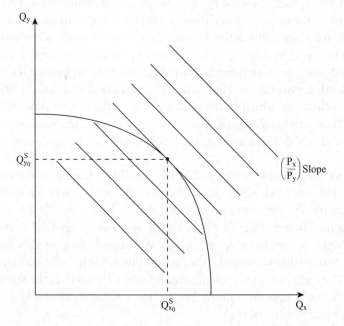

Figure 13.1 Standard trade model – production possibilities and isovalue lines.

x and y, given the technologies and factor supplies of the given country. The frontier is concave with respect to the origin. This reflects the diminishing marginal product with respect to the factor inputs. For example, factors of production can be moved out of industry x and into industry y. This leads to an increase in output in industry y, but at a diminishing rate. Alternatively, factors of production can be moved out of industry y and into industry x. This leads to an increase in output in industry x, but at a diminishing rate.

A country will produce, at some point along the production possibilities frontier, a combination of goods x and y. This *production point* is where the country maximizes the value of output (V_p)

$$V_p = P_x Q_x^S + P_y Q_y^S \tag{13.1}$$

such that the value of output equals the value of good x (i.e., $P_x Q_x^S$) plus the value of good y (i.e., $P_y Q_y^S$) supplied, at given market prices. If we rearrange this equation, we obtain isovalue lines

$$(V_p/P_y) - (P_x/P_y)Q_x^S = Q_y^S \tag{13.2}$$

where the slope is the relative price of good x to y (P_x/P_y). Figure 13.1 shows multiple isovalue lines for a given relative price. The value of output supplied is constant at all points along a given isovalue line. Isovalue lines that are further from the origin represent higher values of output supplied. A country will choose to produce the combination of goods x and y where the isovalue line is tangent to the production possibilities frontier. This is the production point where the value of output is maximized for a given relative price. Production points outside of the frontier are not feasible; and production points inside the frontier are not optimal.

Changes in the relative price results in changes in the production point along the frontier. Figure 13.2 illustrates the effects of changes in the relative price on outputs. The two slope lines in the figure are alternative isovalue lines that correspond with different relative prices of goods x and y. Consider the case where we start with a relative price of $(P_x/P_y)_0$. A decrease in the relative price of good x from $(P_x/P_y)_0$ to $(P_x/P_y)_1$ results in a decrease in output of good x and an increase in output of good y. Similarly, a decrease in the relative price of good y from $(P_x/P_y)_1$ to $(P_x/P_y)_0$ results in an increase in output of good x and a decrease in output of good y.

We can now add consumption to this framework. A country will consume, at some point along an indifference curve, a combination of goods x and y. The indifference curve represents the preferences of a representative agent for a given country. This *consumption point* is where the country maximizes the value of consumption (V_c)

$$V_c = P_x Q_x^D + P_y Q_y^D \tag{13.3}$$

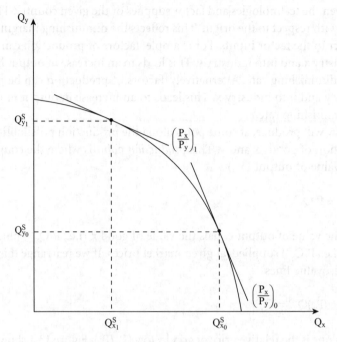

Figure 13.2 Standard trade model – effects of price change on outputs.

such that the value of consumption equals the value of good x (i.e., $P_x Q_x^D$) plus the value of good y (i.e., $P_y Q_y^D$) demanded, at given market prices. If we rearrange this equation, we obtain the relationship

$$(V_c/P_y) - (P_x/P_y)Q_x^D = Q_y^D \qquad\qquad (13.4)$$

where the slope is the relative price of good x to y (i.e., P_x/P_y). Figure 13.3 shows multiple indifference curves. The value of utility is constant at all points along a given indifference curve. That is, the indifference curve represents all combinations of consumption that leave the representative agent equally well off in terms of utility (or welfare). Indifference curves that are further from the origin represent higher values of utility (or welfare).

We can now examine the effects on welfare of moving from autarky to trade. As noted earlier, we can think of the term "welfare" as being synonymous with utility or standard of living or level of development.

In autarky, a country will choose to consume the combination of goods x and y where the value *and* quantity of consumption equals the value *and* quantity of production. This is because without trade, a country can only consume what it produces domestically. The point where this condition holds is where the indifference curve is tangent to the production possibilities frontier.

Figure 13.3 illustrates this autarky scenario at point A. This is the consumption point where the value of utility is maximized under the constraint that the value of

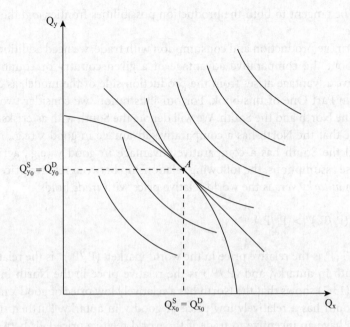

Figure 13.3 Standard trade model – consumption possibilities and indifference curves.

consumption in equation (13.3) equals the value of production in equation (13.1), such that

$$V_c = V_p \tag{13.5}$$

$$P_x Q_x{}^S + P_y Q_y{}^S = P_x Q_x{}^D + P_y Q_y{}^D$$

This is also the consumption point where the quantity of consumption equals the quantity of production

$$Q_x{}^D = Q_x{}^S \tag{13.6}$$

$$Q_y{}^D = Q_y{}^S$$

Consumption points outside of the frontier are not feasible in autarky; and consumption points inside the frontier are not optimal.

Now, when we allow for trade, a country will choose to consume the combination of goods x and y such that the value of consumption equals the value of production as above. However, the quantity of consumption need not equal the quantity of production with trade. This contrasts with the autarky case in that the consumption point can be outside the production possibilities frontier. The constraint that the value of consumption and the value of production equate means that the isovalue line must be tangent to both the production possibilities frontier *and* the indifference curve.

To determine production and consumption with trade, we need additional information about the comparative advantage of a given country or countries. This comparative advantage arises from the production side of the model, as discussed at length in Part One of this book. For our illustration, we consider two country groups – the North and the South. We will denote the South with asterisks. Further, we assume that the North has a comparative advantage in good x (e.g., manufactures) and the South has a comparative advantage in good y (e.g., agriculture). Given these assumptions, the following relationship between relative prices in each country in *autarky* versus the world relative price with *trade* holds

$$(P_x/P_y)^* > (P_x/P_y)^w > (P_x/P_y) \tag{13.7}$$

where $(P_x/P_y)^w$ is the relative price in the world market, $(P_x/P_y)^*$ is the relative price in the South in autarky, and (P_x/P_y) is the relative price in the North in autarky. Equation (13.7) shows that the North has a relatively low price of good x in autarky and the South has a relatively low price of good y in autarky. Further, the North and South have an incentive to trade if the world relative price falls between their autarky prices.

Figures 13.4 (a) and (b) illustrate the production, consumption, and welfare in autarky in comparison with trade for the North and South. In autarky, producers

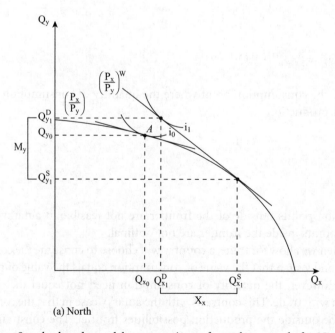

(a) North

Figure 13.4a   Standard trade model – comparison of autarky vs. trade for North.

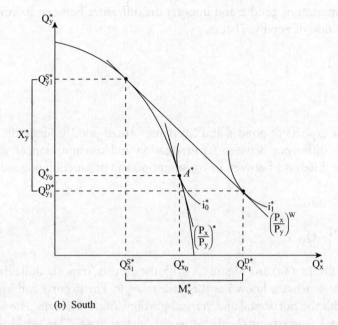

(b) South

Figure 13.4b Standard trade model – comparison of autarky vs. trade for South.

in the North produce the combination of outputs Q_{x0} and Q_{y0}; and producers in the South produce the outputs Q_{x0}^* and Q_{y0}^*. Consumers in the North and South consume these production quantities at points A and A*, respectively. For these combinations, the value of consumption equals the value of production where the isovalue line is tangent to both the production possibilities frontier and the indifference curve in both the North and South. Furthermore, in autarky the quantity of consumption equals the quantity of production in both the North and South. We can also observe the relative autarky prices in equation (13.7) in Figures 13.4 (a) and (b).

Now let's consider what happens when the North and South trade. With trade, production and consumption depend on the relative world price $(P_x/P_y)^w$. For such a world price, producers in the North supply the combination of outputs Q_{x1}^S and Q_{y1}^S; and producers in the South supply the combination of outputs Q_{x1}^{S*} and Q_{y1}^{S*}. Alternatively, consumers in the North consume the quantities Q_{x1}^D and Q_{y1}^D, and consumers in the South consume the quantities Q_{x1}^{D*} and Q_{y1}^{D*}. For this combination, the value of consumption equals the value of production where the isovalue line is tangent to both the production possibilities frontier and the indifference curve in both the North and South. However, the quantity of consumption no longer equals the quantity of production as the production and consumption points are no longer the same with trade. These relationships hold for both the North, in Figure 13.4 (a), and the South, in Figure 13.4 (b).

Figures 13.4 (a) and (b) also show the patterns of trade between the North and South. At the world price, the North exports the difference between its production and consumption of good x and imports the difference between its consumption and production of good y. That is,

$$X_x = Q_{x1}{}^S - Q_{x1}{}^D \tag{13.8}$$

$$M_y = Q_{y1}{}^D - Q_{y1}{}^S$$

where X_x is exports of good x and M_y is imports of good y. Similarly, the South exports the difference between its production and consumption of good y and imports the difference between its consumption and production of good x. That is,

$$X_y{}^\star = Q_{y1}{}^{S\star} - Q_{y1}{}^{D\star} \tag{13.9}$$

$$M_x{}^\star = Q_{x1}{}^{D\star} - Q_{x1}{}^{S\star}$$

In both Figure 13.4 (a) and Figure 13.4 (b), the exports, imports, and relative world price comprise what is known as the *trade triangle*. The exports and imports correspond with the horizontal and vertical portions of the triangle. The hypotenuse of the triangle corresponds with the world relative price. This world price is the "terms of trade".

What then is the effect of moving from autarky to trade? We can see from Figures 13.4 (a) and (b) that trade results in an increase in consumption and an increase in utility (welfare) from i_0 to i_1 in the North and from $i_0{}^\star$ to $i_1{}^\star$ in the South. These increases occur for both the North and the South. That is, with trade, the representative consumer in both the North and the South is on a higher indifference curve. Their standard of living has improved in terms of their consumption possibilities as a result of trade. In other words, international trade raises the welfare of both countries – each country as a whole is able to afford bundles of goods that it could not afford in autarky and thus each country achieves higher welfare with trade.

13.2.2   What are the effects of trade on growth?

Research on the effects of trade on country growth shows both positive and negative effects.[2] That is, trade (or trade liberalization) can increase or decrease the rate of economic growth of countries over time. The findings in the literature show that the direction of the relationship is sensitive to the underlying assumptions of the modeling approaches. In this section, we provide a brief summary of some of the conflicting views in the literature. We then consider how changes in the terms of trade over time (associated with trade) can result in changes in welfare as well as different economic growth rates.

This trade and growth literature includes three types of approaches. The first explores the unequal relationship between developed countries (e.g., the North) and developing countries (e.g., the South). This research tends to focus on the effects of trade on the growth of developed countries with a comparative advantage in manufactured goods versus developing countries with a comparative advantage in agriculture or primary products. For example, the research considers the effects of trade on changes over time (or volatility) in world prices of primary products for which developing countries tend to have a comparative advantage. This research also considers the effects of trade on the relative price of country exports versus imports (i.e., the terms of trade). The prominent findings show that trade (or trade liberalization) leads to decreased growth in countries with a comparative advantage in agriculture (i.e., the South) and increased growth in countries with a comparative advantage in manufacturing (i.e., the North). The findings also show that trade can result in a deterioration in the terms of trade of countries in the South over time.

The second approach considers the effects of trade on growth via the mechanism of capital accumulation. Again, this research focuses on the unequal relationship between the North and the South. In this approach, the North and South are distinguished by their savings rates, and also by the character of their factor markets and institutions. For example, the research shows that high savings rates result in the accumulation of large capital stocks. The primary result is that trade (or trade liberalization) results in growth in capital-intensive industries in countries with high savings rates. That is, trade leads to an increase in the return to capital, which leads to capital accumulation and growth. Countries that tend to benefit from growth through this mechanism are countries of the North.

The third approach focuses on the relationship between trade and growth in a setting where growth is endogenous. A prominent result of this research is that trade has a positive effect on growth by reducing the duplication of research and development (R&D), and by allowing for flows and pooling of knowledge across countries. The findings also show that the effects of trade on growth depend on a country's abundance or scarcity of skilled labor, often referred to as human capital. That is, trade has a positive effect on growth in countries that are abundant in human capital (i.e., the North), and has a negative effect on growth in countries that are scarce in human capital (i.e., the South). Finally, this line of research shows that trade can have a positive effect on growth by creating a *pro-competitive effect*. That is, trade leads to increased competition, which results in an increased return to R&D and growth.

In summary, the literature on trade and growth comprises a variety of approaches that lead to quite different conclusions about the direction and character of the relationship.

We now turn to illustrating one aspect of the effect of trade on growth. Specifically, we consider how changes in the terms of trade over time (associated with trade) can result in different welfare effects as well as different growth rates across countries. Below we illustrate the effects of trade on welfare over time when there are asymmetries between the North and South. To this end, we extend our prior discussion of the Standard Trade model. In this framework, we consider the effects of price shocks on the welfare of the North and South in the presence of trade.

These price shocks can occur as a consequence of trade liberalization, trade restriction, or other external conditions. We start by assuming that the North has a comparative advantage in good x (e.g., manufactures) and the South has a comparative advantage in good y (e.g., agriculture). Further, we assume that the North and South are already trading and then experience a price shock. In particular, we assume that the price of good x (e.g., manufactures) increases relative to good y (e.g., agriculture). This is the same as assuming that the price of good y decreases relative to good x. This shock could be the result of any condition that significantly alters the supply or demand of a good in the world market. For example, if world relative demand for good x (e.g., manufactures) increased, then the relative price of x would increase. Alternatively, if world relative supply of good y (e.g., agriculture) increased, then the relative price of y would decrease. Both of these examples correspond with an increase in $(P_x/P_y)^w$. This price change represents a terms of trade improvement for the North and a terms of trade deterioration for the South.

Figures 13.5 (a) and (b) illustrate the production, consumption, trade and welfare of the North and South before and after a price shock. As shown, we begin by assuming that the countries already produce, consume and trade at time 1. (Note that this contrasts with Figure 13.4 where our starting point is autarky.) The countries then experience a price shock that alters production, consumption and trade at time 2. For the North, the price shock results in an increase in the supply of good x (Q_{x1}^S to Q_{x2}^S) and a decrease in the supply of good y (Q_{y1}^S to Q_{y2}^S). Further, the North experiences an increase in consumption of both goods x (Q_{x1}^D to Q_{x2}^D) and y (Q_{y1}^D to Q_{y2}^D), and an increase in utility (i_1 to i_2). The North has clearly benefited

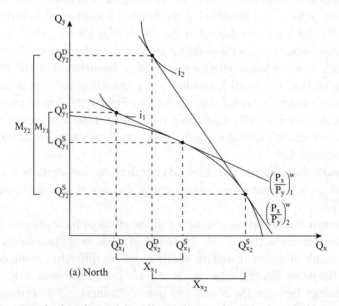

(a) North

Figure 13.5a	Standard trade model – effects of price changes on trade for North.

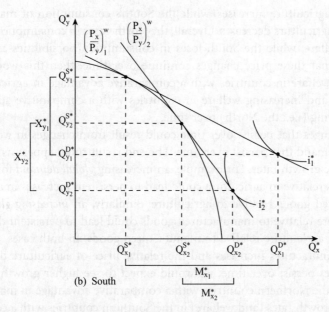

(b) South

Figure 13.5b Standard trade model – effects of price changes on trade for South.

from the improvement in its terms of trade. Similarly, for the South, the price shock results in an increase in supply of good x (Q_{x1}^{S*} to Q_{x2}^{S*}) and a decrease in supply of good y (Q_{y1}^{S*} to Q_{y2}^{S*}). However, the South experiences a decrease in consumption of both goods x (Q_{x1}^{D*} to Q_{x2}^{D*}) and y (Q_{y1}^{D*} to Q_{y2}^{D*}), and a decrease in utility (i_1^* to i_2^*). The South has clearly lost from the deterioration in its terms of trade. Further, we can see that the volume of trade changes as a consequence of the price shock. That is, the North exports relatively less of good x in exchange for relatively more imports of good y. And the South exports relatively more of good y in exchange for relatively fewer imports of good x.

These conclusions can be stated in more general terms. That is, when a country experiences a terms of trade improvement (an increase in the price of exports relative to imports), this results in a shift in production toward the good for which the country has a comparative advantage. It also results in an increase in the country's consumption possibilities and welfare. In contrast, when a country experiences a terms of trade deterioration (a decrease in the price of exports relative to imports), this results in a shift in production toward the good for which the country has a comparative disadvantage. It also results in a decrease in the country's consumption possibilities and utility.

In our example, the price shock alters the patterns of production, consumption, trade and welfare of the North and South in different ways. The North and South both shift production toward manufactured goods, and the volume of trade between the North and South decreases. However, the North's consumption of manufactured goods and agriculture increases, while the South's consumption of manufactured goods and agriculture decreases. Overall, the North gains in consumption possibilities and welfare, while the South loses in consumption possibilities and welfare. Assuming that these price changes continue over time, then this would lead to decreasing welfare in countries with a comparative advantage in agriculture (i.e., the South) and increasing welfare in countries with a comparative advantage in manufacturing (i.e., the North) over time.

Price changes that persist over time could result from changes in world supply or world demand that persist over time. The end result could appear as differences in economic growth rates. For example, an increasing *global demand* for manufactured goods relative to agriculture could lead to persistent increases in the price of manufactured goods relative to agriculture. Similarly, an *increasing global supply* of agriculture relative to manufactured goods could lead to persistent decreases in the price of agriculture relative to manufactured goods. In both cases, the relative price of manufactures increases and the relative price of agriculture decreases. If such changes persist over time, we would expect to see higher growth rates (and welfare) in the Northern countries with a comparative advantage in manufactures, and lower growth rates (and welfare) in the Southern countries with a comparative advantage in agriculture. This example illustrates that trade can affect the welfare and growth of countries differently over time.

13.2.3   What are the effects of trade on income distribution?

Research on the effects of trade on the distribution of income includes studies of trade and the labor market, and studies of trade and poverty.[3] Chapters 2 and 12 cover the prominent findings on trade and wages. In addition to these findings, there is a body of literature that focuses specifically on the effects of trade on the labor market in *developing countries*. This research includes several prominent concerns such as fluctuations in wages and employment, wage inequality, and bargaining power issues. The findings of this literature suggest that trade affects wages, but not necessarily employment. The findings also suggest that trade can lead to increased wage inequality within developing countries. As discussed in Chapter 12, this finding is at odds with traditional trade theory, which predicts a decrease in wage inequality in the South resulting from trade. This puzzle continues to be explored by international trade economists. The literature is also mixed on the effects of trade on wage and employment fluctuations and bargaining power in developing countries.

Finally, research on the effects of trade on *poverty* includes two prominent approaches. The first uses cross-country analysis of trade and growth, and focuses attention on the growth in the income of low income groups. The second uses microeconomic household analysis of trade and growth, and focuses on the channels by which trade affects the income of low income groups. Although this literature is relatively small, it does provide some evidence that trade leads to a reduction in poverty. This reduction in poverty appears to occur both across countries and within countries in regions with greater trade exposure.

13.3 What Are the Effects of Growth on Development (or Welfare) in the Presence of Trade?

As noted earlier, economic growth and economic development are not synonymous concepts. Economic growth is one means by which economic development can occur. Further, the terms *welfare* or *utility* can be used to describe the level of economic development. In this section, we consider the effects of growth on development (or welfare), assuming an open economy setting where countries trade. That is, we examine the effects of growth on development (or welfare) in the presence of trade.

One of the prominent findings of research in this area is that rapid growth in the presence of trade can result in a terms of trade deterioration. *Immiserizing growth* is an extreme case where high growth results in a deterioration in a country's terms of trade that is large enough to decrease the country's welfare. We will illustrate the case of immiserizing growth along with other cases.

Specifically, we consider three types of growth: (1) neutral growth; (2) import-biased growth; and (3) export-biased growth. *Neutral growth* is growth that benefits all industries of an economy in a proportional way. *Import-biased growth* is growth that is biased toward those industries for which a country has a comparative disadvantage. *Export-biased growth* is growth that is biased toward those industries for which a country has a comparative advantage. Below, we consider the effects of these three types of growth on a country's outputs, terms of trade, and welfare. We consider these effects in sequence; that is, first we consider the effects of a country's economic growth on its relative outputs or production possibilities; second, we consider the effects of any relative output changes on its terms of trade; and finally, we consider the effects of terms of trade changes on its welfare. Our analysis involves a three-step process. Combining these steps, we can see the effects of growth on development (or welfare) in the presence of trade.

Country size is relevant to this analysis. By country size, we mean the extent to which the country contributes to the world supply of a particular good, and thus the extent to which the country influences the world price of the good relative to other goods. We consider a country to be "large" if the country contributes enough to the world relative supply of a good to influence the world relative price. Alternatively, we consider a country to be "small" if the country's contribution to the world relative supply of a good is too small to influence the world relative price of that good. Below we illustrate that if a country is small, then economic growth will affect its domestic relative outputs, but will not alter its terms of trade in the presence of trade. Alternatively, if a country is large, then economic growth will affect relative outputs and terms of trade in the presence of trade. These growth-induced changes then affect welfare.

13.3.1   What are the effects of economic growth on relative outputs?

First, what are the effects of growth on the relative outputs of a country, assuming constant relative world prices? Figure 13.6 illustrates these effects for each of the three types of growth. Each component figure shows the production possibilities frontier for goods x and y before and after growth has occurred. Growth is shown by an outward shift in the production possibilities frontier. Case 1 demonstrates neutral growth where the production possibilities frontier shifts out in a proportional manner as a consequence of growth. The result is a proportional increase in output supply of goods x and y. That is, the supply of good x relative to y (Q_x^S/Q_y^S) does not change. Case 2 shows growth biased toward industry x. In this case, the production possibilities frontier shifts further from the origin in industry x relative to y as a consequence of growth. The result is an increase in the output supply of good x relative to y (Q_x^S/Q_y^S). In contrast, Case 3 shows growth biased toward industry y. In this case, the production possibilities frontier shifts further from the origin in industry y relative to x as a consequence of growth. The result is a decrease in the output supply of good x relative to y (Q_x^S/Q_y^S). Each of these changes assumes that the relative price of the goods remains unchanged at $(P_x/P_y)_1$.

In summary, growth that is proportional has no effect on the relative output supply of goods, given constant prices. However, growth that is biased toward a particular industry leads to an increase in the output supply of that industry relative to others, given constant prices. The case of neutral growth provides a baseline for comparison. In practice, neutral growth is not observed, as economic growth is almost always biased in one direction or the other. This bias is a matter of degree. Of course, there are cases where the bias is so slight that it is close to neutral.

13.3.2   What are the effects of output changes on the terms of trade?

Now, let's assume that the country experiencing these growth shocks is large in terms of its contributions to the world supply of good x and/or good y. What, then, are the effects of the above described output changes on world prices? Figure 13.7 illustrates these effects for each of the three types of growth. Each component figure shows the world supply and demand curves for the goods. These curves are *relative* supply and demand curves. Conceptually, they are the same as the familiar supply and demand curves, yet expressed in relative terms. That is, for a given supply curve such as S_1, the quantity of supply of good x (relative to y) increases as the price of good x (relative to y) increases. And for a given demand curve such as D_1, the quantity of demand for good x (relative to y) decreases as the price of good x (relative to y) increases. Further, the curves represent relative supply and demand in the *world market*. That is, they represent the sum of the supply and demand of the countries that comprises the "world". In our example, world relative supply is

$$(Q_x/Q_y)^W = ((Q_x + Q_x^*)/(Q_y + Q_y^*))$$ (13.10)

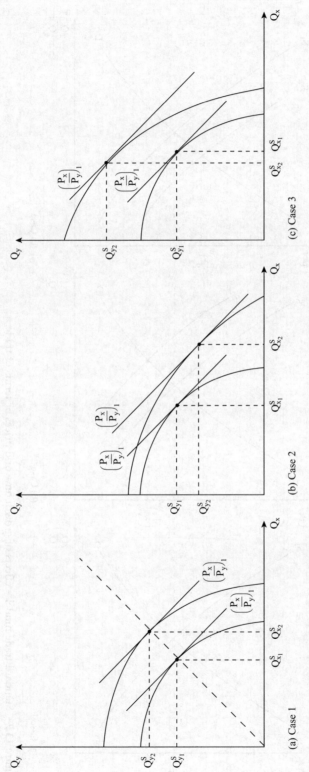

(a) Case 1

(b) Case 2

(c) Case 3

Figure 13.6 Standard trade model – effects of growth on production at constant world prices.

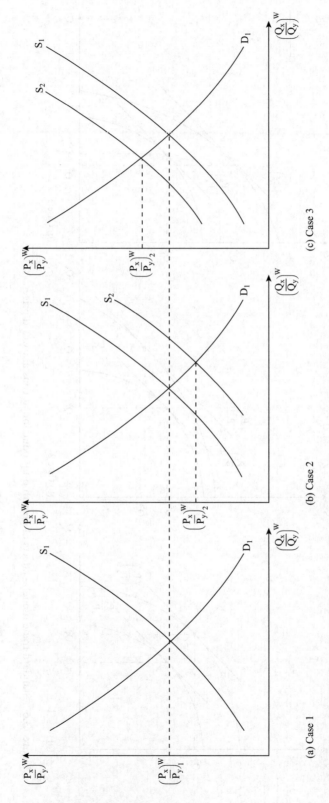

(a) Case 1   (b) Case 2   (c) Case 3

Figure 13.7   Standard trade model – effects of growth on world prices or terms of trade.

The intersection of the relative world supply and relative world demand represents the equilibrium relative world price $(P_x/P_y)^W$.

The effects of growth in a given large country (or group of countries) are shown as a shift in the relative world supply curve. Case 1 illustrates the effects of a neutral growth shock in a large country. As we saw in panel (a) of Figure 13.6, neutral growth results in a proportional increase in the supply of goods x and y. Thus, in panel (a) of Figure 13.7, we see no change in the supply of good x (relative to good y) in the world market. The supply of both goods has increased proportionately. Thus, the relative world supply curve remains unchanged. Case 2 illustrates the effects of growth biased toward good x. As we saw in panel (b) of Figure 13.6, such growth results in an increase in the supply of good x (relative to good y). Thus, in panel (b) of Figure 13.7, we see an increase in the supply of good x (relative to y) in the world market. This results in a decrease in the equilibrium price of good x (relative to y). Finally, Case 3 illustrates the effects of growth biased toward good y. As we saw in panel (c) of Figure 13.6, such growth results in a decrease in the supply of good x (relative to y). Thus, in panel (c) of Figure 13.7, we see a decrease in the supply of good x (relative to y) in the world market. This results in an increase in the equilibrium price of good x (relative to y).

We can interpret these findings in terms of the effects of growth on a country's terms of trade. Recall that *terms of trade* is an expression for the price of a country's exports relative to its imports. If the price of a country's exports increases relative to its imports, this represents an *improvement* in its terms of trade. It is an improvement in the sense that the country can now import more in exchange for fewer exports at the new relative world prices. Conversely, if the price of a country's imports increases relative to its exports, this represents a *deterioration* in its terms of trade. It is a deterioration in the sense that the country now imports less in exchange for more exports at the new relative world prices.

To illustrate, let's extend our previous examples to consider a country such as one in the South that has a comparative advantage in good y (e.g., agriculture) relative to good x (e.g., manufactures). An increase in the price of good x (relative to good y) in the world market is a deterioration in the terms of trade for the South; and a decrease in the relative price of good x to good y in the world market is an improvement in the South's terms of trade. Now, let's assume that the South experiences the various growth shocks shown in Figure 13.6. Assuming that the South is large enough to affect world prices, these growth shocks then result in changes in the world relative prices as illustrated in Figure 13.7. If the South's growth is neutral, then it experiences no change in its terms of trade. If the South's growth is biased toward industry x (its import sector), then it experiences an improvement in its terms of trade $((P_x/P_y)_1^W$ to $(P_x/P_y)_2^W$ in panel (b) of Figure 13.7). Finally, if the South's growth is biased toward industry y (its export sector), then it experiences a deterioration in its terms of trade $((P_x/P_y)_1^W$ to $(P_x/P_y)_2^W$ in panel (c) of Figure 13.7).

Stated more generally, export-biased growth deteriorates the terms of trade; and import-biased growth improves the term of trade.

13.3.3   What are the effects of terms of trade changes on welfare?

Extending the analysis above, we can now consider the effects of growth in a country on its welfare. This analysis combines the findings in the previous two steps. Figure 13.8 illustrates the effects of growth on welfare, for each type of growth. For illustration purposes, these figures focus specifically on a country with a comparative advantage in good y (such as in the South, with a comparative advantage in agriculture). Similar figures could be generated for a country with a comparative advantage in good x. Each component figure shows the effects of growth in the country on its production possibilities, terms of trade, and utility. Recall that utility is a measure of welfare or standard of living.

   Let's first focus on the *neutral growth* shown in panel (a) of Figure 13.8. As shown, the production possibilities increase in the same proportional manner, as illustrated by the even outward shift of the production possibilities frontier. The production point along the frontier changes from p_1 to p_2 as a result of the growth. The relative price line that is tangent to the production possibilities frontier is the terms of trade or relative world price $((P_x/P_y)^W)$. With neutral growth, this relative world price remains unchanged despite the increase in production possibilities. This is reflected by the unchanged slope of the terms of trade line. However, the consumption possibilities increase as a consequence of neutral growth. This is shown by the outward shift of the indifference curve from i_1 to i_2 that is tangent to the terms of trade line. The consumption point along the indifference curve changes from c_1 to c_2. (Recall that trade will occur where the value of production equals the value of consumption; or where the terms of trade line is tangent to both the production possibilities frontier and indifference curve.) Thus, neutral growth results unambiguously in an increase in country utility or welfare. This result applies irrespective of whether the country is large or small.

   Next, let's focus on *import-biased growth* as shown in panel (b) of Figure 13.8. In this illustration, good x is the imported good and good y is the exported good. Growth results in an outward shift in the production possibilities, which is biased toward good x. The production point along the frontier changes from p_1 to p_2 as a result of growth, given constant world prices. The consumption possibilities also increase as a result of growth from c_1 to c_2, given constant world prices. If the country in the illustration is small, then we can stop our analysis here and conclude that import-biased growth results in an increase in utility from i_1 to i_2. However, if the country is large then we need to take into account the effect of growth on world prices. In our illustration, import-biased growth results in a decrease in the relative world price $(P_x/P_y)^W$. This change in world price is shown in the decrease in the slope of the terms of trade line. The effect of import-biased growth in the large country case is a further change in production and consumption possibilities to p_3 and c_3. Thus, import-biased growth results unambiguously in an increase in country welfare. This result holds, irrespective of whether the country is large or small. However, if the country is large enough to affect the world price, then the increase in welfare as a result of growth is even larger (i.e., i_3 instead of i_2).

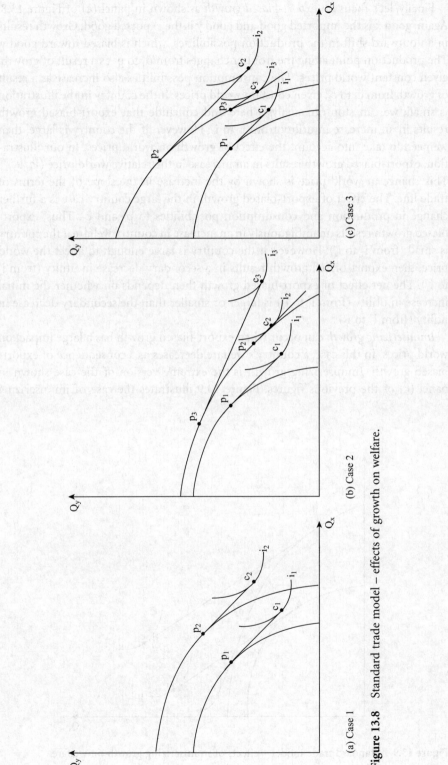

(a) Case 1

(b) Case 2

(c) Case 3

Figure 13.8 Standard trade model – effects of growth on welfare.

Finally, let's focus on *export-biased growth* as shown in panel (c) of Figure 13.8. Again, good x is the imported good and good y is the exported good. Growth results in an outward shift in the production possibilities, which is biased toward good y. The production point along the frontier changes from p_1 to p_2 as a result of growth, given constant world prices. The consumption possibilities also increase as a result of growth from c_1 to c_2, given constant world prices. If the country in the illustration is small, we can stop our analysis here and conclude that export-biased growth results in an increase in utility from i_1 to i_2. However, if the country is large, then we need to take into account the effect of growth on world prices. In our illustration, export-biased growth results in an increase in the relative world price $(P_x/P_y)^W$. This change in world price is shown by the increase in the slope of the terms of trade line. The effect of export-biased growth in the large country case is a further change in production and consumption possibilities to p_3 and c_3. Thus, export-biased growth results unambiguously in an increase in country welfare if the country is small (from i_1 to i_2). However, if the country is large enough to affect the world price, then export-biased growth results in a secondary decrease in utility (from i_2 to i_3). The net effect of export-biased growth then depends on whether the initial increase in utility (from i_1 to i_2) is larger or smaller than the secondary decrease in utility (from i_2 to i_3).

Immiserizing growth can occur when export-biased growth has a large impact on world prices. In this case, a country's welfare decreases as a consequence of export-biased growth. Immiserizing growth is the extreme version of the case shown in panel (c) of the previous figures. Figure 13.9 illustrates the case of immiserizing

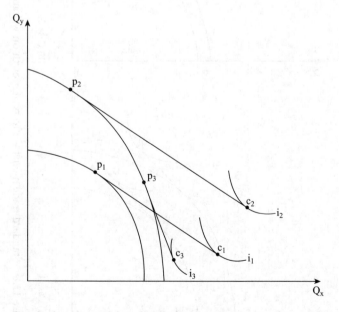

Figure 13.9 Standard trade model – effects of immiserizing growth on welfare.

growth for a country that exports good y and imports good x. As shown, growth biased toward good y results in an initial increase in utility from i_1 to i_2, given constant world prices. This corresponds with an increase in consumption from c_1 to c_2. This growth also results in a large increase in the relative supply of good y to good x as production changes from p_1 to p_2. As the supply of good y increases in the world market, the relative world price of good y falls. That is, $(P_x/P_y)^W$ increases. This results in a secondary shift in production and consumption to p_3 and c_3. In this case of immiserizing growth, the change in the world price is substantial. The result is that the net change in utility (from i_1 to i_3) from export-biased growth is negative. That is, growth leads to a substantial deterioration in the country's terms of trade, which generates a welfare loss.

The findings of this section are useful in several ways. First, they help us to evaluate the benefits and losses from growth at home and abroad. The analysis showed that the distribution of benefits across countries depends on the character of the growth. For small countries that do not influence world prices, growth of all forms results in an increase in country welfare. However, for large countries, the welfare effects of growth in the presence of trade depend on the effects of growth on world prices or the terms of trade. For example, export-biased growth in the South results in a terms of trade deterioration for the South, and an increase or decrease in the South's welfare. That is, the benefits of growth in this case are either diminished but positive, or negative. The negative welfare effect of growth is the case of immiserizing growth. At the same time, this growth in the South results in a terms of trade improvement for the North, and an unambiguous increase in the North's welfare. Alternatively, import-biased growth in the South results in a terms of trade improvement for the South, and an unambiguous increase in the South's welfare. At the same time, this growth in the South results in a terms of trade deterioration for the North, and a decrease in the North's welfare.

These results suggest that although all countries can benefit from growth, the distribution of the benefits is sensitive to the character of growth. For example, if all countries in the South experienced *export*-biased growth (in raw materials and agricultural products) and all countries in the North experienced *import*-biased growth (in technologically advanced substitutes for these same goods), then the terms of trade would improve for the North and deteriorate for the South. Although both the North and South could potentially both benefit from their growth, the North benefits disproportionately more than the South.

13.4 Summary Remarks

What are trade-related development and growth policies, their types, and purpose? Economic development policies seek to raise the standard of living of a population, including that of a country. Such policies include efforts to foster human capital, raise literacy, and reduce poverty, as well as efforts to advance the trade competitiveness of a country in the global market. In contrast, economic growth refers to the percentage increase in the value of output of a country. When measured in per capita terms, economic growth seeks to gauge changes in the standard of living of a population, including that of a country. Economic development and economic growth are not synonymous. Economic growth is one means by which economic development can occur. Development and growth policies of developing countries have been concerned with the objectives of promoting industrialization and addressing income distribution concerns. Prominent trade policies used to promote these goals include import substitution and export promotion policies.

What are the effects of trade on welfare? Research on the effects of trade on country welfare shows a positive relationship. This positive effect occurs through several channels, including: efficiency gains from specialization based on comparative advantage; efficiency gains associated with increased competition; increased consumer access to product variety, which raises utility; and a positive effect on institutions, which has a positive effect on income. We illustrate the first of these effects. We build on the production-side models in Part One. We extend these models to include consumption in a framework known as the Standard Trade model. We show that trade results in an increase in consumption and an increase in utility (or welfare). That is, the standard of living is improved as a result of trade. These changes occur for each trading country as a consequence of the efficiency gains from specialization based on comparative advantage.

What are the effects of trade on growth? Research on the effects of trade on growth shows both positive and negative effects. This literature comprises a variety of approaches, which lead to divergent conclusions. One approach explores the unequal relationship between the North and South that emerges from differences in industries of comparative advantage. Prominent findings include that trade leads to decreased growth in countries with a comparative advantage in agriculture (i.e., the South) and increased growth in countries with a comparative advantage in manufacturing (i.e., the North). A second approach considers the effects of trade on growth via the mechanism of capital accumulation. The North and South are distinguished by their savings rates, which affect the accumulation of capital stocks. Findings include that trade leads to an increase in the return to capital, which leads to capital accumulation and growth in countries with high savings rates (i.e., the North). A third approach focuses on endogenous growth. A prominent result is that trade has a positive effect on growth by reducing the duplication of research and development (R&D), and by allowing for flows and pooling of knowledge across countries. Further, trade has a positive effect on growth in countries that are abundant in human capital (i.e., the North). Trade also has a positive effect on growth via a pro-competitive effect, which increases the return to R&D.

We use the Standard Trade model to illustrate the effects of trade on welfare and growth over time when there are asymmetries between the North and South in comparative advantage. We show that when a country experiences a terms of trade improvement, this results in a shift in production toward the good for which the country has a comparative advantage, and an increase in welfare. In contrast, when a country experiences a terms of trade deterioration, this results in a shift in production toward the good for which the country has a comparative disadvantage, and a decrease in welfare. Thus, a decrease in the price of agriculture relative to manufactures is a terms of trade improvement for the North and deterioration for the South. The North and South both shift production toward manufactures and their trade decreases. However, the North's consumption of manufactures and agriculture increases, while the South's consumption of manufactures and agriculture decreases. The North gains in welfare, while the South loses in welfare. If these changes continue, then this leads to decreasing welfare in the South and increasing welfare in the North over time, along with differences in economic growth rates in the North and South.

What are the effects of trade on income distribution? Research on the effects of trade on the distribution of income include studies of trade and the labor market, and studies of trade and poverty. Research on the labor market includes the findings in Chapters 2 and 12, as well as studies that focus specifically on developing countries. Findings for developing countries suggest that trade affects wages, but not necessarily employment. Findings also suggest that trade can lead to increased wage inequality within developing countries. The literature is mixed on the effects of trade on wage and employment fluctuations and bargaining power in developing countries. Research on the effects of trade on poverty provides some evidence that trade leads to a reduction in poverty both across countries and within countries in regions with greater trade exposure.

What are the effects of growth on development in the presence of trade? We consider three types of growth: neutral, import-biased, and export-biased. We consider the sequential effects of these types of growth on a country's outputs, terms of trade, and welfare. We show that neutral growth causes a country's production possibilities to increase in a proportional manner. The relative world price remains unchanged; however, consumption possibilities increase. Thus, neutral growth results in an increase in country welfare for both large and small countries. Alternatively, import-biased growth causes a country's production possibilities to change in a manner that is biased toward the imported good. This results in an increase in the relative output of that good, given constant world prices, and an increase in consumption possibilities and welfare. If the country is large, then this growth also results in an improvement in the country's terms of trade, which further increases welfare. Thus, both the initial and secondary effects result in an increase in country welfare. Finally, export-biased growth causes a country's production possibilities to change in a manner that is biased toward the exported good. This results in an increase in relative output of that good, given constant world prices, and an increase in consumption possibilities and welfare. However, if the country is large, then this growth results in a deterioration in terms of trade, which results in a welfare decrease. Thus, the net welfare effect depends on the relative magnitudes of the positive initial effect and the negative secondary effect. Immiserizing growth is the case of export-biased growth where welfare decreases in net.

These findings help us to evaluate the distributional effects of growth across countries. For small countries (or group of countries) that do not influence world prices, growth of all forms results in an increase in country welfare. For large countries (or group of countries), the welfare effects of growth in the presence of trade depend on the terms of trade changes. Export-biased growth in the South results in a terms of trade deterioration for the South, and a net increase or decrease in the South's welfare. Concomitantly, this growth in the South results in a terms of trade improvement for the North, and an increase in the North's welfare. Alternatively, import-biased growth in the South results in a terms of trade improvement for the South, and an increase in the South's welfare. This growth in the South results in a terms of trade deterioration for the North, and a net increase or decrease in the North's welfare.

Applied Problems

13.1 Consider the following Standard Trade model. Assume there are two goods (high-technology and low-technology), and two groups of countries (the North and South). Assume that the North has a comparative advantage in high-tech goods and the South has a comparative advantage in low-tech goods. Assume that markets for both goods are perfectly competitive. (a) Diagram the production possibilities for the North and South, and indicate the optimal production and consumption points, given that the North and South trade. (b) Diagram and indicate the effects of an increase in the price of high-tech goods on output, consumption, trade, and welfare in both the North and South. (c) Based on your findings, what is the relationship between the terms of trade and welfare? (d) Now, assume that the South experiences *import-biased growth*. Diagram and indicate the effects of this growth on the outputs, terms of trade, and welfare in the North and South.

13.2 Consider the following Standard Trade model. Assume there are two goods (genetically modified (GMOs) and non-GMOs), and two countries (the United States and the rest of the world (ROW)). Assume that the United States has a comparative advantage in GMOs and the ROW has a comparative advantage in non-GMOs. Assume that markets for both goods are perfectly competitive. (a) Diagram the production possibilities for the United States and ROW, and indicate the optimal production and consumption points, given that the United States and ROW trade. (b) Diagram and indicate the effects of an increase in the price of GMOs on output, consumption, trade, and welfare in both the United States and ROW. (c) Based on your findings, what is the relationship between the terms of trade and welfare? (d) Now, assume that the United States experiences *export-biased growth*. Diagram and indicate the effects of this growth on the outputs, terms of trade, and welfare in the United States and ROW.

13.3 Countries typically experience stronger growth in their export sectors than in their import-competing sectors. Compare the effects of *export-biased growth* on the welfare of: (a) a large country that influences world prices; and (b) a small country that cannot influence world prices.

13.4 National policy makers are often concerned with stimulating the economic growth of their economies. Develop a policy proposal that would: (a) ensure that growth led to higher country utility; and (b) stimulate international competitiveness. Support your proposal with models/diagrams and references to the literature.

13.5 Consider the following questions using your knowledge from this chapter and previous chapters: (a) How has globalization affected income inequality in developing countries? (b) What are the channels through which globalization has affected income inequality?

13.6 Consider the following questions using your knowledge from this chapter and previous chapters: (a) What are the effects of trade policies on the distribution of income in developing countries? (b) How are trade policies linked to prices? (c) How are the price changes linked to welfare effects? (d) How are the price changes linked to labor income effects?

13.7 Arguments supporting *free trade* include the following: (a) economic efficiency; (b) economies of scale; (c) competition and innovation; and (d) endogenous policy conditions. Use your knowledge from this chapter and previous chapters to describe each of these arguments.

13.8 Arguments for *protectionist trade* policy include the following: (a) terms of trade improvement; (b) dynamic infant industry; and (c) domestic market failure. Use your knowledge from this chapter and previous chapters to describe each of these arguments.

Further Reading

Acemoglu, Daron, and Jaume Ventura. 2002. The world income distribution. *Quarterly Journal of Economics* 117: 659–694.

Amsden, Alice H. 2001. *The Rise of "The Rest": Challenges to the West from Late-Industrializing Economies.* Oxford: Oxford University Press.

Bhagwati, Jagdish. 1958. Immiserizing growth: a geometrical note. *Review of Economic Studies* 25: 201–205.

Bhagwati, Jagdish. 1971. The generalized theory of distortions and welfare. In *Trade, Balance of Payments and Growth* (eds J. N. Bhagwati *et al.*). North-Holland, Amsterdam, chapter 12.

Broda, Christian, and David E. Weinstein. 2006. Globalization and the gains from variety. *Quarterly Journal of Economics* 121 (2): 541–585.

Bruton, Henry J. 1998. A reconsideration of import substitution. *Journal of Economic Literature* 26 (2): 903–936.

Dollar, David, and Aart Kraay. 2002. Growth is good for the poor. *Journal of Economic Growth* 7 (3): 195–225.

Edwards, Sebastian. 1993. Openness, trade liberalization and growth in developing countries. *Journal of Economic Literature* 31 (3): 1358–1393.

Feenstra, Robert C. 1996. Trade and uneven growth. *Journal of Development Economics* 49: 229–256.

Feenstra, Robert C., and Gordon H. Hanson. 2003. Global production and inequality: a survey of trade and wages. In *Handbook of International Trade* (eds E.K. Choi and J. Harrigan). London: Blackwell, pp. 146–185.

Findlay, Ronald E. 1984. Growth and development in trade models. In *Handbook of International Economics*, vol. 1 (eds R.W. Jones and P.B. Kenen). Amsterdam: North-Holland, pp. 185–236.

Frankel, Jeffrey, and David Romer. 1999. Does trade cause growth? *American Economic Review* 89 (3): 379–399.

Goldberg, Pinelopi, and Nina Pavcnik. 2007. Distributional effects of globalization in developing countries. *Journal of Economic Literature* 45 (1): 39–82.

Grossman, Gene M., and Elhanan Helpman. 1990. Comparative advantage and long run growth. *American Economic Review* 80: 796–815.

Grossman, Gene M., and Elhanan Helpman. 1991. *Innovation and Growth in the Global Economy.* Cambridge, MA: MIT Press.

Harrison, Ann E. 1994. Productivity, imperfect competition, and trade reform: theory and evidence. *Journal of International Economics* 36 (1–2): 53–73.

Harrison, Ann E. 1996. Openness and growth: a time-series, cross-section analysis for developing countries. *Journal of Development Economics* 48: 419–447.

Hasan, Rana, Devashish Mitra, and K.V. Ramaswamy. 2007. Trade reforms, labor regulations, and labor-demand elasticities: empirical evidence from India. *Review of Economics and Statistics* 89 (3): 466–481.

Krishna, Pravin, and Davashish Mitra. 1998. Trade liberalization, market discipline, and productivity growth: new evidence from India. *Journal of Development Economics* 56 (2): 447–462.

Krueger, Anne O. 1978. *Foreign Trade Regimes and Economic Development: Liberalization Attempts and Consequences.* Cambridge, MA: Ballinger.

Milner, Chris R., ed. 1990. *Export Promotion Strategies: Theory and Evidence from Developing Countries.* New York: New York University Press.

Milner, Chris R., ed. 2004. Constraints to export development in the developing countries. In *The WTO and Developing Countries* (eds Homi Katrak and Roger Strange), London: Palgrave, pp. 213–232.

Pavcnik, Nina. 2002. Trade liberalization, exit, and productivity improvements: evidence from Chilean plants. *Review of Economic Studies* 69 (1): 245–276.

Porto, Guido G. 2006. Using survey data to assess the distributional effects of trade policy. *Journal of International Economics* 70 (1): 140–160.

Prebisch, Raul. 1950. *The Economic Development of Latin America and Its Principal Problems.* New York: United Nations.

Rodriguez, Francisco, and Dani Rodrik. 2001. Trade policy and economic growth: a skeptic's guide to the cross-national evidence. In *Macreconomics Annual 2000* (eds Ben Bernanke and Kenneth S. Rogoff), Cambridge, MA: MIT Press, pp. 261–325.

Rodrik, Dani. 1992. Closing the productivity gap: does trade liberalization really help? In *Trade Policy, Industrialization, and Development: New Perspectives* (ed. G. K. Helleiner), Oxford: Clarendon Press, pp. 155–175.

Romer, Paul M. 1986. Increasing returns and long-run growth. *Journal of Political Economy* 94 (5): 1002–1037.

Sachs, Jeffrey D., and Andrew Warner. 1995. Economic reform and the process of global integration. *Brooking Papers on Economic Activity* 1: 1–118.

Srinivasan, T. N., and Jagdish Bhagwati. 2001. Outward-orientation and development: are revisionists right? In *Trade, Development and Political Economy: Essays in Honor of Anne O. Krueger* (eds D. Lal and R. H. Snape), New York: Palgrave, pp. 3–26.

Trindade, V. 2005. The big push, industrialization, and international trade. *Journal of Development Economics* 78: 22–48.

Winters, L. Alan. 2004. Trade liberalization and economic performance: an overview. *Economic Journal* 114 (February): 4–21.

Winters, L. Alan, Neil McCulloch, and Andrew McKay. 2004. Trade liberalization and poverty: the evidence so far. *Journal of Economic Literature* 42 (1): 72–115.

Notes

1. For studies of the relationship between trade and country income levels, see Bhagwati (1971), Broda and Weinstein (2006), Frankel and Romer (1999), Harrison (1994), Krishna and Mitra (1998).
2. For studies of the relationship between trade and economic growth, see Bhagwati (1958), Findlay (1984), Grossman and Helpman (1991a; 1991b), Harrison (1994), Krisha and Mitra (1998), Rodriquez and Rodrik (2001), Rodrick (1992), and Sachs and Warner (1995).
3. For studies of the effects of trade on income distribution, see Dollar and Kraay (2002), Feenstra and Hanson (2003), Goldberg and Pavcnik (2007), Hasan, Mitra, and Ramaswamy (2007), Porto (2006), and Winters, McCulloch, and McKay (2004).

Part Four

Trade Arrangements

14

Regional and Multilateral Arrangements

In Part One of this book, we discussed the effects of liberalization and protectionism generally, without specifying the policy instruments used to bring about these changes. In Part Two, we considered specific policy instruments that are designed to bring about these changes. We referred to these instruments as traditional trade policies. These include tariffs, export subsidies, and quantitative restrictions. In Part Three, we extended our discussion of policy instruments to include those policies that are designed for non-trade purposes that affect trade as a side effect. We referred to these policies are trade-related policies. These include intellectual property rights, environmental policies, labor policies, and growth and development policies. In this last section of the book (Part Four), we consider the institutional arrangements within which these traditional and trade-related policies are designed, adopted, and managed.

In the current chapter, we will consider two core questions: (1) What are the institutional arrangements for trade policy? (2) What are the effects of alternative institutional arrangements for trade policy? To this end, we examine the effects of regional liberalization, multilateral liberalization, and country exclusion from liberalization arrangements. We also consider whether or not regional arrangements are a first step toward multilateral liberalization; that is, we consider the additional question: (3) Are regional arrangements stepping stones or stumbling blocks to multilateral liberalization? Thus, this last chapter provides a framework for thinking about and comparing the continuously evolving institutional arrangements for trade policy.

Global Trade Policy: Questions and Answers, First Edition. Pamela J. Smith.
© 2014 John Wiley & Sons, Inc. Published 2014 by John Wiley & Sons, Inc.

14.1   What Are the Institutional Arrangements
for Trade Policy?

The prominent institutional arrangements for trade policy include bilateral arrangements, regional arrangements, and multilateral arrangements. These arrangements differ in the scope of countries involved as well as other characteristics.

Bilateral trade arrangements are those where two trading partners agree to reduce or eliminate barriers between themselves. Trade economists typically think of these "partners" as two countries; however, they can also be customs territories, trade blocks, or other informal groups of countries. Bilateral arrangements are voluminous in number. One explanation for their prominence is that arrangements limited to two partners are more politically feasible to negotiate than are arrangements with broader membership.

In contrast, *multilateral trade arrangements* are those where multiple countries agree to reduce or eliminate barriers between themselves. Trade economists typically use this term to refer to agreements that are broader than regional arrangements and not necessarily bound by geography. Because the scope of countries involved is extensive, multilateral arrangements are the least discriminatory form of arrangement. This is because there are few countries left outside the block. Examples of multilateral arrangements include the General Agreement on Tariffs and Trade (GATT) and its successor the World Trade Organization (WTO). Membership to these agreements is extensive. For example, membership of the WTO was 128 at its inception in 1995 and increased to 153 by 2012. In 2012, 26 countries were negotiating their accession to the WTO. Thus, a relatively small number of countries remain outside this multilateral arrangement.

Regional trade arrangements fall in between bilateral and multilateral arrangements in terms of scope. *Regional trade arrangements* are those where "blocks" of countries agree to reduce or eliminate barriers between themselves. The scope of countries involved is partial and typically includes countries that are major trading partners and/or countries in relatively close geographic proximity. This form of liberalization is discriminatory in that countries outside the regional block are treated differently than countries within the regional block. For example, tariff rates on trading partners within the block are eliminated or reduced, while the tariff rates on trading partners outside the block are maintained at higher levels.

There are two primary forms of regional trade arrangement: (1) free trade areas and (2) customs unions. *Free trade areas* (FTAs) are arrangements where the member countries eliminate or reduce trade barriers between themselves on all or most goods. At the same time, the member countries establish or maintain their own individual – and potentially different – bilateral barriers with countries outside the FTA. Examples of FTAs include the ASEAN Free Trade Area (AFTA), Central European Free Trade Agreement (CEFTA), North American Free Trade Area (NAFTA), South Asian Free Trade Agreement (SAFTA), and the US-Singapore FTA.

The number of FTAs has increased dramatically since the early 1990s and there are now more than 100 such arrangements. These arrangements can be overlapping in that countries can simultaneously belong to more than one FTA. For example, the United States is a member of both NAFTA and the US-Singapore FTA mentioned above.

Customs unions (CUs) are arrangements where the member countries eliminate or reduce trade barriers between themselves on all or most goods. However, the member countries establish or maintain common bilateral barriers with countries outside the union. For example, each country within a customs union has the same tariff rate on imports from countries outside the customs union. Such common bilateral barriers in the form of tariffs are referred to as *common external tariffs* (CETs). Examples of CUs include the European Union (EU), Mercosur, the Central American Common Market, the Eurasian Economic Community, the East African Customs Union, and the South African Customs Union. The number of CUs has increased dramatically since the early 1990s, along with FTAs.

The primary difference between an FTA and a CU is the treatment of nonmember countries outside the block. In an FTA, each country within the block maintains its own bilateral barriers with nonmember countries outside the block. In a CU, each country within the block maintains a common external barrier with nonmember countries outside the block. An FTA is more distortionary than a CU in the sense that the differential bilateral barriers with nonmember countries can create additional trade distortions.

One such distortion results from the efforts by nonmember countries that seek access to countries within the block but also seek to avoid high tariff countries in the block. If a nonmember country outside the FTA wants to export to a member country inside the FTA, it can export to the member country with the lowest external barrier (e.g., tariff) and then transship the good to the desired destination within the block. In this way, the nonmember country can skirt the higher barrier of the destination country. For example, consider the case of NAFTA, which includes Canada, Mexico, and the United States. If the United States and Mexico maintain a higher tariff on goods from China than does Canada, the Chinese exporter can export the goods into Canada and be subject to the relatively low tariff rate, and then transship the goods from Canada to Mexico and the United States at a zero tariff rate. This behavior results in distortions including a transfer of tariff revenues to the lowest barrier country as well as costs associated with the reallocation of resources for the purpose of transshipment.

Rules of origin are designed to prevent such distortions associated with FTAs. *Rules of origin* establish conditions that are required for a good to be considered a good originating from a given country. In our example above, the Chinese good being transshipped to the United States and/or Mexico via Canada is eligible for the zero tariff of the FTA only if conditions are met to grant the good a Canadian origin rather than a Chinese origin. Such conditions include *local content requirements* that a particular fraction of the value of the good be produced domestically for the good to be considered a good of a given country. Such rules of origin prevent goods from being passed through countries with the lowest tariff and then being transshipped across countries within the FTA with zero tariffs.

Irrespective of rules of origin, regional trade arrangements, including CUs and FTAs, are by their nature discriminatory against nonmember countries outside the block. This discrimination conflicts with the most favored nation (MFN) principal of the GATT. The MFN status requires that countries cannot offer any other country a more favorable barrier (e.g., a lower tariff rate). However, Article XXIV of the GATT (and its successor the WTO) allows an exception in the case of FTAs and CUs. The conditions for this exception are that trade within the block is substantially free and barriers with nonmembers are lower on average after the establishment of the FTA or CU. The intuition underlying this exception is that regional trade arrangements – although discriminatory – may serve as stepping stones to larger multilateral trade arrangements.

Article XXIV of the GATT states: "The contracting parties recognize the desirability of increasing freedom of trade by the development, through voluntary agreements, of closer integration between the economies of the countries parties to such agreements. They also recognize that the purpose of a customs union or of a free-trade area should be to facilitate trade between the constituent territories and not to raise barriers to the trade of other contracting parties with such territories."

Finally, FTAs and CUs differ in terms of the autonomy of national trade policy-making. For example, with FTAs, the individual countries in the block retain their separate tariff-setting authorities for establishing external tariffs against nonmember countries. In contrast, with CUs, the individual countries transfer this authority to a tariff-setting body of the customs union. Thus, individual member countries in the CUs are not free to negotiate bilateral tariff reductions with countries outside the block. The lack of autonomy (such as in tariff setting) can provide a source of tension among member countries of CUs.

14.1.1   What are the prominent multilateral arrangements for trade policy in practice?

The GATT and its successor, the WTO, are the most economically significant multilateral arrangements for trade policy to date. The GATT was established in 1947 and was succeeded by the WTO in 1995. Under each of these arrangements, "rounds" of negotiations are conducted on a periodic basis. These rounds to date include: Geneva (1947), Annecy (1949), Torquay (1950), Geneva (1956), Dillon (1960–1961), Kennedy (1963–1967), Tokyo (1973–1979), Uruguay (1986–1994), and Doha (2001-present). The Uruguay Round of the GATT resulted in the establishment of the WTO. The purpose of these rounds of negotiations is to reduce trade barriers and to establish rules of conduct for negotiating trade policy. Each successive round builds on the previous agreements, providing for an evolving multilateral trade negotiation process.[1]

Membership to this multilateral arrangement has grown from 23 signatories of the GATT in 1947 to 153 signatories of the WTO to date; that is, membership has increased by more than 127 countries during the course of nine rounds of negotiations. All members can participate in the rounds of negotiations and the results of the rounds apply to members in a nondiscriminatory manner. The principal of nondiscrimination is supported by the MFN clause of the GATT/WTO. This clause guarantees that members are offered the best treatment that any given country offers to another country. That is, concessions offered by one country to another must be extended to all members of the GATT/WTO.

The subjects of the rounds of negotiations have evolved substantially over time. Early negotiations (1947–1961) focused on tariff reductions on manufactured products. Subsequently, since the Kennedy Round (1963–present), the subjects of negotiation have broadened considerably to include non-tariff measures. For example, the Kennedy Round added the subjects of antidumping and customs valuation. The Tokyo Round added the subjects of subsidies and countervailing duties, government procurement, import licensing, product standard safeguards, and special and differential treatment of developing countries. The Uruguay Round added the subjects of services trade, intellectual property rights, trade-related investment measures, pre-shipment inspection, rules of origin, dispute settlement, transparency and surveillance of trade policy, among others.

The modalities of these negotiations have also evolved over time. *Modalities* refer to the rules and procedures for conducting the negotiations. Early negotiations (1947–1961) focused on tariff reductions on an item-by-item basis. Under the *item-by-item method*, countries simultaneously submit to each trading partner requests for tariff cuts on specific products. These requests comprise what is known as "positive lists" of tariffs to be reduced. The participating countries can then either grant the requests or not. These requests are also referred to as concessions. The granting and receiving of *concessions* refer to the exchange of benefits received by exporters in exchange for cost incurred by importers from reductions in trade barriers. For example, when an importer lowers a tariff on a specific product, this importer is said to be granting a concession to the exporter who is receiving the concession. *Reciprocity* refers to cases where countries exchange concessions that are roughly equal.

The modalities negotiated in the Kennedy Round (1963–1967) resulted in changes to this approach. In the Kennedy Round, a linear approach was introduced. Under the *linear method*, countries simultaneously cut tariffs on all manufactured products by an equal percentage. That is, the same percentage cuts are applied across all member countries. At the same time, countries can submit item-by-item requests for exceptions to the linear tariff cuts. These requests comprise what is known as "negative lists" of tariffs to be omitted from the linear tariff reductions. Another significant modality change under the Kennedy Round was the introduction of special and differential treatment for developing countries. For example, the developing countries were not expected to reciprocate the tariff cuts undertaken by developed countries.

Finally, the modalities negotiated in the most recent rounds further modified the earlier approaches. In the Tokyo Round (1973–1979), a formula approach was introduced. Under the *formula approach*, the linear tariff cuts were adapted using a formula such that the tariff cuts would be larger on products that had relatively larger tariffs initially. In the subsequent Uruguay Round (1986–1994), a combination of the formula approach and the item-by-item approach was applied.

These multilateral negotiations under the GATT/WTO have resulted in a significant liberalization of trade. According to the World Trade Report (World Trade Organization, 2007), using the item-by-item approach, the first five rounds of negotiations (1947–1961) resulted in approximately 45,000 concessions. These concessions covered roughly 15,000 product categories, referred to as *tariff lines*. The Kennedy Round, which initiated the linear approach, resulted in a 35% average reduction in tariffs, although the target was 50%. This round also resulted in agreements on customs valuation and antidumping. The Tokyo Round, which initiated the formula approach, resulted in further tariff reductions as well as advances in the liberalization of a broader range of non-tariff measures via voluntary codes of conduct. The Uruguay Round, which used a combination of modalities, resulted in roughly an additional 33% cut in tariffs and a further broadening in the treatment of non-tariff measures. The treatment of non-tariff measures was covered in more than 50 agreements adopted in 1995. This round was also significant in altering the organizational structure through the establishment of the WTO and the associated dispute settlement mechanism. The round also introduced ministerial conferences – biannual meetings where the trade representatives of member countries discuss trade policy in an ongoing manner.

Negotiations since the Uruguay Round have included the ministerial conference in *Seattle*, Washington in 1999. The purpose of this meeting was to discuss the next round of negotiations, but it was stalled by demonstrations as well as disagreement over the agenda. The next ministerial conference was held in *Doha*, Quatar in 2001. This meeting initiated the new round of negotiations referred to as the *Doha Development Round*. Key issues on the agenda included reductions in barriers to agricultural trade as well as improvements in the transparency of antidumping duties. Meetings of negotiating groups in 2002–2003 could not reach agreement on the terms and structure of the negotiations.[2] The next ministerial meeting, held in Cancun, Mexico in 2003, resulted in a stalling of negotiations due to disagreements over liberalization of agricultural subsidies, among other issues. In 2006, the Doha Round of negotiations was suspended. Since that time, efforts have focused on revising the terms and structure of the rules and procedures for conducting the negotiations – the modalities.

14.2   What Are the Effects of Alterative Arrangements for Trade Policy?

We now turn to the effects of alternative institutional arrangements for trade policy. We consider three illustrative cases. The first is the case of regional liberalization (e.g., FTAs or CUs). The second is the case of multinational liberalization (e.g., GATT or WTO). The third is the case of extensive but incomplete multilateral liberalization, where a relatively small number of countries are excluded from the liberalization arrangement. This last case illustrates why countries have an incentive to join large multilateral arrangements and why exclusion from such arrangements is disadvantageous. In each case, we illustrate liberalization by focusing on the elimination of tariffs (using the methods covered in Chapter 5). Liberalization agreements, of course, involve the elimination or reduction of a wide range of trade and trade-related barriers (as discussed in Chapters 4 to 13). To simplify our illustrations, we focus on the tariff as the primary policy instrument within liberalization arrangements.

14.2.1   What are the effects of regional liberalization?

We begin by exploring the effects of liberalization under a regional agreement such as a customs union or free trade area. The question is, does regional trade liberalization increase or decrease the welfare of countries within the block? We will show that the answer to this question is ambiguous. It depends on the extent of the trade that is created from liberalization relative to the extent to which distortions remain and/or are introduced from liberalization. These effects are known as "trade creation" and "trade diversion".

Trade creation results from liberalization when countries shift production away from goods in which they have a comparative *dis*advantage and import these goods from other countries that can produce these goods at a relatively lower cost. Trade creation is the consequence of specialization based on comparative advantage. Trade creation results in an increase in national welfare for both the exporter and importer (as discussed in Part One of the book). Alternatively, *trade diversion* results when countries within a block shift their imports from the lowest cost producers outside the block to higher cost producers inside the block. This diversion arises because of the difference between intra-block tariffs (which are zero) and extra-block tariffs (which are positive).

In the context of a regional trade agreement, trade liberalization can result in trade creation and trade diversion. Tariffs (and other barriers to trade) are eliminated between the countries within the block, which results in trade creation. However, tariffs are maintained against countries outside the block, which can result in trade diversion. A country can import with zero tariffs from lower cost producers within the block or import with positive tariffs from lower cost producers outside the block. The decision of which country to import from depends on the magnitude of the cost differences between the exporters relative to the magnitude of the tariffs.

For example, suppose there is an importer within the regional block with a comparative *dis*advantage in a particular good. This means that the country has a relatively high price of producing the good (say $130). Further, suppose that an exporter inside the block supplies the good at a price of $115 while an exporter outside the block supplies the good at a price of $100. In this case, the exporter outside the block is the lowest cost producer. In the absence of tariffs, the importing country will import from the country outside the block at a price of $100. However, suppose that the tariff imposed on imports from countries outside the block is greater than 15% while the internal block tariff is zero. In this case, the importing country will import from the country inside the block even though the country outside the block is the lowest cost producer. Such trade diversion occurs when importing countries increase imports from member countries even though a non-member country is the lowest cost producer of the good.

To illustrate the effects of regional liberalization on trade creation and diversion – and thus welfare – we consider two cases. The first is the case where the lowest cost producers are outside the regional block that liberalizes trade. The second is the case where the lowest cost producers are inside the regional block that liberalizes trade.

The setup is as follows. Consider the scenario where there are three countries (or groups of countries): A, B, and C. There is one good (or composite of many goods). Country A is a small country with a comparative *dis*advantage in this good. In other words, country A is the highest cost producer of the good and is thus an importer of the good in the presence of trade. In contrast, countries B and C have a comparative advantage in the good and are thus exporters of the good. Both countries B and C are large and supply the good with infinite elasticity into the world market. However, country C is the lower cost producer of the good relative to country B. Further, assume that, initially, country A maintains a tariff on imports of the good from both countries B and C.

Figure 14.1 illustrates this set of assumptions. This figure plots the domestic supply and demand of country A. As shown, the equilibrium autarky price is relatively high, reflecting that country A has a comparative disadvantage in the good. Further, country A faces two infinitely elastic export supply curves of the large exporting countries B and C (S_b^X and S_c^X). The relative positions of these export supply curves show that country C is a lowest cost producer of the good relative to country B. These relative costs are reflected in the relative prices of the good, where $P_c < P_b$. Further, given that country A initially maintains a similar tariff on imports of the good from countries B and C, the tariff-inclusive prices are P_c^t and P_b^t, respectively, where $P_c^t < P_b^t$. Thus, before liberalization of trade, country A will import the good from country C at the tariff-inclusive price P_c^t. These imports are the amount of the excess demand of country A at that price (P_c^t), where $M_3 = Q_3^D - Q_3^S$. Country A will not import from country B prior to liberalization because the tariff-inclusive price of goods from country B (P_b^t) is high relative to the tariff-inclusive price of goods from country C (P_c^t).

Now, suppose that countries A and B establish a regional trade arrangement, and country C is outside of this arrangement. This regional arrangement reduces tariffs within the block to zero. What are the effects of such regional liberalization when the lowest cost producers are *outside* the block? First, trade is created as country A expands her imports. Specifically, country A now imports a larger quantity of the good ($M_2 = Q_2^D - Q_2^S$) at a lower price (P_b) from country B. This liberalization

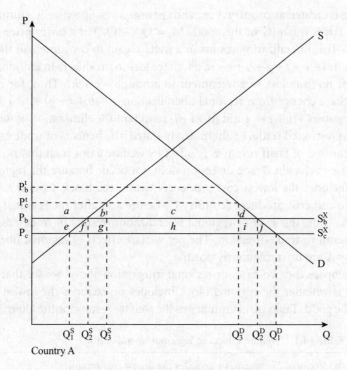

Figure 14.1 Regional liberalization – welfare effects in importer.

results in a welfare gain to consumers in the amount $+(a + b + c + d)$, a welfare loss to producers in amount $-(a)$, and a tariff revenue loss to government in amount $-(c + h)$. Thus, for country A the net welfare change from regional liberalization is $+(b + d) - h$. The net positive areas $+(b + d)$ represent the (partial) elimination of dead weight losses associated with restricted trade, or alternatively stated, the benefits of trade creation. The negative area $-(h)$ represents the net tariff revenue lost, or alternatively stated, a remaining distortion from the limited membership of the regional arrangement. Trade diversion occurs because liberalization is limited to the regional block and the lowest cost producers are outside this block. As a result of regional liberalization, country A now imports from a country within the regional block rather than the lowest cost producer of the good outside the block. That is, country A's imports are diverted away from country C (a nonmember) toward country B (a member). The net welfare effects of the regional liberalization on country A can be positive or negative. This direction depends on whether the net welfare gains from trade creation exceed the net welfare losses from trade diversion (e.g., $b + d > h$ or $b + d < h$).

Alternatively, suppose that countries A and C establish a regional trade arrangement and country B is outside of this arrangement. Again, this regional arrangement reduces tariffs within the block to zero. What are the effects of such regional liberalization when the lowest cost producers are *inside* the block?

First, trade is created as country A expands her imports. Specifically, country A now imports a larger quantity of the good ($M_1 = Q_1^D - Q_1^S$) at a lower price (P_c) from country C. This liberalization results in a welfare gain to consumers in the amount $+(a + b + c + d + e + f + g + h + i + j)$, a welfare loss to producers in amount $-(a + e)$, and a tariff revenue loss to government in amount $-(c + h)$. Thus, for country A the net welfare change from regional liberalization is $+(b + f + g) + (d + i + j)$. The net positive areas $+(b + f + g)$ and $(d + i + j)$ represent the elimination of dead weight losses from restricted trade, or alternatively stated, the benefits of trade creation. In this case, the loss of tariff revenues is offset by welfare gains such that no net negative distortions remain. Trade diversion does not occur because the regional liberalization includes the lowest cost producers within the block. Country A imports from the lowest cost producer (country C) before and after the regional trade liberalization. Thus, this case of regional liberalization results in trade creation, but does not result in trade diversion. The net welfare effects of regional liberalization on country A are unambiguously positive.

If we compare the two cases or regional integration above, we see that the main difference is whether the regional block includes or excludes the lowest cost producer of the good. Table 14.1 summarizes the welfare results for the alternative cases

Table 14.1   Welfare effects of regional liberalization.

(a) Regional liberalization excludes the lowest cost producer

Economic agent	Country A Welfare effects
Consumers	$+(a + b + c + d)$
Producers	$-a$
Government	$-(c + h)$
Country	$+(b + d) - h$
Country (direction)	Positive or negative

(b) Regional liberalization includes the lowest cost producer

Economic agent	Country A Welfare effects
Consumers	$+(a + b + c + d + e + f + g + h + i + j)$
Producers	$-(a + e)$
Government	$-(c + h)$
Country	$+(b + f + g) + (d + i + j)$
Country (direction)	Positive

Note: These cases both assume that country A is the highest cost producer, country C is the lowest cost producer, and country B is in between. Further, country A is an importer, whereas countries B and C are exporters. Case (a) assumes that regional liberalization includes countries A and B, but excludes country C. Case (b) assumes that regional liberalization includes countries A and C, but excludes country B.

of regional integration that are illustrated in Figure 14.1. If the regional block *excludes* the lowest cost producer, then regional liberalization results in trade creation along with trade diversion. If the block *includes* the lowest cost producer, then regional liberalization results in trade creation but no trade diversion. In both cases, there are welfare gains from regional liberalization associated with the trade creation. In the first case, the positive welfare changes are diminished and potentially reversed by trade diversion.

These results apply to regional arrangements including FTAs and CUs. However, in the case of FTAs without rules of origin, additional distortions arise from the differential tariffs maintained by member countries against countries outside the arrangements (e.g., resource reallocation associated with transshipments, and tariff revenue shifts to relatively low tariff countries). If we consider these additional distortions in the FTA case, then it is possible that the welfare effects of regional liberalization are negative for some countries within the regional block. Thus, regional trade liberalization increases the welfare of countries within the block if the welfare gains from trade creation exceed welfare losses from trade diversion plus any additional welfare losses associated with uneven external barriers in the FTA form of regional liberalization.

14.2.2   What are the effects of multilateral liberalization?

Next, we consider the case of multinational liberalization (e.g., GATT or WTO). The extreme version of multilateral arrangement is one in which all countries are included in the agreement. If the scope of countries involved is complete, then the multilateral arrangement is nondiscriminatory. All countries simultaneously eliminate and/or reduce barriers to trade. This liberalization results in trade creation but no trade diversion. In this section, we illustrate this extreme case of complete multilateral liberalization. In the following section, we consider the case where a small number of countries remain outside the multilateral arrangement.

The set up is as follows. Consider the case where there are three countries (or groups of countries). There is one good (or composite of many goods). Country A is a small country with a comparative disadvantage in this good; in other words, country A is the highest cost producer of the good and is thus an importer of the good in the presence of trade. Block R is a group of countries that have formed a large regional trade arrangement. Country A is a member of this arrangement. Block W is all other countries in the rest of the world. We will refer to these country groups as block R and block W. Both the regional block and the rest of world block are large, and supply the good with infinite elasticity to the world market. However, block W is the lower cost producer of the good relative to block R. Further, assume that initially country A maintains a tariff on imports of the good from block W but not on imports from block R, as A is a member of the regional block R.

Figure 14.2 illustrates this set of assumptions. This figure plots the domestic supply and demand of country A. As shown, the equilibrium autarky price is

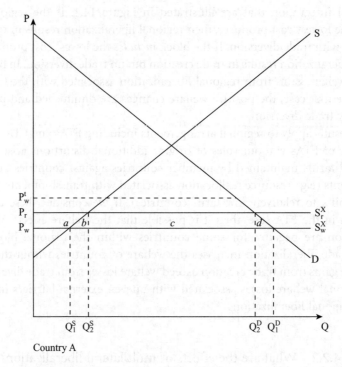

Country A

Figure 14.2 Multilateral liberalization – welfare effects in importer.

relatively high, reflecting that country A has a comparative disadvantage in the good. Further, country A faces two infinitely elastic export supply curves of the large exporting blocks R and W (S_r^X and S_w^X). The relative positions of these export supply curves show that block W is the lowest cost producer of the good relative to block R. These relative costs are reflected in the relative prices of the good, where $P_w < P_r$. Further, country A initially maintains a tariff on imports of the good from block W but not from block R since country A is a member of block R. Thus, before multilateral liberalization, country A will import the good from block R at the regional free trade price P_r. The imports are the amount of the excess demand of country A at that price, or $M_2 = Q_2^D - Q_2^S$. Country A will not import from block W prior to the multilateral liberalization because the tariff-inclusive price (P_w^t) of goods from block W is higher than the free trade price (P_r) of goods from block R.

Now, suppose that all countries establish a multilateral trade arrangement. This multilateral arrangement reduces tariffs on goods from all countries to zero. What are the effects of such multilateral liberalization? First, trade is created as country A expands her imports. Specifically, country A will now import a larger quantity of the good ($M_1 = Q_1^D - Q_1^S$) at a lower price (P_w) from group W. This liberalization results in a welfare gain to consumers in the amount of $+(a + b + c + d)$, a welfare loss to producers in the amount $-(a)$, and no tariff revenue loss to government. Thus, for country A the net welfare change from multilateral liberalization is

Table 14.2   Welfare effects of multilateral liberalization.

(a) Multilateral liberation

Economic agent	Country A Welfare effects
Consumers	$+(a + b + c + d)$
Producers	$-a$
Government	0
Country	$+(b + c + d)$
Country (direction)	Positive

Note: This case assumes that country A is the highest cost producer; block R is a large regional trade arrangement; country A is a member of block R; block W is the rest of the world; and block W is the lowest cost producer.

$+(b + c + d)$. The net positive areas $+(b)$ and $+(d)$ represent the elimination of dead weight losses associated with restricted trade, or alternatively stated, the benefits of trade creation. The net positive area $+(c)$ represents a terms of trade improvement. That is, the relative price of the good that country A imports is now lower. In this case, trade diversion does not occur because there is no discrimination, as no countries are excluded from the multilateral arrangement. Table 14.2 summarizes the welfare effects of this multilateral liberalization.

If we compare this case of multilateral liberalization with regional liberalization (in Tables 14.1 and 14.2), we see that the main difference is that multilateral liberalization results in trade creation only, whereas regional liberalization results in trade creation (although not complete) and can result in trade diversion if the lowest cost producers are outside the regional block. With regional liberalization, the net welfare change of countries is mixed. With multilateral liberalization, the net welfare change of countries is unambiguously positive.

14.2.3   What are the effects of country exclusion from multilateral arrangements?

What if a multilateral arrangement is not complete? That is, what if a small number of countries remain outside the multilateral arrangement? Do these *excluded* countries have an incentive to join the multilateral arrangement? Do the *included* countries benefit from a broadening of membership? The motivation for asking these questions is that in practice, even broad multilateral arrangements such as the GATT and WTO are not complete. So, in this section we ask: What are the effects (including opportunity costs) of country exclusion from multilateral trade liberalization on both members and nonmembers?

To analyze this question, we consider the following illustrative example. Consider the case where there are four groups of countries, including North America (N), Europe (E), Asia (A) and the rest of the world (W). There is one good (or composite of many goods). For this particular good, North America is an importer, and Europe, Asia, and the rest of the world are exporters. In other words, North America is the highest cost producer of the good and is thus an importer of the good in the presence of trade. In contrast, blocks E, A, and W have a comparative advantage in the good and are thus exporters of the good. These exporting blocks are large and supply the good with infinite elasticity into the world market. Suppose that the rest of the world is the lowest cost producer, followed by Asia and then Europe. Further, suppose that initially the blocks of Europe, North America, and Asia have liberalized trade via a multilateral arrangement, but the rest of the world has not yet acceded.

Figure 14.3 illustrates this set of assumptions. This figure plots the domestic supply and demand of North America. As shown, the equilibrium autarky price is relatively high, reflecting that North America has a comparative disadvantage in the good. Further, North America faces the three infinitely elastic export supply curves of the large exporting blocks of Europe, Asia, and the rest of world (S_e^X, S_a^X, S_w^X). The relative positions of these export supply curves show that the rest of world is the lowest cost producer, followed by Asia, and then Europe. These relative costs are reflected in the relative prices of the goods, where $P_w < P_a < P_e$.

Now, suppose that a multilateral arrangement includes all countries in North America, Europe, and Asia, but excludes the rest of the world. Thus, tariffs are main-

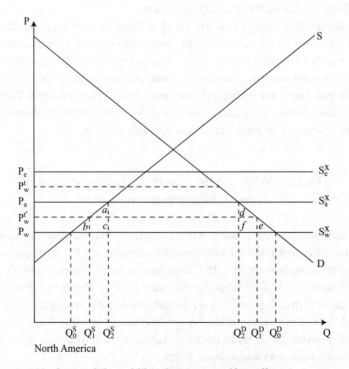

Figure 14.3   Incomplete multilateral liberalization – welfare effects in importer.

tained only on goods imported by North America from the rest of the world. What are the effects of such an incomplete multilateral arrangement on both the importer (i.e., North America) and exporters (i.e., Europe, Asia, and the rest of the world)?

Given this arrangement, North America will import the good at the lowest possible price. If the tariff-inclusive price of the good from block W is higher than the tariff free price of the good from blocks A or E, then North American will import from a block other than W. If we assume a relatively large tariff (t) such that $P_w < P_a < P_w^t < P_e$, then North America will import the good from Asia at price P_a in amount $M_2 = Q_2^D - Q_2^S$. The rest of the world is shut out from trade with North America even though the rest of the world is the lowest cost producer of the good.

Alternatively, if the tariff-inclusive price of the good from block W is lower than the tariff free price of the good from blocks A or E, then North American will import from block W. In this alternative case, we assume a relatively small tariff (t') such that $P_w < P_w^{t'} < P_a < P_e$. In this case, North America will import the good from the rest of the world at price $P_w^{t'}$ in amount $M_1 = Q_1^D - Q_1^S$ even though the rest of the world is excluded from the multilateral arrangement. This alternative case assumes that the cost advantage of block W is sufficiently large that a price advantage is maintained even in the presence of a tariff.

Finally, suppose that the rest of the world accedes to the multilateral arrangement such that tariffs are eliminated against the countries of the rest of the world. Now North America will import from the rest of the world at price P_w in the amount $M_0 = Q_0^D - Q_0^S$. The rest of the world is no longer shut out from trade with North America. Rather the rest of the world is now the primary exporter to North America after accession to the multilateral arrangement.

In these illustrations, both the importer (i.e., North America) and the exporters (i.e., Europe, Asia, and the rest of world) are affected by the exclusion or inclusion of the rest of the world in the multilateral arrangement. When countries within a multilateral arrangement maintain barriers against countries outside the arrangements, trade can be diverted away from the excluded countries even when they are the lowest cost producers of the good. In our example, when North American maintains a relatively large tariff (t) against the nonmember countries of the rest of the world, trade is diverted away from the nonmember countries and toward member countries in Asia. The dead weight loss triangles $(a + b + c)$ and $(d + e + f)$ represent the welfare losses to North America associated with the distortionary effects of the exclusion of countries from the multilateral arrangement. Alternatively, when North America maintains relatively small tariffs (t') against nonmember countries of the rest of the world, North American imports from the rest of the world rather than from Asia. The remaining dead weight loss triangles (b) and (e) represent the remaining welfare losses to North American associated with the distortionary effects of the tariff. Finally, when tariffs are completely eliminated upon accession of the rest of the world to the multilateral arrangement, the dead weight loss triangles disappear, and the volume of imports by North America from the rest of the world increases.

This example illustrates the conflicting interests of the various blocks. North America has an interest in the accession of the rest of the world to the multilateral arrangements. This is because North America will gain in terms of net country welfare. However, the lowest cost producer within the multilateral arrangement (i.e., Asia) has an interest in excluding the lowest cost producer outside the arrangement (i.e., the rest of world) from the arrangement. This is because Asia will no longer export to North America after the liberalization of barriers with the rest of the world. This corresponds with a loss of producer welfare in Asia. Finally, the lowest cost producer outside the multilateral arrangement (i.e., the rest of the world) has an interest in accession to the multilateral arrangement. The opportunity cost of exclusion is the lost producer welfare from foregone exports to North American. The rest of the world gains producer welfare from accession to the arrangement if this block is indeed the lowest cost producer of the good.[3]

In summary, countries initially excluded from a multilateral arrangement do have an incentive to join the arrangement in order to gain access to trade with countries within the arrangement and the corresponding welfare improvements. However, countries initially included in the multilateral arrangement have mixed incentives for broadening membership.

These conclusions focus on the aggregate "national" perspectives of the blocks. There are, of course, welfare changes *within* each block between producers, consumers, and government (as discussed at length in Part Two of this book). Political economy considerations that place different weights on the welfare of these agents would alter the conclusions discussed above. For example, if North America placed a larger weight on the welfare of North American producers relative to North American consumers and governments, then the interest of the block in broadening membership in the multilateral (or regional) arrangement is diminished. Given such political and economic considerations, the answers to the questions posed at the start of this section are not clear-cut.

In practice, it is not unusual for producers to receive greater weight in policy decisions relative to consumers, given the strength of business lobbyists versus consumer groups. This political economy dimension of welfare analysis does not create a gap between the economic theory presented above and practice. Rather, the theory can be extended to account for the different weights placed on the welfare of agents within and across countries. One way to do this (using the illustrations presented in this book) is to consider the case where governments place either full weight or no weight on the welfare of agents. For example, in the results summarized in Tables 14.1 and 14.2, the welfare of consumers could be given zero weight, while the welfare of producers and governments could be given full weight. Under this weighting, when we add together the welfare effects to get the aggregate country effects, the results show a negative welfare effect for the importer considered in these tables. That is, the importer has a disincentive to engage in regional or multilateral liberalization when the welfare of consumers is given relatively less weight. This example reduces to welfare maximization for producers and governments alone, excluding the interests of consumers. Such results (from the unequal weighting of agents) help to explain why governments sometimes choose policies that seem counterintuitive from an economic perspective.

Furthermore, in practice, it is not uncommon for governments to balance various economic and political incentives when deciding whether to join a bilateral, regional, or multilateral arrangement. For example, there are cases where large higher-cost countries (e.g., developed countries) want the lower-cost countries as partners to an arrangement despite the losses to their domestic producers. There are also cases where small lower-cost countries (e.g., developing countries) hesitate to join an arrangement despite the gains to their domestic producers. One explanation is that the small developing countries may feel overpowered by the large countries, which have more seasoned negotiators who can extract better terms for their domestic interests. In such cases, countries initially excluded from an arrangement may not have an incentive to join, despite the potential economic gains that could be accrued. In such negotiations, small countries may perceive that larger weights are placed on the welfare of countries that have relatively strong political bargaining power.

These *political economy* aspects of trade build on and extend the theory foundations presented in this chapter. We encourage the reader to explore the political economy literature for research that considers the *endogenous* determination of trade policy.

14.3 Are Regional Arrangements Stepping Stones or Stumbling Blocks to Multilateral Liberalization?

It is often the case that countries participate in bilateral or regional free trade arrangements because they are easier and faster to negotiate than multilateral ones. There may be a time cost (or opportunity cost) of negotiating a more complete global agreement, even though it could generate larger welfare gains. Firms (or their national delegates) may want to strike bargains faster. This observation has prompted economists to consider whether bilateral and/or regional arrangements facilitate the movement toward broader multilateral arrangements for trade liberalization.

In this final section, we consider whether regional arrangements provide a first step toward broader multilateral arrangements or whether they inhibit movement toward multilateral arrangements. That is, we consider whether regional arrangements are "stepping stones" or "stumbling blocks" to multilateral arrangements. The motivation for considering this issue is that from a global perspective, multilateral arrangements generate larger welfare gains than do regional arrangements. Thus, from an economic point of view, it would be desirable to move directly to a multilateral arrangement. However, if this were not feasible, then it would be desirable if regional arrangements provide a stepping stone to broader multilateral integration over time.

Before considering this issue, it is important to note that the trade creation and diversion that result from liberalization arrangements can take the form of trade in different goods (i.e., inter-industry trade) and/or trade in different varieties of similar goods (i.e., intra-industry trade). Recall that inter-industry trade arises from differences across countries in comparative advantage (as discussed in Chapter 2), and intra-industry trade arises from economies of scale (as discussed in Chapter 3). Section 14.2.3 described the welfare effects of trade liberalization that occur from the creation and diversion of inter-industry trade. But, we should also consider the additional welfare effects from the intra-industry trade that arises from trade liberalization.

To review briefly, intra-industry trade between similar economies arises in the presence of economies of scale. The effect of allowing for trade liberalization is an increase in market size. Access to a larger market results in a decrease in average costs due to the efficiencies of scale. These efficiencies create an incentive for countries to specialize in a given product variety and trade this variety in exchange for another variety exported by a trading partner. Thus, with trade liberalization, firms increase the scale of their production in a given product variety in order to take advantage of the economies of scale. As a result, the prices of these varieties decrease. Consumers have access to increased product variety and lower prices of these varieties. That is, consumer welfare (and national welfare) increases as a consequence of trade liberalization in the presence of economies of scale. The implication is that broader multilateral liberalization arrangements result in a larger market size and larger welfare gains from increased intra-industry trade, as compared with regional arrangements.

Thus, the potential welfare gains from trade liberalization include gains from the creation of both inter-industry trade and intra-industry trade. In multilateral arrangements, these gains are not offset by the welfare losses associated with trade diversion. Thus, if one could move directly to a multilateral form of liberalization, this would be optimal from an economic welfare point of view. In real world practice, however, regional arrangements have proved to be more politically feasible than multilateral arrangements. So, this leads us back to our original question. Are regional arrangements stepping stones or stumbling blocks to broader multilateral arrangements?

The research literature in economics provides arguments on both sides. One *stepping stones* argument is as follows. Regional arrangements typically occur between economies that are relatively similar in sources of comparative advantage (such as endowments). Because the countries are similar, trade liberalization results in relatively small changes in inter-industry trade and thus relatively small changes in factor prices including wages paid to labor and rents paid to capital and land owners (see Chapters 2 and 12). Instead, trade liberalization between similar economies results in relatively large increases in intra-industry trade associated with economies of scale (see Chapter 3). This type of trade does not result in factor price changes that would typically generate political resistance. Thus, political resistance to regional arrangements between similar economies is more modest than between dissimilar economies. According to this argument, a regional arrangement between similar economies can serve as a less politically charged starting point for further liberalization between dissimilar economies.

Another *stepping stones* argument is that regional liberalization can lead to a domino effect, with increasingly broader waves of integration.[4] In this argument, a core group of countries forms a regional arrangement. The countries excluded from this arrangement suffer the adverse effects of trade diversion. That is, trade is diverted away from the lowest cost producers outside the arrangement, to countries within the arrangement (as shown in section 14.2). This diversion creates an incentive for the excluded countries to join the block; that is, joining the block is welfare improving. This process continues in waves of integration, leading eventually to a broader multilateral arrangement.

Alternatively, the research also shows that regional arrangements can be a *stumbling block* to broader multilateral arrangements. One such argument is that even if national welfare is relatively higher under a multilateral arrangement than a regional arrangement, if a regional arrangement is adopted first, it can prevent a multilateral arrangement from being adopted later.[5] The intuition is based on political economy considerations. If regional arrangements tend to occur between relatively similar countries, then the median voter can be better off with regional liberalization. This is because the welfare gains from economies of scale and product variety (associated with intra-industry trade) can exceed welfare losses from changes in factor prices (associated with inter-industry trade). If a subsequent multilateral arrangement occurred between countries that differ in endowments, then the returns to the country's abundant endowments would increase while the returns to the country's scarce endowments would decrease (see Chapters 2 and 12). Consequently, it is possible that the median voter of a country is worse off under the multilateral arrangement even though total welfare of the country is higher. In this case, the regional arrangement is a stumbling block to a multilateral arrangement because political support for broader liberalization cannot be achieved.

Another *stumbling block* argument is that the preferential treatment allowed under regional arrangements can be diminished under a multilateral arrangement and this results in political resistance.[6] Countries receiving preferential treatment under regional arrangements would need to compete with lower cost suppliers under broader multilateral arrangements that do not provide preferential treatment. Such countries would oppose broader liberalization arrangements that dilute their preferential treatment. This stumbling block argument is a political economy argument, which captures the special interests of countries with preferential treatment arrangements.

These stepping stones and stumbling block arguments lead to quite different conclusions as to whether regional liberalization of trade policy leads to a movement toward multilateral liberalization of trade policy or not. The research literature in economics has not reached a consensus on this issue and continues to evolve as the character of liberalization arrangements and international flows evolves.

14.4 Summary Remarks

What are the institutional arrangements for trade policy? The prominent institutional arrangements for trade policy include bilateral, multilateral, and regional arrangements. Bilateral trade arrangements are those where two trading partners agree to reduce or eliminate barriers between themselves. In contrast, multilateral trade arrangements are those where all (or many) countries agree to reduce or eliminate barriers between themselves. Regional trade arrangements are those where "blocks" of countries agree to reduce or eliminate barriers between themselves, via a free trade area or customs union. In a free trade area, member countries maintain their own individual – and potentially different – bilateral barriers with nonmember countries. In a customs union, member countries maintain common bilateral barriers with nonmember countries. A common external tariff is an example of such a common barrier.

Each of these types of trade arrangement is discriminatory in that nonmember countries are treated differently than member countries. This discrimination is allowed under an exception to the most favored national (MFN) principal of the GATT and its successor, the WTO. However, the discriminatory nature of these trade arrangements creates distortions. In relative terms, an FTA is more distortionary than a CU because of the differential bilateral barriers with nonmember countries in the FTA. Furthermore, in an FTA, nonmember countries can seek access to member countries via the country with the lowest external barriers. Rules of origin can prevent such behavior by establishing conditions for a good to be considered as originating from a given country. Finally, multilateral arrangements are the least discriminatory because the broad scope of the countries involved reduces the degree of discrimination.

What are the prominent multilateral arrangements for trade policy in practice? The GATT and the WTO are the most economically significant multilateral arrangements for trade policy to date. The GATT was established in 1947 and was succeeded by the WTO in 1995. Under these arrangements, "rounds" of negotiations are conducted on a periodic basis. The Uruguay Round of the GATT resulted in the establishment of the WTO. The purpose of these rounds is to reduce trade barriers and establish rules of conduct for negotiating trade policy. Each successive round builds on the previous agreements, providing for an evolving multilateral trade negotiation process. Membership to these multilateral arrangements has grown from 23 original signatories of the GATT to 153 signatories of the WTO to date. All members can participate in the rounds of negotiations and the results apply to members in a nondiscriminatory manner.

The subjects of the rounds of negotiations have evolved substantially over time. Early negotiations focused on tariff reductions on manufactured products. The subjects of more recent negotiations have broadened to include many other forms of non-tariff measures. The modalities of these negotiations have also evolved over time. Early negotiations focused on tariff reductions on an item-by-item basis, followed by a linear method, and then a formula approach. In the more recent Uruguay Round, a combination of the formula approach and the item-by-item approach was applied.

These multilateral negotiations have resulted in a significant liberalization of trade. The first five rounds (1947–1961) resulted in approximately 45,000 concessions covering roughly 15,000 product categories. The Kennedy Round (1963–1967) resulted in a 35% average reduction in tariffs and agreements on customs valuation and antidumping. The Tokyo Round (1973–1979) resulted in further tariff reductions as well as advances in the liberalization of a broader range of non-tariff measures via voluntary codes of conduct. The Uruguay Round (1986–1994) resulted in roughly an additional 33% cut in tariffs and further broadening of the treatment of non-tariff measures. Negotiation since the Uruguay Round include a series of ministerial conferences. The 2001 conference in Doha, Quatar initiated the Doha Development Round. Key issues on the agenda were reductions in barriers to agricultural trade and improvements in the transparency of antidumping duties, among others. In 2006, the Doha Round was suspended. Since that time, efforts have focused on revising the terms and structure of the rules and procedures for conducting the negotiations.

What are the effects of alterative institutional arrangements for trade policy? Specifically, does trade liberalization increase or decrease the welfare of countries? To answer this question, we considered the effects of regional, complete multilateral, and incomplete multilateral liberalization of tariffs. In each case, we examine the effects known as trade creation and trade diversion. Trade creation results from liberalization when countries within the arrangement increase trade based on comparative advantage. Trade diversion results from liberalization when countries within the arrangement shift their imports from the lowest cost producers outside the arrangement to higher cost producers inside the arrangement.

What are the effects of regional liberalization? With regional liberalization, tariff reductions among member countries result in trade creation. However, tariffs maintained against nonmember countries can result in trade diversion. The presence of trade diversion depends on whether the lowest cost producer is within the block or not. And if not, it depends on the size of the external tariff relative to the cost differences between nonmember and member exporters. If the regional block excludes the lowest cost producer, then liberalization results in trade diversion if the tariff on nonmembers is larger than the cost difference between producers inside and outside the block. Alternatively, if the tariff is smaller than the cost difference, then the arrangement does not lead to trade diversion. In the latter case, countries in the block continue to import from countries outside the block, but the full benefits of trade creation are not achieved due to the external tariff. In contrast, if the block includes the lowest cost producer, then regional liberalization results in trade creation but no trade diversion. These results apply to FTAs and CUs. However, FTAs without rules of origin produce additional distortions from the differential tariffs maintained by members against nonmembers. Thus, regional trade liberalization increases the welfare of countries within the block if the welfare gains from trade creation exceed welfare losses from trade diversion plus any additional welfare losses associated with uneven external barriers.

What are the effects of multilateral liberalization? The extreme version of a multilateral arrangement is one where all countries are included. If the scope of countries involved is complete, then the multilateral arrangement is nondiscriminatory.

In this case, all countries simultaneously eliminate and/or reduce barriers to trade. This liberalization results in trade creation but no trade diversion. If we compare this multilateral liberalization with regional liberalization, we see that multilateral liberalization results in trade creation only, whereas regional liberalization results in trade creation (although not necessarily complete) and can result in trade diversion if the lowest cost producers are outside the regional block. With regional liberalization, the welfare effect for member countries depends on whether trade creation exceeds trade diversion. With complete multilateral liberalization, the welfare effect for all countries is unambiguously positive.

What are the effects of country exclusion from multilateral arrangements? That is, what if a small number of countries (i.e., the rest of the world) remain outside the arrangement? Do excluded countries have an incentive to join the arrangement? Do included countries benefit from a broadening of membership? The answer to these questions is that there are conflicting interests. Member importers have an interest in the accession of the rest of the world because of the welfare gains from trade creation with the lowest cost producers. However, the lowest cost producers initially within the arrangement have an interest in excluding the lowest cost producer outside the arrangement from joining. This is because original members will have to compete with the rest of the world after their accession. For the original members, the accession of the rest of the world can result in a loss of producer welfare. Finally, the rest of the world has an interest in accession to the arrangement because of the opportunity cost of exclusion – lost producer welfare from foregone exports to member countries. The rest of the world gains welfare from accession. Thus, countries initially excluded from a multilateral arrangement do have an incentive to join the arrangement in order to gain access to trade with member countries and the corresponding welfare improvements. However, countries initially included in the multilateral arrangement have mixed incentives for broadening membership. These conclusions focus on the aggregate perspectives of the blocks. There are also welfare changes within blocks between producers, consumers, and government. Political economy considerations that place different weights on the welfare of these agents can alter the conclusions discussed above.

Are regional arrangements stepping stones or stumbling blocks to multilateral liberalization? To answer this question, we need to recall that trade can take the form of inter-industry or intra-industry flows. Inter-industry trade tends to occur between dissimilar countries and arises from gains associated with comparative advantage. In contrast, intra-industry trade tends to occur between similar economies and arises from gains associated with economies of scale. Inter-industry trade results in changes in the factor prices of abundant and scarce endowments, whereas intra-industry trade does not. This is relevant because regional arrangements tend to occur between relatively similar economies as compared with multilateral arrangements. Thus, regional arrangements produce relatively more intra-industry trade than inter-industry trade and have relatively small impacts on factor prices as compared with multilateral arrangements.

The stepping stones and stumbing blocks arguments build on this intuition. One stepping stones argument is that there is less political resistance to regional arrangements between similar economies because such arrangements produce relatively small changes in inter-industry trade and thus relatively small changes in factor prices. Thus, regional arrangements can provide a less politically charged starting point to future multilateral liberation. The domino effect argument further suggests that regional liberalization can lead to increasingly broader waves of integration. This is because excluded countries suffer the adverse effects of trade diversion, which creates an incentive for them join the block. This continues until a multilateral arrangement is achieved.

Alternatively, a prominent stumbling block argument is that if a regional arrangement is adopted first between similar countries, this can prevent a multilateral arrangement from being adopted later. Since the regional arrangement has relatively small effects on factor prices, the median voter of a country is better off under the regional arrangement, even though total country welfare is higher under the multilateral arrangement. Thus, political support for broader liberalization cannot be achieved. Another stumbling block argument is that the preferential treatment allowed under regional arrangements can be diminished under a multilateral arrangement. Thus, countries that receive preferential treatment would oppose broader liberalization arrangements that dilute this preferential treatment, and a multilateral arrangement cannot be achieved.

The economics literature has not yet reached a consensus on whether regional arrangements are stepping stones or stumbling blocks to multilateral arrangements.

Applied Problems

14.1 Consider the following four types of arrangement for trade policy: (a) bilateral arrangements; (b) customs unions; (c) free trade areas; and (d) multilateral arrangements. Briefly describe each type of arrangement. Then describe the differences between these forms of arrangements, including the relevance of rules of origin, discrimination, and political autonomy in policy making. Be sure to discuss trade creation, trade diversion, and other distortions associated with these arrangements.

14.2 Consider the welfare effects of regional trade arrangements. (a) Does regional liberalization of tariffs increase or decrease the welfare of the countries within the arrangement? (b) Does your answer depend on whether the arrangement includes or excludes the lowest cost producers? If so, how? (c) Does your answer depend on the size of the external tariffs maintained against countries outside the arrangement? If so, how? In answering these question, be sure to articulate underlying assumptions. Also, consider the perspectives of both importers and exporters within the arrangement.

14.3   Consider the welfare effects of a multilateral trade arrangement that includes all countries. What are the effects of complete multilateral liberalization on global welfare?

14.4   Compare regional and multilateral trade arrangements. Which type of arrangement is preferred from a global welfare perspective?

14.5   Consider a trade arrangement such as the World Trade Organization, where only a small number of countries remain outside the arrangement. (a) Do the excluded countries have an incentive to join the arrangement? (b) Do the included countries benefit from a broadening of membership? Identify all underlying assumptions and consider the national perspectives of the included and excluded countries.

14.6   Consider the welfare effects of both regional and multilateral trade arrangements from a subnational perspective. That is, consider the welfare effects of tariff liberalization on: (a) producer welfare; (b) consumer welfare; and (c) government welfare. Consider these welfare effects for both importers and exporters, inside and outside the arrangements.

14.7   Consider a world comprised of countries grouped by level of development including: highly developed countries (H); developing countries (M); and least developed countries (L). Assume that the highly developed countries are the highest cost producers of the good, the least developed countries are the lowest cost producers of the good, and the developing countries are somewhere in between. Further, assume that the highly developed countries import the good and the other two groups export the good, with infinite elasticity of export supply. Assume that initially, the highly developed countries maintain similar tariffs on imports of the good from all other countries. (a) Evaluate the effects of a regional arrangement between the highly developed countries and the developing countries. (b) Evaluate the effects of a multilateral agreement between all three groups of countries. Specifically, consider the effects of these alternative arrangements on: prices; the volume of trade; and welfare. Consider these effects from the perspective of each group of countries.

14.8   Consider a world consisting of three regional "power" blocks (Europe, North America, and Asia) and the remaining "excluded" countries. Evaluate the effects of liberalization within the "power blocks" on the "excluded" countries. State any assumptions that you make. Be sure to consider trade creation and trade diversion, and support your analysis with illustrations.

14.9   If you were a policy maker concerned with maximizing global welfare, what type of trade liberalization would you support (e.g., free trade areas, customs unions, multilateral agreements) and why? Support your answer with illustrations.

14.10 Does trade liberalization increase the volume of international trade? Consider this question from both a national perspective and global perspective. Be sure to identify any assumption that you need to make to answer this question.

14.11 Are regional trade arrangements stepping stones or stumbling blocks to multilateral trade liberalization? Provide at least four alternative arguments.

Further Reading

Anderson, James E. 1998. The Uruguay Round and welfare in some distorted agricultural economies. *Journal of Development Economics* 56 (August): 393–410.

Bagwell, Kyle, and Robert W. Staiger. 2002. *The Economics of the World Trading System*. Cambridge, MA: MIT Press.

Baicker, Katherine and M. Marit Rehavi. 2004. Policy watch: trade adjustment assistance. *Journal of Economic Perspectives* 18 (2): 239–255.

Baldwin, Richard E. 2006. Multilateralizing regionalism: spaghetti bowls as building blocs on the path to global free trade. *World Economy* 29 (11): 1451–1518.

Baldwin, Robert E. 1984. Trade policies in developing countries. In *Handbook of International Economics*, vol. 1 (eds Ronald W. Jones and Peter B. Kenen). Amsterdam: North-Holland.

Baldwin, Robert E. 1985. *The Political Economy of US Import Policy*. Cambridge: MIT Press.

Baldwin, Robert E. 1989. The political economy of trade policy. *Journal of Economic Perspectives* 3 (4): 119–137.

Bhagwati, Jagdish. 1982. *Import Competition and Response*. Chicago: University of Chicago Press.

Bhagwati, Jagdish. 1988. *Protectionism*. Cambridge: MIT Press.

Bhagwati, Jagdish. 2004. *In Defense of Globalization*. New York: Oxford University Press.

Bradford, Scott. 2003. Paying the price: final goods protection in OECD countries. *Review of Economics and Statistics* 87 (1): 24–37.

Coleman, William, Wyn Grant, and Timothy Josling. 2004. *Agriculture in the New Global Economy*. Cheltenham, UK: Edward Elgar.

Corden, W. Max. 1974. *Trade policy and economic welfare*. Oxford: Clarendon Press.

Eaton, Jonathan, and Maxim Engers. 1992. *Sanctions. Journal of Political Economy* 100 (5): 899–928.

Flam, Harry. 1992. Product markets and 1992: full integration, large gains? *Journal of Economics Perspectives* (Fall): 7–30.

Gawande Kishore and Usree Bandyopadhyay. 2000. Is protection for sale? Evidence on the Grossman-Helpman theory of endogenous protection. *Review of Economics and Statistics* 82 (1): 139–152.

Grossman, Gene M., and Elhanan Helpman. 1994. Protection for sale. *American Economic Review* 84 (4): 833–850.

Harrison, Glenn H., Thomas F. Rutherford, and David G. Tarr. 2003. Trade policy options for Chile: the importance of market access. *World Bank Economic Review* 16 (1): 49–79.

Hoda, Anwarul. 2001. *Tariff Negotiations and Renegotiations under the GATT and the WTO: Procedures and Practices*. Cambridge: Cambridge University Press.

Hoekman, Bernard, and Michel Kostecki. 2001. *The Political Economy of the World Trading System*, 2nd edn. New York: Oxford University Press.

Irwin, Douglas A. 1995. The GATT in historical perspective. *American Economic Review* 85 (2): 323–328.

Irwin, Douglas A., Petros Mavroidis and Alan Sykes. 2008. *The Genesis of the GATT*. Cambridge, MA: Cambridge University Press.

Jackson, John H. 1997. *The World Trading System: Law and Policy of International Economic Relations*. Cambridge: MIT Press.

Ju, Jiandong, and Kala Krishna. 2000. Welfare and market access effects of piecemeal tariff reform. *Journal of International Economics* 51 (2): 305–316.

Kemp, Murray, and H. Wan. 1976. An elementary proposition regarding the formation of customs unions. *Journal of International Economics* 6: 95–97.

Krueger, Anne O. 1974. The political economy of the rent-seeking society. *American Economic Review* 64 (3): 291–303.

Krueger, Anne O. (ed). 1996. *The Political Economy of Trade Protection*. National Bureau of Economic Research Project Report. Chicago: University of Chicago Press.

Krueger, Anne O., M. Schiff, and A. Valdes. 1991. *The Political Economy of Agricultural Pricing Policy*. Baltimore: Johns Hopkins University Press for the World Bank.

Krugman, Paul R. 1997. What should trade negotiators negotiate about? *Journal of Economic Literature* 35 (1): 113–120.

Levy, Philip I. 1997. A political-economic analysis of free-trade agreements. *American Economic Review* 87 (4): 506–519.

Limao, Nuno. 2006. Preferential trade agreements as stumbling blocks for multilateral trade liberalization: evidence for the US. *American Economic Review* 96 (3): 896–914.

Lipsey, Richard G. 1960. The theory of customs unions: A general survey. *Economic Journal* 70 (279): 496–513.

Maggi, Giovanni, and Andres Rodriguez-Clare. 2000. Import penetration and the politics of trade protection. *Journal of International Economics* 51 (2): 287–304.

Maggi, Giovanni, and Andres Rodriguez-Clare. 2007. A political economy theory of trade agreements. *American Economic Review* 97 (4): 1374–1406.

Salvatore, Dominick, ed. 1987. *The New Protectionist Threat to World Welfare*. Amsterdam: North-Holland.

Schiff, Maurice, and L. Alan Winters. 2003. *Regional Integration and Development*. Washington, D.C.: World Bank and Oxford University Press.

Schott, Jeffrey. 1994. *The Uruguay Round: An Assessment*. Washington, D.C.: Institute for International Economics.

Stern, Robert, ed. 1987. *US Trade Policies in a Changing World Economy*. Cambridge: MIT Press.

Sumner, Daniel A. and Stefan Tangermann. 2002. International trade policy and negotiations. In *Handbook of Agricultural Economics*, vol. 2B, *Agricultural and Food Policy* (eds Bruce L. Gardner and Gordon C. Rausser), Amsterdam, Netherlands: North Holland Press, pp. 1999–2055.

Trefler, Daniel. 1993. Trade liberalization and the theory of endogenous protection: an econometric study of US import policy. *Journal of Political Economy* 101 (1): 138–160.

Viner, Jacob. 1950. *The Customs Union Issue*. New York: Carnegie Endowment for International Peace.

Vousden, N. 1990. *The Economic Theory of Protection*. Cambridge: Cambridge University Press.

World Trade Organization (WTO). 2007. *World Trade Report 2007: Sixty Years of the Multilateral Trading System, Achievements and Challenges*. Geneva: WTO.

Notes

1. See World Trade Organization (2007) for background on the GATT/WTO and rounds of negotiations.
2. However, agreement was reached on an intellectual property rights issue concerning developing countries' access to pharmaceuticals. Developing countries could now import generic copies of drugs used against diseases of substantial threat (e.g., HIV/AIDS, malaria) and could produce these drugs for export to other developing countries.
3. The discussion of conflicting interests associated with the exclusion of countries from multilateral arrangements also applies to the exclusion of countries from regional arrangements. For example, if Mexico is the lowest cost producer of a good within NAFTA, then Mexico may want to exclude the lowest cost producers outside of NAFTA from joining the regional arrangement. Such countries may include those of the Dominican Republic-Central America-United States Free Trade Agreement (CAFTA-DR), which compete with Mexico in their trade with the United States.
4. See Baldwin (2006) for research on the domino effect argument that regional liberalization is a stepping stone to broader multilateral arrangements.
5. See Levy (1997) for a political economy treatment of this argument.
6. See Limao (2006) for demonstrations of this argument.

References

Acemoglu, Daron 2003. Patterns of skill premia. *Review of Economic Studies* 70 (2): 231–251.

Antweiler, Werner, Brian R. Copeland, and M. Scott Taylor. 2001. Is free trade good for the environment? *American Economics Review* 91 (4): 877–908.

Baldwin, Richard E. 2006. Multilateralizing regionalism: spaghetti bowls as building blocs on the path to global free trade. *World Economy* 29 (11): 1451–1518.

Bergstrand, Jeffrey H., and Peter Egger. 2007. A knowledge-and-physical-capital model of international trade, foreign direct investment, and multinational enterprises. *Journal of International Economics* 73 (2): 278–308.

Bhagwati, Jagdish. 1958. Immiserizing growth: a geometrical note. *Review of Economic Studies* 25: 201–205.

Bhagwati, Jagdish. 1965. On the equivalence of tariffs and quotas. In *Trade, Growth, and the Balance of Payments* (eds Robert E. Baldwin *et al.*). Chicago: Rand McNally.

Bhagwati, Jagdish. 1968. More on the equivalence of tariffs and quotas. *American Economic Review* 58 (1): 142–146.

Bhagwati, Jagdish. 1971. The generalized theory of distortions and welfare. In *Trade, Balance of Payments and Growth* (eds J. N. Bhagwati *et al.*). North-Holland, Amsterdam, chapter 12.

Braconier, Henrik, Pehr-Johan Norback, and Dieter Urban. 2005. Reconciling the evidence on the knowledge-capital model. *Review of International Economics* 13 (4): 770–786.

Brainard, S. Lael. 1997. An empirical assessment of the proximity-concentration trade-off between multinational sales and trade. *American Economic Review* 87 (4): 520–544.

Brander, James A. 1981. Intra-industry trade in identical commodities. *Journal of International Economics* 11 (1): 1–14.

Brander, James A., and Paul R. Krugman. 1983. A "reciprocol dumping" model of international trade. *Journal of International Trade* 15: 313–321.

Broda, Christian, and David E. Weinstein. 2006. Globalization and the gains from variety. *Quarterly Journal of Economics* 121 (2): 541–585.

Campa, Jose, and Linda Goldberg. 1997. *The Evolving External Orientation of Manufacturing Industries: Evidence for Four Countries.* NBER Working Paper No. 5919. Cambridge, MA: National Bureau of Economic Research.

Caves, Richard E. 2007. *Multinational Enterprises and Economic Analysis.* Cambridge: Cambridge University Press.

Chichinisky, Graciela. 1994. North-south trade and the global environment. *American Economic Review* 84 (4): 851–874.

Clausing, Kimberly A. 2003. Tax-motivated transfer pricing and US intrafirm trade prices. *Journal of Public Economics* 87 (9/10): 2207–2223.

Clausing, Kimberly A. 2006. International tax avoidance and US international trade. *National Tax Journal* 59 (2): 269–287.

Copeland, Brian R., and Sumeet Gulati. 2006. Trade and the environment in developing countries. In *Economic Development and Environmental Sustainability* (eds R. Lopez and M. Toman), Oxford: Oxford University Press, pp. 178–216.

Copeland, Brian R., and M. Scott Taylor. 2003. *Trade and the Environment: Theory and Evidence.* Princeton University Press, Princeton.

Copeland, Brian R., and M. Scott Taylor. 2004. Trade, growth and the environment. *Journal of Economic Literature* (March): 7–71.

Davis, Donald. 1996. *Trade Liberalization and Income Distribution.* NBER Working Paper No. 5693. Cambridge, MA: National Bureau of Economic Research.

Deardorff, Alan V., and Robert M. Stern. 2007. Empirical analysis of barriers to international services transactions and the consequences of liberalization. In *Handbook of Services Trade* (eds Aaditya Mattoo, Robert M. Stern, and Gianni Zanini), Oxford: Oxford University Press, pp. 169–220.

Dixit, Avinash K., and Joseph E. Stiglitz. 1977. Monopolistic competition and optimum product diversity. *American Economic Review* 67 (3): 297–308.

Dollar, David, and Aart Kraay. 2002. Growth is good for the poor. *Journal of Economic Growth* 7 (3): 195–225.

Dunning, John H. 1973. The determinants of international production. *Oxford Economic Papers* 25 (3): 289–336.

Ekholm, Karolina, Rikard Forslid, and James R. Markusen. 2007. Export platform foreign direct investment. *Journal of the European Economic Association* 5 (4): 776–795.

Ethier, Wilfred J., and James R. Markusen. 1996. Multinational firms, technology diffusion and trade. *Journal of International Economics* 41 (August): 1–28.

Feenstra, Robert C. 2010. *Offshoring in the Global Economy: Microeconomic Structure and Macroeconomic Implications.* Cambridge, MA: MIT Press.

Feenstra, Robert C., and Gordon H. Hanson. 1996. Foreign investment, outsourcing, and relative wages. In *The Political Economy of Trade Policy: Papers in Honor of Jagdish Bhagwati* (eds R.C. Feeenstra, G.M. Grossman, and D.A. Irwin), Cambridge, MA: MIT Press, pp. 89–127.

Feenstra, Robert C., and Gordon H. Hanson. 1999. The impact of outsourcing and high-technology capital on wages: estimates for the US, 1979–1990. *Quarterly Journal of Economics* 114 (3): 907–940.

Feenstra, Robert C., and Gordon H. Hanson. 2004. Intermediaries in entrepot trade: Hong Kong re-exports of Chinese goods. *Journal of Economics and Management Strategy* 13 (1): 3–35.

Feketekuty, Geza. 1988. *International Trade in Services: An Overview and Blueprint for Negotiations.* Cambridge, MA: Ballinger.

Ferrantino, Michael J. 1993. The effects of intellectual property rights on international trade and investment. *Weltwirtschaftliches Archiv* 129 (2): 300–331.

Findlay, Ronald E. 1984. Growth and development in trade models. In *Handbook of International Economics*, vol. 1 (eds R.W. Jones and P.B. Kenen), Amsterdam: North-Holland, pp. 185–236.

Frankel, Jeffrey, and David Romer. 1999. Does trade cause growth? *American Economic Review* 89 (3): 379–399.

Glass, Amy J. 2000. Costly R&D and intellectual property rights protection. *International Journal of Technology Management* 19 (1/2): 170–193.

Goldberg, Pinelopi, and Nina Pavcnik. 2007. Distributional effects of globalization in developing countries. *Journal of Economic Literature* 45 (1): 39–82.

Gorg, Holger. 2000. Fragmentation and trade: US inward processing trade in the EU. *Review of World Economics* 136: 403–422.

de Gorter, Harry, and Erika Kliauga. 2006. Reducing tariffs versus expanding tariff rate quotas. In *Agricultural Trade Reform and the Doha Development Agenda* (eds Kym Anderson and Will Martin), Washington, D.C.: World Bank and Palgrave Macmillan, pp. 117–160.

Grossman, Gene M., and Elhanan Helpman. 1991a. *Innovation and Growth in the Global Economy.* Cambridge, MA: MIT Press.

Grossman, Gene M., and Elhanan Helpman. 1991b. Integration versus outsourcing in industry Equilibrium. *Quarterly Journal of Economics* 117 (1): 85–120.

Gruebel, Herbert G., and Peter Lloyd. 1975. *Intra-industry Trade: The Theory and Measurement of International Trade in Differentiated Products.* London: Macmillan.

Harrison, Ann E. 1994. Productivity, imperfect competition, and trade reform: theory and evidence. *Journal of International Economics* 36 (1–2): 53–73.

Hasan, Rana, Devashish Mitra, and K.V. Ramaswamy. 2007. Trade reforms, labor regulations, and labor-demand elasticities: empirical evidence from India. *Review of Economics and Statistics* 89 (3): 466–481.

Helpman, Elhanan. 1984. A simple theory of trade with multinational corporations. *Journal of Political Economy* 92 (3): 451–471.

Helpman, Elhanan. 1993. Innovation, imitation, and intellectual property rights. *Econometrica* 61 (6): 1247–1280.

Helpman, Elhanan and Paul R. Krugman. 1985. *Market Structure and Foreign Trade.* Cambridge, MA: MIT Press.

Helpman, Elhanan, Marc Melitz, and Stephen Yeaple. 2004. Exports versus FDI with heterogeneous firms. *American Economic Review* 94 (1): 300–316.

Hindley, Brian, and Alasdair Smith. 1984. Comparative advantage and trade in service. *World Economy* 7 (4): 369–390.

Hoekman, Bernard. 1996. Assessing the General Agreement on Trade and Services. In *The Uruguay Round and the Developing Countries* (eds Will Martin and L. Alan Winters), Cambridge: Cambridge University Press, pp. 88–124.

Hoekman, Bernard. 2006. *Liberalizing Trade in Services: A Survey.* World Bank Policy Research Working Paper No. 4040, Washington, D.C.: World Bank.

Horstmann, Ignatius, and James R. Markusen. 1987. Licensing versus direct investment: a model of internalization by the multinational enterprise. *Canadian Journal of Economics* 20: 464–481.

Horstmann, Ignatius, and James R. Markusen. 1992. Endogenous market structures in international trade. *Journal of International Economics* 32 (1–2): 109–129.

Jones, Ronald W., and Stanley Engerman. 1996. Trade, technology, and wages: a tale of two countries. *American Economic Review* 86: 35–40.

Jones Ronald W., and Sugata Marjit. 1985. A simple production model with Stolper-Samuelson property. *International Economic Review* 26 (3): 565–567.

Jones, Ronald W., and Sugata Marjit. 2003. Economic development, trade, and wages. *German Economic Review* 4:1–17.

Krishna, Pravin, and Davashish Mitra. 1998. Trade liberalization, market discipline, and productivity growth: new evidence from India. *Journal of Development Economics* 56 (2): 447–462.

Krugman, Paul R. 1979. Increasing returns, monopolisitic competition, and international trade. *Journal of International Economics* 9 (4): 469–479.

Krugman, Paul R. 1981. Intraindustry specialization and the gains from trade. *Journal of Political Economy* 89 (5): 959–973.

Krugman, Paul. 2000. Technology, trade, and factor prices. *Journal of International Economics* 50 (1): 51–71.

Lawrence, Robert Z. 1995. *Single World, Divided Nations: Globalization and OECD Labor Markets*. Paris: OECD.

Leamer, Edward. 2000. What's the use of factor contents? *Journal of International Economics* 50 (1): 73–90.

Lee, Jeong-Yeon, and Edwin Mansfield. 1996. Intellectual property protection and US foreign direct investment. *The Review of Economics and Statistics* 78 (2): 181–186.

Levy, Philip I. 1997. A political-economic analysis of free-trade agreements. *American Economic Review* 87 (4): 506–519.

Limao, Nuno. 2006. Preferential trade agreements as stumbling blocks for multilateral trade liberalization: evidence for the US. *American Economic Review* 96 (3): 896–914.

Lopez, Ramon. 1997. Environmental externalities in traditional agriculture and the impact of trade liberalization: the case of Ghana. *Journal of Development Economics* 53 (1): 17–39.

Lopez, Ramon, and Gregmar I. Galinato. 2005. Deforestation and forest-induced carbon dioxide emissions in tropical countries: how do governance and trade openness affect the forest-income relationship? *Journal of Environment and Development* 14 (1): 73–100.

Marjit, Sugata, and Rajat Acharyya. 2003. *International Trade, Wage Inequality, and the Developing Economy: A General Equilibrium Approach*. Heidelberg: Physica/Springer Verlag.

Marjit, Sugata, and Rajat Acharyya. 2006. Trade liberalization, skill-linked intermediate production, and two-sided wage gap. *Journal of Policy Reform* 9 (3): 203–217.

Marjit, Sugata, Hamid Beladi, and Avik Chakrabarti. 2003. Trade and wage inequality in developing countries. *Economic Inquiry* 42 (92): 295–303.

Markusen, James R. 1984. Multinationals, multi-plant economies, and the gains from trade. *Journal of International Economics* 16 (3–4): 205–226.

Markusen, James R. 2002. *Multinational Firms and The Theory of International Trade*. Cambridge, MA: MIT Press.

Markusen, James R., and Anthony J. Venables. 1998. Multinational firms and the new trade theory. *Journal of International Economics* 46 (2): 183–203.

Markusen, James R., and Anthony J. Venables. 2000. The theory of endowment, intra-industry, and multinational trade. *Journal of International Economics* 52 (2): 209–234.

Maskus, Keith E. 1998. The international regulation of intellectual property. *Weltwirtschaftliches Archiv* 134 (June): 186–208.

Maskus, Keith E., and M. Penubarti. 1995. How trade-related are intellectual property rights? *Journal of International Economics* 39 (November): 227–248.

Maskus, Keith E., Kamal Saggi, and Thitima Puttitanun. 2005. Patent rights and international technology transfer through direct investment and licensing. In *International Public Goods and Transfer of Technology under a Globalized Intellectual Property Regime* (eds Keith E. Maskus and Jerome H. Reichman). Cambridge: Cambridge University Press, pp. 265–281.

Mattoo, Aaditya. 2005. Services in a development round: three goals and three proposals. *Journal of World Trade* 39 (6): 1223–1238.

Mattoo, Aaditya, Robert M. Stern, and Gianni Zanini, eds. 2007. *Handbook of Services Trade*. Oxford: Oxford Unversity Press.

Organisation for Economic Co-operation and Development (OECD). 2002. Intraindustry and intrafirm trade and the internationalisation of production. *Economic Outlook*, no. 71, chap. 6, pp. 159–170.

Organisation for Economic Co-operation and Development (OECD). 2006. *Producer Support Estimates* and *Consumer Support Estimates*, OECD Database 1986–2004. Paris: OECD.

Porto, Guido G. 2006. Using survey data to assess the distributional effects of trade policy. *Journal of International Economics* 70 (1): 140–160.

Primo Braga, Carlos A., and Carsten Fink. 1998. The relationship between intellectual property rights and foreign direct investment. *Duke Journal of Comparative and International Law* 9: 163–187.

Ranjan, Priya. 2006. Preferential trade agreements, multinational enterprises, and welfare. *Canadian Journal of Economics* 39 (2): 493–515.

Richardson, J. David. 1995. Income inequality and trade: how to think, what to conclude. *Journal of Economic Perspectives* 9 (3): 33–55.

Robbins, Donald. 1995. *Trade, Trade Liberalization, and Inequality in Latin America and East Asia: Synthesis of Seven Country Studies*. Mimeo, Harvard Institute of International Development.

Rodriguez, Francisco, and Dani Rodrik. 2001. Trade policy and economic growth: a skeptic's guide to the cross-national evidence. In *Macreconomics Annual 2000* (eds Ben Bernanke and Kenneth S. Rogoff), Cambridge, MA: MIT Press, pp. 261–325.

Rodrik, Dani. 1992. Closing the productivity gap: does trade liberalization really help? In *Trade Policy, Industrialization, and Development: New Perspectives* (ed. G. K. Helleiner), Oxford: Clarendon Press, pp. 155–175.

Sachs, Jeffrey D., and Andrew Warner. 1995. Economic reform and the process of global integration. *Brooking Papers on Economic Activity* 1: 1–118.

Samuelson, Paul A. 1939. The gains from international trade. In *Readings in the Theory of International Trade* (eds H.S. Ellis and L.A. Metzler), Homewood, IL: Irwin, 1949, pp. 239–252.

Skully, David W. 2001. *Economics of Tariff-Rate Quota Administration*. US Department of Agriculture, Economic Research Service, Technical Bulletin Number 1893 (April). D.C.: USDA.

Smarzynska, Beata. 2004. The composition of foreign direct investment and protection of intellectual property rights: evidence from transition economies. *European Economic Review* 48: 39–62.

Smith, Pamela J. 1999. Are weak patent rights a barrier to US exports? *Journal of International Economics* 48: 151–177.

Smith, Pamela J. 2001. How do foreign patent rights affect US exports, affiliate sales, and licenses? *Journal of International Economics* 55: 411–440.

United Nations Conference on Trade and Development. 2000. *World Investment Report: Cross-Border Mergers and Acquisitions and Development.* Geneva: United Nations.

Winters, L. Alan, Neil McCulloch, and Andrew McKay. 2004. Trade liberalization and poverty: the evidence so far. *Journal of Economic Literature* 42 (1): 72–115.

Winters, L. Alan, T. L. Walmsley, Z. K. Wang, R. Grynberg. 2003. Liberalizing temporary movement of national persons: an agenda for the development round. *World Economy* 26 (8): 1137–1161.

Wood, Adrian. 1997. Openness and wage inequality in developing countries: the Latin American challenges to East Asian conventional wisdom. *World Bank Research Observer* 11 (1): 33–57.

World Trade Organization (WTO). 1997. *European Communities-Regime for the Importation, Sale, and Distribution of Bananas.* Report of the Appellate Body (September 9). Geneva: WTO.

World Trade Organization (WTO). 2006. *Tariff Quota Administration Methods and Tariff Quota Fill.* Committee on Agriculture Background Paper TN/AG/S/22 (April 27). Geneva: WTO.

World Trade Organization (WTO). 2007. *World Trade Report 2007: Sixty Years of the Multilateral Trading System, Achievements and Challenges.* Geneva: WTO.

Xu, Bin. 2003. Trade liberalization, wage inequality, and endogenously determined nontraded goods. *Journal of International Economics* 60 (2): 417–431.

Yang, Guifand, and Keith E. Maskus. 2001. Intellectual property rights, licensing, and innovation in an endogenous product-cycle model. *Journal of International Economics* 53: 169–187.

Index